D1084031

HALAL FOOD

HALAL

A HISTORY

FOOD

FEBE ARMANIOS

AND

BOĞAÇ ERGENE

OXFORD
UNIVERSITY PRESS

OXFORD
UNIVERSITY PRESS

Oxford University Press is a department of the University of Oxford. It furthers
the University's objective of excellence in research, scholarship, and education
by publishing worldwide. Oxford is a registered trade mark of Oxford University
Press in the UK and certain other countries.

Published in the United States of America by Oxford University Press
198 Madison Avenue, New York, NY 10016, United States of America.

© Oxford University Press 2018

All rights reserved. No part of this publication may be reproduced, stored in
a retrieval system, or transmitted, in any form or by any means, without the
prior permission in writing of Oxford University Press, or as expressly permitted
by law, by license, or under terms agreed with the appropriate reproduction
rights organization. Inquiries concerning reproduction outside the scope of the
above should be sent to the Rights Department, Oxford University Press, at the
address above.

You must not circulate this work in any other form
and you must impose this same condition on any acquirer.

Library of Congress Cataloging-in-Publication Data
Names: Armanios, Febe, 1974– author. | Ergene, Boğaç A., 1971– author.
Title: Halal food : a history / Febe Armanios and Boğaç Ergene.
Description: New York, NY : Oxford University Press, 2018. |
Includes bibliographical references and index.
Identifiers: LCCN 2017042076 (print) | LCCN 2017039349 (ebook) |
ISBN 9780190269050 (hardcover : alk. paper) | ISBN 9780190269067 (Updf) |
ISBN 9780190269074 (Epub)
Subjects: LCSH: Halal food. | Halal food industry.
Classification: LCC BP184.9.D5 A76 2018 (ebook) | LCC BP184.9.D5 (print) |
DDC 297.5/76—dc23
LC record available at https://lccn.loc.gov/2017042076

9 8 7 6 5 4 3 2

Printed by Sheridan Books, Inc., United States of America

CONTENTS

ACKNOWLEDGMENTS

Let me bring you trays of food
And something that you like to drink.
You can use my soft words
As a cushion for your head.

Hafiz (d. 1390)

The aim of this book is to introduce readers to the Islamic conceptualizations of permissible (*halal*) and impermissible (*haram*) food. The book provides an overview of core halal food rules in historical perspective and in contemporary interpretations. It speaks to the authors' shared interest in Islamic law, comparative religious practices, political economy, and food history. And the Persian lyricist and mystic Hafiz's beautiful stanzas encapsulate this book's planning and writing process, which involved many good meals shared between the authors as well as with colleagues, friends, and family throughout the world. We hope that they, and other readers, will enjoy the printed words on the following pages. Of course, any errors or omissions are the authors' sole responsibility.

The project was completed, in part, with research and sabbatical support from the University of Vermont, Middlebury College, and Harvard University. At the University of Vermont, our gratitude extends to the History

ACKNOWLEDGMENTS

Department, particularly Paul Deslandes and Kathy Carolin; the College of the Arts and Sciences; and the Office of the Provost. At Middlebury, we are grateful to the History Department, the Office of the Dean of Faculty Professional Development and Research, the Center for the Comparative Study of Race and Ethnicity, and the Office of the President. At Harvard, the authors benefited from a residential Fellowship at the Islamic Legal Studies Program (ILSP) and from the generous assistance of the Islamic librarians at the Harvard Law Library, who helped us secure key documents for the book. In collaboration with Kristen Stilt, director of ILSP and professor at Harvard Law School, we organized a fruitful and rewarding workshop in May 2016 titled "Animals, Law, and Religion" and learned a great deal about the place of animals as food in various religious and geographic settings in conversations with the workshop participants: Kecia Ali, Beth Berkowitz, David Cassuto, Divya Cherian, David Clough, Bruce Friedrich, Chris Green, Aaron Gross, Dale Jamieson, Justin Marceau, Richard McGregor, Natalie Prosin, Jordan Rosenblum, Sarra Tlili, Anne Vallely, and Paul Waldau. We are grateful for their insights.

We would like to extend special thanks to our friend and colleague Kristen Stilt. She was supportive of this project from its initial inception, was a wonderful conversation partner throughout the writing stages, and offered meticulous advice and important guidance on various chapters. Similarly, we are indebted to Dana Barrow and Andrew Amstutz, both of whom carefully read entire drafts of the book and provided detailed feedback that was critical for the final revision process. Along the way, many friends and colleagues gave their time as well as important insights and pointers for parts of the manuscript. Heather Sharkey warmly shared her teaching materials about food in the Middle East. Jordan Rosenblum helped us consider many of the book's major themes like animal slaughter, animal rights, and food ethics in a more comparative religious framework. Riad Bahhur offered us valuable suggestions and comments on different chapters. James Calvin Davis, Ayda Erbal, Bert Johnson, Chris Rominger, Rebecca Tiger, Julia Welsh, and Ela Yazıcı İnan gave useful pointers on specific sections. Thanks also to Ata Anzali, Yavuz Aykan, Dima Ayoub, Elizabeth S. Bolman, Darién Davis, Bruce Friedrich, Caroline Kahlenberg, Jahd Khalil, Karin Hanta, Noémi Lévy-Aksu, Sujata Moorti, Ellen Oxfeld, Natalie Prosin, Safa Saraçoğlu, and Claire Wilkinson for helping us locate or access sources and answering our queries. Ian Barrow, Rebecca Bennette, and James Fitzsimmons gave much appreciated advice and recommendations.

Several individuals contributed to the book's overall production process. We would like to thank Christi B. Stanforth especially for her superb and thorough reading of various stages of the book manuscript and her detailed editorial suggestions. We truly valued her time, her passion for food studies, and her good cheer. With great care, patience, and attentiveness, Gregory T. Woolston prepared the beautiful maps. We would also like to thank Ayda Erbal, Celeste and Jeff Flynn, Michelle Kim, Hiroko Miyokawa, and Martin Naunov for kindly sharing their photographs. At Middlebury College, several research assistants gathered important materials for the book: Jiya Pandya, David Russell, and Winnie Yeung worked diligently and punctually during the project's earliest stages, while Lex Scott and Elizabeth Weiss assisted with final matters.

The idea for this book goes back to 2013 but later materialized in conversations with Susan Ferber, executive editor of American and World History at Oxford University Press. We are thankful for her professionalism, expertise, and enthusiasm. We would also like to thank the three anonymous reviewers for the press, whose comments and suggestions enriched the final draft. We are appreciative of the care and effort of our amazing production editor Maya Bringe, as well as other members of the production staff, including Patterson Lamb, John Grennan, and Jenny Volvovski.

The seeds for this project were planted in spring 2013 when Febe Armanios began teaching a course titled "Food in the Middle East: History, Culture, and Identity" at Middlebury College and noticed a dearth of accessible yet scholarly readings about halal food to assign her students. Students in that inaugural course, and in its subsequent incarnations, gave important insights and asked discerning questions that, in many ways, inspired the book's organization. We would also like to thank University of Vermont students Nell Cava, Zachary Heier, and Isabella Schechter who read and offered helpful comments on some of the book's first chapters as part of Boğaç Ergene's "Animals in Islamic Tradition(s)" class in spring 2017.

Finally, we would like extend our gratitude to our families. We were fortunate to have and were encouraged by their continuous and enthusiastic support in the process of writing this book.

ABBREVIATIONS

ABV	alcohol by volume
AHC-Europe	European Association of Halal Certifiers
AKP	Justice and Development Party (Adalet ve Kalkınma Partisi) of Turkey
AOI	Thailand's Administration of Organizations of the Islamic Act
AVS	A votre service
CEN	European Committee for Standardization (Comité Européen de Normalisation)
DİB	Directorate of Religious Affairs (Diyanet İşleri Başkanlığı) of Turkey
EFTA	European Union and the European Free Trade Association
ESMA	Emirates Authority for Standardization and Metrology
FAO	Food and Agriculture Organization of the United Nations
FDA	Food and Drug Administration of the United States
GCC	Gulf Cooperation Council
GDP	gross domestic product
GİMDES	Association of Inspection and Certification Research for Food and Material Needs (Gıda ve İhtiyaç Maddeleri Denetleme ve Sertifikalandırma Araştırmaları Derneği) in Turkey

GMOs	genetically modified organisms
GMP	good manufacturing practice
GS 993	Gulf Cooperation Council's Animal Slaughtering Requirements
GSO	Standardization Organization of the Gulf Cooperation Council
GSO 2055	Gulf Cooperation Council's General Requirements for Halal Food
HACCP	hazard analysis and critical control point
HalMQ	Halal Quality Management System of Singapore's MUIS
HFA	Halal Food Authority in the United Kingdom
HMC	Halal Monitoring Committee in the United Kingdom
HMSA	Humane Methods of Slaughter Act of the United States
IFANCA	Islamic Food and Nutrition Council of America
IHI Alliance	International Halal Integrity Alliance
IKIM	Institute of Islamic Understanding in Malaysia
IQS	Islamic Quality Standard for Hotels
ISO	International Organization for Standardization
JAKIM	Malaysian Department of Islamic Development (Jabatan Kemajuan Islam Malaysia)
MAIN	Islamic Religious Councils in Malaysia
MENA	Middle East and North Africa
MeS	MUIS eHalal System
MIHAS	Malaysia International Halal Showcase
MS 1500	Malaysian Standard 1500
MUI	Indonesian Ulama Council (Majelis Ulama Indonesia)
MUIS	Islamic Religious Council of Singapore (Majlis Ugama Islam Singapura)
OIC	Organization of Islamic Cooperation
OIC/SMIIC 1	OIC's General Guidelines on Halal Food
PETA	People for the Ethical Treatment of Animals
SIRIM-Berhad	State-owned "total solutions provider" for Malaysia's industrial sector
SMIIC	Standards and Metrology Institute for Islamic Countries
SMIIC 1	*See* OIC/SMIIC 1
TC1	OIC's Technical Committee on Halal Food Issues
TDA	Trade Description Act

TSE	Turkish Standards Institute (Türk Standardları Enstitüsü)
TUBITAK	The Scientific and Technological Research Institute of Turkey (Türkiye Bilimsel ve Teknolojik Araştırma Kurumu)
UAE	United Arab Emirates
WHC	World Halal Council
WHFC	World Halal Food Council
WHO	World Health Organization

GLOSSARY

ahadith   plural of *hadith*

ahl al-kitab   people of scripture, i.e., Jews and Christians. *See also* kitabi

akçe   a monetary unit in the Ottoman Empire

"Allah Akbar"   "God is great." *See also* tasmiyya

banj   hemp

bid'a   innovation, which is often assumed to be corrupt and illegitimate

"Bismillah"   "In the name of God." *See also* tasmiyya

boza   a lightly fermented drink made from barley, millet, or wheat

dhabiha **(or *zabiha*)**   halal slaughter or a halal-slaughtered animal

dhikr   in Islamic mysticism, devotional sessions

döner kebab   spiced, roasted, and thinly sliced meat of lamb, beef, and sometimes chicken

fard   religious duty or obligation. *See also* wajib

fatwa   a jurisprudential opinion

fiqh   "Islamic jurisprudence" in the sense of jurists' attempts to discover God's design for righteous Muslim life (i.e., Sharia)

hadith   accounts of the Prophet Muhammad's and his companions' sayings and actions; plural, *ahadith*

Hanafi   a Sunni *madhhab*

Hanbali   a Sunni *madhhab*

halal   legally permissible, lawful

haram   forbidden, illegitimate, sinful

hijra   flight, specifically the Prophet's flight from Mecca to Medina in 622 CE

ijma'   juridical consensus, a source for jurisprudential interpretation in Islamic law

infaha   rennet, also known as *minfaha* or *manafih*

isnad   a hadith's chain of transmission

istihala   biochemical transformation of impermissible substances into halal ones

istihlak   dissolution of small amounts of impermissible substances in large amounts
of halal ones

Ja'fari   a Shiite *madhhab*

janaba   state of bodily impurity following sexual intercourse or ejaculation

kashrut   Jewish dietary laws

kefir   slightly fermented, yogurt-like beverage

khaba'ith   *khabith* in plural

khabith   filthy, disgusting, and/or polluting thing

khalifa   a term that most interpret as Allah's vice-regent on earth; others translate it
as steward of the earth

khamr   wine, alcoholic beverages; plural, *khamar*

kımız (kumis, kumiss)   fermented mare's milk

kitabi   Jewish or Christian. *See also* ahl al-kitab

kufr   unbelief

madhhab   Sunni and Shiite school of law

makruh   actions and substances that should be avoided but cannot be considered
categorically forbidden because of a lack of clear or definitive directives in the
Quran or ahadith

mashbuh   suspicious

Maliki   a Sunni *madhhab*

mandub   recommended

maslaha   public interest

mayta   carrion; an animal that dies in a fashion other than ritual slaughter

mi'raj   the Prophet Muhammad's ascension to heaven

mubah   permitted

mufti   a Muslim jurist who issues a jurisprudential opinion (fatwa)

muhtasib   premodern market inspector

mustahab   preferred

nabidh   a lightly fermented drink that the Prophet was reported to have enjoyed

najis (najs)   foul, filthy, and/or impure

naskh   abrogation of earlier Quranic verses by later ones

niyya   intent to perform a religiously sanctioned act

qat   a plant with mind-altering effects indigenous to Eastern Africa *qibla*   the direction of prayer toward Mecca

qiyas   analogical reasoning, a source for jurisprudential interpretation in Islamic law

qullatayn   the amount of liquid in roughly the equivalent of two clay urns, discussed in the context of *istihlak*

rahiq   pure wine

rakı   an anise-flavored alcoholic drink

rijs   filth; dirty, foul, and/or impure things

sahih   sound, reliable

samak   fish; according some jurisprudential opinions the term is inclusive of sharks, whales, cephalopods, crustaceans, and mollusks

sayd   hunting, fishing

Shafi'i   a Sunni *madhhab*

Sharia   "Islamic law" in the sense of God's design for righteous Muslim life; compare to *fiqh*

shechita   Jewish ritual slaughter

shubha   doubt

Sufism   Islamic mysticism

sunna   customs; practices of the Prophet Muhammad and his companions, which became accepted as normative by subsequent generations of Muslims

tahir   pure

tasmiyya   invocation of God's name

tayyib   good, wholesome, pure; plural, *tayyibat*

tayyibat   plural for *tayyib*

ulama   Islamic jurists and legal scholars

umma   Muslim community; plural, *umam*

wajib   religious duties or obligations. *See also* fard

zabiha   see *dhabiha*

zakat   almsgiving to the poor

A NOTE ON TRANSLITERATION

Primarily for the sake of simplicity, we employed for Arabic words a modified version of the *IJMES* transliteration system. We omitted the use of non-*'ayn* or -*hamza* diacritical marks in transliterated words. Names of recognized places, historical figures, or terms such as Ali, Aisha, Rabia, Umar, Ibn al-Arabi, Quran, Shiite, Sharia, and ulama were all included in their most common English spelling without the 'ayn or hamza. Other names directly transliterated from their original Arabic, however, included the 'ayn or hamza. Turkish and French words, phrases, and book titles were given in their familiar modern spelling. We italicized foreign words when first introduced in the text, with exceptions for known words in English like sheikh and mufti.

HALAL FOOD

In 2014, Henna Khan and Talib Hussein, a Muslim-British couple from West Yorkshire, were growing more and more frustrated that one of their three children was repeatedly served ham and jelly sweets at school despite the parents' best efforts to communicate with school administrators about the family's religious dietary obligations. Ham is made of pork, which is not permissible or *halal* for Muslim consumption, and the jelly sweets likely contain porcine-derived gelatin, which most Muslims also consider unlawful. The family's frustration reached such a point that Henna Khan decided to pin bright red "Halal Only" tags to her children's clothing as a protest and to remind school officials to respect her family's religious needs. When interviewed by the press, Khan revealed the extent of her family's dissatisfaction and wondered about the school's (in)actions:

> Every time we complained to the school they say they are going to look into why this [giving non-halal food to Muslim children] is happening, yet these mistakes keep happening. I asked [school administrators] "does this happen to any of the other children?" [to] which they replied "no." This made me question whether someone is doing this on purpose. It has been quite stressful for us since we have moved to the area and I have even been to see the head teacher in tears. We have

never had any problems with the school and the kids all do well here. They just need to give the right meals to the right children.[1]

Khan's words indicate the intensity that "dietary wars" were beginning to reach in British school cafeterias and among the broader public. In the previous decade, Muslim (and also Jewish) parents had increasingly demanded accommodations for religious dietary needs, yet they often met resistance, not just from administrators but also from other parents. The latter opposed catering to minority religious food customs, such as providing pork-free meals or those derived from ritually slaughtered animals, citing any changes to established eating practices as an attack on "fundamental" British values and on their own freedom to eat nonreligiously sanctioned food.[2] In the midst of these tensions, Henna Khan's homemade signs on her children's clothes appeared as emblematic of her family's resistance. They deliberately called attention to the children's religious identities and showed how a halal diet and lifestyle can be a critical, even proud symbol of Muslim faith. The story, more importantly, stood as a general reminder of how eating halal food had become implicated in Muslims' efforts to assimilate and integrate within European culture and society.

Fig. I.1. Henna Khan with her three children (from left to right: Mohammed Talib, Khadija Khan, and Tayyeba Khan), wearing homemade "Halal Only" signs. Used with permission from © SWNS Picture Desk.

This book focuses on the relationship between food rules and Islam, a critical concern for many Muslims. More specifically, it studies sanctioned dietary substances and practices in the Islamic tradition while exploring how halal versus *haram* (impermissible) food considerations evolved over time and in varied Muslim settings. Echoing a central issue raised by the Hussein-Khan family's story, the narrative also examines how Muslims came to think about food in relation to their own identity and that of others, and how—throughout history—they devised systems of food production and consumption that suited their specific needs and demands. While broader halal rules extend to clothing, ritual prayers, speech, and general conduct, this book focuses solely on food and other ingestible substances (e.g., intoxicants like tobacco), which were often addressed in the same Muslim juristic writings.

Concerns about food purity in Islam are as ancient as this religion itself. Over the centuries, what to eat, what to avoid, including restrictions on alcohol and other intoxicants, distinguished Muslims from non-Muslims. It is a cliché that in Islam, people's religious identity is based as much on how they live as on what they believe. And correct eating and drinking are key aspects of a correct Islamic lifestyle. This point was expressed differently, and perhaps with a greater sense of urgency, in the *State of the Global Islamic Economy Report 2016/2017*: "Within the Islamic tradition, a person's spirituality and the purity of one's soul are very much tied to the food and drink we consume. In an age of increasing commercialization, the food we consume can be devoid of God's presence and the reverence for God's creation that Islam requires. It is this gap that much of the Halal Food sector seeks to fill."[3]

Islam's teachings and attitudes about food find their roots in its scripture. God's revelations to the Prophet Muhammad, as recorded in the Quran (Qur'an, Koran), celebrate the act of eating, so long as it is in moderation and so long as believers acknowledge divine benevolence. In Quranic descriptions of paradise, God promises "rivers of water unaltered, rivers of milk the taste of which never changes, rivers of wine delicious to those who drink, and rivers of purified honey, in which they will have from all [kinds of] fruits, and forgiveness from their Lord" (47:15). Such lush ideals sharply, though understandably, contrasted with Arabia's barren desert climate, where scarcity and rationing prevailed. Islamic conceptualizations of permissible and forbidden foodstuffs were therefore tied to topography, geography, and existing modes of sustenance but were also influenced by pre-Islamic food taboos among Jews, Christians, and animists. These groups and their eating habits were frequently referenced and sometimes denounced in the Quran and also in the *ahadith* (sayings of the Prophet Muhammad and his companions; singular form is *hadith*), texts that highlighted the Prophet's *sunna* (or custom), which became normative among subsequent generations of Muslims. The Quran and ahadith contain the core halal dictums—specifically, those against consuming pork, blood, carrion (an animal that dies in a fashion other than ritual slaughter), and alcohol. Later medieval juristic and legal authorities would articulate a more elaborate and rigorous interpretation of these canonical sources.

Yet it is not always easy to determine what constitutes correct eating and drinking according to Islamic legal provisions. In fact, within many modern settings, Muslims' desire to live according to Islamic principles is complicated by their struggle to better interpret and apply those principles to their constantly changing circumstances. Often, ancient Islamic legal interpretations of what constitutes halal are more flexible than modern expectations, as in the case of halal slaughter and who may perform it. In other instances, though, what was once considered "forbidden" might now be "acceptable." For example, in 1983, Iran's Ayatollah Khomeini issued a fatwa that permitted the consumption and trade of sturgeon caviar in response to specific economic needs and despite long-standing prohibitions against sturgeon in Shiite (Shi'ite, Shi'i) Islam.[4] In other contexts, from Malaysia to the United States, Muslims are reexamining the status of practices with no correlates in early Islam's canonical sources, such as prestunned and machine-slaughtered animals, or the use of gelatin or lecithin in food manufacturing. Although conceptualizations of halal food constitute critical bases of religious practice, these conceptualizations are being reconstrued as Muslims adjust to new, sometimes radically different and often Western-imported changes to food production and to their dietary worldviews.

Studying the meaning and history of halal is particularly pertinent in the midst of the present-day "halal revolution."[5] According to one current estimate, the size of the global halal food and beverage market is $1.2 trillion, constituting about 17 percent of the global food industry.[6] The overall spending on halal food and beverage products is predicted to grow at 8.5 percent annually until 2021, when the sector will be worth about $1.9 trillion.[7] Over the past few decades, Muslims have shown an increasing awareness of and demand for Islamic products and services—from food and medicine, to clothing and cosmetics—in an effort to express their pietistic intentions; build stronger, more self-consciously Muslim communities; and, especially among diaspora Muslims, deal with feelings of alienation.[8] This demand has prompted global manufacturers such as Nestlé, Coca-Cola, and Cadbury to stock supermarket shelves with hundreds of halal-approved products. In many ways, these foodstuffs serve a market long ignored by the industry, but their increasing availability also adds to the need for greater standardization and industrial efficiency, which frequently lead to more restricted interpretations of medieval juristic opinions. The book also addresses these questions, particularly as related to halal food processing, certification, and consumption.

In recent years, ethnographic, sociological, and technical research on halal has proliferated. This book differs from past scholarship as a work of history that addresses the nature, development, and significance of halal food provisions, connecting halal's historical formulations with later developments and trajectories. Indeed, many existing works treat halal specifications as static. And yet current anxieties surrounding pork and its by-products are tied as much to recent considerations of hygiene and healthfulness, to the industrial manufacturing of prepackaged foods, and to the rise of Islamic pietism as they are to classical Quranic prohibitions. Likewise, questions pertaining to intoxicants, to meat and its slaughter, and to cooking have both ancient and recent histories. One important contribution of this volume is to explore various conceptualizations of halal food through such dynamic trajectories.

The book's geographic locus follows the spread of Islam itself. The Arabian Peninsula and the Middle East and North African regions were the birthplace of not only the Islamic religion but also its greatest early empires. In these heartlands, medieval jurists formulated dietary laws; and political leaders and legal administrators enforced key food rules. In the late medieval and early modern worlds, grand empires like the Ottomans, the Safavids, and the Mughals, extending from the Balkans and the Middle East to the Indian subcontinent, came into close contact with new cultures, religious traditions, and ingredients that shaped extant dietary habits. Questions of how certain rulers may have dealt with alcohol prohibitions in their territories or whether they allowed the consumption of certain types of seafood over others reveal some variability in the enforcement of halal rules. Much of the historically based material, particularly in the early parts of the book, focuses on the Middle East and North Africa, incorporating case studies from other contexts when relevant.

The development of new halal regulations, the rise of the halal consumer and certification industry, and the construction of a "halal cuisine" in the modern period trace halal's broader global reach. Halal's current epicenters have moved beyond their medieval and early modern bases—Baghdad, Cairo, Istanbul—to encompass Kuala Lumpur, Jakarta, Singapore, London, and Chicago. Muslims living in Europe and North America have larger disposable incomes and a heightened awareness of their religious identity. Many are eager to live modern and cosmopolitan lives and to freely engage in modern consumption habits—from buying the most fashionable clothes to eating at the hippest sushi restaurants—while also shopping for products that allow them to abide by strict pietistic standards. Their expanding conceptualizations of halal—as organic, untainted, healthy, wholesome, and delicious—have drawn, as noted, the attention of global manufacturers eager to meet and profit from this market. Diasporic Muslims such as the Hussain-Khan family therefore play an equal (and perhaps sometimes greater) role than their coreligionists in majority-Muslim countries with regard to how halal food is consumed and molded in today's world.

Rather than follow a strict chronological approach, the book is thematically organized, highlighting core sources, interpretations, and topics. It starts with a basic discussion of the halal prescriptions found in Islam's canonical sources—the Quran and the Prophet Muhammad's example in hadith traditions. As chapter 1 shows, subsequent generations of Muslims built a complex system of dietary regulations based on these sources but always under the sway of a wider set of cultural, economic, and geographical influences as Islam rapidly expanded from its Arabian core. Consequently, although the halal protocols adopted by Muslim jurists were generally consistent with regard to jurisprudential concepts and terminology, they came to reflect a diversity of opinions on the legal status of different dietary practices. Chapters 2 to 4 detail the development of halal prescriptions governing meat, slaughter, and various intoxicants. These chapters trace how medieval and early modern communities came to view core halal rules and then how modern interpretations have subsequently emerged under the influence of various factors including considerations of animal rights and welfare, the economics of food production in industrialized settings (such as factory farms and slaughterhouses), and modern medical information on the health effects of different psychoactive substances.

Chapter 5 explores the global halal business, which expanded considerably over the last few decades. Cultural, economic, demographic, and political factors have contributed to the proliferation of halal commerce and market transactions since the 1980s. Both public and private actors provide services to halal consumers. And, in the international arena, various governments and organizations compete to control greater portions of increasingly lucrative profits via their efforts in standardization, regulation, and certification.

Chapter 6 compares five major halal food standards that were developed over the last two decades by global halal actors: Malaysia, the Organization of Islamic Cooperation (OIC), and the Gulf Cooperation Council (GCC). These alternative standards for halal food production, packaging, and marketing represent competing scripts for what counts as halal in the international arena. Despite their differences, however, they also symbolize how in modern times, governments and their market calculations have become increasingly influential in deciding what counts as permissible and impermissible food in Islamic terms.

Chapter 7 explores halal compliance issues pertaining to modern food additives and manufactured products. It discusses how Muslims have recently come to assess the halal status of gelatin and other animal-derived food additives and ingredients, sodas and energy drinks, and "faux libations" (e.g., non-alcoholic beer or wine) by retooling ancient legal concepts and formulations. At the same time, Muslims' attempts to detect and eliminate the slightest traces of porcine substances and alcohol in manufactured food products and beverages have led to what anthropologist Johan Fischer calls the "scientification of halal,"[9] that is, the use of scientific methods and sophisticated technologies to ensure the purity of halal substances. In this sense, the challenges generated by modern food and beverage industries have brought about an eclectic, pragmatic approach to halal considerations.

Chapter 8 shifts the discussion from business and manufacturing to the ethical and health aspects of halal eating. In particular, it examines how some contemporary Muslims strive to incorporate into their conceptualizations of halal the Quranic concept of *tayyib* ("good," "tasty," "wholesome," or "pure") and are thus intent on producing humanely sourced food that is also good for human health. By reinterpreting the Quranic approval of good and wholesome foodstuffs, proponents of ethical and healthy halal have been developing alternative scripts for halal food alongside the official standards discussed in chapter 6. Many of these scripts attempt to characterize halal food in extralegal terms—to link halal to vegan, vegetarian, organic, free-range, and non-GMO (genetically modified organism) designations. Some intellectuals and activists are also seeking to challenge the capitalist orientation of the worldwide halal business and to refocus Muslims' attention toward more pious and transcendent habits, be they in food consumption or environmental stewardship. Such efforts are still far from widespread among Muslims, even in the West, but their very existence underscores the fact that conceptions of halal still shift and expand.

Finally, the last two chapters explore the halal food phenomenon in popular culture, first as a cuisine (chapter 9), and then as a dining and public eating option in restaurants, fast-food eateries, airplanes, school dining halls, and prisons (chapter 10). Together, these chapters demonstrate how the notion of halal has recently been transformed from an obscure set of religious prescriptions for observant Muslims into something that is increasingly mainstream and even appealing to non-Muslims. This development, noticeable not only in the most cosmopolitan centers of the Western world like New York and London but also in countries such as China and Japan, is likely to continue with the growing pace of globalization and as entrepreneurs become better aware of the business opportunities associated with halal marketing.

CHAPTER 1

I n the 610s, during the nascent days of the Islamic religion, the polytheistic Meccan elites in the western parts of the Arabian Peninsula perse-
cuted, harassed, and at one point even banished the Prophet Muhammad
and his followers for propagating their new monotheistic beliefs. To protect
his followers from growing persecution, the Prophet dispatched dozens to
Abyssinia (modern-day Ethiopia), a Christian kingdom under the governance
of King Negus, who is remembered by Muslims as just and compassionate. The
newcomers wished to live in peace with their Christian neighbors, whom they
sought neither to convert nor to offend.

One day King Negus called their leader, the Prophet's cousin Ja'far, and
asked him why Muslims had turned their back on their ancient religion but
also refused to adopt the Christian faith of their Abyssinian hosts. Ja'far
explained, "We were a people steeped in ignorance, worshipping idols, eating
unsacrificed carrion, committing abominations, and [living in a community
where] the strong would devour the weak . . . . So we [now] worship God alone,
setting naught beside Him, counting as forbidden what He has forbidden and
licit what He has allowed . . . . That is why we have come to thy country, having
chosen thee above others; and we have been happy in thy protection."[1]

Ja'far's response captures early Muslim efforts to distinguish themselves
from their animist and polytheistic ancestors who, among other offenses, ate

improperly sacrificed meat, that is, carrion. Implicitly, Ja'far thus also gave a nod of respect to his Christian hosts. Christians in these lands had long held their own restrictive attitudes toward food, ones that mirrored Jewish rules about which animals can be consumed, who can perform acts of slaughter, and whether meals can be shared with non-coreligionists. Ja'far may have recognized that his explanation would elicit empathy from this royal Christian audience—that the desire to create an autonomous religious community based on specific dietary rules would be viewed with some measure of understanding.[2]

Although stories about food, identity, and difference in the context of the early Muslim community abound in various historical sources—namely, biographies of the Prophet Muhammad or, more commonly, in collections of his and his early companions' sayings—this chapter focuses first on the notion of halal as applied to Islamic dietary practices in the Quran. The Muslim scripture constitutes the earliest and most important source for divine guidance in every aspect of Muslim life, including halal matters. Here relevant sections are contextualized within the historical and geographical setting where the scripture was revealed and related to earlier religious traditions in surrounding regions.

To Muslims, the Quran is the compilation of the revealed words of God, as transmitted by the Prophet Muhammad, and the foundational text for Islamic law. But the Quran, like the Jewish and Christian scriptures, encompasses a wide range of topics; the strictly legal sections are limited in nature and number, as are the verses about licit and illicit dietary practices. For this reason, to develop a jurisprudential system that addresses food matters required an enormous intellectual effort and creativity by generations of Muslim legal minds following the revelatory period. Where the Quran was ambiguous or silent, Muslim jurists (ulama) turned to the corpus of sources known as the ahadith, the collected accounts of the sayings and actions of the Prophet Muhammad and his earliest companions. This trove of reports, some deemed more reliable than others, contains a wealth of information about the dietary customs and habits of the first Muslims. So they, alongside the Quran, became crucial in establishing halal rules and dictums. In addition, jurists formulating dietary precedents relied on an array of legal tools, including analogical reasoning (qiyas) and juridical consensus (ijma'). This chapter also explores the roots of this process, investigating how Muslims, vis-à-vis the Quran and the ahadith, came to determine what food was permissible, what was impermissible, and what lay in between those absolutes.

Fig. 1.1. *The Prophet Muhammad and His Companions at a Feast* (painting, recto; text, verso), illustrated folio from a manuscript of *Siyar-i Nabi* (*The Life of the Prophet*) by Mustafa Darir of Erzurum, 1594–1595. Unknown Artist. Harvard Art Museums/Arthur M. Sackler Museum, The Edwin Binney, 3rd Collection of Turkish Art at the Harvard Art Museums, 1995.824. Photo: Imaging Department © President and Fellows of Harvard College.

Halal in the Quran

According to Muslims, the Quran was progressively revealed to the Prophet Muhammad in the early seventh century CE, beginning around the year 610. The holy book is considered the compilation of the actual words of Allah, the Arabic term for the one God that Muslims worship, as conveyed to Muhammad by the Angel Gabriel. The Prophet continued to receive God's revelations for about twenty years, until his death in 632, when the revelations were amassed by his followers into a single text.

Significantly more is known about Muhammad as a historical figure than about other Abrahamic prophets. He lived in the bustling trade and pagan pilgrimage center of Mecca, located in the Hijaz region of the western Arabian Peninsula. Although he belonged to the Quraysh, the tribal conglomerate that controlled the strategically positioned city, he was not one of its most powerful elites, those who administered Mecca's economic and religious affairs. In fact, both his personal opinions and the revelations he received from Allah were unsympathetic toward the socioeconomic and religious pillars of the city. His message challenged the greedy mercantilism of the Meccan elite and their pagan and polytheistic orientation. Thus, when Muhammad rallied a small community of poorer, marginalized individuals with monotheistic inclinations, Mecca's patriarchs felt threatened. Following a period of intimidation and harassment spearheaded by the Qurayshi elite, Muhammad and his followers were expelled from Mecca in 622, the event known to Muslims as the *hijra* or emigration, and took refuge in the nearby northern oasis of Yathrib, which would later come to be known as Madinat al-Nabi ("city of the Prophet," or "Medina" in short). In Medina, Muhammad established the first full-fledged Muslim community and waged a protracted but ultimately successful military campaign against Mecca, which he conquered in 630.

This chronology provides critical background for the revelations Muhammad received, particularly regarding key halal food prescriptions. In Mecca, the Muslims, surrounded by hostile pagan elements, lived in a defensive position. In Medina, they gradually assumed positions of power—not only over non-Muslim elements of the town, which included the settlement's Jewish inhabitants, but also against their archenemies, the pagans of Mecca. Quranic revelations about ritual prayer, religious practices, and food and eating customs may be interpreted to reflect the Muslims' sense of anxiety and excitement based on evolving circumstances in Mecca and Medina.

In the Quran, the term "halal" refers to objects and practices regarded as lawful and permissible.[3] The opposite of halal is "haram," which is often translated as "forbidden," "illegitimate," "unlawful," and "sinful."[4] The Quran uses these terms or their derivatives to make assertions about the lawfulness and unlawfulness of specific economic transactions, ritual practices, sexual and family interactions, and dietary matters—questions of great import for the earliest Muslims in Mecca and Medina. For example, the Quran states that "Allah has permitted [*ahalla*] trade and has forbidden [*harrama*] interest" (2:275). It is "not lawful [*la yahillu*] for you to inherit women by compulsion" (4:19).[5] Also, "prohibited [*hurrimat*] to you [for marriage] are your mothers, your daughters, your sisters, your father's sisters, your mother's sisters, your brother's daughters, your sister's daughters, your [milk] mothers who nursed you, your sisters through nursing, your wives' mothers, and your step-daughters under your guardianship [born] of your wives unto whom you have gone in" (4:23). During the designated period of pilgrimage to Mecca—a practice that would become enshrined in the Islamic religion during the Prophet's lifetime—hunting land animals is "forbidden [*hurrima*]," but obtaining "game from the sea" is "lawful [*uhilla*]" (5:96).[6]

The Quran states that God created food to sustain and nourish life and encouraged humans to enjoy it in moderation. Thus food represents God's divine power and benevolence (26:79 and 41:10).[7] Clear Quranic prohibitions against specific types of food are provided in a limited number of verses, given below in the chronological order of revelation from the earliest to the more recent:

> 6:145 (Meccan): Say, "I do not find within that which was revealed to me [anything] forbidden to one who would eat it unless it be a dead animal or blood spilled out or the flesh of swine—for indeed, it is impure—or it be [that slaughtered in] disobedience, dedicated to other than Allah. But whoever is forced [by necessity], neither desiring [it] nor transgressing [its limit], then indeed, your Lord is Forgiving and Merciful."

> 16:115 (Meccan): He [Allah] has only forbidden to you dead animals, blood, the flesh of swine, and that which has been dedicated to other than Allah. But whoever is forced [by necessity], neither desiring [it] nor transgressing [its limit]— then indeed, Allah is Forgiving and Merciful.

> 2:173 (Medinan; revealed two years after Muhammad's flight from Mecca): He has only forbidden to you dead animals, blood, the flesh of swine, and that which has been dedicated to other than Allah. But whoever is forced [by necessity],

neither desiring [it] nor transgressing [its limit], there is no sin upon him. Indeed, Allah is Forgiving and Merciful.

5:3 (Medinan; revealed at the time of the final or "farewell" pilgrimage, about two years before the Prophet's death in 632): Prohibited to you are dead animals, blood, the flesh of swine, and that which has been dedicated to other than Allah, and [those animals] killed by strangling or by a violent blow or by a head-long fall or by the goring of horns, and those from which a wild animal has eaten, except what you [are able to] slaughter [before its death], and those which are sacrificed on stone altars . . . . But whoever is forced by severe hunger with no inclination to sin—then indeed, Allah is Forgiving and Merciful.

Although the Islamic scripture outlines distinct rules against the consumption of blood and pork, the revelations are silent about why these substances are considered unlawful. As to other prescriptions, Muslims came to understand "dead animals" (*mayta*) as carrion: that is, any animal that was not ritually slaughtered (*dhabiha* or *zabiha*). Notably, the Quran does not explain what ritual slaughter is or why the explicit intention to kill is important. Animals dedicated to deities other than Allah and ones sacrificed on stone altars, presumably popular practices in pre-Islamic Arabia, are unlawful because they challenge the Quran's strict monotheistic message.[8] In this way, the holy text identifies the "other" by their food and presents the act of eating as a basis of in-group solidarity and out-group exclusion, a clear tendency in later jurisprudential interpretations.

The above prohibitions are not inflexible. In fact, all quotations show that the Quran allows the consumption of prohibited foods in dire circumstances, presumably when necessary for survival.[9] However, the scripture remains silent on what circumstances would make this breach of normative rules acceptable or how much intake of prohibited items would be warranted. The ulama would reflect on these topics, among others, in later periods.

The Quran contains additional directives relevant to food. Some verses deal with fasting, specifically during the holy month of Ramadan, when Muslims are expected to abstain from food, drink, and sexual relations from sunrise to sunset (2:183–187). On the other hand, verse 5:1 states that Muslims are not allowed to hunt while they are performing pilgrimage to Mecca.

Intoxicating beverages also receive attention, although Quranic statements on that topic paint a more oblique picture than those dealing with pig, blood, or carrion.[10] Here are the relevant verses regarding intoxicating substances in the order they were revealed to the Prophet Muhammad.

16:65–67 (Meccan): And Allah has sent down rain from the sky and given life thereby to the earth after its lifelessness. Indeed in that is a sign for a people who listen. And indeed, for you in grazing livestock is a lesson. We give you drink from what is in their bellies—between excretion and blood—pure milk, palatable to drinkers. And from the fruits of the palm trees and grapevines you take intoxicant [*sakaran*] and good provision. Indeed, in that is a sign for a people who reason. And your Lord inspired to the bee, "Take for yourself among the mountains, houses [i.e., hives], and among the trees and [in] that which they construct. Then eat from all the fruits and follow the ways of your Lord laid down [for you]." There emerges from their bellies a drink, varying in colors, in which there is healing [*shifa'un*] for people. Indeed in that is a sign for a people who give thought.

56:16–21 (Meccan): There [in paradise] will circulate among them young boys made eternal. With vessels, pitchers and a cup [of wine] from a flowing spring. No headache will they have therefrom, nor will they be inebriated [or "mad" or "exhausted"; *yunzifun*]. And fruit of what they select. And the meat of fowl, from whatever they desire.

37:43–48 (Meccan): In gardens of pleasure, on thrones facing one another, there will be circulated among them a cup [of wine] from a flowing spring. White and delicious to the drinkers; no bad effect is there in it, nor from it will they be inebriated [or "mad" or "exhausted"; *yunzifun*]. And with them will be women limiting [their] glances, with large, [beautiful] eyes.

83:22–26 (Meccan): Indeed, the righteous will be in pleasure, on adorned couches, observing. You will recognize in their faces the radiance of pleasure. They will be given to drink [pure] wine [*rahiqin*, which was] sealed.

2:219 (early Medinan): They ask you about wine [*al-khamri*] and gambling. Say, "In them is great sin [*ithmuhuma*] and [yet some] benefit for people. But their sin is greater than their benefit." And they ask you what they should spend. Say, "The excess [beyond needs]." Thus Allah makes clear to you the verses [of revelation] that you might give thought.

4:43 (Medinan): O you who have believed, do not approach prayer while you are intoxicated [*sukara*] until you know what you are saying or in a state of impurity [*junuban*], except those passing through [a place of prayer], until you have washed [your whole body]. And if you are ill or on a journey or one of you comes from the place of relieving himself or you have contacted women and find no water, then seek clean earth and wipe over your faces and your hands [with it]. Indeed, Allah is ever Pardoning and Forgiving.

47:15 (Medinan): Is the description of Paradise, which the righteous are promised, wherein are rivers of water unaltered, rivers of milk the taste of which never changes, rivers of wine [*anharun min khamrin*] delicious to those who drink, and rivers of purified honey, in which they will have from all [kinds of] fruits and for-giveness from their Lord, like [that of] those who abide eternally in the Fire and are given to drink scalding water that will sever their intestines?

5:90–91 (later Medinan): O you who have believed, indeed, wine [or intoxicants, al-khamru], gambling, [sacrificing on] stone altars [to other than Allah], and divining arrows are but defilement from the work of Satan, so avoid it that you may be successful. Satan only wants to cause between you animosity and hatred through wine [al-khamri] and gambling and to avert you from the remembrance of Allah and from prayer. So will you not desist?

What these verses demonstrate is that the Quran's treatment of intoxicating drinks, often equated to "wine" in later commentaries, is more ambiguous than its position regarding other prohibited substances.[11] The scripture does not explicitly state that intoxicating drinks are haram; indeed, verses 16:65–67 present them as among Allah's gifts to those who appreciate his power and creation. The verses that mention pleasure-inducing drinks in paradise (for example, 37:43–48) suggest that the problem with their earthly counterparts is not their foul or impure (najis) nature, but their troubling effects: they cause bodily discomfort and inebriation. Without the latter, they are as worthy of paradise as honey, milk, fruits, fowl meat, and wide-eyed maidens.[12]

A more critical attitude toward wine emerges from the Medinan verses, which were revealed when Muhammad became occupied with founding the first Muslim state to govern the first Muslim community, the umma. In this new setting, discussions over alcohol consumption and its mind-altering effects appear to have become more problematic.[13] Yet even these verses present variations in how intoxicants are treated. The first Medinan verse that mentions khamr, 2:219, acknowledges its benefit but declares that its resultant sin is greater than any good. Verse 4:43 again clarifies that alcohol consumption is repulsive for its inebriating symptoms, especially during prayer, when one is expected to be sober. The fact that this verse compares intoxication to bodily impurity caused by ejaculation (janaba) is instructive considering Islam's favorable treatment of licit sex. The religion sanctions sexual intercourse among lawful partners but requires them to take a ritual bath (ghusl al-janaba) before they participate in any religious activity. In a similar fashion, and read in isolation, 4:43 may be interpreted to suggest that alcohol consumption might be acceptable so long as those who drink purify themselves before prayer.[14]

Verses 5:90–91, which are said to have been revealed a mere two years before the Prophet's death, demonstrate the most critical treatment of khamr. Unlike earlier verses, these neither list the desirable attributes of the drink nor distinguish it from its adverse side effects. Instead, the verses compare wine-drinking to pre-Islamic pagan animal sacrifice and describe it as a temptation generated by Satan. Because these verses were revealed so late, their apparent inconsistency with earlier ones has been explained by Muslims with reference to the principle of abrogation (naskh): when they were revealed, 5:90–91's treatment of wine-drinking replaced, or abrogated, earlier scriptural attitudes and became accepted as the new standard.[15]

Food in Pre-Islamic Arabia

One way to understand the Quran's dietary prescriptions is to consider the variety of foods available in pre-Islamic Arabia and the existing religious and cultural traditions pertaining to their consumption. Given the inadequacy of historical sources on this topic, however, only limited observations are possible.

The Arabian Peninsula, birthplace of Islam over 1,400 years ago, is a region of about 1.2 million square miles, surrounded by the Red Sea in the West, the Persian Gulf in the East, and the Indian Ocean in the South. This hot and arid region receives less than ten centimeters or four inches of rain annually in most spots. Temperatures can reach over 120 degrees Fahrenheit (50 degrees Celsius) during daytime in the summer, often followed by steep nighttime cooling. In winter, the temperature scarcely falls under 50 to 60 degrees Fahrenheit (10–15 degrees Celsius), except in a few highlands. Much of the interior is covered with deserts, the western areas by bare rock-strewn mountains. Historically, this rugged topography hinders agricultural production. With the exception of Yemen, located in the peninsula's southwestern corner, the region is dry and barren, unsuitable for cultivation. In most locations, access to the sparse subterranean water resources is difficult, if not impossible. For centuries, wells dug for this purpose were tough to maintain, as they were easily clogged by frequent sandstorms. The combination of the low precipitation rates and permeable sandy soil, which makes water retention during short rainstorms difficult, allow for the growth of vegetation (trees, bushes, shrubs) that are hardy and have longer lifespans in the desert climate but are often unsuitable for a permanent agrarian economy. Date palms, for example, which need little water, were commonly grown primarily at oases in the inner and most arid regions. Cereals and fruits were cultivated in a few spots, but the quality and quantity of production was nothing like the lush agriculture of ancient Egypt, Mesopotamia, and parts of the Levant. Outside of a few important trade centers, a nomadic, herding, and tribal lifestyle prevailed. Before the discovery of oil in the early twentieth century, the nomads of Arabia—the Bedouin—primarily relied on animal husbandry for their survival. They also made a living by alternatively protecting, guiding, or looting trade and travel caravans.

Historian of early Islam Maxime Rodinson described the food of the pre-Islamic Arabs as "typical of the diet of a pastoral people in a desert region with scattered cultivated oases."[16] The Arabian diet depended heavily on milk and milk products from sheep, goats, and camels. Meat consumption was limited,

Fig. 1.2. The Arabian bustard is a medium to large-sized bird, commonly found in Southwest Asia and North Africa. Inhabitants of the Arabian Peninsula have historically hunted this bird, among other animals, for food. "Wikimedia Commons Arabian Bustard," photograph by ©Allan Drewitt, https://www.flickr.com/photos/31003918@N05/5559472710. Accessed July 28, 2017. Licensed under CC BY 2.0.

and the most commonly consumed meat was mutton; pre-Islamic Arabs rarely ate beef or goat. Camels, uniquely adapted to desert conditions and important for long-distance travel and transportation, were slaughtered only in cases of dire necessity. During famines, the Bedouin also drank blood drawn from a living camel, a practice still common among the seminomadic Maasai and Suri peoples of eastern Africa, who use cattle for this purpose. For climatic reasons, pigs and fowl must have been even rarer. Desert animals such as hare, bustard (a large bird mostly found in drylands), lizards, hedgehogs, and mice were consumed, and some Bedouin ate grasshoppers. In the coastal regions, fish complemented the local diet.

Dates, a very important food item, were grown at agricultural oases, where a few settled or semisettled agricultural populations also cultivated beets, leeks, chicory, onions, garlic, cucumbers, and a variety of vegetables from the gourd family. Citron, melons, pomegranates, and grapes are mentioned in ancient sources. Wheat bread may have been consumed on rare occasions, but barley bread was more common among settled populations, if not the Bedouin; indeed, it would become associated in the medieval Islamic period with "low life and austerity."[17] Dates, honey, barley, wheat, and raisins were also used to produce fermented drinks. Although some vineyards did exist, wine from grapes was generally imported and thus expensive. Agricultural production was more prominent in Yemen and southern Arabia, which held many orchards, vineyards, and vegetable gardens.

The Quran's hesitation to impose more dietary restrictions might thus be linked to the region's harsh climatic circumstances. Given the limited nutritional options available to the Arabian peoples, it makes sense that the Quran lists relatively few dietary restraints, a point that the scripture underscores by favorably comparing its own mandates with those imposed on Jews. A more extensive list of dietary requirements would have threatened the quality of life of the earliest Muslims, which is precisely what the Quran seems to avoid. The Quran insists that "Allah does not intend to make difficulty for you" (5:6). Believers should "eat from the good things [al-tayyibati] which We have provided for you and be grateful to Allah" (2:172). And Muslims should not "prohibit [tuharrimu] the good things [al-tayyibati] which Allah has made lawful [ahalla] to you" (5:87).

Quranic dietary requirements could be compared to food traditions among the pre-Islamic populations of Arabia, who abstained from eating the flesh of newborn animals, the hearts of birds, the fat tails of sheep, and testicles. Such

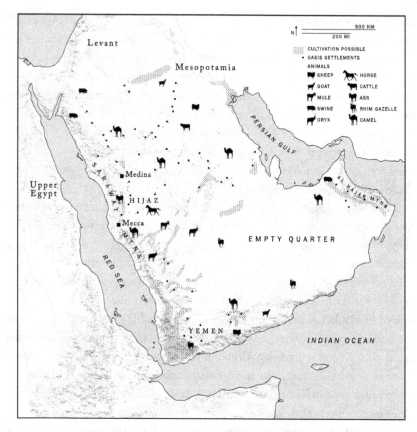

Map 1.1. Potential Food Sources in Pre-/Early Islamic Arabia

Note: Made with Natural Earth Data and Shuttle Radar Topography Mission Imagery (Courtesy NASA/JPL/NIMA).

Sources: Phillip K. Hitti, *History of the Arabs* (London: Palgrave, 2002); Fred M. Donner, *The Early Islamic Conquests* (Princeton, NJ: Princeton University Press, 1981); J. G. Bartholomew, "Land Surface Features of Arabia" (Edinburgh: Edinburgh Geographical Institute, 1904); Sarra Tlili, *Animals in the Qur'an* (Cambridge: Cambridge University Press, 2012).

rules were imposed "rather by custom than by definite code of laws," according to Rodinson.[18] In verse 5:103, the Quran ignores these traditions and criticizes pre-Islamic prohibitions on eating certain types of camels.[19] At the same time, by prohibiting Muslims from killing game and domesticated animals during pilgrimage (5:1), the Quran appears to endorse a parallel sanction that existed before the rise of Islam: in Mecca, families responsible for serving local sanctuaries abstained from consuming meat and milk products on religious holidays. Sources also indicate that Arabian inhabitants occasionally abstained from intoxicating drinks when following through on a vow; for example, one who swore vengeance avoided wine until his or her vengeance was fulfilled. Pre-Islamic Arabs may have also abstained from meat, milk, and wine due to the influence of restrictive Manichean ethics and ascetic Christianity.[20]

Scholars have long recognized the similarities between Quranic food prescriptions and Jewish and Christian guidelines (see Appendix A for a detailed comparison of kosher, Christian, and Islamic dietary regulations). Historical sources reference a visible Christian and Jewish presence in pre-Islamic Arabia. In addition to itinerant monks of diverse backgrounds, Christian communities lived both among the sedentary farmers in the southwestern corner of the peninsula and among nomadic herdsmen in the northwest. Considerable numbers of Jews also populated the region. These presumably included the descendants of refugees who fled from Judea after the Roman suppression of great rebellions in the late first and early second centuries after Christ, as well as indigenous converts to Judaism. Islamic sources specify the existence of Jewish clans and tribes in Medina at the time of the Prophet's arrival and discuss their often-uneasy relationship with the first Muslims. Both the Quran and early Islamic sources indicate a certain awareness of Jewish and Christian customs.

Prohibitions against the consumption of carrion and blood are present in Jewish and Christian traditions (Genesis 9:3–4; Leviticus 17:10–14; Acts 15:28–29).[21] Jewish dietary laws forbid the consumption of pork (Leviticus 11:7; Deuteronomy 14:8), a tendency that might have also existed in pre-Islamic Arabia, and they stress the importance of ritual slaughter, which transforms a live animal into lawful food.[22] Objections to eating at temples where animals are sacrificed for deities other than the one God can also be found in the teachings of Paul, specifically in 1 Corinthians 7–13.[23]

One instructive line of thought here is religion scholar David Freidenreich's observation that the Quran differentiates between Muslims and various non-Muslim communities, based on the food practices of specific groups. Quranic dietary prescriptions distinguish Muslims primarily from polytheists and secondarily from Jews, if not Christians.[24] On the one hand, by selectively endorsing the dietary prescriptions of the other two monotheistic groups, the Quran emphasizes continuity among the three Abrahamic traditions and juxtaposes their followers against contemporary polytheists.[25] This Abrahamic solidarity appears in verse 5:5: "This day [all] good foods have been made lawful, and the food of those who were given the Scripture is lawful for you and your food is lawful for them. And [lawful in marriage are] chaste women from among the believers and chaste women from among those who were given the Scripture before you." While there were disputes regarding how to interpret this verse, it was universally agreed that Muslims should stay clear from the food (and women) of the polytheists. Food and mating prescriptions as identity boundaries move Muslims closer to other monotheistic communities. Verse 5:5 imagines Muslims and members of earlier Abrahamic religions as compatible communities, people who can eat at the same table and mate with each other under certain conditions.[26]

On the other hand, by emphasizing the more restrictive aspects of Jewish dietary regulations, the Quran also differentiates Islam somewhat from Judaism. Verse 6:146 makes the latter point clear: "And to Jews We prohibited every animal of uncloven hoof [kulla dhi dhufurin]; and of the cattle and the sheep We prohibited to them their fat, except what adheres to their backs or the entrails or what is joined with bone. [By] that We repaid them for their injustice. And indeed, We are truthful." The punitive nature of these restrictions is clearer in verse 4:160, according to which God has imposed these dietary prescriptions on the Jews because of their "wrongdoing" and their "averting [people] from the way of Allah." It is noteworthy that the Quran makes no similar statements with regard to Christian dietary standards.[27]

Justifications for Prohibitions against Pork, Blood, and Carrion

The Quran prohibits the consumption of blood, pork, carrion, and the flesh of meat dedicated to deities other than Allah but does not explain why it endorses those first three proscriptions. Since these bans are not unique to Islam and existed among various communities in the pre-Islamic Near East, there might be clues about their roots in Islam within other religious and cultural practices.

Pigs have been bred in the Middle East for millennia. As early as 6500 BCE they were domesticated in what are now Turkey, Syria, and Iraq, and around 5000 BCE they made their appearance in Egypt. Ancient Egyptians had an ambivalent and somewhat dismissive attitude toward pigs, one that may have made its way into Judaism and local Christianity, and later into Islam. Although the poor ate pork, the ancient Egyptian nobility viewed pigs as loathsome creatures.[28] Their ambivalence was echoed in ancient Greek writings: Herodotus deemed pigs unclean; Philo condemned them as "licentious sophists"; and Plutarch remarked that the pig was filthy "because it seems to copulate especially as the moon wanes."[29]

Scholars have also offered different lines of explanation about the pork prohibition specific to the Jewish tradition. One theory, which cultural anthropologist Frederick Simoons has called the "hygienic hypothesis," focuses on the supposed negative effects of pork on human health and sees the prohibition as a way to eliminate this danger.[30] The rationale for this argument rests on claims of rapid pork decay in warm climates, contentions about the unhealthy nature of the pigs' omnivorous diet and unclean living habitat, and the association of pork with trichinosis, a parasitic disease caused by eating undercooked or raw meat. But there are problems with various formulations of the hygienic hypothesis. For one, there are easy ways to prevent the decay of pork in warmer climates, including thorough cooking. And with regard to pigs' dietary habits or their squalor, the Levitical code (and Muslim sources) allow the consumption of the flesh of other animals (such as chickens) that also feed on human refuse and forbids those that are quite clean (such as hares).

As to the connection between trichinosis and pork consumption, a number of factors make this an unlikely basis for the pork prohibition. First, it is possible that the parasite *Trichinella spiralis* appeared in Europe and the Near East relatively recently, not until the thirteenth, sixteenth, or even eighteenth centuries. The connection between the parasite, the pig, and the disease was made only in the nineteenth century, when *Trichinella* was discovered in human cadavers. The disease is difficult to diagnose, its incubation period is long (about ten days), its symptoms vary significantly among patients in both type and intensity, and they also mimic other conditions. So it appears unlikely that the relationship between the disease and pork was obvious to ancient Hebrews. Moreover, the scripture makes no mention of the health effects of pork consumption.[31] Finally, the consumption of other meat, including beef, mutton, and goat, could also have adverse health effects, but these did not lead to any prohibitions.[32]

Another line of explanation was proposed by researchers who explained the ban with reference to the material circumstances of the communities in which pork prohibitions appeared. Simoons dubs this view as the "economic, environmental, and ecological hypotheses."[33] In an arid or semiarid environment, pigs eat food otherwise fit for humans and might also consume more water, a scarce resource, than sheep or goats do. Thus, in most Near Eastern settings, raising pigs might have constituted an economic and ecological luxury, one best avoided by communities pressed for resources. But this explanation too has its shortcomings. Archaeological evidence in the semiarid regions of southern Jordan indicates that some pastoral communities in late antiquity raised pigs despite the harsh climate. In the fourth and fifth centuries, largely nomadic groups in the Negev region may have partly subsisted on pigs in addition to cattle.[34] In fact, pigs seem to have adapted to arid conditions.[35] Furthermore, ancient Palestine contained lush and wooded areas suitable for pigs, yet evidence doesn't show that humans raised pigs in these locations.

Other explanations attempt to make sense of the pork ban with reference to the scripture's own logic and in the context of broader religious concerns, considerations, and taxonomies. For example, according to anthropologist Mary Douglas, the Levitical pork prohibition can be understood through an exegesis of how the scripture orders the universe and classifies living things. That is, certain species of animals, particularly sheep, goats, and cattle, are considered blessed by God. As such, they are deemed normative in the sense that they demonstrate the purest aspects of God's animal creation. Species that are somehow different, on the other hand, are lacking, beneath human consumption, and certainly inappropriate for sacrifice to God. For Douglas, the shunned species lack the "holiness" of the preferred ones because they are not "whole" or pure—they are deficient of certain qualities specific to the norm. Since the species considered holy/whole are all ungulates that chew the cud and have cloven hoofs, the species without these characteristics are lacking and must be spurned, including the camel, the hare, and the pig.[36]

In principle, Christian traditions broke with Levitical dietary laws that forbade pork's consumption. The founder of Egyptian monasticism, St. Antony, allegedly kept a pet pig. Archeological evidence shows that several early Christian monasteries in Egypt raised pigs and sold their meat to supplement their income.[37] Some Christian theologians, however, openly condemned the pig. Clement of Alexandria remarked that "the pig refers to pleasure-loving and unclean desire for food and lewd and defiled license for sex."[38] Shenoute of Atripe also showed little love for swine and frequently maligned dissenters and heretics by calling them "worse than dogs and pigs." Also, Ethiopian Christians closely follow Levitical practices, including those against eating pigs, and in modern times, some Western Pentecostal and charismatic churches have preserved Levitical dietary rules and have either discouraged or prohibited pork consumption.[39]

When Muslims explain the pork prohibition in the Quran, they frequently rely on versions of the hygienic hypothesis rather than exegetical or cultural reasoning. The renowned medieval scholar Abu Hamid al-Ghazali (d. 1111) considered pork filthy, and more recently some Muslim scholars have mentioned trichinosis as a possible consequence of pork consumption.[40] Other researchers have associated pork consumption with swine flu, tuberculosis, anthrax, rabies, high cholesterol, heart disease, hypertension, and other diseases and conditions.[41] Consuming pig fat, adds physician-author Muhammad 'Ali al-Bar, can lead to deadly forms of cancer.[42] All of these interpretations likely stem from the fact that the Quran calls pork *rijs* (here *rijisun*, meaning dirty, foul, or impure) in 6:145 and associates the category of haram with things that are evil, unwholesome, and disgusting.[43] In 7:157 Allah enjoins upon humankind "what is right and forbids them what is wrong and makes lawful (*yuhillu*) for them the good things (*al-tayyibati*) and prohibits (*yuharrimu*) for them *al-khaba'ith[a]*." In the Quran *al-khaba'ith* is a catchall term that refers to all negative qualities, particularly to forbidden foods.[44]

The "economic, environmental, and ecological hypotheses," if valid, might make sense from an Islamic perspective, since Islam and Judaism have close geographic origins. Still, Muslim commentators have generally not pursued these lines of argument in explaining the pork prohibition. Rationales based on the close interpretation of religious texts (i.e., hermeneutics), on the other hand, are difficult to adopt because they make sense largely in the context of Jewish biblical and dietary traditions. Given the relatively limited number of food prohibitions in the Quran, it is difficult to offer a hermeneutical justification similar to what Douglas and others have proposed in their work.

But Muslims have made clear associations between pork consumption and moral degeneration. One common saying in Turkish that can also be found in some religious books on halal and haram might be translated as "Those who eat pork would not mind being cuckolded": that is, their moral standards pertaining to marital affairs would be abysmally low. According to a recent work on halal slaughter, certain animals, including pigs, "possess barbaric and shameless tendencies . . . [thus] they tend to have a morally adverse impact on the consumers."[45] Turkish scholar Yüksel Çayırlıoğlu has also suggested, with ample references to earlier medical literature, that pork fat diminishes vitamin E levels in the human body, which in turn erodes a man's ability to love and, thus, prevents him from being jealous, the latter considered an important masculine attribute. In fact, hogs don't fight over their females during heat as the males of many other species do, which the author presents as evidence for pigs' detestable nature.[46] He also considers pigs lazy, slow, ugly, and foul-smelling. They are so "lecherous" that they show no qualms in copulating with their own sex, and they often eat their own babies.[47] The Hui Chinese Muslims, on the other hand, regard the pig as lacking "moral goodness": among other things, the animal is "unfilial," and filial piety is a prized virtue in traditional Confucian codes.[48] In the context of these attitudes, it is surely inappropriate for human beings, whom the Quran depicts as God's most noble creation, to consume such animals.[49]

Compared to restrictions on pork prohibition, there are far fewer explanations behind the ban against blood and carrion in non-Islamic and Islamic cultures.[50] According to Jacob Milgrom, scholar of the Hebrew Bible, since blood is symbolic of life, the kashrut prohibition against eating or drinking blood—and against animals not slaughtered and drained of their blood according to established prescriptions (i.e., carrion)—is designed to prevent human beings from being desensitized to killing in general.[51] Interestingly, blood (and therefore blood consumption) is considered equally impure in Hindu traditions due to its association with killing.[52] These explanations, however, have not been adopted by Muslim commentators to justify Quranic prohibitions. Instead, and as with the ban against pork, Muslims have used sanitary and hygienic reasons to justify these practices: blood could be a vector for infection and may also carry toxins and waste products harmful to the body.[53] Carrion connotes danger not only because blood may not be properly drained from the corpse but also because the rotting flesh of a dead animal could be bad for digestion and a source of countless diseases.[54]

But religious scholars also have a tendency to resist all nonreligious rationales for Jewish or Islamic dietary requirements. While they generally acknowledge that food prohibitions must exist for the benefit of humankind, which the Quran explicitly suggests (7:157), humans need not fully understand the logic behind them.[55] Legal experts maintain that humans have no right to demand a logical reason to follow God's orders: food prescriptions should be observed simply because they represent God's will or because "God says so."[56] Any attempt to justify them based on health-based, economic, or environmental benefits might offend religious sensibilities.

Post-Quranic Developments in Islamic Jurisprudence

The Quranic restrictions on diet are few and simple compared to biblical prescriptions. However, as the Islamic community grew, dietary requirements expanded and became more systematic as Muslim jurists tried to accommodate the increasing demographic and cultural diversity in the new Islamic empires (Map 1.2).[57] Their efforts would play an important role in the development of Islamic jurisprudence (or *fiqh*) in the centuries after the Prophet's death. In fact, most concepts and terminology that Muslims utilized to formulate religious dietary requirements were shaped by the jurisprudential interpretations articulated after the revelatory period. These interpretations established the legal boundaries of halal and haram and generated a scale of classifications that helped Muslims define the gray areas of dietary provisions. To be sure, the halal and haram concepts became applicable to all sorts of human action and interaction. Here, though, attention is given to what they signify in the context of food, drink, and dietary practices.

Although the binary distinction of haram versus halal is based on the Quran, the scripture does not offer categorical definitions for these terms. Instead the holy text provides statements that are open to interpretation and that could be used by legally oriented minds to further elaborate boundaries for what is lawful and unlawful. One such statement can be found in 7:157, which informs the reader that God enjoins upon humankind "what is right and forbids them what is wrong and makes lawful for them al-tayyibat and prohibits for them al-khaba'ith." This could be a useful verse for legal concerns and prescriptions, provided that the reader knows exactly what the words al-tayyibat and al-khaba'ith meant in seventh-century Arabia. Today, it is common to translate al-tayyibat as good or wholesome things and al-khaba'ith as evil, filthy substances. However, historically speaking, the terms could have had a wider spectrum of related but not identical meanings. At various points in the Quran the word "tayyib" is used to mean good, pious, chaste (for men and women), clean, wholesome, fair, and favorable. Variations of the word could also mean to mollify or to be agreeable, willing, ripe, healthy, and fragrant.[58] Al-khaba'ith, on the other hand, can describe foul, filthy, impure, or disgusting things. Words associated with that term could also refer to wicked, vicious, sinful, corrupt practices; abominations; or obscenities.[59]

This spectrum of meanings associated with halal and haram offered jurists a vast range in determining what should be considered permissible and impermissible.[60] If haram is associated with filth, many later ulama reasoned, then anything that can be considered filthy should be unlawful for human use, even if it is not mentioned in the Quran. But how does one determine what is good and what is evil, what is clean and what is impure, what is acceptable and what

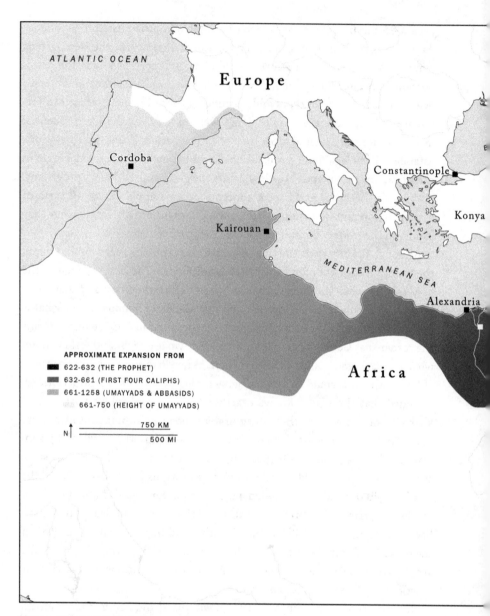

ATLANTIC OCEAN

Europe

Cordoba ■

Kairouan ■

Constantinople ■

Konya

MEDITERRANEAN SEA

Alexandria ■

Africa

APPROXIMATE EXPANSION FROM
■ 622-632 (THE PROPHET)
■ 632-661 (FIRST FOUR CALIPHS)
■ 661-1258 (UMAYYADS & ABBASIDS)
661-750 (HEIGHT OF UMAYYADS)

N ↑   750 KM
      500 MI

Map 1.2. Early Islamic Expansion

Note: Made with Natural Earth Data.
Sources: Roelof Roolvink, et al, *Historical Atlas of the Muslim Peoples* (Amsterdam: Djambatan, 1957);
W. Leisering and H. Schulze, "Die Ausbreitung des Islam," in *Putzger: Historischer Weltaltlas* (Berlin: Cornelsen
Verlag, 1992); "The Expansion of Islam from Antiquity to Colonial Morocco," https://chronicle.fanack.com/
morocco/history-past-to-present/from-antiquity-to-colonial-morocco/.

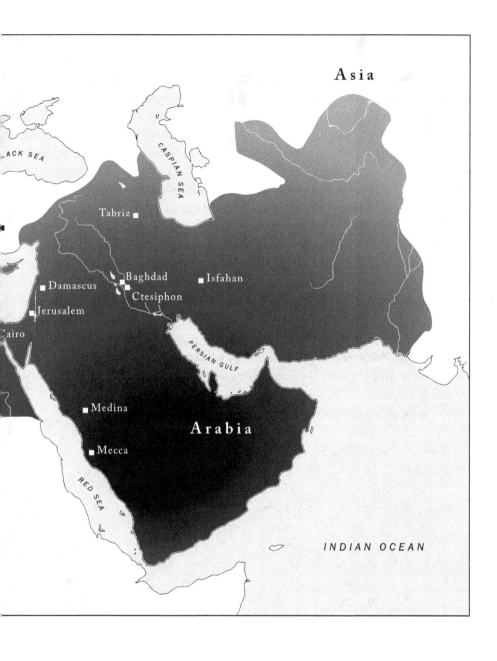

Asia

BLACK SEA

CASPIAN SEA

Tabriz

Baghdad   Isfahan

Damascus
Ctesiphon

Jerusalem

Cairo

PERSIAN GULF

Medina   **Arabia**

Mecca

RED SEA

INDIAN OCEAN

is objectionable if these items were not explicitly named? In some cases, the answer is easy: for example, Muslims agreed that human or animal feces are foul and should be kept away from food, though they are not mentioned in the Quran. Jurists also agreed that the consumption of any substance that might endanger human health is forbidden. Thus a plant- or animal-based poison cannot be regarded as tayyib. Also, the consumption of food and drinks acquired by illegitimate and immoral means, such as bribery or theft, should be prohibited.

It is more difficult to decide on the legal status of many other substances. God told Muslims that pig is rijs or "filth" (6:145), but what about animals not mentioned in the Quran? On the one hand, the Quran says that God "has explained in detail to you what He has forbidden you" (6:119). The holy text also states that "lost are those who . . . prohibited what Allah had provided for them, inventing untruth about Allah. They have gone astray and were not [rightly] guided" (6:140). Finally, "do not say about what your tongues assert of untruth, 'This is lawful and this is unlawful,' to invent falsehood about Allah. Indeed, those who invent falsehood about Allah will not succeed" (16:116). Some Muslims have interpreted these verses as warnings against attempts to expand on halal and haram prescriptions beyond what the scripture explicitly states. The majority of Muslims, on the other hand, admit the primacy of the Quran in providing guidance yet also insist that divine guidance on things permissible and impermissible is not limited to what is plainly stated. In particular, they consider the Prophet's example and the customs of the first generation of Muslims in determining what al-tayyibat and al-khaba'ith might mean.

The Quran orders Muslims to "obey the Messenger . . . . If you obey [the Messenger] you will be rightly guided" (24:54).[61] From the earliest times, Muslims compiled accounts of what the Prophet Muhammad said and did in specific circumstances as understood and transmitted by subsequent generations of Muslims. Called "reports," "narratives," or "sayings" (ahadith; singular hadith), these accounts also included stories of the Prophet's tacit approval of statements or actions by others in his presence. As repositories of Muhammad's prophetic example, the ahadith became normative sources of divine guidance, second in authority only to the Quran. Muslims reasoned that since the Quran was revealed to Muhammad, the Prophet (and his immediate community) understood the scripture better than subsequent generations of Muslims. Islamic traditions also insist that the Prophet, though a fallible human being, was fortunate to receive divine warnings and corrections when he acted or spoke erroneously, thus he was able to correct his mistakes during his lifetime. For these reasons, later Muslims considered it legitimate to use the Prophet and his companions' examples to supplement the Quran in their efforts to (re)create a Quranic lifestyle.

Consequently, after Muhammad's death his "customs," or sunna, as enshrined in the ahadith, helped Muslims to manage their new circumstances. As Islam grew, spread to new areas, encountered new peoples, and found converts from different cultures and backgrounds, jurists made a systematic effort to collect, classify, and scrutinize the ahadith as they negotiated with and responded to changes experienced by the Muslim community. In the process, the numbers of traditions attributed to Muhammad and his close companions reached to the tens of thousands and encompassed every aspect of life, from food choices and leisure activities to practices related to hygiene and sanitation, from marriage and divorce to adoption, from inheritance division to commerce, from love-making to war-making. These texts helped Muslims govern themselves and those whom they ruled; they justified certain choices and condemned others. They became useful tools for governance and critical sources of Islamic jurisprudence.

Later Muslim scholars established that many hadith traditions were inauthentic and did not reflect the Prophet's normative example. In some cases, scholars determined that ahadith had been fabricated presumably to justify personal, regional, and cultural preferences. In others, confusion and poor memory led to inaccurate attributions to the Prophet. Even among more credible traditions, hadith scholars came to differentiate the most reliable (*sahih* or "sound") ahadith from less reliable ones (in three categories of sliding order: *hasan* or "good," *da'if* or "weak," and *saqim* or "infirm"). Weaker ahadith have not been completely dismissed by Muslims, but the sound ones, which comprise only a fraction of all hadith traditions, came to be regarded as the most legitimate bases of legal action and interpretation.[62]

This wealth of information on correct belief and action expanding on that found in the Quran allowed later generations to formulate much-needed social and legal prescriptions. Consequently, ahadith played a major role in the elaboration and systematization of halal and haram food rules in Islamic jurisprudence. The Quran provides the most critical wisdom in halal versus haram differentiation, but without ahadith and the jurisprudential interpretations they inspired, the legal system that distinguishes lawful from unlawful (food) may not have developed. Specifically, in articulating notions of filth and purity, Muslim jurists considered, among other factors, the Prophet's personal standards. For example, some came to regard dogs as impure just like pigs, not because the Quran stated it but because they believed that the Prophet commanded Muslims to kill most dogs: "All dogs were to be killed except for dogs used for hunting and herding livestock."[63] He is also reported to have said that "a vessel should be washed if the dog drank from it seven times: the first and last [wash] with dirt."[64] On the other hand, jurists did not consider cats as filthy because (among other reasons), the Prophet ordered Muslims to wash the vessel that a cat drank from only once.[65]

So ahadith became, in short order, an important source in the development of jurisprudential traditions that systematized and elaborated on halal versus haram distinctions. But even ahadith, despite their richness, could not provide answers for all questions. For this reason, Muslim legal minds used sophisticated jurisprudential methods to address the most difficult legal issues. One such method is a legislative practice known as ijma', or "consensus": the adoption of a single legal prescription, even if not based in the Quran or ahadith, that the ulama agreed upon.[66] For example, there is a broad consensus among Muslim jurists that the consumption of the flesh of an otherwise halal animal would be unlawful if Allah's name was intentionally not invoked during its slaughter. It is best practice among Muslims to mention Allah's name during slaughter to satisfy the Quranic requirement that an animal not be killed as a sacrifice to other deities. Many jurists regarded as acceptable the flesh of animals slaughtered by Muslims without invoking Allah's name, if the latter happens inadvertently. Most, however, deem the intentional omission of Allah's name to be a deliberate affront to Quranic expectations and thus consider the meat of animals slaughtered this way unfit for consumption, although the scripture and ahadith are silent about its status.

Qiyas, or analogical reasoning, is another jurisprudential method in which the legal roots of a particular action are assessed based on the normative texts of Islam. For example, the Quran uses prohibitive language against khamr, often translated as "wine." But the jurists (a great majority of them, at least) decided through analogical reasoning that the Quranic prescription against wine should be expanded to all intoxicants and mind-altering substances, even if these were unmentioned in the Quran or ahadith.

In the centuries following the revelation, and with the help of such jurisprudential considerations, jurists also formulated a gradated system that complicated how Muslims came to think about permissible and impermissible food, drinks, and actions. Within this structure, there developed finer distinctions among food items and dietary practices in terms of degrees of permissibility and impermissibility. Although absent from the Quran or hadith traditions, the juristic classification categorized acts and substances according to whether they are obligatory (*wajib* or *fard*), recommended (*mandub*), permissible (*mubah*), reprehensible (*makruh*), or forbidden.

The first classification, wajib or fard, refers to religious duties or obligations; their omission will be punished according to Islamic law, and their performance will be rewarded in the afterlife.[67] The Ramadan fast, for instance, or almsgiving to the poor (*zakat*) fall into this category. With the exception of the Ramadan fast and some practices associated with slaughter, wajib or fard are largely extraneous categories in regard to dietary practices, since Islam does not require any particular substance to be consumed. Contrast this, for instance, with the sacrament of the Holy Eucharist, of consuming bread and wine in liturgical ceremonies, which is regarded more or less as obligatory practice in several Eastern Christian traditions.

The next three categories—mandub, mubah, and makruh—represent behavior and items that are technically considered within the realm of halal, although generally the category of makruh or reprehensible comes very close to haram. These categories can be seen less as new mandates than as indicative of the complexity of Muslim concerns about food. Considering the variety of opinions about many types of substances and actions, they reflect how certain juristic opinions transcended simple binaries. For example, given that the Prophet's example is so important for Muslims trying to live a divinely guided life, wouldn't it be recommendable or praiseworthy to eat what he personally liked and avoid what he disliked, even though the normative sources of Islam may not have forbidden the latter? One known case of makruh is that of onions, garlic, and leeks: in hadith traditions, the Prophet is said to have abhorred the consumption of these strong-smelling foods, especially in their raw form and among anyone who intended to pray in a mosque. Accordingly, some of the legal schools declared these foods makruh, but only in the context of prayer.[68] Thus the tripartite classification reveals a wide variety of considerations that Muslims encountered in the ahadith and subsequent jurisprudential interpretations, as well as their own cultural/regional preferences. In order to render this increasing complexity more manageable, Muslims differentiated superior practices from merely acceptable ones and distinguished dubious choices from forbidden acts.

Specifically, on the halal spectrum, mandub refers to food and practices that are praiseworthy on the basis of the prophetic traditions or customs of the first Muslim community. But they are not obligatory, thus their neglect does not require punishment. For example, based on the Prophet's custom, Muslims consider it "recommended" to eat a meal before dawn, before the start of a fasting day during the month of Ramadan. It is also "recommended" to eat dates during this meal and to break one's fast at the end of the day with dates, all of which might be related to the Prophet's personal love for this fruit. Exercising care, skill, and compassion when handling animals that will be slaughtered is similarly mandub. Mubah, on the other hand, refers to everything that is not positively forbidden or reprehensible in the Islamic sources and that does not damage human health and well-being.[69]

Makruh, a particularly complex classification, represents an almost liminal space between halal and haram: it refers to substances and actions that should be avoided but cannot be considered categorically forbidden because of a lack of clear and definitive directives in the Quran or ahadith. Some Muslims, particularly those associated with the Hanafi school of law, make even finer distinctions within makruh. What they call *makruh tahriman* refers to something close to being forbidden, where jurists have issued clear directives of aversion regarding a detested act or substance, but their rulings are based on weak or contradictory ahadith or reflect speculative interpretations of canonical sources. For example, many modern Hanafi jurists consider tobacco smoking makruh tahriman but not haram because although tobacco consumption is harmful to human health and therefore should be regarded as khabith, the practice is not mentioned in the Quran or in any sound ahadith. *Makruh tanzihan* (the latter is from the root *n-z-h*, "honest" or "virtuous") refers to an act from which one should refrain, an unvirtuous substance or practice that should be avoided according to the Quran or the ahadith. However, the prohibitive language in the ahadith amounts to recommendations rather than an outright ban. Included in such acts are things disliked by God or criticized by the Prophet, or described as errors or abominations. For instance, a food item that was deemed personally unappetizing by the Prophet but not explicitly banned by him when he observed others consuming it could be makruh tanzihan.[70]

Finally, many jurists recommended that Muslims should err on the side of caution when faced with difficult decisions, especially when they are unable to determine whether a substance or action is permissible (mubah) or reprehensible (makruh). In such doubtful circumstances, those which possess the quality of dubiousness (*shubha*), it is preferable to avoid consuming the potentially offensive item. For example, according to some jurists, if it is not clear that an otherwise halal animal was slaughtered according to legal requirements, then it is better to avoid it if one can afford to do so.[71]

While jurists managed to develop a widely agreed-upon legal system of categorization for permissible and forbidden food practices in the postrevelatory period, intracommunal variations on the application of legal categories quickly proliferated. Food preferences became symbolic of confessional traits. As stated, this is one way the Quran distinguished the new community of believers from polytheistic Arabs, on one hand, and from other monotheistic populations (Jews and Christians), on the other. What has been less recognized in the academic literature on Islamic dietary regulations is that the range of attitudes toward dietary practices also reflected the ethnic, sectarian, and regional differences within the greater Muslim community. Again, questions such as what food items should be regarded as repulsive or whether a dietary practice should be categorized as haram or makruh are at the root of these contentions.

Disparities regarding the consumption of specific food items are most obvious in the breakdown of Islamic jurisprudential schools, which require one final elaboration. Sunni and Shiite schools of law (*madhhabs*) emerged in the medieval era, giving form to the legal thought and legacy of specific jurists as interpreted by generations of scholars who followed them. Initially, in early medieval times, there were dozens of legal schools. Over time, however, the Sunni schools consolidated into four: the Maliki, Hanafi, Shafi'i, and Hanbali schools, named after their founders: Malik ibn Anas (d. 795), Abu Hanifa (d. 767), Muhammad ibn Idris al-Shafi'i (d. 820), and Ahmad ibn Hanbal (d. 855). The most popular Shiite legal school has been the Ja'fari madhhab, named after Ja'far al-Sadiq (d. 765), the sixth Shiite imam.[72]

When it comes to all legal matters, and specifically to questions of food, these schools diverge on how they approach and utilize various "sources of jurisprudence" (*usul al-fiqh*), including hadith traditions, ijma', and qiyas. For example, the Malikis tended to be less restrictive than the Shafi'is in their reliance on and interpretation of hadith traditions. And in Hanafi jurisprudential traditions, analogical reasoning has historically played a central role. Such differences are largely a consequence of regional and intellectual trends that shaped the development of different schools and influenced their attitudes toward specific food items and dietary practices.[73] While the Hanafi school historically came to reflect the earlier Kufan traditions (named for the town of Kufa in Iraq) from which it was derived, the Maliki interpretations remained more consistent with the prevalent jurisprudential inclination of Medina, where the school's founder, Malik ibn Anas, lived his entire life. Even today each school dominates a different geographical area, though that area may also contain communities affiliated with minority madhhabs. In very general terms, the Malikis are prevalent in North Africa, the Hanafis in South and Central Asia, the Shafi'is in Egypt and Southwest Asia, the Hanbalis in north and central Arabia, and the Ja'fari school in modern-day Iran, southern Iraq, and eastern Arabia. Finally, it should be noted that within each madhhab there exists a degree of juristic variation: to speak of a unified Hanbali opinion in an absolute fashion, for instance, would overlook the fact that notable jurists within that school sometimes disagreed about basic interpretations of consumable and forbidden foods. Subsequent chapters survey madhhab-based variations pertaining to the legality of various food items and practices.

Quranic prescriptions regarding halal and haram food items and practices reflected the environmental and historical circumstances of early Muslims. In particular, the parallels and divergences between these prescriptions and pre-Islamic Arabian, Jewish, and Christian traditions became important markers in Muslims' attempts to differentiate themselves from other populations. The long-ago meeting between the Prophet's cousin Ja'far and the Abyssinian King Negus discussed in this chapter's first paragraphs captures these attempts well and also hints at an early Muslim awareness of the centrality of food rules and laws among competing monotheisms.

The Islamic dietary regime grew more complicated over time as Islam spread beyond Arabia and as Muslims incorporated different peoples into their fold. The gradated classification system that emerged in the postrevelationary era represents Muslim jurists' attempts to systematize food rules, when a simpler, binary taxonomy fell short of communal needs and/or expectations. The dietary plurality within the new umma is also reflected in the food-related inclinations associated with specific Sunni and Shiite legal schools, which, in turn, played a key role in canonizing regional and cultural variations. These early developments indicate a capacity for the Islamic law to accommodate change and diversity. However, this should not insinuate a timelessly progressive character for the law. For one thing, and as will be later discussed, the law also developed tendencies and practices that aimed to retain connections to its own roots. For another, how the law responded to new challenges has often been based on contextual factors and influenced by individual jurists' personal proclivities.

CHAPTER 2

H alal food is not exclusively about meat. But questions about what types of meat should be consumed and how they should be sourced occupy a central place in halal considerations. This chapter begins with two broad questions: how were meat consumption and socioeconomic development linked in Islamic history? And how have Muslims viewed the ethics of human-nonhuman animal relationships? Within this broader context, the chapter subsequently explores Muslim attitudes toward eating different types of animals—including those from the sea, for fish have long been a staple food for many Muslims, particularly in coastal South Asia. In the process, the discussion reveals the plurality and disagreements among Muslims pertaining to meat and explains how this diversity came to be and has persisted since the earliest times.

Meat Consumption in Premodern Islamic Settings

Food historian David Waines describes the people of the Arabian Peninsula during Muhammad's time as "frugal and emaciated, so little nourished."[1] Food sources were relatively scarce, and the ahadith characterize pre-Islamic Arabia as a "land afflicted by hunger."[2] According to one account by Aisha, a wife of the Prophet Muhammad, "sometimes a month would come in which [Arabs] did not kindle a fire [for cooking], having only dates and water" for nourishment.[3] Dates, milk products, barley bread, and a limited number of vegetables were the most common types of food in this setting; in fact, a shortage of dates was equivalent to famine.[4] One common refrain in the hadith sources is "scarcity made a virtue of moderation in both food consumption and as a goal of the moral life. Two people's food is enough for three, and three enough for four."[5] The Quran (90:14–16) expresses life's moral goals in several ways but forcefully describes the faithful as those who would "feed on a day of starvation an orphan among relatives or a needy man in desolation."[6]

The Quran mentions animals including sheep, goats, cattle, and camels as seemingly desirable food items, but in Muhammad's Arabia, animal flesh was a rare source of nourishment.[7] Camels were valuable for a variety of purposes and were slaughtered only as a last resort. Similarly, the Arabs of the Prophet's time seldom consumed beef or goat, and enjoyed mutton a little more often.[8] Contemporary sources indicate that the Prophet ate some meat and that he liked it. His favorite food, as reported in various ahadith, was *tharid*, crumbled bread soaked in mutton broth and usually served with bite-sized pieces of meat. However, most early Muslims may have lived a vegetarian or semivegetarian lifestyle because of their environmental and economic circumstances.[9] There are also reports suggesting that the first Muslims viewed meat consumption suspiciously, associating it with exuberance and health problems, perhaps because of its rarity. For example, one medieval commentary on the Shiite text *Nahj al-Balagha*—the collection of sayings and letters attributed to Ali ibn Abi Talib (d. 661), the fourth Sunni caliph and first imam in Shiite traditions, as well as the Prophet's cousin and son-in-law—reports the following statement by Ali: "Do not allow your stomachs to become graveyards for animals."[10] The same source also indicates that Ali ate meat only a few times every year and in very small quantities. Imam Malik's *Al-Muwatta'* reports that Umar ibn al-Khattab (d. 644), one of Muhammad's closest companions and the second caliph of the first Muslim polity, warned Muslims against consuming meat in excess because it could induce addictive cravings.[11]

Meat consumption remained uncommon among lower-class Muslims before modern times. Islamic historian Paulina Lewicka indicates that meat was not a primary staple in medieval Cairo and that the Egyptians, especially the poor, ate little meat.[12] The situation was similar in the late seventeenth century. A European visitor to Cairo remarked in 1693, "The way the Turks [*sic*] live is one continual penance. The meals, even of the richest, are composed of bad

Recipe Box 2.1   Tharid

Thanks to its positive association with the Prophet Muhammad, tharid became a richer and more complex dish in the medieval Islamic period as spices and vegetables were added to give it more flavor and texture. This "simpler" recipe from the tenth-century Baghdadi cookbook by Ibn Sayyar al-Warraq, as translated by Middle East food historian Nawal Nasrallah, captures the dish's basic flavor profile. According to Nasrallah, the addition of sugar was likely an Abbasid-era culinary innovation.

Choose fatty meat, cut it into small pieces, and put it in a pot along with soaked chickpeas, whole onions, salt, and some water. Light the fire underneath the pot and let it cook until meat is done. This will come out as a [white stew].

Divide [water bread] into quarters. Arrange the pieces in a [wide bowl big enough for ten people], and pour some clarified butter or fresh butter all over them. Do this when the bread has just been taken out of the oven and is still piping hot.

Ladle the broth over the bread, putting as much as needed [to saturate the bread]. Pound some sugar and sprinkle it on the bread before you ladle the broth. Arrange meat pieces all around the dish and serve it. God willing.

From Nawal Nasrallah, *Annals of the Caliphs' Kitchens: Ibn Sayyar al-Warraq's Tenth-Century Baghdadi Cookbook*, 338.

bread, garlic, onion and sour cheese; when they add boiled mutton it is a great feast for them."[13] Likewise, Carsten Niebuhr, a late eighteenth-century traveler to Egypt, Arabia, and Syria, observed that the people of Arabia were "a sober frugal nation, which is probably the cause of their leanness, and seemingly stinted growth." Niebuhr confirmed that the locals seldom ate meat and that, when they did, it was usually mutton.[14]

In eighteenth-century Damascus, the poor ate meat infrequently and in surrounding rural regions, they were "condemned to the tedium of barley bread."[15] Throughout the Ottoman Empire, jurisprudential authorities considered bread essential for everyone's survival and held the state and its representatives responsible for its regular supply, but they treated meat as a luxury food and exempted the state from providing it.[16] Steady, unrestricted access to meat was the privilege of well-to-do families, high-level state officials "for whom meat advertised social status as effectively as riding a horse."[17] The Ottoman state devoted significant resources to meat provision only in the capital, Istanbul, whose demands threatened whatever meat supplies were available in the empire's peripheries. In all, meat consumption followed four hierarchical rules: the imperial center claimed meat at the expense of the provinces.[18] Upper classes and the administrative elite claimed it at the expense of the common folk. Free Muslims claimed it at the expense of slaves. And men claimed it at the expense of women.[19]

Given that halal food regulations mostly concern meat, halal prescriptions regarding food presumably did not affect the lives of premodern Muslims as much as they affect modern Muslims, who consume meat with much more regularity and quantity.[20] And class status seems to have been a particularly important factor in halal food matters in premodern times since these issues were more relevant to the wealthier segments of the society than to lower classes. Hence the danger of "presentism" in recent halal food studies: the rise of per capita meat consumption in Muslim-majority communities in recent decades must have caused most Muslims, not only the wealthy but also the poor, to pay much more attention to issues relevant to food purity. Socioeconomic development is not the only factor that has elevated modern halal consciousness, of course (see chapter 5), but it is a critical variable.

Human-Animal Relations in Islam's Cosmological Order

Regardless of how much meat Muslims ate in different eras and settings, Islam condones the human consumption of animal flesh. And halal considerations regarding meat primarily involve how Muslims are supposed to kill and eat animals permitted for human consumption. A more basic set of questions has received little attention until recently: In the Islamic tradition, what justifies humans' killing and consuming animals? What do the ethics of human-animal interactions look like in this religious context? And how did Islamic ethics come to influence the practices identified in halal regulations as pertaining to meat consumption?

In general terms, classical interpretations of Islamic law propose a hierarchical order in the universe.[21] This order is premised on a series of binary

Printed in Colours.   at 70 St Martin's Lane.

SELLER OF SWEETMEATS,
CONSTANTINOPLE.

Fig. 2.1. "Seller of Sweetmeats, Constantinople." The Miriam and Ira D. Wallach Division of Art, Prints and Photographs: Art & Architecture Collection, The New York Public Library. New York Public Library Digital Collections. Accessed July 28, 2017. http://digitalcollections.nypl.org/items/510d47d9-65cb-a3d9-e040-e00a18064a99.

associations, each one juxtaposing two legally unequal entities: Muslims versus non-Muslims; men versus women; and free individuals versus slaves. In these binaries, the former constitute the privileged entities and possess legal rights over the latter. The consequences of this hierarchical order have been well recognized in premodern jurisprudential literature. Muslims have the legal right to govern and tax non-Muslims as long as the latter choose to live in Muslim-dominated territories. Non-Muslims possess limited autonomy in managing their internal affairs, but they are not full-fledged constituents of the Muslim community and thus cannot participate in government as equal partners to Muslims. Similarly, the law privileges fathers, husbands, and brothers over mothers, wives, and sisters. For men but not for women, polygamy is sanctioned, and while husbands can easily divorce wives, the same is not true for women. Finally, classical Islamic law as interpreted by medieval jurists recognizes slavery as a legitimate form of human and property relationship. Human beings, as slaves, can be bought, sold, and gifted to others by their owners, although the law does not permit Muslims to enslave other Muslims, and Muslim slave owners are not required to manumit their slaves who convert to Islam. Islamic ethical prescriptions encourage Muslims to free their slaves, but this is not a legal requirement.

What has received less attention, however, is a fourth binary: the relationship between humans and nonhuman animals. Islamic sources indicate that animals, just like humans, are sentient creations of Allah and possess the right to exist in this universe unmolested. Animals can speak, according to the Quran, and they all praise God. Again like humans, they constitute communities (*umam*, singular umma), which led at least one medieval commentator to speculate that they received prophets from God like all human communities did.[22] Nevertheless, according to most interpretations, the Quran also proposes a hierarchical relationship between humans and animals. Of all Allah's creation, humans are the ones who are created in "the best of stature" (95:4). They are designated by Allah as his vice-regent (*khalifa*) on earth, and animals were created to serve humans' needs.[23] Thus, according to mainstream opinions, humans are allowed to exploit nonhuman animals for their own welfare, keeping some in servile status and killing others for consumption.[24] The status difference between humans and animals becomes even more explicit when God punishes those who violate his commands by turning them into apes and pigs (2:65; 5:60; 7:163-166).[25]

The parallels between the first three pairings and the human/animal pairing are also apparent in the way Muslim commentators described how those in positions of power ought to treat the disadvantaged. According to jurists, Muslim governance of non-Muslims should be tolerant, which is consistent with how most historians have described the circumstances of religious minorities in many premodern Muslim-majority polities. Likewise, the law requires husbands to respect their wives, be cognizant of their rights, and be kind to them. If women need to be disciplined, the punishment should not be excessive nor brutal but should remind women of their responsibilities to male family members. Slave owners are also required to be mindful of their slaves' needs and to treat them kindly. Indeed, historians have often distinguished Islamic forms of slavery from the chattel slavery common in Western settings because of the purportedly benevolent relationship between Muslim slave owners and their slaves.

Islamic prescriptions that regulate human treatment of animals demonstrate a similar character. The Prophet is said to have promised Muslims rewards for showing compassion to animals.[26] He also instructed Muslims traveling with animals to move slowly in areas with vegetation to allow for grazing and to rush quickly through the deserts to protect animals from the elements and insects. He admonished men sitting idly and unnecessarily on their camels, and reprimanded his wife Aisha for treating her camel roughly. He also forbade Muslims to hunt for sport.[27]

The language of compassion toward animals is also clear in halal requirements for slaughter. In fact, halal advocates laud the fact that halal prescriptions call for Muslims to treat animals gently and minimize their suffering before and during killing. For example, Muslims should slaughter animals out of the sight of other animals, lest the act of killing one cause anxiety and panic among others. They are also required to refrain from killing an animal's young within its sight.[28] In many Muslim settings, animals' eyes are covered with a piece of cloth during slaughter to prevent them from seeing their own blood. One critical halal requirement is that slaughter be performed by a sharp object and in one stroke, if possible, to make killing swift and efficient. Killing animals, wild or domesticated, by blunt tools such as mauls, sledgehammers, or the like, which crush bones, renders them carrion and thus unlawful to eat. Halal rules prohibit skinning a slaughtered animal or cutting its bones before the animal is completely dead and its body is cold. In general, Islamic law also requires that animals designated for Muslim use (including but not limited to food consumption) be given plenty of food, water, and other necessities during their lives.

Fig. 2.2. Shepherdess of camel herd. *Al-Maqamat li'l Hariri* (1236–1237), drawings by Yahya ibn Mahmoud ibn Yahya ibn Aboul-Hasan ibn Kouvarriha al-Wasiti. Bibliothèque nationale de France, Département des manuscrits, Arabe 5847, folio 101r. Used with permission.

Recently, however, the broader Islamic discourse of tolerance toward the underprivileged has been criticized as a rhetorical device that perpetuated power differentials between unequal beings. This critique is especially noticeable in Muslim feminist (or women-friendly) interpretations of Islamic jurisprudential sources, which have questioned the assumption that the presumed inequality between man and woman is divinely ordained. Such a critique is relevant for our considerations because classical halal prescriptions, which also promote benevolence in interspecies relationships, take for granted their unequal nature.[29] For example, Islamic historian Richard Foltz has argued that "when it comes to determining compensation for wrongs, the Islamic jurists are clear that . . . a wrong committed against an animal is really seen as a wrong committed against its owner."[30] In this system, "while the rights of non-human animals are guaranteed in the legal tradition, their interests are ultimately subservient to those of humans."[31] Scholar of Arab and Islamic studies Sarra Tlili, on the other hand, has proposed a reinterpretation of basic Islamic sources, including the Quran and the ahadith, which might lead to alternative judicial interpretations that reject the legal inferiority of animals and their subservience to humans. In her eco-centric exegesis of the Muslim scripture, Tlili has argued that although the Quran does allow for the serviceability of nonhuman beings to humans, this does not exclude the possibility that humans could likewise be serviceable to other entities, particularly nonhuman animals.[32] She has also challenged the idea that humans were created to be vice-regents of God, a conception based on an imprecise interpretation of the term "khalifa" in the scripture. Given the fact that the Quran often characterizes humans as tyrannical, temperamental, disobedient, and ungrateful, it is inconceivable for the just and wise God to designate them as his representatives on earth.[33]

Voices resistant to the human/animal hierarchy in Islamic law are not new. *The Case of the Animals versus Man before the King of the Jinn*, a tenth-century epistle composed by a group of Muslim intellectuals collectively known as the Brethren of Purity, disputes that humans have physical, intellectual, or spiritual superiority over animals. According to the epistle, human dominion over animals is solely a consequence of God's mercy to humans, who cannot survive without animals.[34] More prominently, in various brands of Islamic mysticism, dispositions against animal subjugation to and consumption by humans are well known. Tales attributed to some major Sufi figures urge Muslims to identify with animals and sympathize with the pains they experience at the hands of humans. In one such tale of dubious origin, Rabia al-Adawiyya (d. 801), a renowned female Sufi, supposedly chastised Hasan al-Basri (d. 728), another notable Sufi, for approaching animals after having eaten animal fat. Though it is unknown if Rabia was a practicing vegetarian, she is represented in this tale as distressed by the fact that Hasan offended the scared animals, which then refused to come near him. In another tale, Mawlana Jalaluddin Rumi (d. 1273) tells the story of a dervish who warns hungry travelers not to eat young elephants they might encounter because this would cause anguish to their mothers.[35] It would be better, the dervish suggests, for the travelers to satisfy their hunger by eating grass and vegetation. According to the tale, all but one of the travelers did eat a young elephant they encountered, and they were consequently killed by the mother elephant.[36]

Sophisticated Sufi formulations also fundamentally challenge the legal binarism involving humans and nonhuman animals. In scholar of Islamic mysticism Pasha M. Khan's interpretation of *Fusus al-Hikam* (Rightness of Wisdom), for example, the medieval mystic Ibn al-Arabi (d. 1240) rejected the widely recognized hierarchical order that elevated humans above animals. According to Ibn al-Arabi, the rational "intellect" (*'aql*) of humans did not necessarily give them an advantage in appreciating the divine being. In fact, humans' intellect muddled their attempts to make sense of God's complex and seemingly contradictory aspects. On the other hand, all God's creations possessed instinctive "reason" (*nutq*), which is essential to "divine" the creator and his creation. Ultimately, Ibn al-Arabi's mystical thought called for a conceptualization of a single creation ("animal") that did not differentiate among human and nonhuman species.[37]

Modern discourses promoting an Islamic animal ethics—including humane treatment and/or a vegan lifestyle, as will be discussed in chapter 8—often look to Quranic, hadith, or mystical sources to justify their viewpoints. Indeed, several Muslim activists call for renouncing all meat consumption and for an end to animal abuse, and they believe their ethics are the most consistent with Islam's unquestionable call to be merciful and humane toward nonhuman animals.

Land Animals

Despite these opposing voices, the cosmological order that elevates humans over nonhuman animals has been hegemonic among Muslims, and it is this order that justifies the human consumption of animal flesh, albeit according to many jurisprudential considerations. The Quranic position against the pig is clear. The Prophet also spoke unequivocally against the dog, which is why many Muslims consider it filthy and thus inappropriate for human consumption. In addition, there was some dispute over which parts of a halal-slaughtered animal can be consumed: with some exceptions, the medieval juristic tradition allowed the consumption of most body parts of an animal according to halal slaughter rules. Notably, however, the Hanafis excluded the animal's reproductive organs, glands, and bladders (including gall bladders), in part because they contained najis liquids such as urine or semen. On the other hand, Malikis allowed for the consumption of all offal, gall bladders, kidneys, ears, hearts, testicles, and glands, while Hanbalis specifically prohibited the consumption of glands, ears, and hearts.[38]

Furthermore, Sunni and Shiite legal schools have identified animal species and types that should be avoided altogether. Unlike with the pig and the dog, however, the schools' positions on the halal status of these animals vary, sometimes significantly. Table 2.1 shows how classical jurists associated with different legal schools have generally characterized the status of various land animals on which there are disagreements.[39] The first four columns in the table represent the opinions of the four major Sunni legal schools, and the last that of the most dominant Shiite school: the Ja'fari.[40]

Table 2.1 lists animals from the most accepted to the least. At the very top are animals considered halal by most schools: wild donkey and hare. Animals at the bottom—"beasts of prey," elephant, domesticated donkey, and mule—are universally regarded as objectionable, but the strength of the objection varies. Between the top and bottom groups are animals for which there are more pronounced differences of opinion. As the table demonstrates, meat-eating regulations are generally stricter in the Shiite tradition than among Sunnis. Among the latter, Hanafis are closest to the Shiites in terms of their dietary considerations.

The positions summarized are mostly based on hadith traditions and various jurists' interpretations of them. For example, the almost universal opposition to eating "beasts of prey" stems from generally well-established reports in which the Prophet spoke against consuming beasts with canine teeth.[41] The same is true for the prohibition against the domesticated ass.[42] Verifiable ahadith are among the most important sources of Islamic jurisprudence, which, in the absence of the Quranic directives on a particular issue, provide much-needed guidance for Muslims. The challenge, however, is that

Table 2.1. Schools' Positions on Disputed Land Animals

	Maliki (Sunni)	Shafiʻi (Sunni)	Hanbali (Sunni)	Hanafi (Sunni)	Jaʻfari (Shiite)
Wild ass	[yes]	yes	yes	yes	yes
Hare	yes	yes	yes	yes	NO
Rock-badger	yes	yes	yes	no(?)/NO*	NO
Lizard	yes	yes	yes	no	NO
Jerboa	yes	yes	yes	NO	NO
Hyena	no	yes	yes	NO	NO
Horse	NO/no*	yes	yes	yes*/no	yes*/no
Hedgehog	yes	yes	NO	NO	NO
Fox	no	yes	NO	NO	NO
Iguana	–	yes*	yes*	NO*	–
"Creeping things"	yes	yes*/[NO]	yes*/NO	no	NO
"Serpent"	yes	NO	NO	NO	NO
"Birds of prey"	yes	NO	NO	NO	NO
Elephant	NO*	NO*	no*	NO*	[NO]
Domesticated ass	no*	NO	NO	NO	no
Mule	NO	NO	NO	NO	no
"Beasts of prey"	no	NO	NO	NO	NO

Sources: Adapted from Cook "Early Islamic Dietary Law," 259. Additions have been made from Qasmi, *Animal Slaughter*, 24; "Atʻima," *Al-Mawsuʻa al-Fiqhiyya*, 5:133–147; and Benkheira, *Islâm et interdits alimentaires* (these are identified with *).

Key: "yes" = permitted or mubah; "no" = disapproved or makruh; "NO" = prohibited or haram. Square brackets indicate a degree of inference by Cook or by the authors. Question mark indicates a lack of information (per Cook). "Creeping things" is a category that may include insects (with the exception of locust, which is generally permitted), reptiles other than snakes and lizards, and small mammals. It also excludes worms which are "creeping" but generally permitted. "Serpent" could refer to the snake, although it is not clear in Cook's sources. "Beasts of prey" refers to animals with canine teeth, exclusive of the carnivores individually listed in the table. "Birds of prey" are those with talons used for catching prey, but this category is disputed among the different schools: it excludes permissible creatures with talons like turkeys but also—depending on the specific jurist and/or the school—certain types of crows, ravens, kites, bats, owls, storks, swallows, and ostriches.

there are thousands of hadith traditions attributed to the Prophet and the first generation of Muslims; these traditions may be regarded as credible to different degrees, but they are not entirely consistent; and various legal schools differentiate themselves from others largely, though not entirely, by privileging select groups of hadith collections and disregarding others. For example, while hadith traditions recognized by the Maliki school largely originate from Medina, where the founder of that school lived, the traditions that many

Hanafi and Shiite jurists privilege generally come from Kufa (in modern-day Iraq); this may partially explain why Hanafis and Shiites show pronounced similarities in their halal considerations.[43]

Take the case of the lizard. The Maliki, Shafi'i, and Hanbali jurists disagreed with Shiites and Hanafis on the status of lizards. The former's opinions are based on ahadith prominent in Medina, which tend to permit Muslims to eat this creature, while the latter formulated their interpretations on Kufan traditions, which are less lenient. In other cases, minor variations in hadith accounts recognized by various schools justified differences in opinion. For example, most schools forbid "birds of prey" because many ahadith both suggest a ban against beasts of prey and, in close textual proximity, mention birds with talons. Yet the ahadith that Malikis, who consider birds of pray permissible, deem authoritative on the status of "beasts of prey" do not mention birds with talons.[44] At the same time, varied hadith traditions have allowed jurists from the four major Sunni schools to regard other birds with talons, like turkeys, as permitted, since they do not use their talons for catching prey. The schools also diverge somewhat as to the edibility of certain crows, ravens, kites (falcon-like birds), bats, owls, storks, and ostriches.[45]

Furthermore, even when two or more schools base their decisions on identical hadiths, their interpretations can differ based on other considerations discussed in chapter 1. For example, while all schools consider the hadith against beasts of prey authoritative, many Maliki jurists interpreted Muhammad's words as merely discouraging rather than definitively prohibiting them.[46] And others disagreed on whether the fox or hyena should be included in the category of animals with canine teeth. Variations in jurisprudential interpretations can even extend to Quranic statements. Differing opinions on consuming equine flesh (with the exception of wild donkey) are based on (or justified by) how various jurists interpreted the Quranic verse 16:8: "And [God created] the horses, mules and donkeys for you to ride and [as] adornment." Accordingly, most argued that equine animals should not be eaten because they were created to serve other functions. But a minority claimed that the verse contained no indication that "riding" and "adornment" should be the only uses of equines.[47]

As indicated, a relationship may have existed between various schools' attitudes toward specific animals and the circumstances of the region in which they developed as distilled through various sources of Islamic jurisprudence. For example, the Maliki leniency regarding types of meat permissible for consumption may stem from the school's roots in the Hijaz, where

Arabs constantly faced "the nagging reality of scarcity and hunger."[48] More restrictive tendencies found in the Hanafi, Shafi'i, and Hanbali legal schools could reflect the more robust agrarian and economic settings where they flourished.

Aquatic Animals

Halal requirements also specify the legal status of aquatic animals and their capture, processing, and consumption. In general, Muslim authorities have developed different standards for how these creatures should be treated based on specific criteria, so they deserve a special discussion of their own.

The Quran tells Muslims, "Lawful to you is game from the sea and its food as provision for you" (5:96). When it comes to eating seafood, there are two major points of consensus among all Sunni and Shiite traditions: first, there are no mandatory requirements for ritual slaughter of fish. And second, any fish with scales (*fals* or *qishr*) is considered halal so long as it was captured alive. Beyond these two points, the flexibility of 5:96 has engendered some important differentiations about permissible and impermissible seafood among Muslims. In short, non-Shiite and non-Hanafi traditions, especially Malikis, are more open toward eating different varieties of sea creatures (Table 2.2).

In Shiite traditions, only fish (*samak*) with scales are permitted.[49] This means that Shiites have usually ruled out eating sharks, marine mammals, cephalopods (octopus, squid), most crustaceans (crabs, crawfish, lobster), and mollusks (clams, mussels, oysters, scallops).[50] Curiously, an exception has been made for shrimp or prawns. Citing a hadith that refers to shrimp shells as scales or qishr, another that calls shrimp samak, and other traditions that deem it an "aquatic locust" (locusts are generally considered halal), most Shiites have traditionally viewed shrimp as halal.[51] Today, for instance, shrimp appears in various dishes within Iranian cuisine and is especially prominent in springtime dishes cooked with herbs like cilantro, dill, and fenugreek.[52]

The second most restrictive, after Shiites, are the Sunni Hanafis. Jurists in this school allow consumption of all samak, meaning creatures that look like fish and have fins, gills, and so on. By this reasoning, a Muslim can eat shark meat, but since whales, dolphins, and other marine mammals lack gills, they are forbidden. Hanafis generally regard other categories of seafood—shrimp, squid, and clams—as haram. They also specify, as do Hanbalis, that fish should not be eaten or swallowed while still alive.

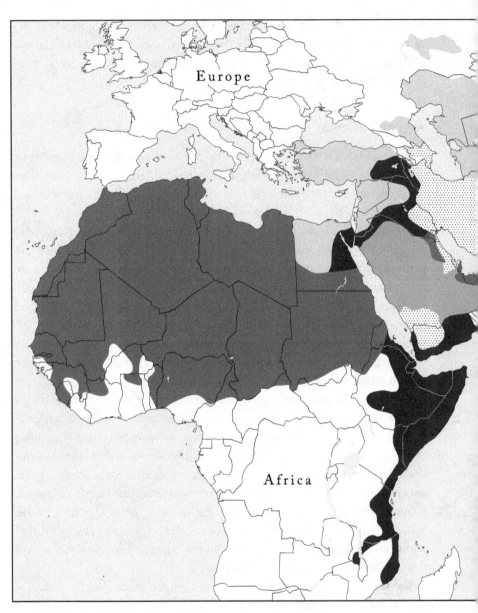

Map 2.1. Predominant Madhhab Affiliations in the Modern Islamic World (Approximate Boundaries)

Note: Made with Natural Earth Data.
Source: Revised and adapted from "Madhhab Map" at Wikimedia Commons, https://commons.wikimedia.org wiki/File:Madhhab_Map3.png.

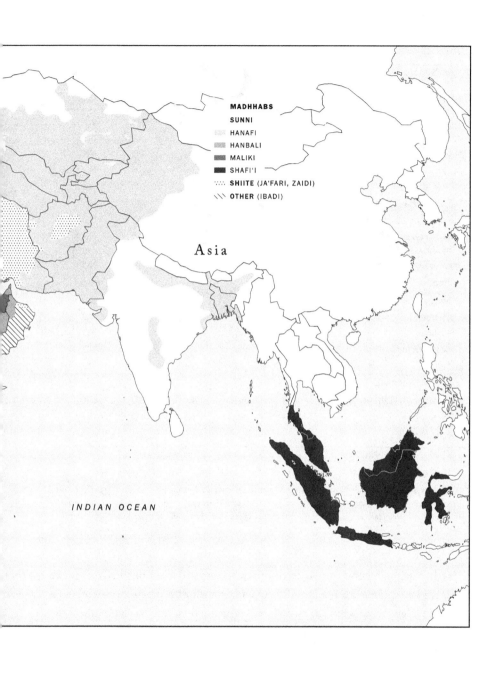

MADHHABS

SUNNI

HANAFI

HANBALI

MALIKI

SHAFI'I

SHIITE (JA'FARI, ZAIDI)

OTHER (IBADI)

Asia

INDIAN OCEAN

Table 2.2. Schools' Positions on Aquatic Animals (Simplified)

	Maliki (Sunni)	Shafi'i (Sunni)	Hanbali (Sunni)	Hanafi (Sunni)	Ja'fari (Shiite)
Fish with scales	yes	yes	yes	yes	yes
Sturgeon	[yes]	[yes]	[yes]	yes	no*
Whales and dolphins	yes	yes	yes	NO	NO
Sharks	yes	yes	yes	yes	NO
Prawns, shrimp	yes	yes	yes	NO	yes
Crabs, crawfish, lobster	yes	no/yes	yes	NO	NO
Squid and octopus (cephalopods)	yes	yes	yes	NO	NO
Clams, mussels, oysters, scallops (mollusks)	yes	yes	yes	NO	NO
Eels	yes	yes	[no]	yes	NO
Isomorphs					
"Sea pigs" or porpoise	no/yes	no	no/yes	no	NO
Sea horses	[yes]	yes	[yes]	no	NO
Sea lions	[yes]	no	[yes]	no	NO
"Sea dogs" or seals	yes	no	yes	no	NO
"Sea cows" or manatees	[yes]	yes	[yes]	no	NO
Sea and land animals					
Crocodiles and alligators	yes	no	no	NO	[NO]
Sea turtles	yes	no	yes	NO	NO
Toads/frogs	yes	no	no	NO	NO

Sources: Cook "Islamic Dietary Law," 237–247; al-Mubarakfuri, *Tuhfat al-Ahwadhi bi Sharh Jami' al-Tirmidhi,* 1:224–231; "At'ima," *Al-Mawsu'a al-Fiqhiyya,* 5:127–132; and Benkheira, *Islâm et interdits alimentaires.*

Key: "yes" = permitted or mubah; "no" = disapproved or makruh; "NO" = prohibited or haram. Square-brackets indicate a degree of inference within the sources. The status of sturgeon and its roe in Shiite traditions (marked with an asterisk) was traditionally haram but was changed to halal by Ayatollah Khomeini in 1983.

Other schools show progressive openness toward seafood. In fact, most jurists in non-Hanafi Sunni traditions view samak as a much more inclusive term that encompasses sharks, whales, cephalopods, crustaceans, and mollusks. Today the world's most populous Muslim country, Indonesia, which has historically followed a Shafi'i interpretation, is one of the world's largest shark catchers. Muslim fishermen in the eastern parts of that country have also been known to practice whaling to procure a critical local food and a profitable source of blubber.[53] This case is a good illustration of the confluence of school-specific rules, geographic location, natural resources, and local subsistence economies.

Recipe Box 2.2 *Maygu Polow:* Rice with Shrimp and Fresh Herbs, Persian Gulf-Style

Shrimp is the only crustacean considered halal by most Shiite interpretations. Here, we have included culinary expert Najmieh Batmanglij's recipe for a spring-time dish traditionally popular in Iran.

Rice:
- 3 cups basmati rice
- 8 garlic cloves, peeled and sliced
- 3 cups freshly chopped cilantro
- 2 cups fresh chopped spring onions
- 1 tablespoon dried fenugreek
- 1/2 cup fresh chopped fenugreek
- 1 teaspoon sea salt
- 1/2 teaspoon pepper
- 2 teaspoons red pepper flakes
- 4 teaspoons hot curry powder
- 1 tablespoon angelica powder (*gol-par*)
- 1 cup oil, melted butter, or ghee
- 1/2 teaspoon saffron dissolved in 2 tablespoons hot water

Shrimp:
- 2 tablespoons oil
- 1 pound raw shrimp, butterflied, or 1 pound white fish fillets, 4-inch length
- 1 tablespoon fresh chopped cilantro
- 1 cup fresh dill
- 1 teaspoon lime powder
- 1 teaspoon curry powder
- 1/2 teaspoon sea salt

1. Wash rice in warm water and drain. Boil 8 cups of water with 2 tablespoons salt.
2. Pour drained rice into pot and boil for 6 to 10 minutes. Stir to loosen sticky grains. Drain in a fine-mesh colander, and rinse with water.
3. In a bowl, mix garlic, all herbs, salt, pepper, pepper flakes, curry, and angelica powder. Set aside.

4. To make rice crust: whisk 1/2 cup oil, 1/4 cup water, a few drops of saffron water with two spatulas of rice. Spread at bottom of pot and then layer with alternating rice and herb-spice mixture to get a pyramid shape.
5. Cover and cook for 10 minutes over medium-high.
6. Mix the rest of the oil with 1/2 cup water and pour over rice. Pour saffron water on top. Wrap pot lid with clean dish towel and cover firmly. Cook for another 50 minutes over low heat.
7. Remove from heat and allow to cool for 5 minutes.
8. Heat 2 tablespoons of oil in a wide skillet until very hot. Dust shrimp with a mixture of lime powder, curry powder, salt, and cilantro. Sear shrimp for 1 minute on each side, until they change color, and then remove.
9. Uncover pot and gently take one spatula of rice at a time without disturbing crust. Mound in a serving dish and place shrimp on top. Detach crust and serve on the side.

From Najmieh Batmanglij, *Food of Life: Ancient Persian and Modern Iranian Cooking and Ceremonies*, 260.

Beyond fish, sharks, whales, and shrimp, other aquatic or semiaquatic creatures have elicited contradictory opinions. For example, based on a hadith containing the Prophet's injunction not to kill them, frogs were prohibited by most schools, except Malikis.[54] Some schools also ban aqueous reptiles like crocodiles and alligators because of their carnivorous tendencies, their fang-like teeth (land animals of this variety are forbidden), and their muddled status as both sea and land creatures. For jurists who have determined that most of a crocodile's life was aquatic rather than terrestrial, consumption of these reptiles is permitted.[55] Sea turtles also spend their life spans both in sea and on land, but again there are mixed opinions regarding their consumption. They are banned by Shiites, Hanafis, and some Shafi'is, but so long as they spend more time in the water, they are considered halal by most Malikis and Hanbalis.

In a few traditions, "isomorphic" sea animals that have Arabic names (or physical markers) bearing resemblance to their haram terrestrial counterparts, such as "sea pigs" (porpoise), "sea horses," "sea lions," and "sea dogs" (seals), are disapproved if not outright forbidden. There are cases to be made, too, that eating "sea cows" (manatees) is halal, since their terrestrial complements are permissible.[56] On the other hand, eels, which resemble snakes, are disapproved by Shiites but approved in most classical Sunni discussions, with the exception of some Hanbali jurists.[57]

In juristic discussions, questions also arose over fish and seafood that die by causes other than fishing (al-samak al-tafi). The classical legal position among Malikis and Shafi'is is that this fish can be consumed so long as it has not rotted and, according to some interpretations, so long as it was discovered afloat in the water rather than on the shoreline. Hanafis, however, view any fish that dies on its own without external impact and floats on the water with its belly up as carrion and haram, as it could harbor harmful disease.[58] Shiite scholars follow a similar logic: fish fit for consumption must be caught while alive.[59]

Fish were among the most popular foods during Islamic rule of South Asia, particularly in the coastal regions. Between the sixteenth and eighteenth centuries, they were widely traded between ports in Sind (western India, Pakistan) and Oman as well as Hadramawt. Reportedly Jahangir, the fourth Mughal emperor (r. 1605–1627 CE), was quite fond of fishing, but he ate only scaled fish: his favorite was a variety of carp known as rohu.[60] In a sense, Jahangir's tastes reflect the Mughals' judicial preferences, which were based on the more restrictive Hanafi interpretations. Ottoman rulers also followed Hanafi jurisprudence, and though fishing was often viewed as a lowly occupation, seafood was widely enjoyed by different classes and religious communities in Ottoman territories. However, in contrast to Jahangir's strictness, and to the possible dismay of Ottoman Hanafi jurists, some menus at the Ottoman imperial palace, notably in the modern period, included shrimp, lobster, and oysters.[61]

As with other foodstuffs, economic needs, political tensions, environmental factors, demographic variables, and culinary trends have recently heightened debates over consumable seafood. For Twelver Shiite jurists, the issue of fish with or without scales was revisited during the earliest years of the Islamic Republic of Iran. Caspian Sea sturgeon, source of the most prized and expensive caviar, is a sea creature ichthyologists (fish scientists) describe as having a few hard, bony scale-like appendages called ganoids. In historical Shiite traditions, the sturgeon and its caviar were both deemed haram. After the Iranian Revolution in 1979, however, the economics of sturgeon fishing and caviar export, in addition to competition with Soviet fisheries, motivated a reexamination of this well-established prohibition. Shiite clergy determined

Recipe Box 2.3   Ottoman Seafood Recipes

Although Ottoman sultans and elites followed the Hanafi legal school, which tended to be more restrictive about seafood consumption, they served varied seafood dishes in their courts, particularly in the nineteenth century when they hosted European dignitaries and wished to display their modernizing efforts, even in culinary matters. Following one impressive banquet that the Ottoman Viceroy in Egypt, Khedive Said (r. 1854–1863), held for some English guests, the book Majmuʿah Atʿimah ʿUthmaniyyah *was produced and translated into English as* Turkish Cookery Book: A Collection of Receipts *(1862). The book features several dishes with oysters, mussels, and scallops.*

Broiled Oysters:
Open as many oysters as are wanted, lay them on a gridiron, sprinkle with your fingers a little salt and pepper over each one, with a few drops of olive oil; set the gridiron on a charcoal fire. When the oysters are nicely broiled and begin to stick to the shells, dish them up in their shells, and serve with lemon.

Fried Mussels with Egg:
Open as many mussels as are required, and remove them from the shells, then dip them in flour, and then in eggs, fry them a nice color in hot olive oil or fresh butter, dish up, sprinkle a little salt and pepper over, and serve hot with lemon.

From Turabi Efendi, *Turkish Cookery Book: A Collection of Receipts*, 12 and 24

that the fish's spiny ganoids now qualified as fish scales, and in 1983 Ayatollah Khomeini issued a fatwa declaring sturgeon and its caviar halal.[62]

Other fish taboos have emerged in connection with the preparation of a specific dish. Since ancient times, Egyptians have eaten a gray mullet called *fesikh* (also, *fisikh* or *feseekh*), especially during the springtime celebration of Shamm al-Nasim (literally, "smelling of the breeze"). Egyptians prepare this fish by drying it in the sun and then salting it, a process that—at least to modern sensibilities—should demand care and hygienic precautions. Poor preparation, however, has often led to numerous cases of poisoning and fatalities. Fesikh was well known to medieval Muslim jurists, most of whom called it *tahir* (pure) unless it was deemed harmful by physicians, in which case it would be forbidden.[63] Following this logic, in 2009 an Egyptian mufti banned fesikh, citing its noxious and putrid odor. The mufti reasoned that Islamic legal interpretations forbade the consumption of any harmful substances.[64] Hence, although the fish in question (a mullet) was halal, its unhygienic preparation yielded a haram product. This juridical reasoning follows a Quranic verse (7:156) that prohibits "disgusting things" or "khaba'ith," a term often invoked to further clarify Muslim dietary taboos.[65]

Let us conclude with a cautionary note that highlights a point implicit within this discussion. Juristic considerations alone cannot explain why Muslims (or subgroups of Muslims) have subscribed to certain dietary practices. References to particular ahadith, or their specific understandings, or opinions based on other sources of Islamic jurisprudence (such as qiyas or ijma') may simply be justifications for regional preferences. Jurisprudential traditions that flourished in varied settings—specifically with regard to meat consumption—were likely influenced by the material and cultural tendencies in these locations as much as they shaped them. This interplay between juridical interpretation and local custom helped determine everything from whether one can eat eel or caviar, hedgehogs or lizards. A nuanced appreciation of how halal standards developed over time and place, therefore, requires a sophisticated assessment of food practices in multiple settings with distinctly different circumstances.

CHAPTER 3

Halal prescriptions developed over long periods, in various settings and in response to many external factors affecting Muslims' lives. The shifts in the notions of halal reflect how Muslims' perceptions of religious purity and proper dietary practice have changed and continue to do so. This tendency is also clear in halal guidelines for animal slaughter. Here, as in many other realms, modern Muslims face pressures to conform to prevailing, often Western, legal and cultural expectations. Halal slaughter rules, originally formulated in preindustrial settings, must now take into account new technologies and associated animal treatment procedures.

This chapter first examines the central guidelines for the proper killing of animals, including differing opinions on how slaughter should be done and by whom, and then focuses on how preslaughter stunning and mechanized killing of poultry, both standard industry practices now, have influenced halal slaughter formulations. This exploration reveals, once again, that Islamic law is a set of living and breathing traditions; thus its complexity—particularly as related to halal food—can be more fully appreciated in relation to new circumstances and challenges, and Muslims' varied responses to them.

Proper Killing of Animals

While Muslims are permitted to kill most animals for sustenance, not all forms of killing are sanctioned as acceptable, for halal slaughter (dhabiha or zabiha) must follow a specific script. What follows is a reflection on the details of this script and an exploration of relevant issues that have caused anxiety and disagreements among Muslims.

Proper slaughter is a central component of halal prescriptions for land animals. In fact, how an animal is killed is precisely what differentiates carrion (mayta) from halal meat. The Quran does not offer extensive details about how slaughter should be performed. The scripture notes, however, that animals appropriate for consumption should not be killed by strangling, beating, a fall from height, or the goring of animal horns (5:3). The same verse also forbids Muslims to eat the flesh of animals killed by birds or beasts of prey.

In the absence of scripturally based guidance, hadith traditions provide additional help. For example, in one account the Prophet instructs Muslims to sharpen their blades and comfort the animal before slaughter.[1] He is also reported to have pressed his foot on the side of a ram, which was presumably lying on the ground, and to have said Allah's name before slaughter.[2] These actions attributed to the Prophet have been widely incorporated into the ritual script of Muslim slaughter.

Slaughter can only be performed on species considered halal. In classical juristic formulations, the slaughterer should be an adult and sane male or female and a Muslim or *kitabi* (Jewish or Christian).[3] The discussion will show, however, that most modern jurists insist on the Muslim faith of the slaughterer. As to the technique: a small animal, such as a ram, sheep, or a goat, is laid down on its left side (where the heart is located), its head facing the direction of Mecca. A big animal, such as a cow or camel, is allowed to remain standing, but again its head should face Mecca. The slaughterer is expected to invoke the name of Allah (*tasmiyya*) before the incision, and the most common way to do this is to say "Bismillah" ("In the name of God") followed by "Allah Akbar" ("God is Great").[4] If the animal is a sheep, ram, or goat, the slaughterer slits the throat using a sharp blade, cutting at least three of the four passages (that is, the carotids, jugulars, trachea, and esophagus) in the throat.[5] However, the head should not be severed. The same procedure is followed for large animals, when possible. But since they are more difficult to control, the slaughterer is also permitted to drive a knife or sharp object in the throat to cause bleeding and eventual death. The law allows the use of sharp blades made of metal, wood, or stone. But the Prophet warned against using bones, human nails, and teeth for slaughter,[6] and Islamic law requires that animals be spared unnecessary suffering and anxiety.

Halal slaughter does resemble Jewish ritual slaughter (*shechita*). In both cases, the preferred method is a rapid incision with a sharp blade to an animal's throat that severs the trachea, esophagus, and major arteries in order to cause a rapid drop in blood pressure, leading to death.[7] Bleeding the animal out is critical in both procedures, and both halal and kashrut regulations regard the blood remaining in the animal as filthy, corrupting, and in need of disposal.[8] The practice of slaughtering larger domesticated animals (such as camels) and prey by bleeding them might also reflect techniques that existed in Arabia before the rise of Islam.

Islamic prescriptions allow for the consumption of the flesh of many wild animal species, as long as they are hunted by Muslims and for the primary purpose of eating rather than pleasure. When hunting (*sayd*), any piercing tools that cause bleeding, such as arrows, spears, and—in modern times—bullets, are allowed so long as the hunter invokes Allah's name at the time of the tool's release. The hunter should slit the prey's throat, after pronouncing the tasmiyya, if the animal is caught before its death. However, if the animal dies before the hunter reaches it, the flesh is still halal so long as the death is caused by the hunting tool that penetrated the animal and caused it to bleed. Prey caught or fetched by hunting dogs or birds are also halal as long as the hunting animals belong to Muslim hunters and do not eat any of what they catch.[9] The meat of animals hunted by non-Muslims is variably and situationally accepted by different Muslim legal schools (see Appendix B).

Sea Animals

In Arabic, the words for hunting and fishing are the same (sayd), and rules for hunting land animals adhere to the general ethos of slaughtering farm-raised animals. A terrestrial hunter, for instance, should utter God's name as he fires his weapon. But since a fisherman is not required to make this utterance, Muslims are permitted to eat seafood and fish caught by any non-Muslims, kitabi or not. This view of seafood as wholesome, regardless of who caught or killed it, stems from a widely cited prophetic saying that "that which is pure water, its dead meat [*maytatuhu*] is permissible."[10]

موجِبُ المَعْذُورِ فِيهِ مُوبِّ إلا إنا الله لا الها إلا أنا القول وخشينا في المسئلة العول

وكما رأيتُنا أن نفيض كما افضنا أو نفيضر فيما افضنا الغرض الغرض لعل العرض عن

الأدبين وتلا أن هذا الأساطير لأولين ثمة كالجنية هاجدة والنفس

الأبّية ناجنه قدلف وأزدلف وخلع الصلف وبذلك أن تلافا ما سلفه تستغيب

سمع السامرة وأوقع كالسهل الهامر وقال

عندي عا جنها دون ما بلا كرب عن الثفات فكتوني با العجب

Fig. 3.1. Camel Slaughter. *Al-Maqamat li'l Hariri* (1236-37), drawings by Yahya ibn Mahmoud ibn Yahya ibn Aboul-Hasan ibn Kouvarriha al-Wasiti. Bibliothèque nationale de France, Département des manuscrits, Arabe 5847, folio 140r. Used with permission.

Fig. 3.2. Slaughter and butchery. Detail from "Preparation for a Feast," folio from a *Divan of Jami* (Iran or Bukhara, late fifteenth century). The New York Metropolitan Museum, Islamic Art Department. Public Domain. Accessed July 28, 2017. http://www.metmuseum.org/art/collection/search/451084?sortBy=Relevance&deptids=14&ft=*&offset=300&rpp=100&pos=363.

With regard to the slaughter of water animals, jurists display leniency: most agree that a freshly caught small fish can be left to die quickly by exposure to air. Shafi'i, Hanbali, and Hanafi jurists consider it reprehensible (makruh) to swallow or cook fish while alive. They also note that a larger fish should be slaughtered from the tail end. In schools that sanction the consumption of sea turtles, jurists recommend slaughtering a turtle according to halal rules for land creatures, presumably by slitting its throat and draining its blood.[11] To avoid prolonging the suffering of large sea animals—specifically, isomorphic sea creatures such as sea cows or manatees—Shafi'i jurists prefer (*mustahab*) but do not mandate that these creatures be slaughtered like land animals: that is, by using a sharp knife to cut the "neck."[12] Where the "neck" is located for some sea creatures, however, is unclear. Since this practice is not mandatory, local fishing traditions have commonly prevailed. For instance, Indonesian whale hunters today often use methods introduced by Westerners in the nineteenth century: over several hours, they harpoon the whale with bamboo spears until the animal tires, then a fisherman jumps into the water and severs the whale's spinal cord.[13]

Disputes and Divergences

Most standard discussions of halal slaughter fail to address regional variations in practice and the complexity of disagreements on specific aspects of slaughter requirements among various Muslim communities. In fact, halal slaughter prescriptions, rather than being a static, ritualized regimen, are a compilation of practices that have been negotiated in different times and places; thus, they mark historical changes in Muslims' views of religious purity and communal identity.

This is very clear, for example, in the question of who can perform the slaughter. The requirement that the slaughterer should be an adult and sane male or female becomes more fluid given that the definitions of "adulthood" and "sanity" have varied by time and place. Also, Muslims have not always been in unison over women's role in animal slaughter. The Quran contains no statement against women's slaughter of animals, and the medieval Islamic scholar Muhammad ibn Isma'il al-Bukhari (d. 870) reports a strong hadith that indicates the Prophet's approval of slaughter performed by a woman.[14] At the same time, in many Muslim settings women's slaughter of animals larger than poultry has been considered unusual. For example, Islamic scholar Georges-Henri Bousquet mentions the existence of a prevalent "superstition" against women's slaughter in Muslim communities of North Africa. He also reports a story originating from Tangier that when women performed slaughters, they placed phallic symbols between their thighs.[15] In certain parts of Anatolia, women are allowed to slaughter animals only when they are not menstruating and only when men are not around.[16] Furthermore, butchery and associated vocations have been traditionally considered men's work in most Muslim societies. Ottoman sources, for instance, indicate that membership in trade organizations that specialized in relevant practices, including butchering, selling organ meat, and making sausage and *pastırma* (a type of cured meat), was limited to men.

By far the most consequential divergences stem from whether meat butchered by non-Muslims can be considered halal. Although modern formulations generally agree that halal slaughter requires Muslim slaughterers, the jurisprudential and historical sources reveal more complex and inconsistent positions on the topic. According to David Freidenreich, the majority of early Muslim jurists permitted the consumption of animals slaughtered by kitabis, by Christian and Jewish butchers, but not by other non-Muslims.[17] This

Fig. 3.3. *A Butcher Shop* (painting, verso; text, recto of folio 29), illustrated folio from a manuscript of the Rawda al-Ushshaq (Garden of Lovers) of Arifi, c. 1560. Unknown Artist. Harvard Art Museums/Arthur M. Sackler Museum, The Edwin Binney, 3rd Collection of Turkish Art at the Harvard Art Museums, 1985.216.29. Photo: Imaging Department © President and Fellows of Harvard College.

distinction rests on the Quranic statement that Allah made lawful to Muslims all good foods "and the food of those who were given the Scripture is lawful for you and your food is lawful for them" (5:5). The scriptures in question here are the Jewish and Christian canons, along with hadith reports indicating that the Prophet accepted and ate roasted meat offered by a Jew.[18]

The question of how verse 5:5 should be reconciled with other Quranic statements such as 5:3 or 6:121 generated different positions on the relationship between halal requirements and the religious identity of the slaughterer.[19] What if a Christian butcher invoked Christ's name before he slaughtered the animal? What if a Jewish butcher said a blessing according to his own religious rites before his incision? Many medieval Muslim jurists ignored this problem completely or explained it away using stock responses. Some argued that 5:5 is one of the most recent revelations and thus "abrogated" all those that came before it.[20] Others suggested that God surely knew about the slaughter practices of Christians and Jews and yet revealed 5:5 as a sign of their special position as people of scripture (ahl al-kitab). Jurists of a more practical bent argued that Muslims should avoid meat slaughtered by Jews and Christians if they clearly heard the latter invoking names other than that of Allah at the instant of slaughter. In the absence of such specific knowledge, they opined, it was permissible to consume this meat.[21]

While these positions generally constituted the medieval Sunni attitudes toward the status of meat butchered by Christians and Jews, Shiite authorities gradually formulated more restrictive opinions. At first the Shiite jurists, like their Sunni counterparts, were relatively accepting of such meat, as long as the slaughterers did not explicitly invoke the name of deities other than Allah during slaughter. During the ninth and tenth centuries, however, Shiites became more concerned about specific practices they associated with Jews and Christians. Rather than simply worrying that these groups might have invoked the names of their own Gods, Shiite authorities came to disdain Jews' and Christians' failure to mention Allah's name during slaughter. This subtle shift in focus led to their more pronounced inclination to resist the consumption of meat slaughtered by Christians and Jews.

From the eleventh century onward, Shiite attitudes became even more discriminating as their jurists justified the prohibition of meat prepared by Christians and Jews, not because of the slaughter-related technicalities but because of these groups' false beliefs and thus their inherent impurity.[22] Shiite jurists used the Quranic statement 9:28, "The polytheists [al-mushrikuna] are unclean [*najasun*]," to justify this interpretation, and by doing so they rejected the privileged positions the Sunnis had traditionally attributed to Jews and Christians relative to other non-Muslim populations. Freidenreich observes that, for medieval Shiites, Christians and Jews were "no different from other idolaters because they do not truly understand God or the divine will . . . . If Jews and Christians possessed accurate knowledge they too would reject Trinitarian theology, abstain from wine, and acknowledge the authenticity of Muhammad's prophecy. Because non-Muslim butchers are ignorant about God, they are unfit to invoke God and therefore incapable of performing a valid act of ritual slaughter."[23] Over time, Shiites developed the idea that contact with any non-Muslims, including Jews and Christians, required ritual cleansing. One interpretation that emerged classified the water that Jews drank as impure and concluded that Muslims should not drink or eat food made with water used by Jews. In this view, only dry and unprocessed food such as grain is safe from contamination.[24]

The transformation observed in the Shiite attitudes toward meat slaughtered by Christians and Jews illustrates yet again the potential for historical change in Islamic religious-jurisprudential interpretations. However, the relatively more liberal Sunni attitudes toward Christian- and Jewish-slaughtered meat remained generally intact until modern times. For example, while manuals for market inspectors (*muhtasib*) from Sunni Mamluk Egypt indicate a preference (though not a requirement) that slaughterers be Muslim,[25] many Muslims in medieval Cairo were suspicious of Muslim butchers' practices and favored meat from non-Muslim butchers.[26] Ottoman sources point to the existence of separate slaughter spaces for Muslims and non-Muslims and identify ten to twelve Jewish slaughterhouses in Istanbul in the eighteenth and nineteenth centuries.[27] Like their Mamluk counterparts, however, Ottoman consumers also shopped from Jewish, if not Christian, butchers. In this regard, Edward William Lane, who lived in Cairo between 1825 and 1828, provides some instructive observations and anecdotes. In one incident, while some Muslim religious figures expressed reservations about buying meat from Jewish butchers, most jurists considered meat slaughtered by Jewish butchers acceptable since they observed halal requirements, including the pronunciation of Allah's name at the time of slaughter.[28]

Only recently, it seems, have Sunni authorities become more restrictive about who should be allowed to perform slaughter. Nowadays, most Sunni formulations require the slaughterer to be a Muslim, which is consistent with

Fig. 3.4. A modern halal butcher in London. Note the hygienic stainless steel shelves and the Quranic verses overhead. Authors' photograph.

older Shiite requirements. The reasons for this change vary and may include, but are not limited to, the following factors:

1. Meat has come to constitute a greater portion of food consumed by increasing proportions of Muslims in modern times. Thus, its purity and Islamic credentials have become a concern for more Muslims, including poorer ones. This may have provoked widespread anxieties that are more endemic to the modern era.
2. The globalization of the meat market has pushed Muslim-majority nations to import their meat from overseas, which has amplified concerns about how meat produced in non-Muslim settings for Muslim consumption is slaughtered and whether halal slaughter rituals are observed in earnest.

3. The popularization of radical and pietistic trends among Muslims since the last quarter of the twentieth century may have played a role in the growth of the Sunni emphasis on Islamic purity and isolation more generally.

4. Intensifying competition among certifying and standardizing bodies over halal standards might have privileged stricter definitions of halal as authentic and led to their popularization in many Muslim communities.

Clearly, the modern era has presented Islamic authorities with challenging new trends and circumstances, including globalization and certification.

Preslaughter Stunning: The Issue of Animal Cruelty

One recent matter of particular concern to Muslims is the preslaughter stunning of animals intended for human consumption, a common practice in Western abattoirs. The global debate over this practice has become highly contentious. In many Western countries, popular opinions of halal slaughter rituals often reflect anxieties about Muslims' cultural integration and their ability to appropriate what many consider to be modern and Western values; halal slaughter objections are thus akin to efforts to ban clothing items such as head scarves and burqinis. Among Muslims, debates about the permissibility of stunning show how distinct political and social variables—even those that originate outside of Muslim-majority settings—might influence halal practices. What follows is a discussion of how preslaughter stunning arose in the modern meat industry and how it came to shape halal slaughter formulations and procedures.

Preslaughter Stunning in the West

The modern experimentation with humane slaughter techniques, particularly preslaughter stunning in the West, goes back to the second half of the nineteenth century. The techniques were intended to spare animals designated for human consumption from the anxiety and pain associated with slaughter. Older stunning methods included rendering the animal unconscious by a blow to the head with a poleaxe or mallet, or by firing a bullet into its brain. Two of the first modern techniques, used from the second half of the nineteenth century, were gassing (mainly with carbon dioxide and nitrogen) and electro-cution. The early twentieth century brought experimentation with penetrating and nonpenetrating captive-bolt appliances, the pistol-like heavy rods used to subdue an animal prior to slaughter. These devices are placed against the ani-mal's forehead and then discharged by gunpowder or compressed air. When the device is discharged or triggered, a metal bolt strikes the skull with such great force that it renders the animal unconscious. The bolt is "captive" in the sense that it is retractable and remains connected to the barrel of the pistol after discharge. In penetrating devices, the bolt enters the skull and damages the brain tissue. This mechanism sometimes causes death by itself, but slaugh-terers often ensure death by following up with exsanguination, severing the spinal cord, or injection of a deadly chemical substance into the bloodstream. The nonpenetrating types (such as ones with mushroom bolt-heads) are not supposed to kill animals, but in unskilled or inexperienced hands, they can require multiple strikes to an animal's skull. Also, animals stunned by non-penetrating captive-bolt pistols are more likely to gain consciousness before slaughter.[29] Historically, while captive-bolt stunning is more common among larger animals such as cattle, gassing and electrocution have often been used on sheep and pigs.

The first modern advocacy organizations for animal welfare were founded in Europe in the late nineteenth and early twentieth centuries. These groups pushed for legislation mandating what they considered to be humane slaughter; they generally favored preslaughter stunning, and their activ-ism sometimes targeted minority groups. For example, in Switzerland, the pressure exerted by animal welfare groups led to an 1893 referendum that banned the kosher slaughter practice known as shechita, since Judaic legal interpretations object to preslaughter stunning.[30] In England, the Humane Slaughter Association actively promoted the use of mechanically operated stunners, trained butchers in humane slaughter techniques, and played a critical role in the introduction of the Slaughter of Animals Act in 1933, which required the use of captive-bolt stunning techniques on cattle and calves and the electrical stunning of pigs butchered in commercial slaugh-terhouses.[31] In Norway, from the 1890s onward the animal rights associa-tion Dyrebeskyttelsen led a popular public campaign against what they saw as the inhumane slaughter of livestock, calling for new legislative reforms.[32] Other North European countries soon followed, making similar legislative changes.

Concerns over animal welfare constituted an important rationale, but not the only one, for preslaughter stunning. Other factors included the safety of the slaughterers, who often had difficulty controlling the animals, especially when killing cattle. In addition, animal welfare arguments were often voiced in the context of growing European anti-Semitism. In early twentieth-century Germany, the relationship between pro-stunning advocacy and anti-Semitic sentiments was pronounced. Barely three months after Hitler became the chancellor of Germany in 1933, shechita was outlawed.[33]

Bans on non-stun slaughter were also adopted in the Netherlands (1920), Norway (1930), Sweden (1938), Poland (1938), Italy (1938), Slovakia (1939), and, after 1940, in countries occupied by the Nazis.[34] In the United Kingdom and the Netherlands (until German occupation), exemption from stunning was allowed in cases of religious slaughter in the name of religious freedom.[35] But in other locations, religious slaughter without stunning was completely prohibited until World War II ended.[36] After the war, although preslaughter stunning became even more prevalent in Europe, religiously based exemptions were introduced in many countries due to the adoption of Europe-wide regulations on animal protection. The European Convention for the Protection of Animals for Slaughter, signed in 1979, required preslaughter stunning but also included leeway for the case of "slaughtering in accordance with religious rituals."[37] The *Council Directive 93/119/EC of 22 December 1993 on the Protection of Animals at the Time of Slaughter or Killing*, which lists the requirements of the European Union (EU) for humane slaughter, necessitated stunning but also permitted exemptions "in the case of animals subject to particular methods of slaughter required by certain religious rites."[38]

To further complicate matters, the wording of the directive also allowed for discretionary policies among signatory countries.[39] Consequently, some European nations have been more hesitant than others to acknowledge religious slaughter exemptions or have recognized them in incremental and case-by-case bases. Iceland, Liechtenstein, Luxembourg, Norway, Sweden, and Switzerland have allowed no exemptions from preslaughter stunning. While the Netherlands and Germany acknowledged the acceptability of shechita immediately after World War II, they waited until 1975 and 1982, respectively, to grant Muslims comparable exemptions. But a few other countries— including France, the United Kingdom, Spain, and Italy, among others—have been less hesitant to grant exemptions from stunning and more accommodating of minority concerns on a wholesale basis.[40]

In 2009, *Council Regulation No 1099/2009 on the Protection of Animals at the Time of Killing* amended and replaced *Council Directive 93/119/EC*. The new regulation maintains the Member States' responsibilities to ensure the welfare of animals intended for human consumption but also upholds the special status of religious slaughter. More specifically, it confirms "derogation from stunning" as a religious right and also exempts slaughterers from keeping the trachea and the esophagus intact in religious culling.[41] At the same time, and just like the Directive it replaced, the Regulation allows for a "level of subsidiarity to each Member State" on issues related to conflicting freedom of religion and animal welfare matters.[42]

The issue of preslaughter stunning is still controversial in Europe and continues to pit influential animal- and minority-rights supporters against each other.[43] A court in Poland banned religious ritual slaughter in 2013, but the decision was overturned by the Constitutional Court in 2014 when Jewish groups challenged it.[44] In 2014, Denmark eliminated the religious exemptions for non-stun slaughter after a long public debate, despite the objections of Danish Jewish and Muslim groups.[45] In 2015, the British Veterinary Association called for an official ban on non-stun slaughter, and the issue has been hotly debated in the British public before and since.[46] In 2017, Belgium's Wallonia, which constitutes more than half of the country's territories and one-third of its population, banned non-stun ritual slaughter, effective from September 2019.[47] Public disputes have contained frequent references to Europe's racist and colonial history, remarks about human cruelty toward other animal species, and complaints about how science is utilized and interpreted by the opposing side.[48]

In the United States, the Humane Methods of Slaughter Act (HMSA), enacted in 1958 after several failures, accepted humane slaughtering as "the public policy of the United States" and required the federal government to purchase meat only from processors that stunned animals "by a single blow or gunshot or an electrical, chemical or other means that is rapid and effective, before being shackled, hoisted, thrown, cast, or cut."[49] But because the meat industry and many Orthodox Jewish groups fought the HMSA, the final legal wording prescribed no penalties for slaughter practices that failed to conform with the humane slaughter requirements. In fact, the law also included amendments that defined non-stun religious slaughter as humane.[50] Twenty years later, in 1978, preslaughter stunning became mandatory for all nonreligious commercial meat providers, whether they sold meat to the federal government or not, and criminal penalties were applied to the violators.[51]

The HMSA has been generally interpreted to cover livestock only, and not poultry, despite numerous unsuccessful attempts to include the latter.[52] Thus the act cannot be used as a basis for a criminal charge at the federal level of inhumane slaughter of poultry. The mechanized nature of poultry slaughter in most plants involves hanging birds by their legs upside-down and dragging their heads through electrified water before slaughter by a mechanical knife. The use of electrocution has recently become an industry standard mainly to speed up slaughter, not to minimize anguish to animals. In fact, many industry insiders and animal rights activists have noted that the process is anxiety-ridden for the animals and often causes broken limbs. In some cases, the birds survive the electrocution and mechanical knife and are thrown alive into scalding hot water tanks.[53] In 2005 the Humane Society of the United States filed a lawsuit against the United States Department of Agriculture demanding that the language of the HMSA be extended to poultry, but in 2008 they lost the case. Parallel attempts to pass legislation requiring poultry to be slaughtered humanely as defined in the act have also failed in the US Congress.[54] Nevertheless, and despite these failures at the federal level, some state versions of HMSA (for example, those enacted by California, Indiana, Pennsylvania, and Michigan) count poultry among animal species that should be subject to humane (including ritual) slaughter regulations.[55]

Finally, preslaughter stunning is a requirement in New Zealand and Australia. These countries are major exporters of lamb and sheep to Muslim countries in the Middle East and South Asia, and they primarily utilize reversible stunning (by electrocution) prior to slaughter. While Australia, where Muslims represent about 2.5 percent of the population, allows exemptions from stunning in cases of religious slaughter, New Zealand, where Muslims constitute about 1 percent of the population, does not.[56]

The various stunning techniques—their effectiveness, how they compare to non-stun slaughter, and so on—have been passionately debated for decades. Proponents of non-stun shechita and halal slaughter have long argued that religious slaughter, in the hands of well-trained and experienced slaughterers, causes minimum pain for animals and that Jewish and Islamic preslaughter treatment of animals reduces their anxiety.[57] These groups have also pointed out that the various procedures followed to stun animals could themselves cause pain, even injury, to animals and that they unnecessarily prolong the killing process. This is a legitimate concern: numerous instances of "misknocks" and "misplaced shots" have been documented in American slaughterhouses.[58] The question of whether stunning minimizes pain during slaughter has also been explored by scientists, yet these studies have not generated clear results, or at least results clear enough to convince all parties to the debate. Researchers agree that modern stunning techniques are generally effective in rendering animals unconscious and less prone to technical or operator-caused failure than earlier methods. They also argue that animals continue to feel pain and experience trauma in non-stun slaughter for a considerable time after the incision on the throat and neck area. A 2004 EU-commissioned European Food Safety Authority report, which provides a comprehensive review of the scientific literature on the topic, reports that "without stunning, the time between cutting through the major blood vessels and insensibility, as deduced from behavioural and brain response, is up to 20 seconds in sheep, up to 25 seconds in pigs, up to 2 minutes in cattle, up to 2.5 or more minutes in poultry, and sometimes 15 minutes or more in fish."[59]

The scale of public concern and debates in numerous Western settings, since the late nineteenth century, about how to slaughter animals with the least amount of suffering is unprecedented among Muslim populations. The gradual involvement of Muslims in preslaughter stunning debates is an indirect consequence of their integration into a global capitalist market for labor and products. More specifically, Muslims became increasingly occupied with non-Muslim animal slaughter techniques and their halal compliance due to the growing international livestock and meat trade between Muslim importers and non-Muslim exporters, and also due to the mass emigration of Muslims to the West in the second half of the twentieth century. It is also relevant that these developments have taken place in the broader context of popularization of Islamic puritanical aspirations since the late twentieth century.

Is Preslaughter Stunning Halal?

An important and controversial jurisprudential issue that Muslims have recently considered is whether preslaughter stunning is permissible according to Islamic law. Since millions of Muslims now live in Muslim-minority settings or are reliant on meat imported from non-Muslim exporters, Muslims have been wrestling with the question of the practice's permissibility. True, many non-Muslim countries grant exemptions to the stunning requirement for religious purposes. Yet preslaughter stunning is now an industry standard because it renders the slaughter process faster, more efficient, less dangerous for humans, more compliant with animal welfare concerns, and cheaper. Today, however, the question of whether preslaughter stunning is halal preoccupies not only Muslim consumers but also meat suppliers to Muslim markets, as well as state regulators in countries with significant Muslim populations.

Since preslaughter stunning is a modern issue, classical jurisprudential treatments of halal slaughter contain no direct prescriptions and few indirect clues regarding its legal status. There is consensus among medieval jurists that the act of slaughter should be as swift and merciful as possible: that both the slaughterer and the animal face Mecca denotes the act's sacredness and its ritualism.[60] More recently (and based on ancillary inferences), modern Muslim jurists have taken three general positions with regard to stunning:

1. Permitted with no limitations, if performed by "People of the Book"
2. Permitted with limitations
3. Not permitted

The first position is based on the Quranic verse 5:5: "This day [all] good foods have been made lawful, and the food of those who were given the Scripture is lawful for you and your food is lawful for them." Accordingly, any form of slaughter performed on animal species considered halal by "People of the Book" (i.e., Christians and Jews or kitabis) in ways that are acceptable to them, and even if these contradict Islamic slaughter methods, results in consumable meat for Muslims. Perhaps the most recognized modern supporter of this position is the Egyptian Sheikh Yusuf al-Qaradawi, who, referring to verse 5:5 and citing the opinions of the medieval legal scholar Ibn al-Arabi, has argued that "imported meats, such as chicken and canned meat, originating with the People of the Book are halal for us, even though the animal may have been killed by means of electroshock or the like. As long as (Jews and Christians) consider it lawful in their religion it is halal for us."[61]

Interpretations based on 5:5 deem lawful any type of slaughter performed by Jewish and Christian butchers on halal species, even if it might violate explicit halal slaughter standards, including the invocation of the name of God before the killing, the complete postslaughter bleeding of the carcass, and some stunning techniques most Muslims object to. However, many Muslims are uncomfortable with the potential conflicts between Islamic and non-Islamic procedures of animal killing, especially as those living in Western settings have access to meat harvested through a variety of methods. Doubt (shubha) is an important legal consideration in Islamic jurisprudential traditions, and many jurists have argued that if a Muslim has doubts about whether a particular act is lawful or unlawful in terms of its nature or consequences, it is best to avoid such an act just to be safe.[62] Also, certain modern jurists who sought additional grounds to disregard the application of 5:5 have expressed doubts about the extent to which Muslims could be sure that a butcher with a "Jewish" or "Christian" name or ancestry was not really an "atheist" or "pagan" or "materialist" or "communist."[63]

The second and third positions about the permissibility of stunning are based on the Quranic prescriptions related to how animals intended for consumption should not be killed, such as verse 5:3: "Prohibited to you are dead animals, blood, the flesh of swine, and that which has been dedicated to other than Allah, and [those animals] killed by strangling or by a violent blow or by a head-long fall or by the goring of horns, and those from which a wild animal has eaten, except what you [are able to] slaughter [before its death], and those which are sacrificed on stone altars."[64] Proponents of the first position, those who consider 5:5 binding in determining the status of Jewish and Christian harvested meat, are required to observe these prescriptions only if the slaughterer is a Muslim. But those who are hesitant to consider 5:5 requisite believe that the prescriptions listed in 5:3 and other parallel verses relevant for considerations related to stunning should apply to all meat, whether slaughtered by Muslims or by People of the Book.

Relevant to the Quranic prescriptions about how animals should not be killed are later jurisprudential elaborations regarding the status of meat harvested from ill, injured, or incapacitated animals. On this issue, premodern jurists made slightly divergent pronouncements. One opinion, as formulated by Abu Hanifa, the eighth-century founder of the Hanafi school, is that the slaughter of an animal so incapacitated that it appears to be dead (just like a stunned animal would be) is allowed as long as the slaughterer knows for certain that it is alive. If that certainty is not possible, however, then the animal's flesh would be halal only if the body moves or bleeds during slaughter. According to other prominent Hanafi jurists, including Abu Yusuf (d. 798) and Imam Muhammad Shaybani (d. 805), the animal intended for slaughter should demonstrate explicit signs of life (bayan al-hayat al-mustaqirra) before slaughter, and if it might be ill, injured, or incapacitated, it should be clear that the animal would live on its own for at least one and a half days. Still others argued that an ill, injured, or incapacitated animal that cannot move or bleed as much as a healthy animal would during slaughter is carrion and should not be consumed. A small group of jurists suggested that animals destined to die because of illness or injury should not be slaughtered at all.[65]

The group of interpretations that we have dubbed "permitted with limitations" insists that as long as the stunning procedures can be guaranteed not to kill the animal (that is, they are "reversible") and do not harm or hurt the animal before slaughter or affect the drainage of blood from its body, they can be used to produce halal meat. The flesh of a stunned animal that demonstrates signs of life, such as reflexive, muscular movements at the time of slaughter, is permissible. The meat of animals that do not show these signs is carrion. This "permitted with limitations" position has the support of many Muslim legal authorities, including those in distinguished fiqh (jurisprudence) academies in India, Mecca, and Jeddah.[66] In 1982, during the process of considering the Muslim exemption from preslaughter stunning, the government of West Germany requested and received a legal opinion from Sheikh Muhammad Al-Najjar, from Al-Azhar University in Cairo, that proclaimed the acceptability of preslaughter stunning in Islam.[67] Also included in this list is the Shiite cleric Ali Khameini, Iran's second and current Supreme Leader.[68] Numerous Muslim experts in Belgium, France, Canada, the United States, and the United Kingdom also allowed the use of select stunning methods in the slaughter process.

Proponents of the second position ("permitted with limitations") object to the use of some common stunning techniques for halal slaughter, mainly for practical reasons. For example, since penetrating captive-bolt pistols often lead to death before slaughter, and animals that die in the process cannot be efficiently identified, they should be avoided in principle. Gas chambers could also cause death for lamb and poultry and thereby render their flesh unlawful for consumption. Head-to-body electroshock is often not considered halal compliant either, since it can lead to cardiac arrest. The preferred stunning techniques for the proponents of the second position are head strikes by nonpenetrating, mushroom-headed captive-bolt pistons for cattle; head-only electroshock for smaller animals such as sheep and goats; and water bath electrocution for poultry.[69] All of these methods have been shown to have fewer accidental death rates. On the other hand, while some authorities recognize the permissibility of stunning for larger animals, they also prohibit the electrocution of poultry because it often leads to death.[70]

The third and final position on preslaughter stunning ("not permitted") differs from the previous one ("permitted with limitations") not in principle, but because of its skepticism about whether any stunning technique can consistently satisfy strict Islamic slaughter standards. Like the second position, it has proponents among both Sunni and Shiite authorities. Among Shiite jurists, Ali al-Sistani, Iraq's Grand Ayatollah, is known to be against preslaughter stunning.[71] At the same time, the Pakistani Sunni cleric Sheikh Taqi Usmani's frequently cited opinions have been influential in justifying the antistunning position. According to Usmani, Muslims should avoid preslaughter stunning for these reasons:

1. Any stunning technique, even "reversible" ones, could kill animals, and in commercial slaughterhouses, slaughterers do not stop and make sure every stunned animal is alive before slaughter. Short of a thorough medical examination of every animal, which would render slaughter significantly more expensive in commercial establishments, it is difficult to differentiate a stunned animal from a dead one. In other words, because stunning undermines the slaughterer's ability to ascertain whether an animal is alive before slaughter, it generates the potential to mistake haram meat for halal. Here, too, doubt (shubha) appears as a legal concern. According to Sheikh Usmani, "There is no doubt that it will be unlawful to use stunning if it causes the death of the animal or if there is a fear that it will cause the death of the animal, and such an animal will also be considered unlawful to consume once it is stunned. As long as there remains doubt in this method, the safest thing to do is to avoid using it."[72]

2. All stunning could affect the intensity of blood drainage from the body after slaughter. According to Usmani, "Stunning the animal before slaughter causes slackness in the animal and contractions in its heart, causing the amount of blood which comes out of the animal to be less than normal."[73] Also, "scientists have proved that stunning causes blood hemorrhage and blood inside the meat. Consuming blood is forbidden in Islam."[74]

3. Some believe that all stunning procedures, even when performed without operator error or technical mishap, cause pain, anguish, and anxiety for animals. It is unnecessary, in this view, to subject animals to stunning because traditional, non-stun halal slaughter is the most effective and humane method of killing, as recognized by modern scientific research.[75]

As mentioned, scientific research on how slaughter methods with or without stunning affect animals has generated inconsistent results. Parties on both sides tend to cite studies in agreement with their specific positions. At the same time, proponents of non-stun halal slaughter tend to believe that traditional Islamic methods of slaughter, because of their connection to the prophetic custom, must be the best method. According to one sound hadith, the Prophet said: "Allah decreed to be good/kind [*ihsan*] in everything [you do]. If you kill, do the killing well. If you slaughter, do the slaughtering well. He among you [who slaughters] should sharpen his blade and comfort his animal to be slaughtered."[76] This report indicates that the traditional slaughter method is the best way to kill an animal and that only a sharp blade can give an animal relief from suffering. Any suggestion, based on scientific research or otherwise, that is inconsistent with these assertions might constitute a *bid'a*, or corrupt innovation. In a religion that locates its golden age in the time of the Prophet and idealizes the practices of the first generation of Muslims in principle, a call for change from accepted practices can potentially be interpreted not only as degeneration but also as an insult to the Prophet's example.

Mechanical Slaughter

Another modern development Muslims must currently contend with in their considerations of halal slaughter is the mechanical slaughter of poultry. The process refers to an automated procedure whereby mechanical blades slit the throats of poultry that are hung upside down by their legs on an assembly line. This stage is often preceded by a stunning operation, in which the birds' heads are dipped into electrified water baths to render them unconscious. Mechanized slaughter is a poultry industry standard because of its low cost; this method allows modern slaughterhouses to process tens of thousands of birds each day. Humans intervene in the process only by turning the mechanical blades on and off and, at some facilities, by manually slaughtering those birds partially or completely missed by the blades.

From the perspective of halal-conscious consumers, mechanized slaughter of poultry can raise multiple problems. First, since halal slaughter protocols often relate to the qualities and actions of the slaughterer, the limited human involvement in the mechanized process seems problematic. For this reason, modern legal authorities have debated whether the equivalent of a slaughterer actually exists in mechanized slaughter and, if so, who that person is. Also, jurists have debated whether, to what extent, and by whom the tasmiyya requirement can be performed during mechanized slaughter.[77] And some have deemed questionable the legal status of meat harvested from poultry that die during electrocution, are slaughtered improperly by mechanical blades, or are altogether missed by blades. When the blades miss the birds or merely injure them, the animals that are not caught and manually slaughtered by overseers die in scalding chambers, which renders them carrion.

As with preslaughter stunning, there are multiple positions regarding the status of mechanized poultry slaughter that range from "permitted, if performed by the 'People of the Book'," to "permitted with limitations," to "not permitted." The "permitted" position applies to meat harvested from mechanically slaughtered poultry only in premises operated by Jews and Christians. Since such poultry represent "the food of those who were given the Scripture," they should be acceptable for Muslims according to verse 5:5. The "permitted with limitations" position, may again appear to shift the attention from the identity of the operators to their specific actions and responsibilities, but since the latter concern how animals are killed (and, thus, the ritualism associated with slaughter) the operators' religious beliefs remain relevant.[78] According to this position, mechanized slaughter could generate halal meat if certain conditions are observed. For example, many who support this practice equate the person who operates the mechanical blades with the traditional slaughterer and suggest that the operator should pronounce the tasmiyya when he or she turns on the machine. The tasmiyya would be valid for every animal slaughtered before the machine is turned off. This interpretation is based on the opinion, common especially among classical Hanafi jurists, that one tasmiyya is adequate for the slaughter of multiple animals if it is performed by a single, uninterrupted sawing movement.[79] The proponents of "permitted with limitations" insist that mechanical operators ensure that any bird that dies during electrocution is discarded as carrion. Overseers should also identify the animals missed by mechanical blades and manually slaughter them after pronouncing the tasmiyya. The proponents of this position contend that at least the operators and overseers in mechanized poultry plants should be Muslims.[80]

Finally, those who consider mechanized slaughter of poultry impermissible object to the equivalency proposed between the machine operator and the slaughterer and argue that in the absence of a proper slaughterer, the killed animals should be considered carrion. The Hanafi opinion cited in the

Fig. 3.5a and Fig. 3.5b. Halal chicken imported from Brazil to Egypt, with detail. Several Islamic countries, including Egypt, have come to rely on imports of chicken and other meats from non-Muslim countries such as Brazil (Fig. 3.5a). In Fig. 3.5b, the right part of the graphic indicates that the chicken was fed a "100% vegetarian diet" and the halal marker toward the bottom notes that the chicken was "slaughtered by hand according to the Islamic Sharia." Authors' photographs.

previous paragraph does not constitute a proper analogy, they note, because in mechanized slaughter poultry are consecutively killed by the blades, one after the other, not simultaneously as a result of a single sawing movement by the slaughterer. Since the operator of the mechanized blades cannot be regarded as the slaughterer of thousands of birds, his or her tasmiyya would be valid only for the first bird whose throat was slit by the machine, not for subsequent ones. The live or audio-recorded tasmiyyas that might be continuously pronounced during the mechanized slaughter would not fulfill the tasmiyya requirement because they are not pronounced by an "actual" slaughterer.[81] For some Muslim jurists, such issues, and many others, make it very doubtful that mechanized poultry slaughter—a Western invention—could satisfy halal standards.[82]

Halal-compliant industrial cattle, sheep, and goat slaughter have not raised similar types of concerns. While the slaughterhouses that harvest halal non-poultry meat en masse have largely adopted modern slaughter tools and technologies, such as v-shaped transport chutes, carcass conveyor lines, and various forms of stun and kill boxes (including rotating ones), the actual slaughter in these facilities is still performed by hand, one animal at a time. This situation provides the slaughterer with the opportunity to check that the animal is properly stunned, to see that it is subjected to halal-compliant stunning procedures, and to personally invoke the tasmiyya before each killing.[83] On the other hand, many halal-compliant industrial slaughterhouses have received criticisms not only for causing unnecessary pain and distress for animals (just as their non-halal counterparts) but also for neglecting other types of halal slaughter requirements, such as turning the heads of animals toward Mecca before slaughter and preventing them from observing the slaughter of other animals.

Before the modern period, Sunni jurists were relatively accommodating toward meat slaughtered by Jews and Christians. In most premodern Islamic settings where producers, slaughterers, and consumers of meat shared similar religious sensitivities and practices pertaining to food, halal slaughter requirements likely caused little consternation. So long as Islamic expectations were presumed to be generally upheld, most Sunni jurists allowed Muslims to be relatively lax about the meats they consumed. According to one well-known hadith, the Prophet Muhammad allowed his followers to eat the meat offered to them by a Bedouin, although they did not know whether the latter had mentioned the name of Allah during slaughter. "Invoke the name of Allah," the Prophet said, "and eat."[84] Accordingly, most premodern juristic authorities discouraged Muslims from inquiring about the meat that they purchased from Muslim butchers, on the assumption that the latter would perform the slaughter according to halal requirements. They reasoned that even if a Muslim forgot to mention Allah's name before slaughter, this could only be unintentional and thus did not render the meat impermissible. Being excessively scrupulous about the issue could offend meat vendors and generate public discontent, which should be avoided at all costs. After all, the Quran says, "Allah intends for you ease and does not intend for you hardship" (2:185).

But in the modern period, Muslims became increasingly reliant on meat producers outside Islamic lands, and many, though not all, saw less reason to assume that the meat they consumed satisfied halal standards, even if the slaughter was performed by "People of the Book." Today, while some Muslims still maintain that stunning and mechanical slaughter are acceptable, many others believe that these practices are tolerable only under certain conditions. The prevalence of this still relatively conciliatory position indicates that a great number of Muslims are willing to reconsider and renegotiate their understanding of permissible meat in conversation with both the principal sources of their religion and the practices of other communities.

Nevertheless, it is also true that significant portions of Muslims completely reject stunning and mechanized slaughter of poultry, and that such segregationist attitudes may be gaining popularity. Indeed, between 2011 and 2013 the percentage of cattle and sheep killed in the United Kingdom by non-stun halal prescriptions rose by nearly a third, to one-half.[85] In Australia as well, industry insiders have observed a parallel pattern stimulated by foreign Muslim demand, mainly in the Middle East.[86] Likewise, Poland, Czechia, Hungary, Lithuania, Latvia, Hungary, and Bosnia-Herzegovina have embraced non-stun slaughter methods, and the rising demand may motivate other countries in Europe and elsewhere to follow suit.[87]

CHAPTER 4

I bn Ishaq's eighth-century biography of the Prophet Muhammad reports that during the *mi'raj*—the Prophet's miraculous ascension to heaven, accompanied by the Archangel Gabriel, to meet with God—he was offered two vessels, one containing milk and the other wine, to quench his thirst. When Muhammad drank from the vessel with milk and left aside that with wine, Gabriel told him: "Thou hast been [rightly] guided unto the path primordial, and hast guided thereunto thy people, O Muhammad, and wine is forbidden to you."[1] The text does not reveal whether the wine offered was earthly, which could lead to inebriation, or heavenly, which Muslims will enjoy in the afterlife with no mind-altering consequences. Islamic scholar Omid Safi suggests that it was the latter, since it is farfetched to imagine that the Prophet would be given an illicit drink.[2] However, if the wine was heavenly, which the Quran blesses as "a joy to those who drink it" (47:15), then why would Gabriel commend the Prophet's choice? The story captures wine's ambiguity in the early Islamic textual traditions: wine, at least in heaven, is worthy of being extended to the Prophet, yet to avoid it is also praiseworthy.

This chapter considers this ambiguity in early Muslims' attitudes toward alcoholic drinks and other psychoactive substances and discusses how later judicial and societal formulations—in premodern and modern times—sought a greater degree of certainty, particularly in the face of

Fig. 4.1a and Fig. 4.1b. Illustrated folio from a manuscript of *Habib al-Siyar* (*Friend of Biographies)* depicting the Prophet Muhammad's ascension to heaven (*mi'raj*), with detail of angel presenting a beverage (Persian, sixteenth century). Used with permission from Fundación Cultural Oriente at islamoriente.com. http://fotografia.islamoriente.com/sites/default/files/image_field/Obras_ maestras_de_la_miniatura_Persa-_%E2%80%9CAscensi%C3%B3n_del_profeta_del_Islam_ %28P%29%E2%80%9D_-_hecho_en_el_siglo_16_dC._2.jpg and http://fotografia.islamoriente. com/sites/default/files/image_field/Obras_maestras_de_la_miniatura_Persa-_hecho_en_el_ siglo_16_dC._tomado_de_libro_Habib_us-Siar_I%2C_de_la_historia_general_del_mundo_2.jpg.

Fig. 4.1a and Fig. 4.1b. Continued

habitual societal violations or the introduction of novel illicit substances. Along with meat, the status of intoxicants has been a focal topic in halal matters. Muslim attitudes toward alcohol and other inebriating substances reveal distinct historical complexities.[3] Most modern treatments of the topic define Islamic notions of purity and impurity ahistorically and consider their formulations enduring and coherent, assuming that they were definitively established during the Prophet's time. As with most aspects of Islamic law, however, the legal and societal standing of many food items, drinks, and substances evolved in protracted, geographically specific, and often nonlegal fashions, and not in entirely consistent ways. What follows is a survey of Islamic attitudes toward a few specific psychoactive substances and an exploration of their status within Islamic legal and social understandings. The discussion delves into how Muslims interpreted and enforced the alcohol-related rules in various contexts and how they subsequently applied those formulations to other psychoactive substances not mentioned in the canonical sources, including cannabis, opium, coffee, and tobacco. The chapter also explores nonlegal dispositions on alcohol and other mind-altering substances that influenced their broader acceptability in Islamic settings.

Alcohol in Islamic Societies

According to standard halal considerations, alcoholic drinks are just as najis (impure or filthy) as pork, blood, and carrion.[4] Most legal experts have regarded all intoxicating beverages as forbidden. Yet opinions against the consumption of alcoholic drinks have been ignored by many Muslims in every historical period and geographical setting—arguably much more so than prohibitions against pork, blood, and carrion. This is largely because, as food sources, pork, blood, and carrion have many alternatives. However, the case against alcoholic drinks is primarily due to their intoxicating qualities; nonalcoholic libations offer no real substitute (but see chapter 7). And as intoxicants, alcoholic beverages have served important social, cultural and medicinal functions since the earliest times. They can be social lubricants and their consumption has often been tied to virtues such as companionship, manliness, and elite identity. They have also been used to relieve daily boredom, depression, and the bodily effects of physical labor, as well as for healing the body. Thus, prescriptions against alcoholic drinks, if implemented fully and faithfully, would have had much wider consequences among Muslim peoples than those against pork, blood, and carrion.

The Quran describes intoxicating beverages in a manner different from other forbidden substances: before condemning "strong" drinks, the scripture recognizes their desirable, positive effects.[5] The gradual transformation of Quranic language on what the scripture calls khamr may reflect the protracted and deliberative process in which the first Muslims engaged. The hadith literature also suggests that alcohol prohibitions might have elicited some resistance within the early Muslim community.[6] That there are many more ahadith

on alcohol than on pork, blood, and carrion consumption is one indication of how Muslims struggled with this particular issue, which is unsurprising given that the people of Arabia had had access to and had enjoyed a variety of alcoholic beverages since ancient times.[7]

Disagreements in historical and jurisprudential sources also abound on various aspects of alcohol prohibition. For example, Islamic sources offer inconsistent statements on the nature, alcohol content, and legal status of *nabidh*, a lightly fermented drink that the Prophet was reported to have enjoyed.[8] Also, debates arose on how to apply the prohibition against khamr, frequently translated as "wine made from grapes," to other alcoholic drinks not specifically discussed in the Quran. While most jurists would agree that anything that has the propensity to inebriate should be considered khamr, others, including Abu Hanifa, the eponymous founder of the Hanafi school, as well as some earlier Iraqi jurists, insisted that Quranic prescriptions against alcohol can only be applied to drinks made from fermented grapes, and perhaps dates, because the term "khamr" specifically referred in the scripture to these potentially intoxicating beverages and only when they were consumed in large amounts. Therefore, they argued, fermented drinks made from wheat, barley, corn, and honey in quantities too small to intoxicate should not be considered haram.[9]

However the term khamr is defined, its prohibition extends beyond matters of consumption: Muslims are also forbidden to produce, store, buy, or sell khamr and to offer it to others. Those who spoil khamr that belongs to Muslims are not subject to punishment or compensation because khamr is not a substance that can legally be owned by Muslims.[10] Jurists agree that a denial of any of these assertions constitutes evidence of unbelief (or *kufr*).

Jurists also debated how to punish those who consumed alcohol. The Quran does not prescribe any specific punishment for consuming khamr (or pork, carrion, or blood, for that matter). The Prophet and his successor (the first caliph) Abu Bakr (d. 634) did determine the punishment for drunkenness, however: forty strikes by palm branches or sandals. The second caliph, Umar (d. 644), increased the punishment to eighty strikes, possibly because Muslims were disregarding the alcohol prohibition.[11] Also, while one hadith suggests that the Prophet prescribed the execution of repeat offenders,[12] another indicates that capital punishment may not be appropriate in such cases.[13] Islamic historian David Waines notes that in tenth-century Córdoba, some judges were patient with public exhibitions of drunkenness because the punishment for

Fig. 4.2. A feasting scene. *Al-Maqamat li'l Hariri* (1236–37), drawings by Yahya ibn Mahmoud ibn Yahya ibn Aboul-Hasan ibn Kouvarriha al-Wasiti. Bibliothèque nationale de France, Département des manuscrits, Arabe 5847, folio 33r. Used with permission.

this offense "is not spelt out explicitly in either the Quran or in sound hadith from the prophet."[14]

Alcohol use might have been lower in pre-Islamic Arabia than in neighboring regions. As Islam spread to the Mediterranean basin and within "greater Iran" (including Mesopotamia, the Caucasus, and eastern parts of Central Asia), encompassing "the world's oldest wine-growing and wine-drinking cultures,"[15] the alcohol prohibition likely faced more serious challenges. While some pre-modern Islamic polities, such as al-Moravids and the Wahhabis, attempted to ban alcohol consumption (often in uncompromising fashions), in most places alcohol prohibitions were more lenient and less consistent, and their intensity varied over time. In fact, the law was often simply ignored. And regional attitudes sometimes tempered jurisprudential interpretations. In Islamic Spain, for example, and following Abu Hanifa's example, some jurists differentiated grape wine from other alcoholic drinks and permitted the limited consumption of the latter. A few even suggested that if wine made from substances other than grape, such as honey, was permitted for consumption, then any beverage with comparable alcohol content, including grape wine, was also permissible.[16]

In medieval Egypt, societal attitudes toward alcohol consumption might have hardened over time. Until the thirteenth century, there was a general tolerance toward the consumption of various forms of alcohol, where people had relatively easy access to wine, beer, and other fermented drinks.[17] Under various Egyptian regimes, attitudes toward alcohol use were eased, then hardened, then relaxed again, in a cyclical fashion. However, attacking alcohol, particularly wine, became common during Mamluk times (1250–1517), a period known for more distinct Islamicization and for the increased marginalization of Egypt's non-Muslim communities (and presumably their alcohol-tolerating habits). After the thirteenth century, "wine disappeared from the corner shop," and, by the fifteenth century, wine drinkers were regularly punished and ostracized.[18] Even the relative laxity of the Hanafis toward non-khamr alcoholic beverages was replaced by more prohibitive interpretations around the same time, presumably under intense Maliki and Shafi'i criticism and pressure.[19]

While religio-legal opinions about alcohol became more stringent in Egypt and possibly elsewhere, alcohol consumption was never completely eradicated; in fact, it remained popular throughout parts of the Islamic world. In premodern times, wine-induced exhilaration appeared as a common and celebrated trope in high and low literature, where it was invoked literally and metaphorically by admired writers and poets. Most Muslims may have stayed away from alcohol, yet contemporary observers frequently commented on the bustling taverns in Muslim metropolises and the habits, practices, and culture associated with alcohol consumption elsewhere.[20] In his writings, Evliya Çelebi, a famed seventeenth-century Ottoman traveler, often referred to Istanbul's vigorous wine culture, mentioned the types of alcoholic drinks popular in the

Balkans and Anatolia (such as the anise-flavored *rakı and beer-like boza*), and described how he tactfully resisted wine offerings at parties hosted by the Ottoman sultan and the governor of Tabriz.[21] Many Western travelers to the Ottoman Empire observed the Ottoman indulgence for wine, and one specifically noted the "outrageous drunkenness of the Turkes."[22] When Lady Mary Wortley Montague, the wife of an English diplomat, drank rakı with a high-ranking Ottoman gentleman in the early eighteenth century, he pronounced "that all creations of God are good, and designed for the use of man . . . the Prophet never designed to confine those that knew how to use it with moderation."[23]

The early modern Islamic polities of the Ottoman and the Safavid empires did issue periodic bans on alcohol use, especially during times when they faced social, economic, and military difficulties and natural disasters and wanted to bolster the public image of their religious devotion and credentials.[24] Such bans often received support from pious groups and puritanical movements, such as the Ottoman Kadızadelis in the seventeenth century. These bans were almost always short-lived, though, and minimally effective in decreasing alcohol consumption. At times the rulers backing these prohibitions themselves drank alcoholic beverages, as did many prominent members of their administration. For example, Murad IV (d. 1640), who pursued one of the bloodiest temperance campaigns in Ottoman history, was a known alcoholic.[25] According to Islamic scholar Shahab Ahmed, many Muslim rulers shared this affliction:

> The consumption of wine was . . . prohibited in legal discourse, but positively valued in nonlegal discourse—especially amongst those social and political elites who instituted and secured the structures of the state and the very legal institutions that regulated the society. Thus the Mughal Emperor, Babur, writes disarmingly in his autobiography about his life-long struggle with the bottle, the diplomatic gifts of the Safavid Shah Abbas to the Great Mughal Jahangir included a choice selection of wine, and the Ottoman Sultan Ibrahim, remembered as Sarhosh ("the Drunk") was popularly reputed to have undertaken the conquest of vine-rich Cyprus for the express purpose of lubricating his habit. Babur noted further of his royal cousin, Baysongur, whom he recognized as a "just, humane, fine natured prince of learned-virtue," that "he was excessively fond of wine; when not drinking, he would perform his prayers."[26]

Wine consumption remained especially popular in urban areas and among the upper classes. Mystics and members of the military establishment also

Fig. 4.3. Mughal "Prince Feasting on a Balcony." Folio from the Davis Album (India, late seventeenth—early eighteenth century). The New York Metropolitan Museum, Theodore M. Davis Collection. Public Domain. Accessed July 28, 2017. http://www.metmuseum.org/art/collection/search/448487?sortBy=Relevance&deptids=14&ft=*&offset=400&rpp=100&pos=423.

consumed alcohol in significant amounts, although their beverage of choice may have been the cheaper kind, such as boza, a fermented beer-like drink made from millet or wheat.[27] According to Evliya Çelebi, there were about 300 boza-houses with more than 1,000 employees in seventeenth-century Istanbul.[28] The Ottomans not only accommodated the production and consumption of alcohol but also financially benefited from these activities. For example, during the sixteenth century the state levied taxes on the extensive wine-production enterprises in the Christian- and Muslim-owned vineyards of Ottoman Crimea.[29] In the same period, boza-houses in the Balkans made monthly tax payments to local authorities.[30] The state itself also owned dozens of lucrative boza manufactories in the fifteenth and sixteenth centuries. One such establishment in Edirne generated about 200,000 akçes in 1477, a considerable profit by fifteenth-century standards.[31]

Modern legal systems in most Muslim countries are only partially, if at all, aligned with Islamic legal principles.[32] Thus the laws and regulations regarding the production, sale, and consumption of alcoholic beverages range widely throughout the Islamic world. In Turkey, alcohol is available for public consumption, although since the early 2000s it has been heavily taxed and regulated by the conservative government of the Justice and Development Party. Until recently, the Turkish state had a monopoly on the production and sale of alcoholic beverages.[33] Before the civil war in Syria in 2011, the situation was similar there. Public access to alcoholic beverages is also easy in Lebanon, and the country is well known for the abundance and high quality of its domestic wine production. In Egypt, alcohol production, sale, and consumption are legal, but alcohol is heavily taxed and faces major taboos, as the society has grown more pious and stringent in recent times.[34] In Iran, Pakistan, and Malaysia, only non-Muslims can legally acquire alcohol. In Saudi Arabia, alcohol is available for no one, Muslim or non-Muslim, and can be brought into the country only by diplomatic missions, in their diplomatic pouches, for their own use.[35]

Today, compared to global averages, Muslims tend to consume less alcohol according to World Health Organization (WHO) statistics.[36] In fact, according to the organization's 2004 report, twenty-five of the thirty countries that were reported to have the lowest alcohol consumption rates are Muslim-majority, and all six have zero liters of annual per capita consumption. All but four of the forty-three Muslim-majority nations surveyed in the report had consumption rates below the global median. Two of these four countries (Azerbaijan and Kyrgyzstan) were former Soviet Republics with significant non-Muslim (Russian) populations. The other two, Burkina Faso and Lebanon, also have large non-Muslim communities. While the report's findings might have been skewed by underreporting, especially in Muslim settings where alcohol consumption is generally stigmatized or even punishable by law, the report also notes a wide range in consumption rates across Muslim-majority nations (from zero to almost seven liters per adult in a given year), suggesting that attitudes toward alcohol vary widely. Furthermore, there is some indication that alcohol consumption per capita has been increasing among Muslims in recent years.

Opium and Cannabis

The Quran and ahadith do not contain specific references to opium or cannabis. There is also little mention of them in literary or legal sources produced by the earliest generations of Muslims, perhaps because their knowledge of these substances was minimal. For opium, if not cannabis, this is curious because it had been cultivated in Egypt and Mesopotamia since the fourth millennium BCE, and many local cultures were quite familiar with its medicinal properties and its recreational use.[37] Muslims began to encounter hashish after Islam spread to Iran and India, where cannabis had long been in use.[38] When people of these regions converted to Islam, they did not stop consuming the plant. Inner Asian migration to the Middle East also played a role in the spread of cannabis use.[39]

Given the silence of the Quran and ahadith on these substances, many later jurisprudential prescriptions regarding their use were largely based on analogy, an interpretive technique that involves applying Quranic and hadith-based prescriptions to new problems and circumstances. Since the Prophet had reportedly declared that "every intoxicant is khamr," most jurists inferred that opiates and cannabis should also be considered haram.[40] Others cited the consensus (ijma') among jurisprudential authorities that the substances' negative effects on individual and societal health was reason to ban them. One problem with these positions, however, is that "analogy" and "consensus" are considered more indirect sources of jurisprudential interpretation than the Quran or the ahadith, so their use as bases for a legal prescription is limited. For analogy, the applicability of the khamr prohibition demands a uniform and airtight parallel between alcohol and these substances with regard to their effects on the human mind. In fact, a small number of jurists wondered whether and to what

Figs. 4.4a–4.4d. Tiles with wine cups and poppies from Karatay Medrese Museum in Konya, Turkey. Glazed tiles found at the Kubad Abad Palace excavation depicting male and female figures holding wine cups and surrounded by poppy plants (Seljuk period, thirteenth century). Authors' photographs.

extent opium and cannabis could be considered as intoxicating as alcohol.[41] Another problem in this regard is that neither the Quran nor hadith traditions explicitly define "intoxicating."[42] In the case of jurisprudential consensus, a dissenting opinion by a single well-regarded jurist would challenge the legitimacy of the prescription.

Opium and cannabis use became increasingly suspect among jurists. Nevertheless, the agreement to ban these substances still remained less

Figs. 4.4a–4.4d. Continued

pronounced than the prohibition on alcohol, at least until very recent times, when, finally, Muslim jurists agreed almost universally that they should be prohibited. The ambiguity in judicial attitudes against nonalcoholic psycho-active substances in the premodern period is evident in the well-established practice of substituting opium and cannabis use when individuals attempted to stop or limit their alcohol consumption. Mustafa Ali, a famous sixteenth-century Ottoman commentator on social and political affairs, mentions the prevalence of opium use among Ottoman religious classes, including Sharia judges, imams, and mosque functionaries.[43] Opium and cannabis use was also popular—possibly more so than alcohol—among the lower echelons in Ottoman, Safavid, and Mughal lands. This preference likely had to do with cost—alcohol, specifically wine, was relatively expensive compared to opium and cannabis—and the more ambiguous legal status of opium and cannabis may have also played a part. Regional variations also existed in the popularity of different psychoactive substances. Carsten Niebuhr, an eighteenth-century traveler to Ottoman lands, observed that while "Arabs" were fond of hashish, tobacco, coffee, and qat, "Turks" and "Persians" regularly used opium.[44] Lane agreed that "hasheesh" use was popular among lower classes in nineteenth-century Egypt, but opium addiction was rare.[45]

The relative ambivalence toward opium and cannabis in the premodern period was later replaced by strict legal hostility toward their consumption. Shiite Iran after the 1979 Islamic Revolution, for example, took an uncompromising position against psychoactive substance production, use, transportation, and distribution, a tendency also visible in some Sunni countries such as Saudi Arabia and Pakistan since the 1980s. In a well-cited statement, Ayatollah Khomeini insisted that "one side [of us] has to fight drugs; and one side has to fight alcoholic drinks."[46] This stance counters the pre-Revolution clerical approach to drugs, which was, according to political scientist Maziyar Ghiabi, "remarkable by its lack of condemnation, even more so in view of the substantial use of *waqf* lands [lands pledged to the funding of religious-charitable foundations] in the opium economy up to the mid-20th Century."[47] More recently, in 2014, the chief mufti of Saudi Arabia and the president of the Council of Senior Scholars, Sheikh Abdul Aziz Al ash-Sheikh, called for tough action against those who smuggle, promote, and sell drugs. He described these intoxicants as "more dangerous than atomic bombs" because they "kill the heart and strip humans of all morals and values."[48] Modern Muslim jurists generally agree that the recreational use of these substances must be totally forbidden since they are inebriating and have proven ill effects on the human body and mind.

Such hardening of opinions also appears in the harsh punishments that many Muslim-majority countries impose on those who illegally produce, use, transport, and distribute psychoactive substances. In Indonesia, Malaysia, Iran, and Saudi Arabia, it is routine to execute drug traffickers, including those who are foreign nationals.[49] China, Singapore, and Vietnam are the only other countries that regularly execute offenders of narcotic laws.[50] Of the thirty-three countries whose laws call for the death penalty for drug trafficking, eighteen are Muslim-majority.[51] Of the 2,020 executions performed in Iran between 2012 and 2014, 1,137 were for drug offenses.[52] Saudi Arabia executed eighty-eight individuals for drug offenses between 2012 and 2014, which constituted about one-third of all executions (267) in the country.[53] In 2015, there were 480 drug offenders on Malaysia's death row, although the country executed only two individuals in 2012 and 2013.[54] In relative terms, prison sentences for drug use and possession tend to be longer and the threshold of punishment lower in many Muslim countries compared to most non-Muslim-majority nations.[55]

According to the *2014 World Drug Report* published by the United Nations Office on Drugs and Crime,[56] five of the top ten nations in a country-based comparison of opiate abuse are Muslim-majority. At the very top of the list is Afghanistan, the most important opium-producing nation in the world; there the opium use rate is 2.65 percent among adults (between ages fifteen and sixty-five). Other major Muslim-majority opium users are Iran (2.27 percent), Azerbaijan (1.50 percent), Pakistan (1 percent), and Malaysia (1 percent).[57] On the other hand, two Muslim-majority nations (Syria and the United Arab Emirates; both 0.02 percent) are among the ten least opium-abusing nations, and five (including Turkey, Algeria, and Saudi Arabia; 0.03 percent to 0.06 percent) are among the twenty-five least opium-abusing.[58] But cannabis appears to be less popular among Muslim populations than opium. No Muslim-majority nation is listed among the top ten cannabis abusers, and only Egypt is in the top twenty-five, with a use rate of 6.24 percent.

Coffee and Tobacco

The introduction of coffee (late fifteenth to early sixteenth century) and tobacco (late sixteenth to early seventeenth century) in the Middle East,[59] and later to other parts of the Muslim world, generated concerns and deliberations among jurists, paralleling those for opium and cannabis. Yet the possibility of making a legal case against these substances by way of analogy was even more limited. Although some scholars attributed intoxicating qualities to coffee and tobacco, many found this argument unconvincing.[60] Instead, several critics claimed that coffee and tobacco were bad for health and should be considered among those filthy substances against which the Quran warns.[61] Still others mentioned the waste of time and money associated with coffee and tobacco consumption, including idle socialization in coffeehouses. A few even likened tobacco smoke to the hellfire depicted in the Quran and its smell to that of onion and garlic, which the Prophet was said to detest.[62]

Fig. 4.5. "A cup of coffee on the heights of Subeibeh." According to the caption, "All the imple-ments for preparing it are shown in the foreground—the iron saucer in which to roast the ber-ries, the pestle and mortar for pounding them, and the water boiling on the fire of crackling twigs." Also note the various instruments used for smoking, including a hookah and a pipe (Ottoman Palestine, late nineteenth century). Dorot Jewish Division, The New York Public Library. New York Public Library Digital Collections. Accessed July 28, 2017. http://digitalcollections.nypl. org/items/510d47d9-5ea0-a3d9-e040-e00a18064a99.

Attempts to define the legal status of non-alcohol-based psychoactive substances further represent the expansive potential of Islamic legal consid-erations. Many Muslims came to define Sharia, or Islamic law, as how God intended them to live their lives, and so it followed that Sharia would regu-late each aspect of daily life, from commercial interactions to government and administration, from marriage to inheritance, from dietary practices to recre-ation and entertainment. A great number of Muslim jurists, therefore, worked to keep jurisprudential considerations relevant and fitting in the face of chang-ing circumstances.

According to the prominent theologian Abu Hamid Muhammad al-Ghazali (d. 1111), the law functions to protect the religion, lives, intellect, material pos-sessions, and progeny of Muslims, a consideration that became popular among subsequent jurists. Technically, therefore, any threat to Muslims' individual or communal well-being, whether stated clearly in the primary sources or not, can be mitigated by the law. In fact, the concern with "public interest" (or *maslaha*) has long been one of the well-established bases of Islamic legislation and legal enforcement. For this reason, at least partially, medical and socioeconomic aspects of coffee and tobacco use became important for jurists and administrators aiming to regulate their consumption. Even though the Quran and ahadith did not specifically mention them, and even if they could not be considered "intoxicants" in the same ways as other psychoactive substances, the use of coffee and tobacco could still be condemned if it harmed Muslims in any way.

Yet claims about their adverse health effects were disputed by many, especially in the premodern era.[63] There were attempts to condemn them because their consumption was associated with waste and with negligence of religious duties, and because the places where they were publicly consumed were centers of frequent social and political turmoil, but these attempts were contentious.[64] Any good in excess could cause harm, many argued, and only a few users of tobacco and coffee did bad deeds. More legally minded users of tobacco and coffee, including some jurists and judges, specifically warned their peers about the sin of pronouncing unlawful what God intended to be lawful.[65] Consequently, these substances inspired a variety of legal opinions, ranging from those that declared them halal to those that considered them makruh to those that pronounced them outright haram.[66] Following more restrictive interpretations, various Islamic governments in the premodern period attempted to punish violators and closed coffeehouses and Sufi lodges where coffee and tobacco use were prevalent. Yet these enforcements were almost always temporary, and as both substances became increasingly popular, more segments of the society resisted any restrictions.

Disputes over coffee were more or less settled after the withering of puritanical movements in the seventeenth and eighteenth centuries. On the other hand, as with cannabis and opium, Islamic legal attitudes against tobacco consumption may be hardening in the last few decades. As medical evidence of smoking's adverse health effects became conclusive, more Muslim legal experts developed a critical attitude toward tobacco.[67] A survey of recent legal opinions on tobacco indicates that most religious authorities now regard tobacco use, production, and trade as makruh or haram, mainly because research has proven smoking's ill health effects on smokers and those around them. In addition, modern jurists have recycled arguments against tobacco by premodern

Fig. 4.6. "The Coffee Shop." Smoking and coffee drinking in Cairo (ca. 1846–1849). General Research Division, The New York Public Library. New York Public Library Digital Collections. Accessed July 31, 2017. http://digitalcollections.nypl.org/items/510d47e0-0edb-a3d9-e040-e00a18064a99.

scholars, including its noxious smell, its filthy nature, its association with financial waste, and its supposed propensity to detract Muslims from worship. This contemporary divergence in opinions about coffee and tobacco is remarkable because earlier jurists generally subscribed to parallel opinions on these substances; that is, they considered both either permissible or impermissible. Perhaps the modern scientific attention to coffee as a potentially beneficial substance has played a role in these discrepancies.

Despite the recent intensification of religiously based criticism against smoking, tobacco use is quite popular in modern Muslim communities, perhaps related to, among other factors, the tobacco industry's enhanced emphasis on non-Western markets in order to make up for its losses in the West. By the early twenty-first century, studies showed the prevalence of smoking as ranging between 16 percent (in Oman) to 77 percent (in Yemen) among male populations in Muslim-majority countries. In sixteen of twenty-two Muslim-majority countries examined, the rate was 30 percent or above for men. In

SKETCH IN A COFFEE HOUSE

Fig. 4.7. "Sketch in a Coffee-House, Constantinople." Lithograph from 1854. Note the hoo-kah smoker in the background. The Miriam and Ira D. Wallach Division of Art, Prints and Photographs: Art & Architecture Collection, The New York Public Library. New York Public Library Digital Collections. Accessed July 28, 2017. http://digitalcollections.nypl.org/items/510d47d9-65da-a3d9-e040-e00a18064a99.

eleven, the rate was 40 percent or above.[68] The corresponding rates are 28 percent in the United Kingdom and 30 percent in India.[69] What's more, tobacco consumption appears to be growing among Muslims: while smoking decreased in many regions of the world between 1990 and 1997, in the Middle East during the same period it increased by 24 percent.[70]

Tobacco's popularity among Muslims has drawn major international authorities into public disputes pertaining to its permissibility. Most notably, beginning in the 1980s the World Health Organization (WHO), a central force behind global antismoking campaigns, made deliberate efforts to link religion with tobacco-related issues by collecting and publishing fatwas against smoking.[71] The tobacco industry responded by establishing contacts with religious experts, though clearly in the minority, who could cast doubts on prohibitive opinions.[72] In response to claims made by antismoking jurists, representatives from the tobacco industry, possibly in consultation with sympathetic religious advisers, directly invoked Islamic law to devise religiously based counterarguments and to demonstrate how legal traditions can affirm smoking's permissibility.[73] Some attempts by these nonspecialists appear remarkable in their legal eruditeness and include a number of well-established pro-smoking arguments: they point to the lack of any specific provision against smoking in the Quran or ahadith; argue that the analogy between tobacco smoking and khamr drinking is invalid based on how differently these substances alter the human mind; and affirm the baselessness of claims that smoking causes financial waste because of an Islamic legal principle stating that expenditure on what is permissible cannot be considered an extravagance.

Some modern jurists have found several more reasons to resist declaring tobacco haram and instead consider it merely makruh, or detestable. For example, they hesitate to pronounce this popular practice unlawful and to thus condemn hundreds of millions of Muslim smokers as sinners. As to the widely acknowledged health issues, these jurists note that smoking is not harmful to every primary or secondary smoker. Thus, its indulgence should be prohibited only to those for whom it causes a harm. This last point is consistent with the tobacco industry position that the health effects of tobacco consumption should not be generalized from its effects on specific individuals or groups.[74] It is also consistent with a well-established opinion in Islamic legal traditions that if substances otherwise considered permissible prove to be harmful to specific individuals (such as those with allergens), they are forbidden only to those people.[75]

What is noteworthy in this public relations battle is how Western organizations on opposing sides of the issue—none of which are otherwise identified with or representative of Islam—have promoted an Islamic religio-legal discourse in their attempts to engage and influence Muslim consumer habits. This, they believe, is the best way to speak to and convince the broader Muslim public. Nonreligious reasoning (medical, economic, cultural) has been subsumed and instrumentalized into religious-legal arguments.

One could expand on this survey by considering jurisprudential opinions regarding many other substances: for example, qat[76] and nutmeg.[77] But the lines of argumentation and disagreement among jurists with regard to those substances, and many others, closely resemble ones already examined.

Broad Observations Regarding the Religio-Legal Status of Intoxicating Substances

A few general observations can be made on halal and haram considerations pertaining not only to alcohol and other psychoactive substances but also to foods and dietary practices:

1. Halal and haram are far from static classifications within Islamic legal considerations. Their roots are in the Quran, as revealed to the Prophet during his lifetime, and also later in ahadith compiled by the Prophet's followers, but these concepts have not stayed frozen. Rather, relevant jurisprudential deliberations over halal and haram began from the earliest Islamic periods and have continued to generate multiple strands of interpretation in response to changing needs and circumstances. At one level, the system has remained steady and coherent with regard to terminology and conceptual apparatus, because jurists' interpretive discourses continually engaged the principal sources of religion and authoritative jurisprudential opinions from earlier periods. At another level, however, the jurists' formulations sought to accommodate new challenges and developments, which led to multiple, sometimes contradictory formulations. In fact, the law has itself developed procedures, such as analogy, juristic consensus, and wider considerations of public benefit, to expand its reach when faced with new practices and circumstances. Thus, successive attempts at judicial interpretation are products of a system that aspires to be "conservative" in terms of its relationship to its own past yet also flexible in its capacity to respond to change and to regenerate itself within limits. The expansive nature of Islamic law, its ability

to remain relevant in novel circumstances, is very much a consequence of its conservative dynamism.

2. The conservative nature of Islamic law is methodological in character; it has little to do with the overall values or political orientations of Islamic legal traditions. Indeed, as one can see from the discussion of alcohol and other intoxicants, Muslim jurists selectively following the same legislative methodology can devise interpretations that reflect contradictory agendas. The inherent complexity within most Islamic jurisprudential sources, including the Quran, allows for such a plurality even though jurists rely on a cautious and often restrained legal approach.

But when it comes to alcohol and most psychoactive materials, prevalent halal and haram considerations have become increasingly restrictive, especially in the modern period—a tendency also observed in Muslims' attitudes toward some other substances, products, and practices (see chapters 3, 5, and 7). For centuries, the legal statuses of various mind-altering substances were subject to jurisprudential debate and disagreement in the Islamic world. Now there seems to be a growing consensus that the use of alcoholic drinks (of all kinds), cannabis, opium, and tobacco should be forbidden for one reason or another, although objections against coffee consumption have faded.[78] Muslims' enjoyment of psychoactive substances has not necessarily declined over time, since the legal script is not the only factor that influences their choices (see below). But as concerns with human health, economic waste, and political sedition prompted jurists to prohibit consumption of intoxicants, they also validated a more forceful stance by the law and its representatives and subjected Muslims to a less lenient religious governmentality.

True, legal arguments can be and have been used to resist the law's increasingly hindering tendencies. Some jurists have advised peers to be concerned about (erroneously) pronouncing as unlawful what God intended to be lawful. But the effectiveness of this argument might be limited. After all, and as stated, Muslims are often urged to avoid what is "doubtful" and stick to what is clear of doubt.[79] Thus when concerns are raised about the lawfulness of a particular dietary substance or practice and cannot be immediately rejected or refuted, that substance is likely to be categorized as impermissible.[80]

3. At the same time, legal considerations do not present the whole story on food, drinks, or other substances.[81] In attempting to understand why certain substances have been popular or not (regardless of whether they are halal or

haram), one must remember that there have always been multiple discourses on alcoholic and other psychoactive substances. The law has provided one script—albeit an inherently complex, multistranded one—that has influenced Muslims' attitudes toward dietary practices. Although the legal script is an important focus in this study, it is important not to confuse Islamic law with "Islam" in its broadest sense.[82]

For example, medical considerations have also influenced Muslims' attitudes toward intoxicants. True, legal experts often use the presumed adverse effects of a specific substance to justify its prohibition. At the same time, the medical script could also be utilized to co-opt, resist, or challenge legal opinions against intoxicants. For example, a few Muslim physicians, especially in early Islamic history, mentioned the possibility that alcohol consumed in moderate amounts could have positive health effects.[83] This is what the Persian philosopher-scientist Abu Zayd al Balkhi (d. 943) says about the benefits of wine in *The Welfare of Bodies and Souls*:

> The best drink that humans, through their reason and understanding[,] have devised a means of producing is the refined grape-drink among whose properties is that it intoxicates. It is, of all beverages, the most noble in essence, most superior in consumption, and most beneficial—if taken in moderation and not to excess . . . . The benefit of a substance to the body lies in what the substance provides the body by way of health and strength, whereas its benefit to the soul lies in what the substance provides the soul by way of happiness and animation . . . . Among its virtues is that it acts to produce a marvelous effect within the capacities of the soul by bringing forth from it that which was not seen to present in it prior to drinking: such as the capacities for courage and magnanimity—which are known to be the noblest of human capacities—this even if these things were lacking in a person before: thus, wine gives courage to the coward and makes generous the miser. It also increases that which is already present in a person: such as the capacities for understanding, memory, intellect, and sharpness of thought; for it is known that these virtues increase in a person when he has reached the midway state of drinking—before he is overcome by inebriation.[84]

The medical value of other psychoactive substances in careful hands has also triggered Muslims to (re)consider the opinions of legal authorities.[85] In fact, information on how these substances could remedy humoral imbalances in the human body remained influential throughout the Muslim world until modern times. Perhaps these opinions have recently been marginalized, but that does not mean that there is unanimity about whether psychoactive substances are acceptable.[86]

Other nonlegal scripts had a marked yet scarcely discussed influence on Muslim perceptions of acceptable and unacceptable substances. For example, in premodern polities, consumption of alcohol and psychoactive substances was prevalent among high-status groups, including the Safavids, Mughals, and Ottomans. Historians have associated their consumption with prevailing notions of sociability, manliness, and leadership in these contexts, notions that mirrored those in many non-Muslim cultures. Praise for and enjoyment of wine was a common trope in historical chronicles and high literature.[87] The ancient Iranian and Central Asian attachment to the "fight hard and play hard" principle continued in successive Muslim dynasties inspired by similar traditions. In Safavid monarchical understandings, rulers showed their manly prowess by participating in long drinking parties before and after their battles. Early Safavid Shahs were not expected to observe existing prohibitions because they believed that these substances did not affect them in the way they affected others.[88] The inscription carved into the lip of the Mughal ruler Jahangir's wine cup, for example, praises its owner's leadership claims and qualities: "God is Most Great. The king of the seven lands. The emperor of emperors who spreads justice. The knower of the signs, real and metaphorical. Abu-l-Muzaffar Nur-ud-Din Jahangir, the king, son of Akbar, the king [and] righteous-warrior."[89] The connection between wine drinking and claims to political power is also evident in the coin struck by Jahangir in 1611, which depicts the emperor holding a wine cup.[90]

A final example of a nonlegal script can be found in the mystical traditions of Sufism. Wine and drunkenness were central to Sufi poetry and embodied the obliteration of oneself prior to achieving ultimate union with the divine.[91] In fact, affirmative attitudes toward psychoactive substances were so prevalent in certain forms of Sufism that prohibitive government measures often exclusively targeted Sufi groups. It is possible that in many Muslim-majority settings, hashish, coffee, qat, and tobacco became common first among the Sufis: these substances suppressed appetite, stimulated the human mind and body, and thwarted sleep, all desirable qualities because of Sufis' lengthy nighttime prayer and *dhikr*, the devotional sessions organized in remembrance of God. Their use also aided the spiritual experience and the sense of connection with the divine that Sufis sought.[92] Assorted versions of this mystical script, which prioritized the spiritual experience over legalistic and this-worldly concerns, justified the use of mind-altering substances. In some cases, a defense of their consumption was made by legal experts who themselves happened to be Sufis.[93]

In closing, the story of the Prophet being offered a choice of wine or milk likely took decades to evolve and was ultimately recorded more than a century after the Prophet's death. This might signal the multiple inclinations toward intoxicating substances that arose in early Islamic times. It is conceivable that while wine might have been more acceptable earlier (i.e., during the initial stages of the mi'raj narrative's formulation), it was later deemed objectionable. The claim that Gabriel praised the Prophet's rejection of ("earthly" or "heavenly") wine might thus suggest a subsequent, more restrictive stance inserted within a previously more lenient narrative, which would explain the apparent ambiguity in the story. In the same way, over time "Islam" came to encompass many layers of dispositions about mind-altering substances, which have been in constant interaction and negotiation.

These dispositions are not only legal in nature. Indeed, the multitude of nonlegal scripts on food, alcohol, and other mind-altering substances further complicates the meaning of "acceptable" and "unacceptable" in Muslim-majority settings beyond the legal implications of these words. The existence of such a wide range of views might caution against black-and-white judgments: should a particular food item, drink, or substance be considered offensive for Muslims just because, at some point or another, some (or even most) jurisprudential opinions opposed it? Whatever the answer may be, the law was not the sole determinant of its broader appeal.

CHAPTER 5

The halal food and beverage market has expanded dramatically over the past two decades, and opportunities to make money from halal food production and sales continue to multiply. The *State of the Global Islamic Economy Report 2016/2017* estimates the size of the halal food and beverage market as of 2015 at about $1.2 trillion[1] in fifty-seven Organization of Islamic Cooperation (OIC) countries, constituting perhaps as much as 17 percent of global food expenditures.[2] Halal-certified food and beverage products generated about $415 billion in the same year.[3] The report projects that by 2021 Muslims will spend more than $1.9 trillion on food and beverage, a great portion of which will be halal, whether certified as such or not.[4] Among Muslims, halal services and products have a clear advantage over their competitors.[5] For this reason, major brands are investing in halal products targeting Muslim countries and markets. Companies such as Tesco, Unilever, and Nestlé have been expanding their halal-certified product lines for some time. McDonalds, Quick (Burger), Starbucks, Burger King, and KFC have also demonstrated sensitivity to Muslim concerns and built separate lines for halal and nonhalal products.[6]

After providing a background for the rise of the global halal food business in the twentieth century, this chapter offers a general layout of major players within the halal food and beverages market and describes their involvement in modern halal economies. It pays special attention to services provided by private halal certifiers and to the modern state's involvement in global halal affairs. As will become clear in the discussion, interest in halal food matters is stimulated by a wide range of goals: religious, altruistic, profit-seeking, and political. This diversity of motivations among the many actors involved makes modern halal matters particularly complicated.

Why Is Halal Business Expanding?

There are about 1.6 billion Muslims worldwide, constituting about 23 percent of the world's population. Demographic studies indicate that Islam is one of the fastest-growing religions, and by 2050, according to Pew Research Center, Muslims may be as numerous as Christians, currently the largest religious group in the world at 2.2 billion. Muslim nations are concentrated in the Asia-Pacific region, constituting about 62 percent of the overall Muslim population worldwide. Muslims of the Middle East and North Africa (MENA) make up about another 20 percent. Historically, the proportions of Muslims in Europe and the United States have been low, but these populations have been growing, mainly because of migration. In Europe, their numbers have increased by 140 percent in the last decade or so, outpacing the rise in non-Muslims, and Muslims currently constitute about 6 percent of the European population. The Pew Research Center projects their proportion in the European population to be 10.2 percent by 2050. In the United States there are about 3.3 million Muslims, representing about 1 percent of the overall population. By 2030 that figure is expected to rise to about 1.7, and by 2050 to 2.1 percent.[7]

At the same time, the economies of Muslim-majority countries, like those of most other countries, have experienced significant growth since the middle of the twentieth century. According to World Bank data, the combined annual per capita gross domestic product (GDP) levels in MENA grew at an average rate of about 2.0 percent (in constant prices) per year between 1966 and 2014. In Turkey as well as Malaysia, Pakistan, and Indonesia—three large Muslim-majority countries outside MENA—the corresponding averages are 2.6, 3.9, 2.2, and 4.0 percent, respectively.[8] Consequently, it would be safe to assume that consumption patterns in many parts of the Muslim world have shifted toward higher-value goods, technology-intensive products, and superior food choices.

Collectively, these demographic and economic trends are important because they indicate a global rise in the overall and per capita purchasing power among Muslims, which naturally stimulates halal commerce from food to toiletries and pharmaceuticals. But the proliferation of the global halal economy can also be traced to reasons beyond the rise in Muslim populations or the relative improvement in their economic circumstances. Halal shopping is a choice after all, even for Muslims, and nondemographic and noneconomic factors also play a part in consumers' decisions.[9] There is relatively little scholarship about this topic but some researchers have highlighted important elements in relation to global halal consumption trends.

The Rise of Pietistic Interpretations of Islamic Identity

There may be a connection between the upsurge in global halal businesses and the recent popularization of pietistic interpretations of Islam. The rise of Islamic radicalism since the 1970s, which represents a critical reaction to Western-rooted values, philosophies, forms of government, and institutions associated with failed attempts of modernization in many Muslim-majority settings, has led some Muslims to support what they regard as authentic and uncorrupted Islamic lifestyles. Modern Islamic radicalism, as formulated by influential figures such as Sayyid Qutb, Abu'l Ala Mawdudi, and Ayatollah Khomeini, sees non-Islamic social, political, and cultural influences as sources of contamination and degeneracy. Even in those realms where Western influences are acceptable (e.g., technology), they must be carefully appropriated and only in ways consistent with Islamic values.

Such purist tendencies have played an important role in the imaginations of many modern Muslims. Alluding to the Prophet's "flight" (or hijra) in 622 from Mecca, then under the control of the new religion's polytheistic enemies, to Medina, the new home of the fledgling Muslim community, Islamist thinkers emphasized the need for true Muslims to separate themselves from the degrading influence of their godless and immoral surroundings and to live more consistently with Islamic values and traditions. Today's palpable halal sensitivity likely reflects, at least in part, a growing pietism and an isolationist penchant attributed to early Islamic times. At the very least, among most ordinary Muslims, greater attention to halal matters represents an inclination to "moralize the marketplace by embracing Islamized products."[10]

In addition to influencing the purchasing choices made each day by ordinary Muslims, a few governments in Muslim-majority nations have also made efforts to promote pietistic halal economies within their territories. It is no coincidence that the foundation of the Shiite Islamic Republic of Iran in 1979, a major turning point in the rise of global Islamist politics, also represents the start of an important phase of the international halal food movement. Immediately after the Revolution, Iran banned all imported meat not certified as halal. Around the same time, Saudi Arabia's Sunni rulers began making efforts to ensure the halal status of their meat imports by funding foreign intermediary organizations that could certify those meat products.[11] Other Muslim countries soon followed and began to Islamize their food trade and production. Most recently, in Malaysia and Turkey, official interest and investment in halal matters have coincided with their governments' conservative orientations.

Reconstitution of Identity in the Muslim Diaspora

In part, the movement toward halal food might also be an indirect consequence of the mass emigration of Muslim populations to Europe and North America in the second half of the twentieth century. In the early 1960s, many European countries, particularly West Germany, the United Kingdom, the Netherlands, France, and Belgium, first turned to South and Central European populations to provide labor for economic development, and then they invited Middle Eastern, North African, and South Asian workers, the vast majority of whom were Muslims. Initially intended to be temporary, Muslim immigration to Europe became permanent as Muslims settled in their host countries, married locals or brought their families to these lands, and had children of their own. Today 19 million Muslims live in Europe. France and Germany have the largest Muslim minorities on the continent, 4.7 and 4.8 million, respectively, constituting about 7.5 and 6 percent of their populations. Muslims comprise about 5 percent (3 million) of the United Kingdom's population. Significant populations also exist in Bulgaria, the Netherlands, Belgium, Italy, Sweden, Greece, and Austria.[12]

In diasporic settings, halal consciousness and other symbols of Islamic piety can represent an assertion of a distinctive identity, a way to resist the assimilative aspects of Western modernity. One common characteristic of many younger Muslims living in the West is the desire to anchor themselves in what they consider their "original" religious and cultural roots, against the confusing and potentially disruptive impulses in their immediate surroundings.[13] Although this tendency requires them to reinvent Islam as a homogeneous entity,[14] the urge stems from feelings of anxiety and rejection common among disenfranchised minorities in the West. It also speaks to how globalization is experienced by these groups; it reflects their feelings of displacement and dysfunction.[15] As individuals feel more marginalized or oppressed, they create safe spaces in their new host countries—for example, by using the homeland's language in the household, celebrating its festivities, and adhering to certain religious and traditional practices.[16]

In this sense, globalization paradoxically spurs the deliberate re-creation of a unique local identity for those who feel threatened by its implications.[17] For many Muslims in the West, particularly the youth, eating halal food is symbolic of a much sought-after authenticity in the face of globalization, like observing gender segregation; similarly, Muslim women may choose to wear a head scarf, hijab, or niqab, and men may choose to grow facial hair. Attempts to develop a distinct halal cuisine (see chapter 9) can be regarded as another facet of these trends.[18]

Supply-Side Stimulation in Halal Markets

The recent heightening of Islamic sensitivities with regard to consumption has generated a multitude of economic opportunities for private and public actors on a global scale. The halal industries that have emerged and proliferated in the last few decades have not only capitalized on the demand for halal products but have also contributed to its further growth. This phenomenon is not unique to Islam. Many Christian revivalist trends in recent US history were not so much the outcomes of shifts on the "demand side" of the religious marketplace—that is, results of social, cultural, and demographic changes among religious consumers—as they were consequences of shifts on the "supply side"—that is, in the manufacture and marketing of religious products, including novel interpretations of religious doctrine.[19] In the process, suppliers of religious products generated greater demand for their services by fine-tuning their marketing schemes.[20]

Similarly, suppliers of halal notions, definitions, and products have played a critical role in making halal even more relevant to modern Muslim and non-Muslim populations by stimulating concerns that consumers may not have even known they had.[21] Until very recently, the halal status of pharmaceuticals, soft drinks, or imported chocolate raised few concerns for consumers. But once suppliers began to offer versions of those products that they implicitly or explicitly claimed to be halal-compliant, they raised consumer consciousness and consequently contributed to the development of the halal market.[22]

Also relevant is the fact that those attempting to broaden appeal to halal products sometimes expand on the meaning of halal by attributing to their products certain qualities that reflect modern consumer sensitivities. Halal food marketed as "good" in every sense of the word might attract more customers, including those who do not identify themselves as Muslims.[23] Thus, if suppliers can convince potential buyers that their products are hygienic, healthy, and/or ethically produced because they are halal, they can expand their markets by drawing hygiene-, health-, and ethically conscious consumers to halal labels. To be convincing, such an effort may require suppliers to demonstrably appropriate certain steps and procedures in the production of halal food and may also complicate existing certification processes. Nevertheless, the potential market benefits might make these efforts worthwhile.

Global Halal Business: The Game and Its Players

The dramatic expansion of the halal food and beverage market is visible in everything from meat products to packaged and preprepared snacks and meals to a robust halal restaurant culture. In 2013, Muslims' expenditure on food and nonalcoholic beverages was highest in the MENA region, excluding GCC countries ($319 billion); followed by East Asia ($226 billion), South Asia ($212 billion), Central Asia ($204 billion), sub-Saharan Africa ($114 billion), and GCC countries, including Bahrain, Kuwait, Oman, Qatar, Saudi Arabia, and the United Arab Emirates (UAE) ($93 billion)[24] (Table 5.1). The collective global Muslim food and beverage market is larger than that of China ($776 billion), the United States ($754 billion), Japan ($473 billion), and India ($403 billion).[25] The OIC countries suffer from a major food trade deficit, forcing them to rely on non-Muslim-majority countries for their supply of critical items. In 2013, OIC members had a $79 billion food and beverage trade gap.[26]

International meat (including poultry) and live animal commerce constitutes about 30 percent of the global halal food market.[27] This is one area where most Muslim majority nations are reliant on other countries: according to the *State of the Global Islamic Economy 2014–2015 Report*, about 85 percent of meat

Table 5.1. Top Muslim Food Consumption Markets
by Size (2013)

Country	Size (billions)
Indonesia	$190.4
Turkey	$168.5
Pakistan	$108.4
Iran	$97.0
Egypt	$94.8
Bangladesh	$59.9
Saudi Arabia	$52.7
Russian Federation	$43.7
India	$41.1
Nigeria	$37.7
Iraq	$35.4
Algeria	$35.4
Sudan	$27.0
Morocco	$24.5
United Arab Emirates	$21.3
Malaysia	$16.6
Kazakhstan	$14.5
United States	$12.8
Azerbaijan	$12.5
France	$11.9
Yemen	$11.5
China	$10.1
Germany	$9.9
Kuwait	$8.7
Tunisia	$8.4

Note: State of Global Islamic Economy Report 2016/2017, 27, provides
the following estimates (based on 2015 data) for a more limited
number of countries (in billions): Indonesia: $155; Turkey: $112;
Pakistan: $106; Egypt: $78; Bangladesh: $69; Iran: $59; Saudi
Arabia: $48; Nigeria: $41; Russian Federation: $37; India: $35.

Source: State of Global Islamic Economy 2014–2015 Report, 49.

and live animal imports to OIC countries come from non-OIC countries.[28] In
2013, the top five meat and live animal exporters to Muslim-majority countries were Brazil ($4.7 billion), India ($2.1 billion), Australia ($1.6 billion), the
United States ($1.2 billion), and France ($0.8 billion). Turkey was the most
important Muslim-majority exporter of meat and live animals to OIC countries

($0.5 billion),[29] followed by Pakistan ($0.2 billion). Major importers were Saudi Arabia ($2.7 billion), UAE ($1.5 billion), Egypt ($1.3 billion), Malaysia ($0.9 billion), and Iraq ($0.9 billion).

Other halal consumables imported by Muslim countries include confectionery, canned and frozen food, dairy and bakery products, organic food, beverages, and herbal substances. In particular, the demand for prepared and prepacked foodstuffs that conform to halal standards has been increasing; so has the desire for halal substitutes to haram additives often found in yogurts, biscuits, and chocolates, specifically additives like pork gelatin or alcohol.[30] Muslim-majority nations suffer from trade gaps in such categories as well, if not at the same level observed in the meat trade.[31]

The world's largest multinational corporations control a significant portion of the global halal food and beverage trade. These include BRF (Brazil), Allanasons (India), American Food Groups (USA), and Cargill (USA) in the meat sector; Nestlé (Switzerland), Kraft (USA), Al Islami (UAE), Saffron Road (USA), Tahira Foods (UK), and Arman (China) in food processing and management; Tesco (UK), Carrefour (France), BIM (Turkey), Marrybrown Sdn Bhd (Malaysia), Kudu (Saudi Arabia), and Lulu (UAE) in retail; and SMIIC (OIC/Turkey), International Halal Integrity Alliance (Malaysia), JAKIM (Malaysia), IFANCA (USA), ESMA (UAE), and MUI (Indonesia) in regulation, compliance, and research and development.[32] More recently, Spanish, Japanese, Mexican, and Chinese companies have made attempts to enter the market because of its profit and growth potential.[33] It's worth noting that companies based in non-Muslim majority markets, such as the American producer Saffron Road, are also increasingly eager to market their halal and "wholesome" products to non-Muslim consumers.

Halal Certifiers and Certification

The rise of a global halal economy has inspired the development of new organizations to authenticate and certify the thousands of halal food products flooding today's markets. Growing Muslim immigration to non-Muslim nations makes the prospect of halal certification particularly critical. In many Western settings, most consumers, regardless of their religious affiliation, know little about how their food is produced, transported, and sold. Vendors servicing Muslim customers (be they Muslim or not) often cannot directly verify the halal credentials of their suppliers, and the multiple and competing halal

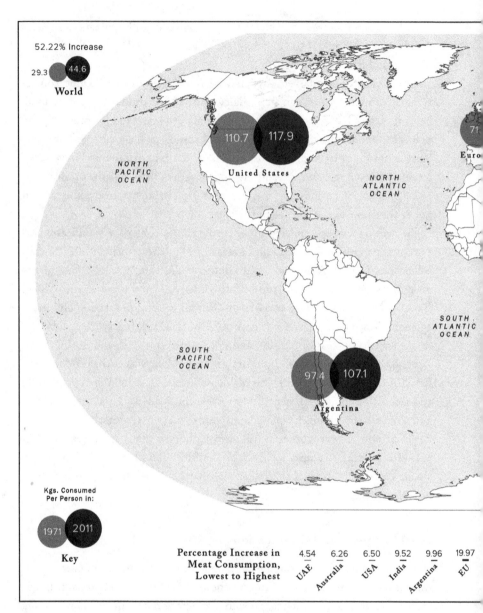

Map 5.1. Meat Consumption per Person in Select Countries

Note: Made with Natural Earth Data. Meat includes ovine, offals, pig meat, poultry, and other animals (hunted ones).
Source: Calculations based on information available at FAOSTAT, http://www.fao.org/faostat/en/#data.

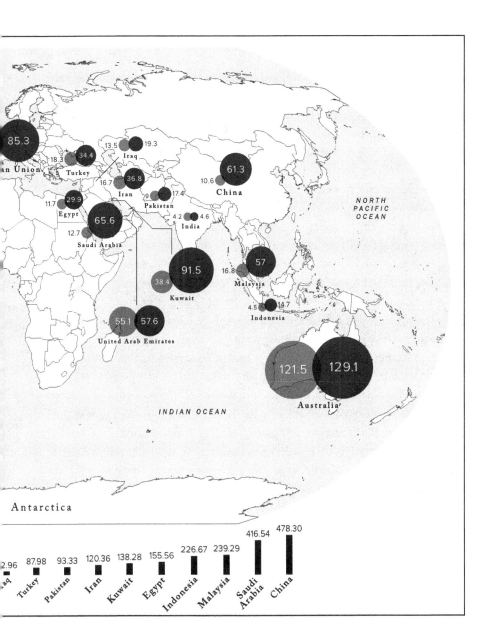

85.3

an Union   Turkey   13.5   19.3   Iraq   China   61.3   NORTH
         18.3   34.4   PACIFIC
              16.7   36.8   10.6   OCEAN
         11.7   29.9   Iran   9   17.4
              Egypt   Pakistan
         12.7   65.6   4.2   4.6   India
              Saudi Arabia
                        91.5   57
                   38.4   16.8   Malaysia
                        Kuwait   4.5   14.7
                                    Indonesia
         55.1   57.6
              United Arab Emirates

                        INDIAN OCEAN

                        121.5   129.1
                             Australia

Antarctica

2.96   87.98   93.33   120.36   138.28   155.56   226.67   239.29   416.54   478.30
aq   Turkey   Pakistan   Iran   Kuwait   Egypt   Indonesia   Malaysia   Saudi Arabia   China

standards confuse sellers and consumers alike.[34] Muslim diasporic communities often originate from different locations and are therefore familiar with varied (and often contradictory) halal traditions. For this reason, the halal movement in the West continually inspires intra-Muslim deliberations on issues of food purity and religious authority.[35]

Halal certification has also become important in the many Muslim-majority countries that rely on imported food. Even if the beef or mutton that, say, Kuwaiti consumers purchase from Australia was slaughtered according to strict halal prescriptions, it may be difficult to ensure that the meat did not become contaminated during transport. Furthermore, modern food production has become impossibly complicated and industrialized in ways that challenge ordinary consumers' ability to ascertain quality, freshness, or religious compliance. Prepackaged foods rely on complex additives, emulsifiers, enzymes, and flavorings for taste and preservation. These may contain porcine residues, alcohol, or other najis substances. Industrial slaughterhouses and packaging establishments might process foods intended for both Muslim and non-Muslim consumers. Even the paper, plastic, and printing on food packages have become an issue, since they may contain glue, ink, and other impermissible substances.[36] The globalization of the food market and the mechanization and industrialization of food production have made it easier and cheaper to feed millions of Muslims, but from a religious standpoint, it has become more complicated to ensure that Muslims eat only "pure" products. And traditional methods of regulating food purity are mostly inadequate in the face of these challenges. Local imams serving Muslim immigrant communities in the West may not have intimate knowledge of food production and transportation processes. The traditional guilds of the old age, which provided self-regulation among Muslim farmers, butchers, and traders, have no place in the new global halal market. Muhtasibs, premodern authorities who inspected markets and enforced halal standards, no longer exist; and even if they did, their responsibilities would require a radical redefinition to meet current needs.[37]

One, often profit-oriented response to rising consumer doubts has been the emergence and proliferation of third-party halal certifiers—agencies, associations, councils, or federations.[38] These organizations, which are often private, profess expertise in halal regulations and knowledge of food preparation, packaging, and transportation methods. Through this dual specialization, religious and industrial, they present themselves as equipped to provide fee-based halal authentication and certification services for companies and private consumers.[39] These groups inspect food products, production facilities and techniques, and labeling and transportation processes, and certify products they deem halal-compliant. Many also offer monitoring services after initial certification to ascertain that client companies remain vigilant in observing halal standards.[40]

Halal certifiers and regulators range from committees established by mosque congregations to wider-based Muslim associations, from nongovernmental and semigovernmental organizations to government bodies.[41] Due to the relative ease of entry to the sector, which often requires modest levels of investment,[42] the number of halal certifiers has been increasing rapidly: in the early 1990s, there were only a handful, but by mid-2015 their number was estimated to be 150, at least according to one partially complete list.[43] Table 5.2 lists the countries with multiple certifiers according to the same compilation.

Additionally, each of the following countries has at least a single certifier: Azerbaijan, Bosnia-Herzegovina, Burkina-Faso, Colombia, Croatia, Denmark, Gambia, Guiana, Indonesia, Iran, Kenya, Kirgizstan, Kuwait, Lebanon, Lithuania, Mali, Mauritius, Morocco, Mozambique, Norway, Oman, Qatar, Portugal, Senegal, Serbia, Spain, Switzerland, Sweden, Thailand, UAE, and Yemen.[44]

The list suggests that third-party certifiers exist mainly in non-Muslim settings with large Muslim minorities (France, Germany, the Netherlands, and the United Kingdom) and in countries that are major food (mainly meat) exporters to Muslim markets (Australia, Brazil, and the United States). Halal certifiers appear to serve two major and often-simultaneous functions: they guide Muslim consumers in their shopping choices, and they authenticate the halal compliance of products produced in non-Muslim countries aimed for export to Muslim markets where they must fulfill state-enforced halal regulations. Certifiers in Muslim nations like Malaysia and Turkey also verify imports from outside and exports from within their own countries.

The annual cost of certification can range from a few thousand US dollars for small shops to tens of thousands for large corporations and abattoirs.[45] The cost also varies considerably based on a company's reputation, the type of services it provides, the location of the business and/or the certifier, and the nature of the products requiring certification, among other factors. Hence it can be tough to determine the revenue or profit levels within the certification industry. However, following recent charges in Australia about how halal

Table 5.2.   Countries with Multiple Certifiers (2015)

Argentina	2
Australia	15
Bangladesh	2
Belgium	2
Brazil	6
Brunei	2
Canada	4[a]
Chile	2
China (incl. Hong Kong)	4
Egypt	2
France	4
Germany	7
India	4
Italy	6
Japan	4
Malaysia	2
The Netherlands	4[b]
New Zealand	4
Pakistan	3
Philippines	2
Poland	3
South Africa	2
Sudan	2
Taiwan	3
Turkey	2
United Kingdom	5[c]
United States	12[d]
Vietnam	4

Notes: a: Zabihah.com lists five certifiers for Canada; see http://
www.zabihah.com/aut (accessed May 29, 2016; b: Van Waarden
and van Dalen claimed that in 2013 there were thirty or forty certifiers of variable credentials and reputations in the Netherlands;
"Halal and Moral Construction of Quality," 212; c: Zabihah.com
lists nine certifiers operating in the United Kingdom; d: Zabihah.
com lists nineteen certifiers for the United States.

Source: m-haditec, "Halal-Certification Worldwide."

certifiers use their profits (some allege that they may be funding terrorism),
Australian certifiers' financial records came under scrutiny. That country's
press reported that in 2014 the Australian Federation of Islamic Councils, one
of the most prominent certifiers, generated a revenue of about $4.5 million,

about two-thirds of which ($2.9 million) was profit.[46] A separate inquiry determined that in 2014 the country's largest meat exporter, JBS Australia, spent $1.8 million to obtain different types of religious approvals inside or outside the country.[47] While most big corporations claim that these expenses are not passed on to their customers, small businesses admit that minimal costs are reflected in their prices.[48]

In addition to helping the food industry meet religious standards, halal certifiers maintain that they serve altruistic purposes; they also present themselves as arbiters of religious law, helping Muslims eat according to Islamic standards in a world of increasing corruption and danger of contamination.[49] The certifiers also embody market-friendly Islam's response to the growing anxiety about food purity. The most successful are those who can reliably and continuously address concerns about food in an environment where traditional (direct) mechanisms of quality control have largely disappeared and where food production has become more technical and internationalized. Halal certification allows food and service providers to be competitive. Certification by particularly reputable organizations that also provide postcertification monitoring services (such as the French AVS: A votre service, or At Your Service)[50] could be costly but often makes economic sense, since many consumers are willing to pay more for products that provide an extra measure of religious peace of mind.

There are major differences among certifiers in terms of their menu of services (certification only; certification + sporadic monitoring of vendors/producers; certification + constant monitoring); the halal standards they follow; their target markets (local or international); their levels of professionalism and transparency; and, consequently, their service costs. For example, two major British certifiers, Halal Food Authority (HFA) and Halal Monitoring Committee (HMC), differ in what they consider halal-compliant slaughter techniques. While the former accepts preslaughter stunning, the latter does not. The two also diverge in how they issue certificates: whereas the HFA provides meat suppliers with a wholesale certification of the entire slaughter and transportation process, the HMC claims to follow a more comprehensive verification process, which involves certification of several points in the chain of production and distribution, from the slaughterhouse to the processing plant, then the butcher, then the retailer.[51]

Differences between HFA and HMC might be indicative of "generational" variation of services expected of halal certifiers.[52] The HFA, which was founded in 1994, may represent what anthropologist Florence Bergeaud-Blackler has labeled the "first generation of certifiers," presumably older organizations that

Fig. 5.1. A Halal Monitoring Committee (HMC) label on a meat product at a London supermarket. Authors' photograph.

focused on international trade and addressed the needs of food producers and merchants rather than representing the voices of consumers. If a meat producer requires halal certification to export its products, it might choose to work with these organizations which have affiliations with or are recognized by international networks or state/public organizations. First-generation certifiers are also accustomed to handling trade arrangements that involve substantial orders and contracts.

On the other hand, the "second-generation" certifiers—such as the HMC, whose operations go back only to the early 2000s—aim to represent consumers' needs and prioritize domestic markets. They often work with local merchants who directly market their products to consumers and who are thus particularly sensitive to consumers' expectations of halal compliance. Second-generation certifiers proclaim a higher level of transparency and appear more vigilant in their monitoring efforts than earlier counterparts, which are sometimes considered to be overly bureaucratic and perhaps too acquiescent to industry needs. While preslaughter stunning, a widespread industry practice in the meat sector, has been either considered halal-compliant or avoided as an issue of concern by first-generation certifiers, many (perhaps most) second-generation certifiers, including the HMC, oppose stunning.[53]

Competition among the increasing number of certifiers encourages many to fine-tune their services according to consumers' perceived needs and to develop strategies that target different clients. The major US halal certifier Islamic Food and Nutrition Council of America (IFANCA)[54] has begun to offer its clients a service it calls a "Five Star Halal Identification System," which is adaptable to the needs of Muslim consumers who observe different standards of halal.[55] This program targets clients who would like to demonstrate that their products' halal quality exceeds IFANCA's entry-level guarantee that "the meat they purchase meets the basic criteria for halal slaughter (or *zabiha*)." IFANCA uses its Crescent-M ("M" for moon) logo on meat to certify conformity with its basic slaughter criteria: that the meat was not derived from an impure animal species, that the animal's blood was completely drained during slaughter, and that the meat was uncontaminated by impure materials during or after the slaughter. For higher fees, however, IFANCA could also certify

1. If the animal was slaughtered by a Muslim.
2. If the animal was slaughtered by a traditional horizontal cut across the neck.
3. If animals were fed an all-natural diet of plant origin.
4. If the factory/slaughterhouse met animal welfare guidelines.
5. The animal was not stunned prior to or after the cut on the neck for bleeding purposes.

For client companies that want this extra level of certification, the organization uses a label that contains five stars under that Crescent-M logo; a shaded star indicates each corresponding criterion that has been met. In creating this new label, the organization may have been influenced by policies practiced by the health- and organic-food oriented grocery chain Whole Foods, which in 2008 developed a five-step Animal Welfare Rating Program that progressively rewards points to farmers and ranchers who are more attentive to animals' living, dietary, and health needs.[56]

IFANCA's five-starred system offers some instructive clues about modern interpretations of halal rules. Sunni sources disagree on whether Muslims must perform halal slaughter and on the legal status of preslaughter stunning. Although slaughter by multiple (vertical or horizontal) cuts does not necessarily render the flesh impermissible, Islamic sources consider a single, clean cut across the animal's throat as the ideal form of culling.[57] Criteria 1,

Fig. 5.2. IFANCA Five-Star Logo.

2, and 5, if met, are consistent with more discriminating interpretations of halal slaughter. For companies merely interested in standard halal compliance, IFANCA's "basic criteria" guarantee would serve their purposes. Companies interested in proving that their slaughter methods are consistent with more discerning halal expectations might choose to pay the extra fees IFANCA charges for its starred logo.

Being able to differentiate among certifiers based on their various definitions of halal allows consumers to satisfy their own specific halal expectations and thus benefits the overall market. This strategy of catering to varied consumers is apparent in IFANCA's third and fourth criteria.[58] These requirements (i.e., animals intended for slaughter "were fed an all-natural diet of plant origin" and the "plant/slaughterhouse met animal welfare guidelines") are not grounded in classical halal slaughter expectations; rather, they deliberately expand on the meaning of halal in ways consistent with modern human health and animal welfare requirements.[59] The industry believes that halal's general appeal to a broader public might grow if the term becomes identified with human health and animal welfare, in addition to representing classical understandings of Islamic meat purity.[60]

State-Based Regulation Efforts

In many non-Western settings, states have become directly involved in halal matters and have made significant attempts at halal regulation. These countries include, among others, Malaysia, Indonesia, Singapore, Turkey, Iran, and the Arab Gulf countries, and their influence in halal business is quite different from that of private halal certifiers. Although most certify the halal compliance of products intended for Muslim consumption in their lands, they also manage national halal affairs in a centralized fashion. These states run structured bureaucracies that shape policies on religious issues, legislative organs that design legal and institutional frameworks required for efficient administration of halal matters, and executive branches that police and enforce the state's halal regulations. State-run scientific entities (such as laboratories, research centers, and universities) test the halal compliance of products and develop technologies needed for market expansion. As massive economic and commercial entities, states invest in industrial infrastructures, provide incentives for companies whose standards and interests align with their own, and dissuade or punish those whose interests diverge. Through their own halal accreditation services, they also differentiate between what they consider reliable and unreliable certifiers. Finally, whether alone or in partnership with other states or international nongovernmental organizations, these states influence global halal affairs and developments more effectively than private organizations.

From a long-term perspective of Islamic history, the modern state's level of involvement in the religious sphere is unprecedented. One salient aspect of premodern Islamic jurisprudential traditions is that they resisted within limits attempts by political authorities to privilege particular versions of jurisprudential and legislative interpretations at the expense of others. Historically, the state played a relatively limited role in the development of Islamic law and legal institutions. Instead, the community of believers (umma) and their contextually determined inclinations constituted the primary basis for many aspects of Islamic jurisprudence. This precedent may help to explain why, from early Islamic times, some within the Muslim scholarly community tended to regard political authority with suspicion and to question its claims to religious legitimacy and legislative authority.

Granted, political and religio-legal authorities were not always at odds. In fact, even in early Islamic history political rulers were expected to "enjoin [religiously sanctioned] right behavior and forbid wrong ones."[61] Although there was a wide range of opinions about what constituted right and wrong and how political authorities were supposed to enjoin and/or forbid such behavior, all sides believed that the law and state were mutually dependent: religious law needed political authorities for enforcement, and political authorities needed religious legitimacy. In later periods, the state's association with religion became more institutionalized: late medieval and early modern

Islamic states (such as the Fatimids, Mamluks, Safavids, and Mughals) developed complex religious-bureaucratic structures, which not only helped administer their respective territories but also established and reproduced religious legitimacy for the ruling political elite.

In this regard, perhaps no other premodern polity was as successful as the Ottoman state, which managed to create a highly bureaucratized and considerably sophisticated state Sunnism after the sixteenth century. The Ottoman jurists also issued interpretations that were aligned with the state's interests and instrumental to its struggles against domestic and international rivals. The Ottomans appointed many religious scholars as state functionaries, founded and patronized religious colleges that formulated state-centric jurisprudential opinions, and built a centralized legal-administrative system where religio-legal authorities enforced Sharia and state law.

Yet even the Ottoman Empire was not a modern state, at least not until the late nineteenth century. Its religio-bureaucratic institutionalization and overall ability to govern the daily aspects of the lives of its subjects paled in comparison to modern states', and its bureaucratic apparatus was never the most important source for legal-religious interpretation. For example, although the Ottomans made occasional attempts to ban the use of alcohol in public spaces, their ability to define and enforce acceptable (and, thus, unacceptable) forms of Islamic practice remained limited. The Ottomans, like other premodern Islamic polities, also lacked the ability (or need) to build infrastructural and industrial frameworks for the production and marketing of halal merchandise appropriate from the state's religious point of view. The economic resources and organizational capacity of the modern state, although they vary from one state to another, are more substantial than those of the premodern state, which allow the former to appropriate a more pronounced role in the governance of the religious sphere and in formulating (and enforcing) religiously sanctioned policies. In this sense, the efforts and policies of modern polities are an unparalleled development that demonstrates how Islam came to be defined and governed by the state, at least within its boundaries.

Since the 1950s Muslim states have claimed unprecedented moral and social functions "to implement the prescriptions which would make society whole again, restoring its sociability and its Islamic identity."[62] In various formulations of these functions, the state appeared as the actor that could identify and meet all types of societal needs and enacted measures, ranging from economic to religious. Programs that aimed at rapid and socially responsible economic development (as in "Islamic socialism," popular in the 1950s and 1960s) reflected these tendencies and expanded to noneconomic sectors, including education, health care, and, most crucially, religion. The modern state became a "repository of expertise," colonizing the world of religious learning and interpretation, at the expense of other private actors, including the traditional scholars or ulama.[63] While "Islamic socialism" and many of its policies lost popularity after the 1970s, the state's role as the ultimate religious arbiter remained prominent in most Muslim countries worldwide.

Eventually the modern state's attempts to govern religion led to the bureaucratization of Islam.[64] Well-staffed and funded institutions proclaim to serve prevailing religious needs and, in the process, define acceptable practice. Key state services include religious education; formulation of officially sanctioned religious positions and policies that range from personal matters of faith to interfaith relationships, from Islamic finance to food regulations; public dissemination of this information through state-sponsored publications and other forms of outreach; building, maintenance, and staffing of places of worship; acquisition and supervision of the use of funds dedicated to specific religious functions (such as zakat, or charity); monitoring the activities of private religious groups; and sanctioning those that are deemed unacceptable from the official point of view. These bureaucratic bodies are run by theologically trained state employees, the new ulama, often in the thousands, who facilitate the state's incursion into its citizens' lives and reinforce its status as the hegemonic arbiter of religion. This process, in turn, undermines traditional religious plurality by suppressing groups and interpretations deemed threatening to the state's religious vision. In other words, state-sponsored bureaucratized Islam homogenizes religion within national boundaries.

Especially since the early 2000s, modern states' direct involvement in halal matters has revealed economic as well as religious concerns and motivations. Because the halal food industry is globally valued at hundreds of billions of dollars and is forecast to grow substantially, the prospect of becoming a key player in halal business entices individual governments. By defining halal standards, regulating halal practices, certifying halal vendors, and investing in domestic and international halal industries, states not only proclaim their central role in governing religion but also position themselves to capitalize on the potential windfalls associated with the lucrative global halal business. Still, a plurality of attitudes toward halal prevails within the global economic arena, precisely because no one individual state or even regional alliance possesses the exclusive ability to govern this realm. States face competition from other states and international governmental alliances with their own interests, agendas, and definitions of halal. Their interaction and rivalry encourage a constant reconsideration of halal definitions.

A Selective List of Global Halal Actors

One of the more influential countries in the international halal business, and perhaps the best-studied one, is Malaysia, which uses its involvement in halal matters as a symbol of its Islamic identity, a means for long-term economic development, and a tool for regional and interregional influence. More than 5 percent of Malaysia's entire exports, which total $12 billion as of 2012, is based on halal products, and the top destinations of those exports are China, the United States, Singapore, the Netherlands, and Japan. In terms of value, food and beverages constitute about one-third of this trade.[65]

In the last couple of decades, successive Malaysian governments have developed a vision to turn the country into what they call a "hub" for international halal commerce and industry, and they have made a concerted and multidimensional effort to realize this vision. To this effect, the state has established numerous agencies and departments responsible for long-term planning and coordinated execution of the state's vision. More specifically, the state has pursued public relations campaigns to expand the country's influence and share in the global halal business; invested in research and development of halal products, processes, and technologies within the country and for export; sought to enhance Malaysia's competitiveness and commercial ties in the international arena; and offered tax exemptions, grants, and favorable loans to private companies that serve Malaysia's halal vision and objectives. Furthermore, the country has organized international halal fairs, the most notable of which is MIHAS (Malaysia International Halal Showcase, established in 2004), which attracts actual and potential consumers and producers from all over the world, and has opened carefully designed halal industrial parks that attract multinational corporations involved in halal business.[66]

Malaysia's efforts to develop halal-compliant services and products have been strategically focused on specialized food production, animal husbandry, and halal ingredients, in which the country has identified major growth and profit potential. The state has also undertaken measures to enhance the country's place in the global regulation, monitoring, and enforcement of halal standards. A primary means of accomplishing the last objective is to formulate halal standards that serve as a blueprint for other international bodies and organizations. Malaysia's attempts to design its halal standards go back to the mid-1970s. Yet the first comprehensive guidelines intended for international usage were developed in the early 2000s through a cooperative effort by a multitude of state agencies, universities, and private organizations. The first version of these guidelines, titled *The General Guidelines on the Production, Preparation, Handling, and Storage of Halal Food* (*Malaysian Standard* [or *MS*] *1500*), was issued in 2000 (referred to as *MS 1500:2000*) and went through two revisions, first in 2004 (*MS 1500:2004*) and later in 2009 (*MS 1500:2009*). These guidelines cover topics that range from halal slaughter, processing, distribution, storage, hygiene, and sanitation to packaging and labeling. The Malaysian Department of Islamic Development (Jabatan Kemajuan Islam Malaysia or JAKIM) is the official body authorized to oversee the implementation of halal standards. JAKIM also provides accreditation services to private certifiers all over the world, ones that enforce Malaysian standards in their halal assessment services.

Malaysia's attempts to dominate the international halal business have been rivaled by other actors. For example, within the OIC, which represents fifty-seven Muslim states, Malaysia's efforts to have its halal guidelines recognized as the gold standard of global halal were resisted.[67] One reason is that other states and organizations have been developing competing halal guidelines with an eye toward becoming influential actors in the booming halal business. Competitors include other early standard-setters, such as Indonesia and Singapore, whose halal guidelines had also received international recognition. Indonesia's active involvement in halal regulation and standardization dates back to the late 1980s and initially emerged over purity concerns in food items intended for domestic consumption. With over 200 million Muslims, Indonesia is not only a major market for but also a potentially significant supplier of halal products.[68] The country has recently positioned itself to take advantage of the growing global opportunities and to become what one government minister in 2011 called the "Halal Center of the World," presumably in contradistinction to Malaysia's self-proclaimed global "halal hub" status.

Until recently, the agency responsible for issuing halal certificates was the Indonesian Ulama Council (Majelis Ulama Indonesia, or MUI), the country's official authority on Islamic affairs.[69] But in 2014, following widely publicized bribery allegations involving MUI and Australian meat exporters, the Indonesian government limited MUI's role in the halal affairs and set up a new body, the Halal Product Security Agency, to issue halal certificates according to new procedures.[70] Until that time, complaints by exporters to Indonesia about difficulties in obtaining necessary religious permissions and licenses were common, as were charges of corruption.[71] Public scandals involving MUI had embarrassed the government. For example, in 2000 MUI falsely claimed that the popular food seasonings and taste enhancers produced by the Japanese company Ajinomoto contained pig-based substances and declared them haram. This ruling was subsequently overturned by the president of Indonesia, Abdurrahman Wahid.[72] In 2009, pork-based ingredients were found in a few products that MUI had previously certified as halal.[73] In 2010, MUI granted a halal certificate to pharma giant Novartis AG for its Menveo vaccine, a decision subsequently challenged by IFANCA authorities, who claimed that the medicine was not pork-free.[74] Indonesia's recent reform attempts in halal administration aim for simplicity, transparency, and credibility. In addition to establishing a new halal authority, the government passed a new law in October 2014, Law No. 33 on Halal Product Assurance, which intended to create a one-stop state-run system for halal certification of food and beverages, cosmetics, and pharmaceuticals.[75] This legislation is part of an attempt to develop a national and comprehensive certification system that resembles the one in Malaysia.[76]

In Singapore, the Islamic Religious Council of Singapore (or Majlis Ugama Islam Singapura; MUIS) determines halal standards and provides accreditation; MUIS began halal certification in 1978 because of domestic concerns about food purity.[77] Like Malaysia and Indonesia, Singapore has sought to join the growing global halal business[78] by gaining international recognition for its agency's halal certification. In 2006, the government implemented the MUIS eHalal System (or MeS), based on a web platform that streamlines and speeds up all phases of halal certification from application to online payments. Two years later, MUIS introduced the Singapore MUIS Halal Quality Management System (HalMQ), which aligned its requirements with the International Organization for Standardization (ISO) and the Hazard Analysis and Critical Control Point (HACCP) standards to ensure food safety. In 2010, MUIS made HalMQ compulsory for receiving certification; the organization argues that this move enhanced compliance, increased the credibility of Singapore's certification process, and improved the international competitive advantage of companies with the MUIS certification.[79]

Malaysia, Indonesia, and Singapore are examples of three older state players in the global halal business.[80] These countries have tried to ensure their hegemonic positions in halal markets by founding and supporting nongovernmental organizations (NGOs) that could globally recognize and promote their leadership and standards. For instance, the World Halal Food Council (WHFC) was founded in Jakarta by Indonesia's MUI in 1999 with the aim of coordinating the efforts of global halal bodies and certifying organizations.[81] Currently the WHFC has forty member organizations, the majority of which (twenty-two) are halal certifiers in Europe and the Americas. Most of these organizations are first-generation certifiers, and they are inclined to promote a "liberal view of halal standards," allowing mechanized slaughter and preslaughter stunning.[82] By contrast, the International Halal Integrity (IHI) Alliance, an NGO based in and with strong connections to Malaysia, was formed in 2007 and promotes the "integrity of the halal market concept in global trade."[83] One distinct aspect of the IHI Alliance is that it does not call for the enforcement of a single global standard. Instead it recognizes the variability of halal standards and proposes a cooperative framework of accreditation that can accommodate such variations.[84] This policy choice aligns with Malaysia's latest international halal strategy.

More recently, other aspiring standard-setters have also emerged in the global halal arena. Unlike their Southeast Asian counterparts, these latecomers became initially involved in halal politics not because of domestic concerns about food purity but as a direct result of the halal trade's global opportunities for economic gain and international influence. The Gulf Cooperation Council (GCC)—Bahrain, Kuwait, Oman, Qatar, Saudi Arabia, and the United Arab Emirates—is one of these bodies that makes up for its latecomer status by invoking the Arabian Peninsula's central role in the development of Islamic law and civilization and by utilizing the region's significant financial capital. The GCC organizes annual meetings and conferences dedicated to halal issues, and in 2008 the council launched its own standard: *GSO 1931/2008: Halal Food.*[85]

Turkey is another aspiring standard-setter, whose involvement in international halal business has further complicated halal matters. As in the Gulf countries, in Turkey the demand for halal certification emerged as a foreign-trade instrument in the mid-2000s. In addition, the rise of the Justice and Development Party (Adalet ve Kalkınma Partisi, or AKP), which desires to enhance Turkey's leadership role in and establish stronger connections with the Muslim world, has turned halal certification and standardization into a globally competitive project. Within the country, the official Turkish Standards Institute (Türk Standardları Enstitüsü, TSE) has been issuing halal certificates since 2011 in collaboration with the Directorate of Religious Affairs (Diyanet İşleri Başkanlığı; DİB),[86] although private certifiers have operated in Turkey since the mid-2000s. TSE's standards for domestic certification are developed by the Standards and Metrology Institute for Islamic Countries (SMIIC), a subsidiary of the Organization of Islamic Cooperation and a body in which Turkey has a strong influence. Efforts to establish uniformity in metrology, laboratory testing, and standardization among member states in the OIC go back to the 1980s, and since 2008 the organization has worked to produce its own halal standards, a process in which the TSE has been very prominent.[87] SMIIC, headquartered in Istanbul, was established in 2010. As of 2017, it has thirty-three member and three observer states.[88] SMIIC's efforts at halal standardization led to the production of three OIC/SCMIIC guidelines: *OIC/ SMIIC 1:2011, General Guidelines on Halal Food, OIC/SMIIC 2: 2011, Guidelines for Halal Certification Bodies* and *OIC/SMIIC 3: 2011, Guidelines for Accreditation Bodies Accrediting Halal Certification.*

Although SMIIC is a subsidiary of the OIC, a body comprising fifty-seven Muslim states, not all OIC members have accepted the SMIIC standards, as they constitute an obstacle to the economic and hegemonic aspirations of other member states, including Malaysia and the Gulf countries.[89] The development of multiple, competing halal standards has frustrated efforts to generate a single universal benchmark and has led some actors, such as Malaysia, to adopt a defensive strategy of promoting selective openness within the international halal market, presumably to protect existing Malaysian gains and influence. The IHI Alliance's recognition of variable standards strongly reflects this more accommodating position.

Turkey has also been a leading actor in the development of European halal standards. Since 2010, the European Committee for Standardization (CEN) has pursued its own standard. CEN is one of three European Standardization Organizations (along with the European Committee for Electrotechnical Standardization and the European Telecommunications Standards Institute) that have been officially recognized by the European Union and the European Free Trade Association as being responsible for developing and defining voluntary standards at the European level.[90] CEN is an umbrella organization that brings together the national standardization bodies of thirty-three

European countries and provides a platform for the development of common European standards for various types of products, materials, services, and processes, since the diversity of certification is especially pronounced in Europe. Many certifiers adopt and enforce standards designed by non-European countries such as Malaysia, Indonesia, and Singapore, an issue of concern for European authorities. Overall, CEN aims to produce a halal standard for the European market, one that would help market integration and lessen transaction costs.

The effort to design a halal standard for European Union countries was initially spearheaded by Austria. Turkey, although not a member of the EU, became prominently involved from the very beginning: it is Europe's largest Muslim-majority nation and has played a central role in the development of SMIIC standards. Turkey's geographical proximity to and historical connections with Europe, its significant commercial interests in European markets, and the sizable Turkish-speaking communities in various parts of the continent also justify Turkey's major role. In 2013, CEN established a Technical Committee (CEN/TC 425, "Project Committee—Halal Food") for this task, and the Turkish Standards Institute (along with the Austrian Standards Institute) was assigned to serve as secretariat of this body.

Before concluding, it is worth mentioning that the intensified competition over the meaning and control over halal has led to significant conflicts among various players at the international level, including, most prominently, Malaysia and other OIC member states. While Malaysia had earlier hoped and pressed for the OIC's recognition of its national guidelines, the SMIIC developed an alternative standard, which undermined Malaysia's hegemonic claims in the international arena.[91] Also well known is the conflict over market domination between CEN (the European Committee for Standardization) and many independent Muslim certifiers operating in Europe. From the start, CEN's efforts to coordinate "European halal" received resistance from several certifying bodies and the international organizations backing them. For example, the World Halal Council (WHC), an umbrella organization composed of over twenty global certifying agencies from different parts of the Muslim world, criticized CEN and demanded a halt to its efforts, stating, "Halal is a pure Islamic issue and Halal standardization and certification cannot be a working field for non-Muslims."[92] Thus, central to WHC's opposition to CEN's initiatives are disagreements on who can speak for Muslims, interpret their religious inclinations, and—simply put—tell them what they can and cannot eat, global concerns that are unlikely to disappear in the near future.

The modern halal movement stems from many factors, including Muslims' desire to carve out a space that they regard as their own and to assert an identity independent of influences they consider alien and threatening. Very much a reaction to the Western political, economic, and cultural domination of Muslim-majority regions in the twentieth century, this urge also reflects how modern Muslims have come to imagine their past: an almost utopian era at the very beginning—the golden age of the Prophet—followed by periods of gradual degeneration that put greater moral and spiritual separation between the first generation of Muslims and each subsequent one.[93] From a pietistic perspective, symptoms of this separation can be recognized in every habit, practice, and institution adopted by Muslims since the seventh century: from Byzantine and Sassanian forms of kingship, to use of tobacco from the New World, to public displays of affection between sexes, to all Western legal, economic, and political institutions appropriated by Muslim rulers. Religio-political currents that have been popular since the 1970s have sought to regenerate authentic Muslim communities by stripping away all those layers of innovation and returning to ideal forms of social existence, defined with reference to the Prophet's time.

Herein lies the paradox of global halal business, including, but not limited to, halal food economies. While modern aspirations of a halal lifestyle have been boosted by Islamist political movements that reject many aspects of Western capitalism and its individualistic and consumerist inclinations, halal business demonstrates distinctly market-oriented, profit-seeking tendencies, driven by local, regional, and international competition and conflict among its multiple actors.[94] The proliferation of private certifiers in many Western settings exemplifies these tendencies, as such groups claim to provide the combined religious and technical expertise required for halal certification and have creatively diversified their services to satisfy Muslims' desires for a purer lifestyle. In the global arena, the sector has been dominated by large corporations and by states, which have the political, economic, and bureaucratic means to govern halal business within their own borders, often as monopolistic actors.

The global halal business is one venue where market-oriented, state-defined modern Islamic attitudes have revealed themselves in unprecedented ways. But it is also worth noting that many Muslim groups advocate resistance to bureaucratized forms of Islam and to Islamic capitalism. Though they are clearly in the minority, these groups, some of which are discussed in chapter 8, are working to develop alternative and what they consider to be more authentic visions of a halal lifestyle.

CHAPTER 6

C hapter 5 highlighted the prominent role that various states and international and multistate organizations have recently come to play in
the global halal business. In continuing this theme, the present chapter examines how three such actors define what counts as halal (and, therefore,
what does not) as depicted in their official halal standards pertaining to food,
beverages, and other related substances. While these standards are by no means
representative of all contemporary definitions of halal (others include organic,
vegan-vegetarian, and ecologically sensitive approaches), they represent
bureaucratic scripts by which major halal players with hegemonic aspirations in
the Islamic world and ambitious economic expectations govern religion. These
standards are also indicative of what has become of halal dictums under the
purview of the modern state and the influence of global capitalism.

The discussion begins with an examination of Malaysian halal standards,
which went through three successive revisions (in 2000, 2004, and 2009) that
collectively illustrate how state-sponsored discourses on halal evolved over
time and under the influence of many factors, including, but not limited to, the
state's religious considerations, industry needs and requirements, and international competition. The chapter then compares the most recent (2009) version
of the Malaysian Standard with its two major counterparts, one formulated
by the Gulf Cooperation Council (GCC) and the other by the Standards and

Metrology Institute for Islamic Countries (SMIIC) of the Organization of Islamic Cooperation (OIC). This comparison reveals the different strategies that major international actors have utilized in competing for influence over international halal business; it also highlights how alternative characterizations of modern halal diverge from one other.

Malaysian Halal Standards

Legal regulation of halal food practices in Malaysia dates back to the mid-1970s. Two orders—"Trade Descriptions (Use of Expression 'Halal') Order 1975" and the "Trade Descriptions (Marking of Food) Order 1975"—that were developed under the Trade Description Act (TDA) of 1972 (hereafter *Malaysia TDA 1972*) defined the term "halal" and explained how the label should be used within the food industry.[1] These are brief documents and, compared to later formulations, are imprecise about factors of concern to halal regulators. For example, the first order characterizes halal food using only four criteria:

a) Neither it [i.e., halal food] consists of, nor contains, any part or matter of an animal that a Muslim is prohibited by Hukum Syarak (or Shari'a-based directive) to consume that has not been slaughtered in accordance with Hukum Syarak.

b) Does not contain anything which is considered to be impure according to Hukum Syarak; and

c) Has not been prepared, processed or manufactured using any instrument not free from anything impure according to Hukum Syarak; and

d) Has not in the course of preparation, processing or storage been in contact with or been in close proximity to any food that fails to satisfy paragraph (a), (b) or (c) or anything that is considered to be impure according to Hukum Syarak.[2]

The second order merely states that "any meat or offal, including that of poultry that are fresh, chilled, frozen, or cooked, canned or preserved in any other manner,"

a) Shall not be supplied [as halal] unless it is marked by a label, tag or any other form of mark that such food is Halal.

b) All uncooked meat and offals [sic], including poultry, shall not be supplied [as halal] unless it is marked by a label, tag or any other form of
mark indicating that such meat or offal had or had not been chilled or
frozen.[3]

Shortcomings in *Malaysia TDA 1972* would appear over time and prompt the
Malaysian government to clarify (and further complicate) halal definition
and matters. For instance, the 1972 Act had failed to name which state body
was empowered to issue the halal label and therefore opened up the possibility for private and possibly fraudulent labeling practices. Also, it was unclear
who should enforce halal-related offenses: existing laws demanded that the
Department of Islamic Development Malaysia (JAKIM), otherwise responsible
for carrying out halal audit and monitoring, must cooperate with the Ministry
of Domestic Trade, Cooperatives, and Consumerism in law enforcement and
prosecution.

To address these shortcomings, the state issued "Trade Description
(Certification and Marking of Halal) Order 2011" under a new law, the Trade
Description Act of 2011 (*Malaysia TDA 2011*). The latter clearly designated
JAKIM at the federal level, and Islamic Religious Councils (MAIN) in individual states, as the appropriate authorities to issue halal certificates for any
food, goods, or related services.[4] Also, *Malaysia TDA 2011* explicitly defined
what constituted halal falsification and prescribed punishments for these
offenses. Finally, the document designated JAKIM as an independent enforcement agency that could prosecute civil cases against the fraudulent use of the
halal logo.[5]

The expansion of JAKIM's jurisdiction over halal matters exemplifies the
Malaysian state's increasing role in governance of Islamic practice since the
1980s and especially during the 2000s.[6] Clearly Malaysia was trying to define
halal more precisely and to standardize the term's meaning in food, beverages,
and other substances. The updated 2011 definition is only moderately more
detailed than *Malaysia TDA 1972*, which described halal food narrowly,[7] but
the reason for this seeming oversight is not hard to find: by the time *Malaysia
TDA 2011* was issued, the state had already prepared three different editions
of Malaysian Standard 1500, or *MS 1500*, all of which had explained in detail
halal rules in food production, handling, processing, labeling, transportation,
storing, and sale processes. By naming JAKIM as the "competent authority"
responsible for the enforcement of *MS 1500* in its certification, monitoring,

and enforcement activities, *Malaysia TDA 2011* recognized the binding relevance of earlier regulatory standards. These critical documents—the three successive versions of *MS 1500*—demonstrate how the Malaysian state defined halal food, and how and why this definition may have changed over time due to an assortment of domestic and/or international factors.

To many observers, the Malaysian state's Islamization represents a response to a growing Islamic radicalism and opposition that began to surface in the 1980s.[8] In this struggle over political legitimacy, the state promoted what some scholars have called a state-sponsored, "moderate" Islam. Besides stabilizing domestic political tensions and, possibly, fostering the state's interventionist character internally, state-led initiatives were also intended to enhance Malaysia's global role in the Islamic world.[9] Broadly, these policies included the creation and development of state institutions—JAKIM and a plethora of others—that defined, supported, and regulated Islamic life and practices. State policies helped develop a bureaucratized Islam that aimed for both procedural rationalization in the modern application of Islamic principles and a homogenization of Islamic life and practices within national borders.[10]

In addition to symbolizing the Malaysian state's vision for Islamization, the country's political leaders considered *MS 1500* a tool for long-term economic development and integration into Islamic markets. Malaysia was an early arrival in the global halal food sector and the earliest version of the standard was likely the first of its kind to have any international appeal. Yet the subsequent versions of the document, and in particular the third edition (*MS 1500:2009*), were issued at a time of increasing global competition, when other states and international organizations were formulating rival guidelines, which ended up influencing the Malaysian standard as much as being influenced by it. Finally, the desire to propel the standard into global use led the document's authors to pay attention to several other international standards on food safety, hygiene, and sanitation.

Malaysian Standard (MS) 1500:2000, "General Guidelines on the Production, Preparation, Handling and Storage of Halal Food," represents the state's first attempt to fully define what halal practices and compliance entail.[11] This edition, like later ones, was developed under the coordination of SIRIM-Berhad—a state-owned "total solutions provider" for Malaysia's industrial sector[12]—for the Department of Standards Malaysia, which operates under the Ministry of Science, Technology and Innovation. *MS 1500:2000* was formulated "through consensus by committees which comprise a balanced representation of producers, users, consumers, and others with relevant interests as may be appropriate to the subject in hand."[13] More specifically, the "Working Group on Halal Foods" that composed *MS 1500:2000* included an array of state representatives, from the trade, agricultural, and veterinary sectors; the Department of Islamic Development Malaysia (JAKIM); and a small number of industry representatives (e.g., from Nestlé).[14] The Food and Agricultural Industry Standards Committee that supervised the working group also included representatives from health, agricultural, trade, and marketing ministries; Malaysian universities; and private business interests.[15] JAKIM, however, did not have a representative on the oversight Food and Agricultural Industry Standards Committee—a situation that would change during subsequent revisions.

The standard's ambitious nature and its place in Malaysia's long-term economic and political aspirations is evident in how the document depicts halal standardization and compliance, as a "means [of] advancing the national economy, promoting industrial efficiency and development, benefiting the health and safety of the public, protecting the consumers, facilitating domestic and international trade and furthering international cooperation."[16] Malaysia had planned to become a developed nation and a prominent global leader in these sectors by 2020 through a process of selective investment in certain industries and technologies, including halal industries: the state had supported the establishment of halal science laboratories in universities and the development of advanced technologies for food inspection. Malaysia's evolution into a frontrunner in this arena entails expertise in traditional Islamic sciences and a technological sophistication Malaysians could skillfully apply in modern production and marketing schemes.[17] In addition to addressing the state's domestic political concerns, *MS 1500* serves these ambitions by providing "practical guidelines for the food industry on the preparation and handling of halal food and to serve as a basic requirement for food product and food trade or business in Malaysia."[18] In meeting these goals, the guideline includes definitions of relevant terminology as well as specifications related to food purity from religious and hygienic perspectives.

At first glance, the document appears to lean slightly in a pro-Shafi'i direction, at least in the way it defines Sharia: "Shariah Law means Islamic Law based on the *Al-Quran, Al-Hadith* (traditions of the Messenger of Allah), *Ijma'* (consensus of Muslim scholars) and *Qiyas* (deduction or analogy) according to the Shafei or any one of the Hanafi, Maliki or Hanbali Schools of Thought or fatwa approved by the relevant Islamic Authority. A particular food becomes halal or non-halal by Shariah Law if it is considered so through any one of the above mentioned sources."[19] However, since *MS 1500:2000* and its subsequent editions were designed to accommodate the expectations of a broader community of (Sunni) Muslims, this pro-Shafi'i stance seems to be only superficial, perhaps a largely symbolic nod to the historically Shafi'i inclinations of Malaysian Islam.

The standard defines halal food as food that does not contain "components or products of animals that are non-halal . . . or products of animals which are not slaughtered according to Shariah Law."[20] Halal food should also be free from any ingredient considered najis (or "impure"), and it cannot be prepared by using equipment that is "contaminated with things najis." Food that came in contact with nonhalal food or najis substances during processing, packaging, storage, or transportation cannot be regarded as halal.[21] In all of these definitions, halal food is presented as a category of exclusion (as what is not nonhalal and/or what is not najis), yet the document glosses over historical debates and disagreements about what constitutes nonhalal and najis food items. The guideline aims to provide a simple and practical depiction of halal and of how this concept may be applied to the modern food industry. Past concerns of Islamic scholars might have muddled the task at hand; perhaps this is why they were avoided.

The document's simplified approach toward historical and theological categories is also apparent in how it defines najis as things "that are themselves not permissible such as pork and all its derivatives, blood and carrion" and as otherwise-halal food "that is contaminated with things that are not permissible" and "that comes into direct contact with things that are not permissible."[22] While examples of potential food items considered "impure" are useful for practical industry concerns, the definition is notable for its circularity. The document earlier defines halal (or "permissible") as food that is non-najis and subsequently defines najis as impermissible substances.[23] According to Islamic legal traditions, however, not every impermissible food item is najis. For instance, mules and donkeys are non-najis according to many jurists, but eating their flesh is still not permissible.

The guideline next identifies nonhalal land and aquatic animals. The former includes animals not slaughtered according to Islamic standards: pigs, dogs, beasts and birds of prey (animals with long pointed teeth and talons); "animals enjoined by Islam to be killed [such] as mice, scorpions, snakes, crows, centipedes, etc."; "animals that are forbidden to be killed such as, [*sic*] bees and woodpeckers"; creatures "considered to be filthy by the public such as lice and flies"; and animals that live both on land and water, such as crocodiles, turtles, and frogs.[24] While the denunciation of pigs is based on the Quran, dogs are condemned because of the negative hadith reports attributed to the Prophet Muhammad. These requirements are largely consistent with majority Sunni and Shiite opinions, with the exception of Malikis and Hanbalis, who generally do not object to the consumption of turtles. Many Maliki jurists are also comfortable with the consumption of toads and frogs.

MS 1500:2000 takes a liberal position regarding seafood, noting that "aquatic animals are those which live in water and cannot survive outside it, such as fish. All aquatic animals are halal except those that are poisonous, intoxicating or hazardous to health."[25] This statement, while consistent with majority opinions in the Shafiʻi, Maliki, and Hanbali schools, contradicts the Hanafi and Shiite opinions regarding shellfish defined most broadly, as well as their views of squid, octopus, and whales. And while Hanafis generally consider sharks as halal, Shiites do not. Here the standard's position on aquatic animals might reflect its Shafiʻi inclinations,[26] and/or its aspiration to be globally appealing to the widest cross-section of Muslims.

Predictably, the standard forbids all drinks, plants, and micro-organisms that are "poisonous, intoxicating, or hazardous to health," but it does not explain how a poisonous substance may not be hazardous to health. On the other hand, the document makes no reference to the halal status of tobacco, despite its well-known negative health effects and the growing number of modern fatwas against its use.[27] Nor does *MS 1500:2000* define what the term "intoxication" means, thus making it difficult to ascertain the status of substances like qat or even nutmeg. At the same time, "food and drinks that are processed through DNA biotechnology of animals that are non-halal by Shariah Law are not halal."[28] This statement illustrates the standard's aim to make religious traditions relevant to modern concerns. References to biotechnological requirements of halal food production, along with (in subsequent editions) concerns about genetic modification, could stem from Malaysia's heavy investment in science and medical technologies in the service of religion. According to religion scholar Romi Mukherjee, such a process represents not only the "scientization of halal" but also the "halalization of science" in that the state's involvement in scientific and technological development remained strictly limited to areas benefiting the state's broader objective to claim Islamic legitimacy.[29]

Given the document's emphasis on the application of halal requirements to the food industry, the absence of any mention of biochemical transformations of najis substances into halal ones (*istihala*), or the dissolution of small amounts of najis substances in large amounts of halal ones (*istihlak*), is curious. What's more, the two subsequent versions of the *MS 1500* continued to skirt these notions.[30] As will be discussed in chapter 7, these issues are directly relevant to the halal status of many modern food additives—particularly gelatin produced from porcine substances or from animals slaughtered in non-Islamic ways (non-zabiha). *MS 1500:2000* categorically rejects the inclusion of these materials into the halal category,[31] and so does its later incarnations, despite the existence of more lenient opinions among numerous scholars of Islam.

MS 1500:2000 requires that slaughter be performed by Muslims who are familiar with Islamic slaughter requirements.[32] Given Malaysia's considerable reliance on foreign meat,[33] this should be regarded as a stringent prescription, and it might reflect the authors' concerns about the standard's acceptability in non-Malaysian contexts: an accommodating position might have undermined the standard's value among more conservative Muslims. Also, *MS 1500*'s stance on the slaughterer's religious identity might signal Malaysian Islam's appropriately orthodox credentials. One objective of Malaysia's attempts to become a global leader in Islamic (and halal) matters has been to discredit the perception that, due both to the country's geographical position far from the "heartland" of Islam and to its population's multireligious and multicultural character,[34] Malaysian Islam has been peripheral, syncretistic, and thus inferior in nature. These same reasons presumably explain why the document specifies tasmiyya as a requirement before slaughter, indicating that its abandonment, even inadvertent, renders a slaughtered animal's flesh nonhalal. This too is consistent with more conservative formulations of halal requirements as interpreted by classical jurists.

On the other hand, the standard is more accommodating in regard to preslaughter stunning through electrical, mechanical, or pneumatic methods, so long as the animal is "fully alive" before the slaughter, the stunning equipment is operated by a Muslim, and this equipment has not been previously used to stun nonhalal animals. Given that preslaughter stunning had long been an industry standard in the meat sector, a conservative interpretation here would have threatened the standard's global appeal. At the same time, the condition of having a Muslim stunner might be a concession and the document stresses that the flesh of animals that die during stunning cannot be considered halal.[35] Also, if a stunner accidentally breaks an animal's skull, the meat from that animal is not halal. The act of slaughtering nonpoultry involves severing the animal's trachea, esophagus, veins, and arteries.[36] Slaughter of poultry by mechanical blades is acceptable as long as the equipment is operated by Muslims and the tasmiyya pronounced every time the machine is turned on.

In the realm of "product processing and handling," the document reveals acute concerns about contamination. Equipment and facilities used to prepare, process, and handle halal food should be completely free from najis substances. If machines, devices, or utensils had been used for nonhalal food items, they should be cleaned "as required by Shariah Law with the supervision of Muslim supervisors."[37] The standard does not explain what this cleaning may entail. However, some contaminated devices are irredeemable: "The use of machines previously used for processing food containing pork is strictly not permitted, even after proper cleaning and washing."[38] Also, halal products should be strictly separated from nonhalal substances when stored, displayed, and sold. Packaging and labeling practices should conform with the same expectations. In particular, packaging materials may not contain nonhalal substances and must be made with clean equipment that hitherto had no contact with najis materials. Halal food labels must display essential information such as contents, ingredients, manufacture dates, and producers' details.

Interestingly, *MS 1500:2000* treats the issue of hygiene the same way it treats the possibility of pollution with nonhalal substances. "Hygiene and sanitation," the document declares, "is a prerequisite in the preparation of halal food. It includes the various aspects of personal hygiene, clothing, equipment and the working premises for processing or manufacture of food."[39] Thus the standard defines halal as freedom from both ritually and hygienically impure substances, which fuses correct religious and scientific attitudes toward food. By this standard's reckoning, halal food is good for human beings both in the present life and in the hereafter. This conflation of ritual and hygienic purity imbues halal with a medical meaning. Halal food production requires the quarantine of unclean substances from pure ones and the sterilization of tools and equipment; otherwise the (spiritual and material) well-being of the body that consumes the food is in danger.

These religio-hygienic concerns capture the type of alternative modernity that Malaysian Muslims have proposed against Western modernity. While the latter is based on the separation of this-worldly concerns from spiritual considerations, Malaysian formulations of Islamic modernity—particularly those put forth by two of the country's prime ministers, Mahatir Mohamed (r. 1981–2003) and Abdullah Ahmad Badawi (r. 2003–2009)—aimed to promote material and economic development without compromising Islamic requirements.[40] Various versions of *MS 1500* served this perspective by proposing a holistic (both spiritual and scientific) form of purity in industrial food production, processing, and handling.

MS 1500:2004

MS 1500:2004, the first revised edition of the 2000 version, bears a slightly modified title: "Halal Food—Production, Preparation, Handling, and Storage—General Guidelines."[41] As with the 2000 standard, SIRIM-Berhad served as secretariat in this document's preparation. One major difference between the two versions is that the organizing committees appear to have been redesigned. *MS 1500:2000* was developed by the "Working Group on Halal Food" under the "supervision" of the "Food and Agricultural Industry Standards Committee," whereas *MS 1500:2004* was formulated by the "Technical Committee on Halal Food" under the "authority" of the "Halal Standards Industry Standards Committee."[42] It is unclear what led to this change, but the numbers of state bodies and agencies involved are certainly greater in the 2004 version. JAKIM had representation in both committees for the 2004 version. Also, the new committees included the Institute of Islamic Understanding (IKIM), a state-owned organization that aims to promote Islamic values, and the Muslim Consumers' Association, neither of which appeared in the 2000 version.[43] These details might indicate that the 2004 document received an even higher degree of religio-bureaucratic scrutiny, an impression the text supports. Interestingly, Nestlé and Ilham Daya were absent from the later document.[44]

Significant textual variations exist between *MS 1500:2000* and *MS 1500:2004*, particularly in the relevant terminology. For example, the 2004 version defines Sharia as follows: "*Shariah* law means the laws of Islam in the *Mazhab* of Shafie or the laws of Islam in any other *Mazhab*s of Maliki, Hambali [*sic*] and Hanafi which are approved by the Yang di-Pertuan Agong to be in force in the state or fatwa approved by the Islamic Authority."[45] The mention of Yang di-Pertuan Agong, Malaysia's elected monarch, is new to the 2004 version and seems to emphasize the discretionary power of the state and its representatives in deciding what constitutes the law and what does not. It may also signify the growing role of political authorities as the ultimate arbiters of correct religion. As mentioned below, what sets this definition apart from those in (competing) standards prepared by other international bodies is its relatively complex characterization of Islamic law: the text points to multiple Sunni legal interpretations (e.g., the reference to the four schools), while also recognizing the role that political authorities play in legal formulation and enforcement.

In defining halal food, the 2004 version describes it as, among other things, "food that is safe and not harmful";[46] this definition is consistent with *MS 1500:2000*'s overall conflation of ritual purity and scientific cleanliness, but such a definition is literally absent in the earlier text.[47] Indeed, *MS 1500:2004* puts additional emphasis on food hygiene and sanitation in the definition of halal and contains detailed clauses about waste management and storage; prevention of contamination from harmful substances such as fertilizers, pesticides, veterinary drugs, and fecal matter; and protection of food products from plastic, glass, chemicals, metal shards from machinery, dust, harmful gas and fumes, and excessive food additives.[48] In addition, the document lists as non-halal "food and drinks containing products and/or by-products of Genetically Modified Organisms (GMOs)."[49] These details all reflect heightened sensitivities within the global food industry.

But ritualistic matters also receive special attention in the 2004 document, particularly in its elaboration on the meaning of najis. In addition to those substances earlier defined as impure, *MS 1500:2004* labels as najis "any liquid and objects discharged from the orifices of human beings or animals such as urine, excrement, blood, vomit, pus, sperm, and ova of pigs and dogs except sperm and ova of other animals," and "carrion or halal animals that are not slaughtered according to *Shariah* law."[50] Also, while the 2000 version of the standard is silent on the issue, *MS 1500:2004* explicitly counts alcoholic beverages among najis substances. Additionally, the document differentiates among the degrees of najis: severe ("*mughazallah*"), medium ("*mutawassitah*"), and light ("*mukhaffafah*").[51] It later becomes clear that these newly inserted variations are important for cleansing different forms of impurity.

Perhaps where *MS 1500:2004* differs most from its predecessor is that of ritual slaughter. The 2004 standard provides a very detailed depiction of the process, accompanied by helpful illustrations of incision points for different species of animals. The document reminds the Muslim slaughterer about the importance of performing the act of slaughter purposefully, with intent (*niyya*); Muslims are expected to initiate their daily ritual prayers with a similar attitude. Also, although both the 2000 and the 2004 standards state that the preslaughter tasmiyya must be correctly invoked, only the 2004 document specifies the required Arabic words: "Bismillah al-rahman ar-rahim" or "In the name of Allah, the most gracious, most merciful."[52] The newer document also provides instructions about how the actual slaughter should be conducted:

> Slaughtering shall be done only once. The "sawing action" of the slaughtering animal is permitted as long as the slaughtering knife or blade is not lifted off the animal during the slaughtering; bones, nails, and teeth shall not be used as slaughtering tools; the act of halal slaughter shall begin with an incision on the neck at some point just below the glottis [Adam's apple] and after the glottis for long necked animals.[53]

These may sound like technical instructions, but they are also based in established Islamic traditions, thus their correct performance carries ritual significance. In this way, the 2004 document nudges the reader to carefully follow the ritual script composed by the earliest generations of Muslims, including the Prophet Muhammad and his closest companions.

Because *MS 1500:2004* presents halal slaughter procedures as part of a technical guideline, it is a good example of bureaucratized halal ritualism. While bureaucratization bolsters the modern state's claims of rational and efficient government, in the case of halal, it also functions to codify religion's spiritual claims. In other words, the standard converts divine laws into an orderly and streamlined technical procedure in which their meanings are fixed and rendered easy to follow. Also relevant here is how the document describes procedures to purify devices, utensils, and equipment that were previously used for nonhalal purposes. *MS 1500:2000* is silent on this process. In *MS 1500:2004*, however, the issue is specifically addressed in Appendix C, "Method of washing and ritual cleansing (*dibagh*), according to *Shariah* law for *najs al-mughallazah* [or severe *najs*]." According to this discussion, which gives a step-by-step depiction, impure equipment should be washed seven times:

C1. (a) one of which shall be water with soil;
  (b) the first wash shall be to clear the existence of *najs*, even if a few washes are needed. The water from first cleaning shall not remain behind and the next wash shall be counted as the second wash;
  (c) and the amount of soil used is just enough to make a suspension.[54]

There is no obvious scientific reason to wash impure equipment seven times instead of three, or five, or ten. Nor is the purpose of using soil in the purification process necessarily self-evident, at least to the casual reader. However, for those familiar with the prophetic traditions an explanation is unnecessary for the document emulates the example of the Prophet, who said, according to one hadith, "if a dog licks an urn, then wash it seven times, the seventh with soil," and, according to another, "if a dog licks your utensils, cleanse them seven times, the first with soil."[55] The document also insists that purified devices, utensils, and equipment should be used exclusively for processing halal food after conversion: "repetition in converting the line to *najs al-mughallazah* line and back to halal line, shall not be permitted."[56]

In short, *MS 1500:2004* appears more committed to satisfying Muslim religious sensitivities than the 2000 version does. One last piece of evidence for this claim can be seen in the two documents' treatment of preslaughter stunning. While the 2000 standard makes no judgment about the latter's halal status, the 2004 version calls it "not recommended."[57] The 2004 document also provides a more detailed description of acceptable and unacceptable methods of stunning, including a table of precise voltage strengths of currents appropriate for stunning different types of animals. One wonders, however, why the document does not simply prohibit stunning instead of merely discouraging it. The document's authors may have hoped to acknowledge conservative sensitivities, yet also keep their standards relevant for a global industry where stunning is common practice. In that sense, stunning presents a conundrum wherein authorities may want to satisfy two contradictory expectations.

The first edition of the Malaysian Standard defined modern halal as relevant to both religious and hygienic purity. While the 2004 version both expands the hygiene- and sanitation-related requirements and provides a more detailed script of halal ritualism, the text focuses more on the latter. Without rejecting the overall vision of the standard's original authors, the later writers seem intent on reminding readers that halal compliance requires Muslims to follow a strict ritual regimen, which may have been established by earlier jurists but would be enforced by the modern state and its agents. Thus the 2004 version makes a stronger case for its authors' religious sensitivities than the earlier version does.

However, even though it contains more religious clauses, it would be wrong to suggest that *MS 1500:2004* is more spiritually driven than its earlier version. In fact, the text disenchants religion by incorporating it into a bureaucratic framework, alongside medical, scientific, and technological scripts, to enhance the standard's governmental utility. In the words of Indonesian journalist and poet Goenawan Mohamad, this script "lies very close to the heart of the secularist agenda. Instead of invoking the sacred in the face of the Other—the Other being the divine, the mortals, the sky and the earth—in unique moments of epiphany and inspiration . . . (it) flatten(s) it to the ground and render(s) expression of piety nothing more than a civic duty."[58]

MS 1500:2009

The Malaysian Standard was revised for a second time in 2009.[59] Because there are no available records or minutes of the working group and committee meetings that generated *MS 1500*'s 2004 and 2009 versions, it is difficult to know why a new version was released. Furthermore, no academic studies to date compare subsequent texts or appropriately contextualize them. This is why any attempt to explain later changes is bound to remain speculative. That being said, during the decade that the Malaysian state produced these three versions it had not only intensified efforts at bureaucratic Islamization but was also facing and responding to increased international competition that challenged Malaysia's claims to economic and institutional hegemony in global halal affairs. The 2009 modifications to *MS 1500* may be, at least in part, related to these broader trends.

Technically, the same parties responsible for the 2004 version—the two committees and the secretariat—also conducted the 2009 revisions. But the membership of these committees further expanded to include additional state agencies.[60] While *MS 1500:2000* required the cooperation of about twenty public and private bodies, the 2009 document was produced by about thirty state departments and agencies, which indicates that the political authority was attempting to address a greater variety of concerns and interests.

Like the 2004 version, *MS 1500:2009* contained some noticeable changes, in both religious and practical matters. On the former, one interesting addition was made to the definition of Sharia law. The 2009 authors inserted the following sentence before repeating the 2004 passage that mentions the four Sunni legal schools and acknowledges the political authority's role in legal interpretation: "*Shariah* law is the orders of Allah which relate to the action of the people who are being accountable (*mukallaf*) by obligation, option or *al wadh'u*."[61] This potentially significant addition reminds readers that the standard is ultimately based on God's wishes, despite variations in different legal interpretations and the political authority's role in their enforcement. The international standards formulated by the OIC/SMIIC and the GCC also contain similar wording (see below).

Regarding slaughter, only minor differences exist between the 2004 and 2009 guidelines. *MS 1500:2009* recommends that slaughter should take place while the slaughterer is facing the direction of Mecca, which enhances the ritualistic aspect of the process.[62] It also acknowledges the acceptability of alternative forms of tasmiyya ("Bismillah" and "Allah al-akbar" in addition to "Bismillah al-rahman ar-rahim").[63] Importantly, the 2009 document requires slaughterers to have certificates of their professional credentials "issued by a competent authority,"[64] which indicates further bureaucratization between 2004 and 2009 or the influence of other international standards requiring similar documents. With regard to aquatic animals, the document forbids the consumption of those that "live in *najs* or [are] intentionally and/or continually fed with *najs*,"[65] a condition that is not mentioned in earlier versions but does appear in the OIC/SMIIC and GCC formulations.

A major difference between the 2004 and 2009 versions is that the latter lists no instructions for the mechanical slaughter of poultry. Although the document provides no reason for this omission, the implication is clear: despite widespread concerns about the halal status of mechanical slaughter, the process does not constitute any actual or potential problem for the 2009 authors so long as those involved in poultry slaughter observe general halal slaughter requirements described in the text. This is a lenient position compared to other international standards and may have enhanced the standard's global appeal.

Perhaps the most important change in *MS 1500:2009* is the discussion of the three subtopics listed in the text as "3.2 Premises," "3.6 Storage, transportation, display, sale and servings of halal food," and "3.7 Packaging, labelling and advertising."[66] The 2000 and 2004 documents do not list details about the premises (including buildings and land) appropriate for halal food production, nor do they specify very elaborate transportation, sale, or advertisement requirements. But *MS 1500:2009* specifies that the premises in which halal food production takes place should be structured so as to prevent any form of contamination by nonhalal and nonhygienic substances. They should facilitate proper sanitation, prevent pest infestation, and allow for appropriate supervision of product flow during production and processing. In a similar fashion, halal food should be completely separated from nonhalal substances in every phase of transportation, storage, and sale processes: all vehicles and storage spaces should be dedicated to halal food. Advertisements for halal food items should neither be misleading nor contradict Islamic legal principles—for example, by displaying indecent elements. Thus, if the 2004 document aimed at enhancing the religious credentials of the standard in relative terms, the 2009 formulation appears to be intent on facilitating the most comprehensive and detailed technical application of halal requirements within industrial food production, transportation, and marketing. Here again, the correspondence with other halal international standards, particularly the OIC guidelines, is noticeable.

Overall, and from a historical perspective, *MS 1500:2009* reveals how halal notions have evolved from the Prophet's time to our age of industrial capitalist food production. Compared to the brief and seemingly straightforward instructions in the Quran, the latest version of the Malaysian Standard is quite long and defines halal compliance as a complex task, relevant to almost all stages in the food chain and requiring constant technical and bureaucratic supervision, industrial regulation, and enforcement.[67] In the twenty-first century, the standard makes the state an essential component of proper public and religious order. In other words, the document legitimizes the state's involvement in every aspect of its (Muslim) citizens' lives.

Table 6.1 provides a shorthand comparative depiction of the changes in *MS 1500* over time. Each column in the table indicates how a particular version of the standard is different compared to the previous version. Thus, in order to appreciate how *MS 1500:2009* evolved from *MS 1500:2000* readers should consider the variations not only between the 2009 and 2004 versions but also between the 2004 and 2000 versions.

Competing International Standards

OIC/SMIIC 1:2011

The *OIC/SMIIC 1:2011: General Guidelines on Halal Food* (hereafter *SMIIC 1*) represents an international alternative to *MS 1500:2009*.[68] The SMIIC (Standards and Metrology Institute for Islamic Countries), composed of thirty-three member and three observer states as of late 2017, is a subsidiary of the OIC, which has fifty-seven member states and is thus the second largest international organization after the United Nations. A founding member of the OIC, Malaysia was involved in the production of an earlier document

Table 6.1.   Variations in Subsequent Versions of *MS 1500*

	MS 1500:2004 compared to MS 1500:2000	MS 1500:2009 compared to MS 1500:2004
Length	Longer, more detailed	Longer, more detailed
Authors	Greater number of state agencies among authors Religious agencies better represented No industry representatives	Greater number of state agencies among authors
Definition of Sharia	Includes reference to state's authority to interpret and enforce law	"Sharia" represents God's will, first and foremost
Technical variations	Emphasis on food hygiene, safety, sanitation; concerns over contamination GMOs are nonhalal	Additional clauses on premises, storage, transportation, display, sale, packaging, labeling, and advertising Call for further bureaucratization of halal regulations and enforcement (e.g., slaughterers' credentials)
Religious characteristics	Emphasis on religious aspects of halal rules Emphasis on halal ritualism (regarding slaughter in particular) Distinctions among degrees of religious (im)purity Detailed, religiously prescribed purification techniques Alcoholic beverages are najis	Minor elaborations on ritual procedures
Stunning and mechanical slaughter	More circumspect toward pre-slaughter stunning and mechanized slaughter of poultry	No reference to mechanical slaughter of poultry
Overall	Holistic, bureaucratized depiction of technical *and* religious procedures	Better alignment with international food standards and codices

(issued in 2009) called "OIC Standards—General Guidelines on Halal Food," which constituted a reference document for *SMIIC 1* (issued in 2011); the two documents have significant similarities. However, Malaysia did not have a seat on the Technical Committee on Halal Food Issues (TC1) that developed *SMIIC 1*.[69] TC1 included Pakistan and several Arab and African nations, notably representatives from Algeria, Cameroon, Egypt, Gabon, Gambia, Iran, Jordan, Libya, Morocco, Saudi Arabia, Senegal, Sudan, Tunisia, Turkey, and

UAE. Four countries—Azerbaijan, Bangladesh, Bosnia and Herzegovina, and Mauritania—had observer status.[70]

MS 1500:2009 and *SMIIC 1* resemble one other in many ways. The two documents serve identical functions: they simplify and bureaucratize halal food requirements in a comprehensive manner. The simplification effort is evident in the way each document brushes over regional, historical, and theological variations in order to make halal instructions practical and easy to follow for consumers and industry actors. And here again, the bureaucratization drive reflects a desire to apply halal requirements to every possible link in the industrial food chain. By simplifying the historical and theological complexity of halal considerations, the documents can seamlessly integrate halal measures and procedures into industrial production. Also, both contain information and prescriptions on a wide variety of topics, ranging from the sources of halal food, to rules of slaughter, attributes of tools and machinery used for food processing, processing lines, handling, transportation, storage, and labeling.

But the two documents differ in significant ways. The first is in how each defines Sharia or "Islamic Rules." *MS 1500:2009* recognizes madhhab-based differences and the political authority's role in the interpretation of law. But *SMIIC 1* overlooks such complications and defines "Islamic Rules" as "what ALLAH Legislates for Muslims which derive its rules from the Holy Qur'an, and the honorable Prophet Muhammad (peace be upon him), practices (Sunnah)."[71] This simple formulation rhetorically elevates the status of the document as a direct tool of God's will and ignores any complications associated with the articulation and enforcement of Islamic law.[72] It is not surprising that the document fails to mention madhhab distinctions, since OIC nations represent all possible madhhab and sectarian affiliations. Also, given that the OIC is an international body comprising fifty-seven countries, the document could not privilege a single political authority's interpretation of Islamic law, as the Malaysian Standard does. Consequently, the document is silent about how potential contradictions between its stated prescriptions and national regulations should be resolved.

Both *MS 1500:2009* and *SMIIC 1* open with terms and definitions (Section 2 in *MS 1500*, Section 3 in *SMIIC 1*). The short Section 4 of *SMIIC 1*, which lists all products and services covered in the document ("4.1 Meat and meat products," "4.2 Milk and dairy products," and so on), has no clear counterpart in *MS 1500*. Substantive discussions of "Halal Requirements" commence in Section 3 of *MS 1500:2009* and Section 5 of *SMIIC 1*. The two documents agree on

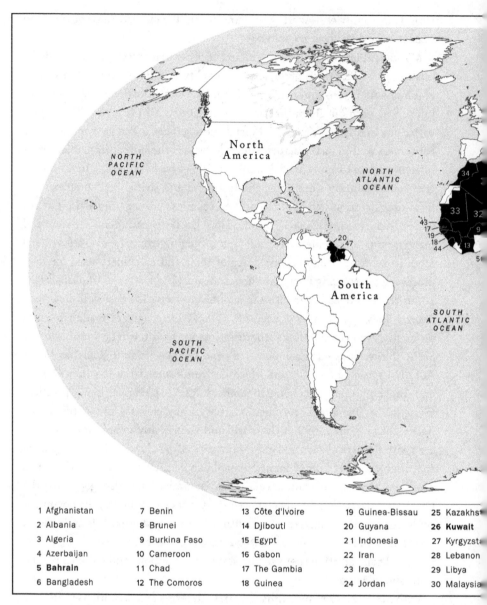

Map 6.1. Map of OIC and GCC Member States

Note: Made with Natural Earth Data.
Sources: For OIC, see http://www.oicun.org/#nogo. For GCC, see http://www.gcc-sg.org/en-us/Pages/default.aspx.

1	Afghanistan	7	Benin	13	Côte d'Ivoire	19	Guinea-Bissau	25	Kazakhst
2	Albania	8	Brunei	14	Djibouti	20	Guyana	26	**Kuwait**
3	Algeria	9	Burkina Faso	15	Egypt	21	Indonesia	27	Kyrgyzst
4	Azerbaijan	10	Cameroon	16	Gabon	22	Iran	28	Lebanon
5	**Bahrain**	11	Chad	17	The Gambia	23	Iraq	29	Libya
6	Bangladesh	12	The Comoros	18	Guinea	24	Jordan	30	Malaysia

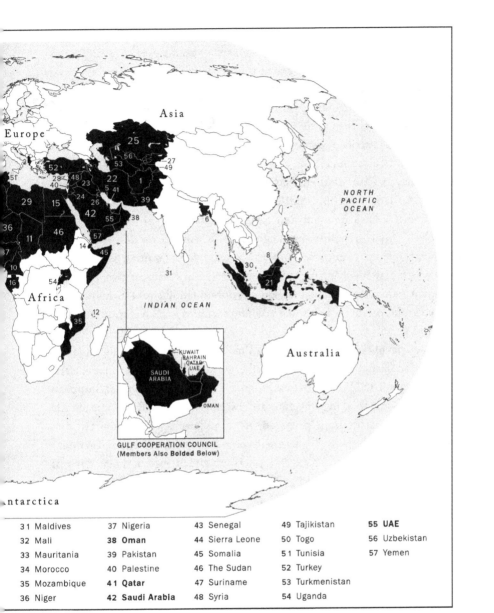

31	Maldives	37	Nigeria	43	Senegal	49	Tajikistan
32	Mali	**38**	**Oman**	44	Sierra Leone	50	Togo
33	Mauritania	39	Pakistan	45	Somalia	51	Tunisia
34	Morocco	40	Palestine	46	The Sudan	52	Turkey
35	Mozambique	**41**	**Qatar**	47	Suriname	53	Turkmenistan
36	Niger	**42**	**Saudi Arabia**	48	Syria	54	Uganda

55	**UAE**
56	Uzbekistan
57	Yemen

what animals are considered halal or haram for consumption.[73] The slaughter requirements described are also largely similar. For example, *MS 1500:2009* and *SMIIC 1* both require slaughterers to be Muslim and to be certified by "a competent authority." Slaughtering tools and equipment should be dedicated to halal slaughter. And the slaughtering act should be performed by sharp blades,[74] skillfully, and in ways that minimize pain to animals.[75] In both documents the act of slaughter is described as severing the animal's trachea, esophagus, carotid arteries, and jugular veins.[76]

The Malaysian Standard emphasizes hygiene and sanitation as important qualities for halal food. But *SMIIC 1* appears to be even more sensitive on this issue: it makes frequent and extended references to food safety. For example, *SMIIC 1* requires preslaughter veterinary inspection of animals and postslaughter examination of the carcass for potential health problems, which may involve laboratory examination of meat samples. Also, the document requires that slaughterhouses contain landing areas where health checks can be performed, carcass-washing facilities with water under pressure, and vessels with hot water and antiseptic liquids for disinfecting and sterilizing slaughter tools. Any dirty animals should be washed and allowed to dry before slaughter, and meat should be chilled and stored in conditions no warmer than 4°C.[77] These prescriptions are consistent with most European and international food hygiene and safety standards, and *SMIIC 1* specifically requires that halal foods be "prepared, processed, packaged, transported, and stored in such a manner that they are in compliance with hygiene and sanitary requirements of Codex CAC/RCP 1 ('Recommended International Code of Practice General Principles of Food Hygiene') and other relevant Codices and other international standards." This statement enhances the impression that *SMIIC 1* is directly linked to renowned and globally recognized best-practice expectations.[78]

In another parallel with European regulations, *SMIIC 1* emphasizes the need for "humane" treatment of animals. For example, the standard instructs that "the slaughtering procedure should not cause torture to animals" and specifies that "if animals have arrived from long distance, they should first be allowed to rest before slaughtering." Also, "animals to be slaughtered shall be led into the slaughter area . . . through a corridor using humane methods. At the end of the corridor that animals are led through [for] slaughtering, it should be ensured that animals waiting in the line are prevented from seeing those being slaughtered, with the help of a curtain or a partition system."[79]

Given *SMIIC 1*'s emphasis on humane slaughter, it is striking that the document discourages preslaughter stunning more strongly than the Malaysian Standard does: for ovines and bovines "all forms of stunning and concussion (loss of consciousness) shall be prohibited."[80] Curiously, however, after this strong statement the document acknowledges that stunning may be "necessary and expedient" in order to "calm down or resist violence by the animal."[81] Thus the reason for stunning is not animal welfare but practical (and economic) efficiency and human safety. And even in such cases, *SMIIC 1* allows stunning only by electroshock. In the case of poultry too, the document first "prohibits" stunning before it offers an exception, permitting electrocution "if it is necessary or expedient."[82] The Malaysian Standard, by comparison, recognizes a wider range of stunning methods for bovines, including what it calls "pneumatic percussive stunner"[83]—that is, nonpenetrating captive-bolt stunners. It also provides more detailed instructions for correct stunning procedures than *SMIIC 1* does, accompanied with useful illustrations.

The issue of preslaughter stunning aside, *SMIIC 1* generally appears to be more engaged with international codices and standards on food matters than the Malaysian Standard, and it attempts to demonstrate that its own prescriptions are largely in tune with prevalent attitudes and sensitivities in those documents. The document's prescriptions for various aspects and phases of the food chain are more detailed and comprehensive than those in *MS 1500:2009*. For example, *SMIIC 1* contains specific sections on milk and dairy products, eggs and egg products, cereal and cereal products, vegetable and animal oils and fats, fruit and vegetables and their products, sugar and confectionery products, honey and its by-products,[84] and dietary supplements, many of which go unmentioned in the Malaysian Standard.

Furthermore—and unlike *MS 1500:2009*—*SMIIC 1* specifically mentions potentially questionable substances such as rennet and gelatin.[85] Also in contrast to the latest version of the Malaysian Standard, *SMIIC 1* considers genetically modified foods permissible so long as they are not derived from nonhalal substances.[86] Following medieval Islamic discussions, *SMIIC 1* describes halal slaughter procedures for hunted animals and what to do with prey captured by hunting dogs and birds.[87] The Malaysian Standard does not. The document further promotes automation and the use of rail systems to lift and move animals for slaughter, which makes it easier to handle the meat and perform hygiene procedures.[88] In addition, while halal requirements in the mechanical slaughter of poultry are addressed in *SMIIC 1*,[89] *MS 1500:2009* is completely silent on the issue, even though an earlier version of the document (*MS 1500:2004*) contains an entire appendix on the topic.

Finally, *SMIIC 1* includes almost verbatim the Malaysian Standard's specifications regarding ritual cleansing for premises previously used for nonhalal slaughter and its pronouncements on "liquid and objects discharged from the orifices of any human beings or animals."[90] While the direction of influence between *SMIIC 1* and the Malaysian Standard in technical and practical matters is unclear, in religious matters it is likely from the latter to the former since *MS 1500:2009* largely replicates the instructions in *MS 1500:2004*.

Overall, and like the Malaysian Standard, *SMIIC 1* represents the hybridity within Islamic modernity. Ritualistic prescriptions, such as turning the head of the animal toward the direction of Mecca during slaughter, are immediately followed by suggestions about how to reduce an animal's suffering (e.g., by not keeping it raised by its hind legs for a long period) and instructions about how to disinfect the slaughter equipment and lines according to scientific methods. The document aims to specify and enforce expectations that originate from very different sources. On the one hand, the text claims to represent the will of God. On the other, it prescribes good manufacturing practices as determined in codices and regulations formulated by nonreligious bodies. Moreover, by treating religious prescriptions as technical requirements, similar to those that apply, for example, to hygiene or sanitation, it too brings religion's guidelines down to earth.

GSO 05/FDS/2055—1:2014: Halal Products[91]

The GSO, the Standardization Organization of the Gulf Cooperation Council, is composed of the national standard bodies of the GCC member states: Bahrain, Kuwait, Oman, Qatar, Saudi Arabia, and the United Arab Emirates. In 2014 the GCC released a new version of its halal standardization: *GSO 2055*, a revision of an earlier 2009 version. *GSO 2055* or the Gulf Standard was prepared under the coordinating direction of the United Arab Emirates.

Like *SMIIC 1*, *GSO 2055* provides a seemingly simple characterization of "Sharea," which it defines as the revelation that Muhammad received "in relation to the beliefs, sentiments and acts of the ordered, whether conclusive or presumptive."[92] The document contains no reference to specific schools of Islamic law, likely because different legal schools prevail among the GCC nations: for example, while Oman's population is predominantly Ibadi, the Kuwaitis are majority Sunni-Maliki, and the Saudis are generally Hanbali.[93] *GSO 2055* also resembles *SMIIC 1* in that it contains few references to local governments that interpret and enforce divine law. Consequently, and perhaps in the spirit of medieval Islamic juristic rulings, the document gives the impression that its prescriptions, both religious and technical, are unimpeded representations of God's will.

Textually, the document is reminiscent of *MS 1500:2009* and *SMIIC 1* in its aspiration to be comprehensive. It requires that halal regulations be followed "in all phases of [the] food chain," including "receipt, preparation, packaging, labeling, transportation, distribution, storage, display and Halal food service."[94] At the same time, in certain respects the Gulf Standard is less comprehensive. Although halal food should be "devoid from Najasah (impurity) contamination that is forbidden by Islamic rules,"[95] *GSO 2055* does not elaborate on what "Najasah" entails, nor does it try to differentiate degrees of impurity. Also, the Gulf Standard agrees with its Malaysian counterpart that facilities and places of service converted to halal food production and processing "should go through cleaning processes in accordance with Islamic rules before commencing Halal production,"[96] but unlike *MS 1500:2009*, it does not explain these rules.[97] Finally, compared to both the Malaysian and OIC/*SMIIC* Standards, the Gulf Standard provides less detailed instructions for acceptable slaughter and stunning practices.

While *MS 1500:2009* aims to demonstrate the relevance of halal considerations for humans' physical and spiritual well-being and also gives instructions for implementing halal compliance at every phase of the industrial food chain, *GSO 2055* says very little along these lines. Although it states that halal food "should not contain any toxic substances and hazardous pollutants which may be considered harmful to health,"[98] it makes no direct reference to hygiene or sanitation. In fact, the document never explicitly states that hygiene should be regarded as an aspect of halal food preparation. In this regard, *GSO 2055* seems reticent to expand on the health aspects of halal, and when it does, it does this indirectly by requiring compliance with separate guidelines.[99] In terms of halal compliance in various stages of food production and processing, the Gulf Standard acknowledges the importance of halal and nonhalal segregation but does not specify how to accomplish this separation.

More significantly, the three documents also contain some doctrinal inconsistencies, even contradictions. For example, unlike the Malaysian and OIC/ *SMIIC* Standards, the Gulf Standard considers permissible those animals slaughtered according to Jewish and Christian traditions.[100] And while the Malaysian and OIC/SMIIC Standards require slaughter to be performed only by Muslims, *GS 993*, a separate GCC document that *GSO 2055* designates as binding in the slaughter process, acknowledges that the slaughterer could be "kitabi"—that is, Christian or Jewish.[101]

Another important variation arises on the issue of stunning. The Malaysian Standard regards as acceptable preslaughter stunning by electrocution for all animals and by nonpenetrating captive-bolt stunners for bovines. *GS 993* rejects "beating on head or similar action, such as using of bolt shot pistol or nonpenetrative percussion or stunning by carbon dioxide" for all animals.[102] In that sense the Gulf document is closer to *SMIIC 1*. However, while *MS 1500:2009* and *SMIIC 1* permit electrical stunning for poultry via "water bath stunner," *GS 993* categorically forbids the use of electrical stunning "in the case of birds."[103] Finally, *GS 993* states that stunned animals must demonstrate signs of life before their ultimate death by slaughter (such as by making "movements") for their flesh to be considered halal.[104] This point is more consistent with Shafi'i and Hanbali expectations and reflects the opinions of the medieval Hanafi jurists Abu Yusuf and Imam Muhammad. If animals fail to demonstrate these signs, they should be considered carrion.[105] No such precise requirement exists in the Malaysian or OIC/SMIIC Standards, although both state that stunned animals must be alive before slaughter. Regarding the act of slaughter, *GS 993* requires the severing of the animal's trachea, esophagus, and jugular veins, but not the carotid arteries.[106]

There are also a few more minor differences among the documents. While *MS 1500:2009* considers genetically modified food (and food that contains genetically modified substances) as nonhalal, the Gulf and OIC/SMIIC Standards do not, as long as genetic modification does not involve association with nonhalal substances.[107] Also, while *GSO 2055* declares permissible the consumption of any aquatic animals, defined as animals "which live in the water and cannot survive outside," it requires "all kinds of fish with scales, shrimp and fish egg of fish with scales including their byproducts" to be clearly labeled "scaled fish," and "all other aquatic animals including their byproducts" to be labeled "non-scaled fish."[108] A similar requirement exists in the OIC/SMIIC document but not in the Malaysian Standard. Finally, unlike *SMIIC 1* but similar to *MS 1500:2009*, the Gulf document makes no reference to the mechanical slaughter of poultry, indicating that its authors tacitly accept this form of slaughter.

Table 6.2 summarizes how *SMIIC 1* and *GSO 2055* differ from *MS 1500:2009* and from each other (if indirectly).

Table 6.2. International Halal Standards in Comparison to *MS 1500:2009* (Only Differences Are Listed)

	SMIIC 1 compared to *MS 1500:2009*	*GSO 2055* compared to *MS 1500:2009*
Authors	International committee in which interests of various states are represented	Regional, multistate committee composed of the representatives of Gulf states
Definition of Sharia	Simplified definition. No reference to school-based variations	Simplified definition. No reference to school-based variations
Products covered	Greater variety of products included in the standard	
Technical variations	Emphasis on food hygiene, safety, sanitation, transportation, labeling rules, etc. GMOs are acceptable Aquatic animals with scales should be explicitly labeled as such Emphasis on humane treatment of animals (except in regulations regarding stunning)	Less emphasis on food hygiene and safety as aspects of halal GMOs are acceptable Aquatic animals with scales should be explicitly labeled as such
Religious variations	Degrees of religious impurity receive no attention	Degrees of religious impurity receive no attention Lacks information on methods of religious purification
Slaughter (including stunning and mechanical slaughter)	Only electroshock may be used for stunning. Mechanized slaughter acceptable Contains prescriptions about hunting	Jews and Christians may perform slaughter Lacks detailed information on acceptable slaughter practices Carotid arteries of nonpoultry need not be severed during slaughter Electroshock allowed only for ovines and bovines No stunning allowed for poultry Animals should demonstrate clear signs of life after stunning.
International appeal	Explicit attempts of alignment with international regulations and codices	

To conclude, a summary of key findings in this chapter may be warranted. A comparison of the three successive versions of the Malaysian Standard has revealed that between 2000 and 2009 the standard appropriated a more overtly religious character as it adopted a variety of ritualistic practices associated with classical halal traditions. During this period, the standard's technical complexity also became more pronounced, and it became increasingly more comprehensive in its coverage of different phases of the food chain. In a way, the Malaysian Standard paralleled the state's simultaneous attempts to effect Islamic modernization and to garner political and economic influence in the Islamic world: the state has steadily burnished its Islamic credentials but has also invested in scientific and technological endeavors that serve its political/ideological vision and interests.

Thus *MS 1500:2009*, the latest version of the standard to date, is remarkable in that it aims to mesh a plurality of concerns in a comprehensive manner. Like other halal standards (if in different degrees), this text mixes attitudes toward food and food production drawn from disparate historical and contemporary sources. The document purposely erases the boundaries between ritualistic and scientific realms and generates a flattened, horizontal plane of "rules," devoid of epistemological peaks and valleys. In seeking to formulate a single set of regulations that fulfills both spiritual and material functions, the Malaysian Standard can appear monodimensional, deliberately avoiding any and all historical complexity.

A comparison of the three most current international halal standards—*MS 1500:2009, SMIIC 1*, and *GSO 2055*—reveals similarities in how they offer comprehensive and appealing guidelines for the thriving global halal business sector. Significant variations, however, signal the plurality of opinions and inclinations among their authors. For example, all three reflect the religious, legal, and historical characteristics of their backers. Also, while *SMIIC 1* sought a more seamless integration between halal standards and internationally accepted hygiene and industrial good practice, *GSO 2055* was less ambitious in expanding the meaning of halal to include hygiene and food safety. *MS 1500:2009* appeared to be particularly invested in promoting both the religious credentials and the technical expertise and assiduousness of Malaysia's governing bodies. Overall, the existence of multiple halal standards with unique characteristics and preferences is indicative of the relative persistence of plurality embedded within traditional Islamic jurisprudence amidst broader (and potentially contradictory) trends in the modern period.

Official standards, however, are only one modern discourse on halal food. Other discourses, less official yet equally modern, include the wholesome and sophisticated aspects of halal eating and the complications of halal manufacturing processes.

MANUFACTURED PRODUCTS

Since the late twentieth century, producers of halal foodstuffs, beverages, pharmaceuticals, and other items have targeted a booming Muslim population, recognizing that younger generations have greater purchasing power, a keener awareness of their religious identity, and a growing desire to articulate their faith. At the same time, a fast-paced lifestyle and a rise, globally, in the numbers of working women have increased the demand for culinary shortcuts. Packaged products such as canned, boxed, or frozen foods, baby foods, snacks, pasta, cheeses, soups, spice blends, condiments, stocks, and nonalcoholic beverages represent convenience, tastiness, and even status, but they have also raised an array of questions about halal compliance. The key relationship in this new marketplace is no longer between the consumer and her butcher; rather, she increasingly relies on her supermarket—and often, by extension, a multinational corporation and a halal certifier—to verify each product's ingredients and ascertain its precise halalness.

This tendency has emerged in the context of an upsurge in manufactured food consumption. A 2015 report predicted that the global packaged food market was on target to reach $3.03 trillion by 2020, and Asia-Pacific (which includes populous majority-Muslim countries like Pakistan, Indonesia, and Malaysia) represents the fastest-growing region.[1] In the Middle East and North Africa, the same industry was valued at $41.1 billion in 2014 and forecast to grow to $52.4 billion by 2019.[2] One study estimates that in 2015, OIC countries spent about 33 percent of their total food trade expenditures (worth about $61 billion) on importing processed and manufactured food, and only 19 percent on importing animals and animal products.[3] Of note here, the corporate giant Nestlé has become the global leader of processed halal foods— including marquee products like Maggi chicken bouillon and Nido powdered milk—although the market has also drawn several multinational firms such as Wal-Mart, Carrefour, Kroger, and Metro that have become major purveyors of halal products.[4] But this prevalence of packaged foods has raised concerns about halal authenticity. To make products stable, hygienic, aesthetic, and/or palatable, many manufacturers add natural or artificial preservatives, flavors, and colors, and such additives have complicated the application and understanding of halal rules. Some producers have solicited fatwas to support their ingredients or products, although other religious scholars or certifying bodies might dispute their validity. Because there are no universal halal standards, concerns about how to make the most halal-compliant products have widened.

Contemporary debates over halal authenticity are consequences of food-manufacturing processes that are, like animal slaughter, increasingly industrialized.[5] Consumers who may follow strict religious dietary rules and others, including vegans and vegetarians, feel more and more uneasy that animal-derived substances, such as gelatin, infuse countless food items. In the context of halal practices and interpretations, these unknown ingredients have prompted the need for a new type of "halal literacy," as Middle East scholar Faegheh Shirazi calls it, one that includes an awareness of how to read, decipher, and judge labels.[6] One goal of this chapter then, is to explore some of the manufactured foodstuffs that Muslims consume each day and see how specific additives, preservatives, derivatives, stabilizers, and by-products can present complicated issues for ordinary buyers seeking to demystify food labels.

A related question involves foodstuffs that contain small traces of haram or najis substances. Alcohol naturally occurs in things like bread or fruit juices and can also be used as a carrier in flavorings like vanilla or almond extract. It might be part of the production process before it is distilled out of, say, a nonalcoholic beer or wine. What is the tiniest percentage of alcohol that is acceptable within a manufactured product? How is the halalness of such products determined, and how have colas marketed as "halal" or beers labeled as "zero-alcohol" been designed, both in terms of their ingredients and branding, to meet demands for a more Western and halal lifestyle?

Before delving into these issues, this chapter explains two classical Islamic legal concepts: istihala and istihlak, both of which have played critical roles in determining (or obscuring) the halal compliance of varied foods manufactured in modern times.

Istihala

Istihala derives from the Arabic root *h-a-l* or *h-w-l*, meaning "to change or be transformed." It can be translated, therefore, as the process by which one substance is fundamentally converted into a new one.[7] More specifically in the context of halal food, istihala describes the alteration of an impure (najis) material into a pure (tahir) and therefore consumable one. When discussed by medieval Muslim jurists, istihala was applied to a limited number of examples, like the conversion of wine into vinegar, or bones into dust. Many jurists believed, for instance, that carrion hide could be purified into tahir leather through the tanning process, which fundamentally alters its nature. The process could also apply to the case of soap made out of animal fats derived from carrion or najis animals.[8] In the medieval literature, there are disagreements about how istihala takes place, but it could occur through burning, charring, and composting, among other means. In the modern period, and for the purposes of later discussions, Muslims have used this term to describe the human-caused biochemical modification of varied foods.[9]

At the heart of jurisprudential debates is the following question: if the starting product is suspicious (mashbuh) or impure (najis), can the end product still be deemed pure (tahir) and therefore halal? The answer varies considerably among different legal schools—and often within the same school as well—because jurists look at two separate issues: the legality of the istihala process in and of itself, and the purity (and therefore halal status) of the resulting product. In this regard, most classical discussions reference a hadith-based example of wine turning into vinegar: can the resulting vinegar—ostensibly a different substance—be consumed by Muslims even though it derives from wine? All Sunni and Shiite legal schools agree that if wine was completely left alone and then turned into vinegar by itself, the resulting vinegar can be ingested.[10] However, if human intervention—for instance, the addition of salt or onions, or moving the wine from a sunny to a shady place—resulted in wine turning into vinegar, then both the human intervention and the vinegar's consumption are disputed.

Among Sunni jurists, Hanafis are the most liberal in their approval of human-induced istihala and the resulting vinegar as halal. The Prophet Muhammad, they note, enjoyed vinegar as a condiment and made no distinction as to whether that vinegar was produced by a natural transformation or by human intervention. His praise of vinegar was categorical.[11] The majority opinion in the Maliki school condemns human-caused istihala, but most Malikis allow the consumption of vinegar produced through this process.[12] The Shafi'i and Hanbali schools also oppose human-induced istihala, but individual scholars associated with these schools hold conflicting views about the resulting vinegar.[13] For most Shiite jurists, as for most Hanafi interpreters, istihala can fully transform a najis substance into a tahir one so long as its original najis essence has been extinguished or completely altered.[14]

So how does the medieval juristic tradition influence modern discussions? The extent to which the example of wine turning into vinegar can be applied to other foods or materials has been widely debated, even though the istihala concept rarely makes an appearance in global documents defining halal standards. But as will be discussed, Muslim juridical experts and religious bodies have recently invoked istihala, primarily in the context of food additives and medicines derived—through a biological or chemical process—from questionable animal sources, and in the manufacturing of one of the most ubiquitous animal-derived substances: gelatin.

Istihlak

In Arabic, istihlak (root h-l-k) is often translated as "consumption." In discussions of food purity, however, it refers to the dissolution of a small amount of an impure substance (e.g., blood) into a much larger amount of pure substance (e.g., water). That is, the pure water "consumes" or absorbs the impure blood. With reference to food, istihlak arises when trace amounts of a prohibited product—for instance, blood or alcohol—make their way into a consumable item. So while istihala refers to the biochemical transformation of one material into another, istihlak deals with the degree of contamination of a pure material with an impure one. Muslim jurists addressed these questions in separate terms.[15]

For most jurists, the istihlak of a tiny amount of impure material within a larger pure one is acceptable, so long as the small impurity does not change the color, taste, or smell of the clean substance. In determining cleanliness (and usage or intake), the relative size and makeup of the clean substance matters. The thing jurists most commonly offer as an example of a clean substance is water. Here, and in contrast to istihala, Hanafis are the most restrictive. A majority argues that the clean substance must be substantially large, roughly the size of a body of water that is at least forty-eight square meters. Seawater, rivers, and ponds, for instance, are the cleanest. For Hanbalis and Shafi'is, if the clean substance is running or flowing water, then no amount of impurity could alter its cleanliness. Otherwise, within a body of still water, the size of the clean substance must amount to at least *qullatayn*, the equivalent of two clay urns commonly used to store water. The exact volume of this measure is in dispute, but some modern estimates suggest that qullatayn is somewhere between 160 and 200 liters.[16] Shiite jurists have a similar view regarding the possibility of istihlak, which for them depends on whether the water is flowing, or, in the case of still water, its size.[17] For Malikis, the concern is not the size of the pure substance but whether the unclean substance has altered the taste, smell, or color of the clean one. If not, then the clean material can be used or consumed.[18]

Most of these examples focus on water, and some Hanafi, Shafi'i, and Hanbali jurists argue that what is valid for water may not necessarily apply to other substances. Clean water can easily reveal impurities. But other substances (e.g., a sugary drink or fruit juice) may hide slight changes in taste, smell, or color. Some Hanafi scholars go as far as to argue that the rule is only applicable to water. If nonwater substances are contaminated in the slightest, they should be declared impure and najis. Conversely, other jurists argue that the rule for water can be applied to other circumstances.[19]

These questions have resurfaced because trace amounts of alcohol and other nonhalal substances can be found in popular soda drinks, juices, "nonalcoholic" brews, medicines, and food flavorings. However, for modern religious scholars, producers, and consumers seeking to determine the halal compliance of diverse food products, historical discussions of istihlak provide diverse and sometimes contradictory answers.

Gelatin and Animal-Derived Food Additives

Today, interpretations of istihala are applied to common food additives and preservatives—most important, gelatin. Gelatin is a protein extracted from animal or fish collagen that comes from skin, hide, connective tissue, and bones. As a food and binding agent, it has existed for over 2,000 years, but it became commercially available only in the late nineteenth century with the rise of the industrialized food industry, where it is used as a thickener and stabilizer.[20] In processed foods, gelatin is omnipresent and difficult to avoid. Few people would guess, for instance, that fruit juices and sports drinks are often clarified with gelatin or that popular dairy products like low fat butter, yogurt, ice cream, sour cream, and cottage cheese may be stabilized with gelatin—or that gelatin is often used in the process of clarifying wine or beer, before final bottling, to remove proteins, cloudiness, or yeasts. Most countries do not require manufacturers to label the source of their gelatin—that is, whether it was derived from pigs, cattle, poultry, and/or fish. Although more expensive (and slightly less effective) vegetable-based substitutes like agar-agar, carrageen, pectin, and gums have been made available, nearly all gelatins produced and used today come from nonvegetable sources.

The question of gelatin's consumption and its potential conflict with religious dietary rules was first confronted by the American Orthodox Jewish community in the 1930s. At that time, Orthodox rabbis in the United States were asked to determine the kashrut status of unfamiliar manufactured foods: soft drinks, packaged cakes, and cookies that contained a catalogue of organically derived substances like glycerin or gelatin. Until the 1950s, many accepted a medieval interpretation of a rabbinic concept comparable to istihala called *ponim chadashos* (roughly translated as "chemical transformation"); ponim chadashos determined that unclean food products transformed into a new and unrecognizable form could be deemed kosher. In particular, they argued, industrially produced gelatin—even if it might have derived from non-kosher-slaughtered animals—was chemically and completely altered into an edible kosher substance. Later some rabbinic experts challenged this ruling. Their "rethinking of kosher law," according to food historian Roger Horowitz, showed that stringent religious interpretations were becoming more prevalent, and in time many Orthodox Jewish experts rejected the consumption of commercially manufactured gelatin and products containing it.[21]

In later years Muslim populations grappled with similar questions as manufactured food products containing gelatin became more prevalent in non-Western industrializing nations. How might Muslims follow halal rules with the full knowledge that most gelatin originated from porcine or non-zabiha animal sources? In 2013, it was estimated that close to 40 percent of the world's gelatin came from pigs; most of the remainder came from conventionally slaughtered mammals or poultry. In that year, the world's total production of gelatin was 373.3 kilo tons; Europe—particularly Germany, Italy, France, and Spain—consumed 147.5 kilo tons.[22] Small amounts of fish skins, which are more expensive, have been used to make gelatin, but they are often mixed with porcine and bovine by-products. This situation has led some Muslim leaders and governments to call for stricter labeling standards and for efforts to produce gelatin following religiously sanctioned methods.

For contemporary Muslim scholars, any gelatin derived from vegetables, zabiha or halal-compliant slaughter, and seafood is considered permissible. However, Muslims have debated whether the chemical and industrial processes that generate gelatin from pigs or carrion could render this colorless, odorless, and tasteless product halal. Some suggest that gelatin production represents istihala and therefore even gelatin from pigs can be deemed as acceptable and halal. But others argue that the transformation of pig or any non-zabiha cartilage and bones is insufficient to fully alter the molecular and genetic structures of the original najis substance.[23]

As in the Orthodox Jewish case, opinions on gelatin's consumption have become progressively conservative. In 1995, a meeting of the Kuwait-based Islamic Organization for Medical Sciences acknowledged the effectiveness of istihala and declared that gelatin "made of unclean animals' bones, skin and tendons is clean and permissible for consumption."[24] Iraq's respected Shiite scholar Ayatollah Sistani has also offered a flexible approach toward most commercially produced gelatin whose origins are unknown, deeming the final substance fully altered and therefore halal.[25] However, following the more recent trajectory of stricter halal interpretations, there are heightened demands for rigorousness in gelatin production and consumption. For instance, a group of Malaysian researchers recently concluded that istihala could not apply to gelatin derived from haram sources, since during the industrial process the core molecular composition of the original product (e.g., pig skin or bones) remains intact. Most gelatins are therefore unclean. IFANCA, the largest American halal certifying agency, agrees and warns that since gelatin is "generally derived from pig skins and cattle bones . . . it must be avoided."[26]

The Turkish halal certification body GİMDES (Gıda ve İhtiyaç Maddeleri Denetleme ve Sertifikalandırma Araştırmaları Derneği, or Association of Inspection and Certification Research for Food and Material Needs)[27] has also noted that gelatin cannot be purified through istihala and that any products made from nonhalal gelatins are unfit for consumption.[28] In 2008, GİMDES further warned consumers that a German drug company that lists gelatin as a common ingredient in its European products had altered its labels, erasing gelatin from labels on medications exported to the Turkish market.[29] This incident raised the question of how Muslims might deal with gelatin's pervasiveness not only in food (which one can likely avoid) but also in medications (which are often a life-saving necessity). Many drug tablets and capsules, in addition to some injectable medications, contain some type of animal-derived substance or gelling agent.[30]

Currently, few Muslim legal experts would object to medications that may contain nonhalal products, especially in the absence of halal-compliant alternatives and in cases of necessity. However, to meet growing demands in the food and medical fields, Islamic organizations, governments, and private businesses have also tried to promote halal gelatin production.[31] In 2011, Malaysia's Halal Industry Development Corp started exploring the use of palm oil as a gelatin source, and in 2012, Malaysian and Saudi Arabian universities began to investigate gelatin derived from camels.[32] Some progress has also been made through collaboration with commercial manufactures. In 2015, one of the oldest and largest producers of gelatin, the French-originated Rousselot Pharmaceutical Gelatines, announced that through its exclusively fish-skin product labeled "Rousselot 275 FG," it had "integrated cultural differences and diverse needs around the globe to provide gelatines that are Kosher or Halal approved by the competent authorities."[33]

Overall, though, these initiatives have yet to make a visible dent in a market heavily dominated with porcine and/or non-zabiha sources. It is likely that this area will see major growth in the coming years; it is less certain how rapidly the industry will develop to meet increased consumer demands and more restrictive guidelines. For now, the halal gelatin output is only a tiny fraction of the global production of this omnipresent additive.[34] Muslims living in non-Muslim countries have often turned to products containing gelatin labeled "kosher," which, despite their questionable status among some Orthodox Jews, are generally deemed an acceptable substitute in the absence of halal correlates.[35] The reliance on kosher products in diaspora settings, out of seeming necessity, is a reminder of the occasional overlaps between current kosher and halal interpretations even if the same substance might raise very different concerns for Jewish and Muslim scholars as related to chemical composition, religious food regulations, and modernization.[36]

Debates over gelatin have extended to other common additives in packaged foods. For example, lecithin, an emulsifier or a fatty substance, can be derived from plant sources (especially soy) but also from egg yolks and animal parts. Used to homogenize water and oil, it is often mixed into chocolates, breads, baked goods, candy bars, cooking sprays, and margarines as well as some medications. Other emulsifiers derived from plants or animals are mono- and diglycerides found in shortening, baked goods, and peanut butter. L-cysteine, an amino acid that is frequently added to commercial breads and used as a "dough conditioner," is most often made from mammal or human hair and is therefore not usually halal.[37] Likewise, carmine, a red dye frequently used in food colorings and baked goods (e.g., red velvet cake) that is obtained from the dried coccus cacti insect, is haram. Lipase and pepsin are frequently extracted from pig organs, so unless they are shown to be vegan, many argue, they should be considered haram.[38]

Various certification agencies have worked hard to raise red flags about all of these products and enzymes, probiotics, amino acids, food colorings, sweeteners, and flavorings.[39] With these additives as with gelatin, organizations like IFANCA take the most conservative position—deemed as the most suitable common denominator—and prescribe avoidance of anything questionable (mashbuh) and the consumption of only those products whose origins are known to be halal.[40] On its website, IFANCA has also prepared a comprehensive list of doubtful ingredients to help Muslim consumers make more informed decisions.[41] Meanwhile, in 2017, Malaysia's JAKIM launched Verify Halal, an app that helps consumers verify the halal status of numerous food products.[42] Muslim shoppers in the United States, on the other hand, can use a variety of phone apps—like Scan Halal or Halal Food SN—to scan barcodes at their local supermarkets to determine an item's permissibility (halal, mashbuh, or haram).[43]

Chocolate

The global confectioneries market, particularly for chocolate, is growing rapidly, with rising sales in Islamic countries like Saudi Arabia, the United Arab Emirates, and Indonesia.[44] As with other markets, Malaysia is becoming one of the biggest players, with its 2016 overseas trade of cocoa-related products reaching $1.3 billion.[45] For consumers and manufacturers alike, the halal compliance of chocolate, therefore, has become more and more significant and raises questions tied to gelatin, animal-derived emulsifiers, and/or the potential presence of alcohol. Given the increased global demand for chocolate, major international producers have been eager to certify their products as halal—even those containing gelatin.[46]

In 2014, Cadbury, one of the world's largest chocolate manufacturers, came under fire after the Malaysian Health Ministry discovered pork DNA in some of its popular treats. The company immediately withdrew the offending chocolates and assured consumers that other Cadbury products sold in the country are definitively halal.[47] Perhaps to gain an edge over its rivals, Belgian chocolatier Guylian emphasizes that its products are made under the supervision of the EuroHalal Office of Control and Halal Certification and are free of any "haram or questionable (mashbouh) ingredients."[48] But to compete more directly and to corner a more elite and local market, as early as 2007 a London-based company called Ummah Foods launched its halal line of chocolates, which is free of animal fats and alcohol but also relies on no alcohol in cleaning factory machines and even uses animal-fat-free glue for its wrappers.[49] Not only has the company chosen to brand itself with the name Ummah, a word that traditionally refers to the broader Islamic community, but the company's manufacturing provisions also appear to comply with some of the strictest national and international halal standards.

Finally, in dealing with misconceptions about the ingredient known as chocolate liquor or cocoa liquor, IFANCA and various other certifying agencies have clarified that despite the use of the word "liquor," this substance—found in chocolate candies, bars, and cakes—is nothing more than alcohol-free ground-up cocoa nibs. This ingredient is definitively halal in and of itself, IFANCA has reassured its followers.[50] It should be distinguished, however, from (haram) chocolate truffles, bonbons, and bars made with actual liquor.

Cheese/Rennet

Today, the consumption of cheese provokes equally important but somewhat less heated debates than those plaguing emulsifiers, gelatin, or alcohol. In premodern times, however, cheese may have been the gelatin of its day. Cheese-related concerns for Muslims following halal prescriptions fall into three separate questions. First, was the milk used to make cheese derived from forbidden animals? Second, what is the source of the rennet (Arabic: *infaha*, *minfaha, manafih*) used to coagulate the milk in the cheese production process? Third, was the cheese cured or matured using any haram or questionable products (e.g., alcohol)?

The first question, regarding milk, has historically caused less trouble for Muslim jurists: milk is produced from living mammals, so in general the issue of proper slaughter is moot.[51] But the question of porcine milk has been raised. In some Shiite traditions, the flesh of an animal of halal species known to have nursed on pig milk until maturity, as well as all by-products of that animal, are considered fully haram. The Maliki tradition, on the other hand, explicitly forbids the consumption of pig milk.[52]

Although some have questioned the source of vitamins added to most commercial milks, which could be derived from animal (pork or cattle) emulsifiers, most milk available for consumption in the global market has been deemed halal.[53] So cheese and its halal qualities are mainly judged by the type of rennet used to make it. Rennet is an enzyme derived from the stomachs of suckling calves, pigs, lambs, and goats. After an animal is slaughtered, the stomach is cleaned, sliced, and soaked with salt and vinegar, and the filtered solution is used to coagulate the milk into cheese. In principle, halal rennet comes only from halal-slaughtered animals or from plant or microbial sources. Synthetic rennet can be used and is generally permissible, although it has raised concern among those opposed to genetically engineered or modified food. Among all Muslims, cheese made from pork rennet is absolutely forbidden. If the origin of rennet is fully unknown, however, different Islamic legal traditions have been more flexible toward the resulting cheese. This flexibility has changed in recent years as Muslims have become more rigorous in their halal interpretations.[54]

Some of the same qualms that arose with regard to meat slaughtered by non-kitabi non-Muslims have parallels in rennet and cheese. Among Sunnis, most Hanafis supported the consumption of this type of cheese, yet many (if not all) Hanbali, Maliki, and Shafi'i jurists opposed it. As to rennet and cheese produced by Jews and Christians (and similar to meat), historical trends of acceptance are now giving way to more stringent positions. Also, most premodern Sunni jurists agreed that rennet/cheese whose origin is absolutely unknown is considered mubah, or permissible, but this tendency too may be changing (see Table 7.1).[55]

Shiite scholars reject all meat slaughtered by non-Muslims, including Jews and Christians. But when it comes to rennet/cheese derived from that meat,

Table 7.1. Halal Status of Rennet

Origins of Rennet	Legal Opinion
Permissible animal, slaughtered according to halal principles (zabiha)	Halal for all Sunni and Shiite schools.
Permissible animal, slaughtered by Christians or Jews (kitabis)	Historically, halal among Sunni schools; disputed among Shiites. Recently, more stringent opinions may be emerging among Sunnis.
Permissible animal, killed or slaughtered by non–People of the Book, using nonhalal rules (carrion)	Historically, halal according to Hanafis, haram for Shafi'is and Malikis, disputed among Hanbalis; disputed within various Shiite interpretations. Recently, more stringent opinions may be emerging among Sunnis.
Vegetable	Halal for all Sunni and Shiite schools.
Of unknown origins	Historically, permissible for Sunnis and most Shiites. More recent opinions would classify it as doubtful and, thus, to be avoided.
Impermissible animals (e.g., pig)	Haram among all.[a]

Sources: Based on Salih al-'Awd, *Sina'at al-Ajban al-Haditha wa Hukm Akliha* (Beirut: Dar al-Kutub al- 'Ilmiyya, 2009); Michael Cook, "Magian Cheese: An Archaic Problem in Islamic Law," *Bulletin of the School of Oriental and African Studies* 47, no. 3 (1984): 449–467.

Note: a: One minor opinion holds that it would be acceptable to consume rennet from nonpermissible animals since the rennet undergoes istihala and is transformed into cheese. Even in this view, zabiha-derived rennet would still be preferred if available. See Çayırlıoğlu, *Helal Gıda*, 259–260, 366.

the Shiite position is more complex. Some jurists have suggested that consuming that cheese would be lawful if its origins were unknown. Others have maintained that the origin of any cheese sold in a Muslim-owned market matters little, even if it came from carrion. In a sense, a Muslim seller and his market imbue trust among buyers and denote purity on a questionable product. Today this flexible approach seems to prevail, at least among certain Shiite scholars: Iraq's Ayatollah al-Sistani has ruled that cheese imported by Muslims from non-Muslim countries, whose rennet origins are unknown, is permissible.[56]

It is difficult for modern consumers, particularly those in non-Muslim countries, to verify the origins of rennet, as labels often obscure or omit that information. The recent move toward greater strictness suggests that in navigating food choices, a lack of knowledge should actually produce suspicion and avoidance of the unknown.[57] The latter, some Muslim scholars have argued, should be the standard for pious believers seeking to protect their halal lifestyles, especially in non-Muslim-majority settings.

Recognizing the potential expansion of the halal market, some commercial cheese producers have trumpeted their adherence to different religious or dietary standards. Cabot Corporation in Vermont, for instance, uses vegetarian, kosher, and halal-friendly rennet for most of its cheeses and advertises its IFANCA-certified products as such.[58] A point of confusion arises, however, with regard to cheese rinds. Some artisan cheesemakers "wash" their ripening cheese with alcohol (in lieu of or in addition to a saltwater brine) to develop distinctive bacteria and flavors. In the case of these "drunken" or "stinky" cheeses, as they are often called, Islamic scholars would likely vary in their interpretation. Invoking the concept of istihlak, whether directly or indirectly, many may argue that trace or small amounts of alcohol in cakes, chocolates, cheeses, or medicines are considered permissible. On the other hand, the most rigorous interpretations prohibit consumption of any alcohol-containing products, particularly if the addition of alcohol was known. Tellingly, a cheese made with vegetarian or synthetic rennet but ripened with alcohol washes would likely be considered vegetarian but would be deemed haram in stricter Islamic interpretations.

Traces of Alcohol in Modern Food Products

Modern scholars and halal certification agencies have disputed the issue of small or trace amounts of alcohol naturally found or artificially added in various foods and drinks. Following medieval discussions of istihlak, many argue that if only a tiny (unspecified) amount of alcohol is present and it does not alter that product's color, taste, or smell, it will not intoxicate and is therefore permissible. However, the question of what constitutes "small" or "trace" amounts in a modern context, where scientific tests can precisely measure alcohol content, has stirred wide debate. "Smallness," for medieval jurists, hinged on whether a najis substance altered water's appearance, taste, or smell. Prompted by the rise in industrial manufacturing of packaged foods, discerning Muslims today have demanded fatwas, state decrees, and/or clear statements from certification agencies specifying the precise measurement, the exact percentage, of acceptable alcohol content in a particular food product. The classical juristic debate had focused on whether Sharia prohibitions opposed (all) alcohol or if they were (only) against its intoxicating nature.

In contemporary contexts, when it comes to trace amounts of alcohol, one originally Hanafi position is often applied. Some early Hanafi jurists argued that alcohol per se is not najis; rather, intoxication is condemned. Since a minute amount of naturally occurring alcohol would not intoxicate, today several scholars and Islamic organizations seem to have adopted this rationale, if implicitly, particularly with regard to trace alcohol in necessary medications.[59]

There is an emerging trend, however, toward specifying what—to some Muslim observers—sometimes seems to be an arbitrary percentage of acceptable alcohol levels. It is quite common for products containing sugar—breads, juices, and colas—to undergo minimal and natural fermentation that leaves trace amounts of alcohol. Groups like the American certification agency IFANCA indicate that the standard of acceptable alcohol is 0.5 percent in ingredients (or components) and less than 0.1 percent in the final product.[60] A fatwa issued by an Egyptian cleric in 2008 indicated that an alcohol level of 0.5 percent in a final product was acceptable.[61]

The case of allowable alcohol percentages in Saudi Arabia, where the Hanbali school predominates, reveals additional complexities. In the early 1980s, the limit for alcohol level (specifically in bottled drinks, like popular nonalcoholic malt drinks or "beers") was reported in international news outlets as 0.1 percent.[62] More recent sources, citing the Saudi Society of Food and Nutrition, implied that nonalcoholic beer manufacturers who get their levels below 0.5 percent have achieved acceptable measures, but then added that nonalcoholic drinks available in the Saudi market were at 0.0 percent.[63] In a well-known fatwa, Saudi Sheikh Muhammad ibn Salih al-'Uthaymin (d. 2001) also affirmed that all nonalcoholic "beer" sold in the Saudi market was halal.[64]

Other recent international rulings vary widely. Malaysia's JAKIM first issued a fatwa in 1984 stating that "alcohol produced as by product in food process [sic] is not najis and can be consumed." But in 2010, in a turn toward less lenient regulations, the group ruled that ethanol naturally found in food and drink must not exceed 0.01 percent, although products surpassing that level could be appealed to the country's Fatwa Committee.[65] The Majlis Ulama Indonesia (MUI) indicated that 1 percent is acceptable, while Thailand's Administration of Organizations of the Islamic Act (AOI) noted that the level should be no more than 1.5 percent in naturally fermented products. In Singapore, the Majlis Ugama Islam Singapura (MUIS) specified that the maximum level is 0.5 percent.[66]

Some Muslim critics see these percentages as overly subjective, as an arbitrary number that came neither from the Quran nor from the Sunni legal tradition. If natural fermentation is an ongoing process, they argue, a product might at various points of its life span contain 0.07 percent or 0.1 percent of alcohol: what was the "red line," some pondered, past which such a product was forbidden?[67] Against discussions of agreeable percentages, an opposing group invokes varied hadiths to argue that substances that intoxicate in large amounts could have a similar undesirable effect in smaller amounts. These commentators maintain that any alcohol (e.g., in medications or in foods) should be avoided, particularly if alternatives are available. Here the principle of istihlak cannot be invoked, they note, since it should apply only to water, not to other substances.[68]

Traditional Brews

Fermented beverages that are neither wine nor beer and generally (but not always) have a lower alcohol content have a long history in both the Islamic and non-Islamic worlds. Such drinks can be produced out of any sugar-containing fruit, dairy product, or grain, including honey, rice, apples, figs, raisins, dates, palms, berries, milk, barley, millet, and wheat. Many of these drinks were carefully addressed in Islamic legal, literary, and culinary sources and continue to play an important role in modern discussions of "trace" alcohol within manufactured drinks.

One traditional brew that was widely discussed in the historical texts is nabidh, a slightly fermented drink that the Prophet Muhammad enjoyed according to hadith literature. Medieval jurists and culinary authorities deliberated over the contents and preparation of this beverage, which is commonly produced from mashed dates, raisins, or other dried fruits, but could also be made from spelt, palms, barley, and honey. Their discussions often focused on whether and/or to what extent this beverage contained alcohol.[69] These questions still attract attention. In fact, in recent years, and in line with the intensified bureaucratization and "scientization" of halal, several studies have been conducted to determine the exact alcohol levels in nabidh. In these experiments, the goal was to evaluate alcohol content in a drink that the Prophet enjoyed but that, according to hadith literature, he specified must be consumed within three days of its preparation, presumably to limit its fermentation. Halal scientists believe that if the alcohol level in a nabidh drink that was allowed to be fermented for three days can be determined with accuracy, then an absolute percentage of alcohol within foods and drinks might be better assessed. One Malaysian study, published in 2010, used a variety of dates and raisins to create nabidh and attempted to replicate the storage process described in hadith literature (i.e., using a closed container to avoid contact with oxygen and additional natural yeasts). The study concluded that a 0.78 percent of naturally occurring ethanol should be acceptable for halal standards, based on the highest possible level of alcohol in nabidh after three days of fermentation as specified by the Prophet.[70]

This research captures how religious halal prescriptions might affect food manufacturing and consumption habits in Malaysia and elsewhere. Scientific experiments were designed and shaped by inferences drawn from hadith literature. For many, results from the use of precise instruments such as gas chromatography, mass spectrometers, and laboratory analyses of ethanol samples affirmed that a more scientific approach is needed in determining an appropriate halal benchmark.

In light of these discussions, several popular traditional drinks are also being reconsidered for their halal compliance. For example, since ancient times, boza (or *buza*) has been enjoyed in Egypt and Mesopotamia, and later in several parts of Africa, Asia, Russia, and most of the Ottoman Empire. Boza is a lightly fermented beer made from cereals like barley, wheat, rice, millet, among others; a thick, souplike, "tangy-sweet beverage," it is often consumed cold, with a dash of cinnamon or ginger, and served with some roasted chickpeas. Royal cooks made a special sweet, lower-alcohol boza for Ottoman sultans, but a stronger, more intoxicating boza was consumed throughout the empire, particularly in Arab lands and the Crimea, as well as in Central Asia.[71] Samples of modern Egyptian boza, which is commonly store-made by local vendors, show that the beverage can contain alcohol levels of 3.8 percent, although other studies revealed up to 7 percent. For this reason, in all likelihood, Dar al-Ifta'—Egypt's premiere Islamic legal research center—issued a fatwa in 2013, during the brief reign of the country's first Islamist government, indicating that this brew was haram. However, the ruling clarified that this restriction did not apply to a similarly named beverage in countries where the drink is produced as a soft drink.[72]

Perhaps the fatwa was referring to a particular version of boza that is popular in places like Turkey, which is generally sweeter and lower in its alcohol content (between 0.03 and 0.39 percent, according to one source).[73] Turkey's official science and technology research institution, TÜBİTAK (Türkiye Bilimsel ve Teknolojik Araştırma Kurumu; the Scientific and Technological Research Institute of Turkey), has declared that alcohol is definitively present in boza, even if in small amounts.[74] Yet one of Turkey's larger manufacturers, Akman Boza, reassures customers that the product they buy on supermarket shelves is free of alcohol and that it should not ferment further unless it sits in the refrigerator for longer than a month or two. On the other hand, and without reference to alcohol content, another major Turkish brand called Vefa Boza notes that the fermentation process will continue if their boza remains unconsumed and recommends, therefore, that the product be drunk immediately.[75] Boza continues to enjoy popularity in Turkey and is being billed by some as the country's original and oldest "energy drink."[76]

In the dairy category, drinks include *kımız* (*kumis, kumiss*), a fermented mare's milk beverage enjoyed among Muslims and non-Muslims from Central Asia, including Kazaks, Kyrgyz, and peoples of Turkic or Mongol heritage. This beverage is commonly homemade, and its alcohol level can range between 0.7 and 2.5 percent.[77] More commercialized nowadays and more commonly found in supermarkets, both in Euro-America and throughout the Muslim world, is *kefir*, a slightly fermented, yogurt-like beverage that originated in the Caucasus Mountains and is produced by mixing milk (cow, sheep, goat, but also soy, coconut, and rice) with kefir grains (proteins and yeasts) to produce a sour, fizzy, mildly alcoholic product. A popular Caucasian legend reports that the drink has been made there since the seventh century, when the Prophet Muhammad gave local inhabitants kefir grains and the secret recipe.[78] These days kefir (or "dairy champagne," as it is sometimes called) is mass produced. In the United

Fig. 7.1. Bottled boza by Vefa, one of Turkey's most recognized brands. Authors' photograph.

States, the American company Lifeway has led kefir production and promotes its drink as wholly alcohol-free.[79] But kefir is also prevalent throughout the Muslim world, and although there is some dispute over its halalness—alcohol levels could range between 0.3 and 1 percent—it is marketed as an acceptable "health drink," a medicinal beverage whose nutritious probiotics are a beneficial part of a modern diet.[80]

Soft Drinks and Colas

The question of halal compliance has been disputed more vehemently around sugary soft drinks, flavor solvents, and "nonalcoholic" beverages than around traditional fermented drinks, even though the latter can have far higher alcohol levels. Possible reasons include the foreign origins of these drinks and the fact that traditional drinks, made from fruits, grains, or dairy, are thought to imbue healthfulness and healing, whereas sugar and corn syrup have been implicated in a variety of modern diseases, such as obesity and diabetes.

For many decades—that is, in the days when colas were reliant on animal-derived ingredients—cola-based drinks raised alarm among religiously observant Jews.[81] For Muslims, however, recent issues surrounding manufactured colas have focused on their alcohol content and Western origins. A 2012 French study confirmed that some Coca-Cola and Pepsi drinks contain 0.001 percent alcohol.[82] Several large manufacturers were quick to insist that they add no alcohol to their products. On its British website, Coca-Cola notes that "more than 200 countries . . . have consistently recognized the drink as a nonalcoholic product. This includes countries where Islam is the major religion."[83] Halal Hub, an American-based group whose mission is to act as an advocate for halal food and dispel "misconceptions of common food products," has also certified these types of drinks as halal.[84] But certain ulama have issued fatwas categorically prohibiting some soft drinks—not necessarily (or only) because of their haram qualities or even their unhealthfulness but because at various points in recent history, especially following the 2003 US invasion of Iraq, consuming them was seen as complying with perceived American imperialist agendas, which several Muslim leaders adamantly opposed.[85]

As part of an ongoing effort to stimulate interest in and promote market shares of "local" halal products, Muslim soft drink manufacturers have introduced their own products to compete with the name brands. Some companies, like Qibla Cola (UK, founded 2003) and Mecca-Cola (France, then UAE, founded 2002), attempted to brand themselves not only as halal but also as advocating political stances popular among their Muslim consumers, such as supporting the Palestinian cause. The religiously themed names of these colas (*qibla* is the prayer direction Muslims must face: i.e., toward Mecca) reveal a conscious marketing strategy to legitimize the product's authenticity to consumers. Mecca-Cola struggled financially for several years but seems to be making a modest comeback; on the other hand, Qibla Cola's UK-based operation went bankrupt in 2005.

Brands like Zamzam Cola[86] in Iran (a Pepsi subsidiary founded in 1954; later, following the 1979 Revolution, an independent corporation) and Cola Turka in Turkey (established in 2003) have weathered the economic competition by urging consumers to support a national product. Cola Turka was produced and marketed by the Ülker group as a domestic alternative to Coca-Cola and Pepsi-Cola. Ülker emphasized the halal compliance of its product (though without commenting on the halal status of its rivals) to successfully compete against these international giants in Turkey, the Middle East, and many European countries with significant Muslim populations.[87]

Extracts

In the United States, "extracts" (e.g., of vanilla or almond) sold in the spice sections of most supermarkets are flavors suspended in a solution that is, according to the US Food and Drug Administration's (FDA) rules, at least 35 percent alcohol.[88] IFANCA has suggested that vanilla extract is an "ingredient" (and not a final food product) that would never be consumed in its pure form. Therefore, mixing vanilla with ethyl alcohol in order to make it soluble and "easy to use" is permissible in the preparation of halal foodstuffs.[89] In the Islamic world, Malaysia's JAKIM was one of the first to issue a fatwa addressing the use of alcohol as a food solvent; this practice is allowed, according to the 1988 ruling, provided the "alcohol is not produced from 'liquor production'" (*arak*, which here seems equivalent to khamr or any alcoholic beverage) and "the quantity of alcohol is minimal and it is not intoxicated [*sic*]."[90] Although these opinions do not explicitly say so, their logic is likely based on the istihlak principle. Most home chefs or manufacturers would use only a small amount of vanilla extract in a given recipe or product, so the taste, smell, or color of the final cake, cookie, or ice cream would not be tainted by the presence of alcohol. It is worth noting here that throughout most of the Islamic world, and perhaps to avoid questions of halal compliance altogether, a powder product (vanillin mixed with sugar crystals) has been widely used for decades.

Faux Libations: The Case of Nonalcoholic Beer

Trends of growing piety and attentiveness to a halal lifestyle have come to a head with the Western-driven marketing industry, which transformed the idea of drinking alcohol into a global status symbol for urban elites, one associated with affluence, style, and a refined taste. In the latter part of the twentieth century, the rise in worldwide consumption of alcohol correlated with the spread of Western entertainment glamorizing this habit. In many developing countries, French wines became the standard; marketing campaigns successfully promoted American whiskey; and Dutch or German beers were coveted by various consumers. In Gulf countries like Saudi Arabia, the influx of foreign workers affiliated with the oil industry, the rise in satellite television broadcasting, and a concurrent population boom influenced local consumption habits and made alcohol even more attractive as a status symbol, a way for young urban elites to set themselves apart from rural people. Although prohibited by rigorous Islamic codes, alcohol came to represent affluence or aspirations of affluence, a (partly) Westernized lifestyle, modernity, and a general cultural superiority.[91]

The halal-market-oriented response to alcohol's allure, specifically in Muslim countries where consumption is legally banned or heavily curtailed, has been the rise in production of faux libations—that is, nonalcoholic beers, wines, champagnes, and liquors. These products were produced and marketed in ways comparable to their alcoholic counterparts in non-Muslim countries. Often sold in stylish bottles with eye-catching labels, they stood out clearly from colas and from traditional and lightly fermented beverages like boza and kefir. Of all the products discussed thus far, nonalcoholic beer best captures the overlaps in halal product branding, manufacturing, production, testing, and consumption.[92]

In the West, the modern commercial manufacturing of faux libations dates back to the first half of the twentieth century, when low- or no-alcohol beers emerged out of necessity during both World Wars due to shortages of raw materials like barley. Also, during the United States' Prohibition era (1919–1933) beers with an alcohol by volume (ABV) of no more than 0.5 percent, dubbed "near beers," became a popular way for manufacturers to keep their factories open.[93] In post-Prohibition America, some nonalcoholic or near beers were still available, but most had limited appeal, and the market stagnated for some time.[94]

Globally, the nonalcoholic drinks industry picked up again in the 1970s and 1980s. In Switzerland, a law was passed that prohibited the serving of alcohol in highway diners, so Swiss restaurateurs needed a solution, and beer brewers met that need by producing near beers. In the early 1980s, the market further shifted in Euro-America, where a new health and dietary consciousness, in addition to widespread campaigns against drunk driving, helped accelerate demand.[95] And in the 1960s and 1970s, Western expatriates living and working in Saudi Arabia desired a near-beer product that met local laws and standards (at that time, reportedly 0.1 percent ABV).[96] After years of tolerating the drinking habits of Americans working at the Arabian-American Oil Company (ARAMCO), in 1952 the Saudi king issued a royal decree banning the sale and transport of all alcohol. Home brewing became popular, but expatriates who wanted to consume brews with Saudi colleagues, friends, and clients—in more public settings—demanded a truly nonalcoholic brew.[97]

In response to all of these demands, Moussy—a nonalcoholic beer made by the Swiss brewer Cardinal of Fribourg (now a part of Carlsberg)—was introduced to Switzerland in 1973 and to Saudi Arabia and other Gulf countries in 1982.[98] Today Moussy is by far the most popular nonalcoholic beer in the Arab Gulf. Moussy owns and operates a local brewery in Saudi Arabia, and as of 2015, the product boasts a 38 percent market share of the nonalcoholic beer market in that country.[99] Although its earlier ABV is unknown, today the malt beverage's ABV reportedly ranges from 0.01 percent in its flavored brews (peach, strawberry, apple, and pomegranate) to 0.025 percent for its "classic" flavor.[100] Nonalcoholic beers like Moussy were originally made by brewing traditional beer, fermented with yeast, and then dealcoholizing it through a specialized distillation process. Not all alcohol can be removed through this method, however, and it is likely that Moussy later altered its techniques to meet more stringent Islamic demands, specifically laws that prohibit the physical presence of any breweries in Saudi Arabia.

Moussy's success in the Gulf inspired several international and regional producers, and soon many new products came into play. Birell, made by local producer Al-Ahram, emerged in Egypt in 1986 and has become that country's most popular nonalcoholic beer.[101] Some brands began to distinguish themselves through a stricter production process, which no longer relied on any yeast or alcohol fermentation. Companies in Germany and elsewhere developed new products that promised to revolutionize this sector: GranMalt, an instant "sweet, crunchy, 00 per cent alcohol-free granulated beer," was promoted as an easily shipped product that is compatible with any strict anti-brewery laws and is easily mixed with water and other flavorings to create a nonalcoholic brew.[102]

These innovations likely transformed manufacturing facilities throughout the Islamic world. In Saudi Arabia, the second most popular nonalcoholic beer after Moussy was Barbican, which was brought to the region in 1983 by the UK-based Bass Brewery.[103] But in 1997 the brand was purchased by the Saudi group Aujan, and the company eventually built a bottling plant in Dubai and a canning plant in the Saudi city of Dammam. Again, to meet stringent laws forbidding the presence of breweries, the Saudi-owned Barbican was produced without any fermentation. Notably, the use of stylish packaging and labeling signaled the manufacturer's attempts to appeal to a new, younger generation of consumers. Aujan redesigned the Barbican bottle and made it more "slim and sexy, with superior graphics."[104] Barbican is prohibited from using ads that rely on suggestively clad women, so its sales campaigns began to target youthful Muslim "bros" who aspire to a more Western lifestyle, noting that their product was "developed with master brewers in Germany" and reminding customers that "Barbican has always stayed in tune with the youth of the region. It is synonymous with being a brand that understands them and speaks their language. Barbican is courageous, chivalrous, loyal, genuine, and open."[105] These promotions have worked. The brand more than doubled its domestic sales within ten years, from 18 million liters in 2004 to 37 million liters in 2013.[106]

Joining this crowd of producers, in 1998, an Egyptian entrepreneur named Ahmed Zayat, then-owner of Al-Ahram brewing company, launched a malt beverage called Fayrouz. Egypt's highest religious authority, Al Azhar, quickly certified the drink as halal, a stamp of approval much coveted by Al-Ahram's competitors. Sales took off, and by 2000, plans were made to sell the product in Africa and South Asia, in addition to different Arab nations.[107] Soon the Dutch brewing giant Heineken recognized the viability of this global market, and in 2002 it acquired Fayrouz (and Al-Ahram) from Zayat.[108] Both Fayrouz and the more established Birell continue to enjoy popularity in Egypt, even if regular beer outsells these drinks.[109]

Several other local nonalcoholic brands have made a splash in the Middle East: Delster, brewed in the Islamic Republic of Iran since 1979, is one of the region's oldest. The Palestinian craft beer brewer in the West Bank, Taybeh

Fig. 7.2. Nonalcoholic beer sold in a Cairo supermarket. Authors' photograph.

launched a nonalcoholic version of its product following Hamas's victory in Gaza in 2005. In Lebanon, the local brand Laziza has enjoyed considerable success. In 2013, the *Economist* reported that the Middle East accounted for one-third of global sales of nonalcoholic beer. Explaining this beverage's success, one industry expert suggested that "drinking beer, even the non-alcoholic variety, taps into a popular desire for a globalised lifestyle that neither fruit juice nor even Coca-Cola can offer."[110]

Nevertheless, not all Muslim countries or halal certification authorities have embraced these trends. In 2011, when Barbican first came to Malaysia, JAKIM challenged its halal compliance, noting that its own tests on the product registered an ABV of 0.5 percent—far higher than Malaysia's permissible level of 0.01 percent. The product's Malaysian wholesaler retorted that the product contains no alcohol and that it had been good enough to be sold in places like Mecca "for the past 25 years."[111] After swift reconsideration, JAKIM conceded.[112] Still, while sanctioning "malt soft drinks" like Barbican, JAKIM has refused to approve products with "beer" in their name, regardless of their alcohol content. IFANCA has yet to certify any nonalcoholic beer or wine as halal, arguing that the "concept itself has alcohol-related connotations."[113] Indonesia's MUI has also refused to certify these beverages: a 2003 fatwa indicates that "it is prohibited to consume food/beverages that give rise to taste/aroma, or animals that are prohibited." The chairman of MUI's Fatwa Commission, KH Ma'ruf Amin, further justified this position, stating that "if something is pointing in the direction of haram, it is the way to haram."[114]

Nonalcoholic or faux libations have generally failed in the Turkish market.[115] One reason the demand for such drinks is lower in Turkey is that although alcohol taxes have recently risen, their production, sales, and consumption are all legal in the country (unlike in Saudi Arabia or Iran). Thus, rising costs aside, Turks who want to consume alcohol face no legal obstacles or deterrents. On the other hand, for pious Turks, refraining from faux libations altogether makes sense, as there are still heated debates over whether trace alcohol renders them haram.[116] In a hardline stance against these drinks—including nonalcoholic malt drinks, wine, or champagne—in 2016 Turkey's GİMDES lambasted these products as tools devised by "satanic powers" to threaten Muslims' health and faith.[117]

Despite this resistance, nonalcoholic beer remains the most popular faux libation in the Islamic world. Its success has opened the way for other products. Nowadays, nonalcoholic (and often halal-certified) wines, champagnes, and even whiskey appeal to the halal-conscious. A few California wineries, including Sutter Home's Fre, have produced dealcoholized wines for several years, bringing it to the Middle East in 2006. Advertising flavors like merlot, white zinfandel, moscato, and brut, the drink does not hide its intent to serve as a suitable alternative for the real thing.[118]

High-end, halal-authenticated entries have also emerged from traditional winemaking powerhouses like Italy and Spain. Italy's Alternativa wines have been billed as fully halal, and the Córdoba-based Halal Institute of Spain has certified local nonalcoholic wines like VINCERO, Al Andalus, and Lussory, opening the way for their consumption in Europe and possibly throughout the Islamic world. Their makers boast of using local varietals like Tempranillo grapes for these prestige-oriented beverages, and most of them are "0.0 percent" ABV.[119] For several connoisseurs, nonalcoholic wines and champagnes have failed to impress in terms of taste and price point. But some brands, like Lussory's Gold 24K—a sparkling 24-karat-gold-infused nonalcoholic white wine—have been marketed as high-end luxury drinks and have become popular in opulent restaurants in Dubai, where a bottle of Lussory's Gold can sell for $150.[120]

For many Muslims, close attentiveness to the most detailed labels on manu-factured foodstuffs—"halal literacy"—has become a necessity and a regular part of their grocery shopping experiences. Different certifying agencies have worked to create more uniform standards that could be easily applied in any international context, to simplify halal questions by finding common denom-inators. In many ways, their task mirrors that of early Islamic scholars: the goal is simply to eliminate contact between their foods and najis substances like pork, carrion, and alcohol. However, halal's technical implications have become increasingly complicated and their reach wide-ranging. In dealing with industrialized and scientifically based food production, attention is given to the molecular and genetic detection of pig or carrion fragments in cheese or chocolate, or to the precise measurements of alcohol content in soda or boza. Certifying agencies and bodies, which support an array of food manufactures, can radically differ in their verdicts, to the point that it becomes difficult for producers and consumers to ascertain halalness. As in the meat industry, with regard to slaughter regulation, the growth of packaged foodstuffs will likely give rise to rigorous verification of each ingredient, each factory, and each final packaged product, using the strictest standards that may satisfy a range of dis-criminatory customers.[121]

CHAPTER 8

F or some Muslims today, even the most jurisprudentially correct or complete halal label is an inadequate indicator of food quality and best dietary practices. Can Muslims be sure that genetically modified organisms (GMOs) or the use of pesticides in grain, fruit, and plant cultivation, while possibly halal according to most legalistic definitions of the term, are healthy for their families? If not, how can they consider these products and practices permissible in religious terms? Is it acceptable for farm animals to be given growth hormones or antibiotics, or does this practice sully the meat for Muslim consumption? Could the act of killing and eating any animal ever comply with the religious injunction to treat animals with compassion? How can Muslims move away from the burgeoning market-driven model toward a more deliberately conscientious and ethical halal lifestyle? Such questions are on the minds of many modern Muslim believers and prompt them to contest, if not reject, commercially geared halal labeling, certification, and manufacturing processes.

In order to articulate their viewpoints and find guidance, some Muslims have looked to the Quranic concept of tayyib in matters of environmental stewardship, animal welfare, food ethics, and healthy living. The Quran states: "O mankind, eat from whatever is on earth [that is] lawful (halal) and good/wholesome (tayyib)" (2:168). It also says, "All good foods (al-tayyibat) have been made [by

Allah] lawful (*uhilla*; from the same root as *halal*)" to Muslims (5:5). These scripturally based pronunciations unequivocally link the notion that when it comes to food, halal and tayyib go hand in hand. This is why one way to expand on the meanings of halal according to modern concerns and expectations has been to define (and redefine) the meaning of tayyib. In other words, improvisations on the alternative meanings of halal take place within the lexicological boundaries of tayyib, in the many shades of "good" and "wholesome."

This chapter maps out the various meanings of tayyib as found in Islam's earliest sources, including the Quran and medieval judicial texts, to highlight the concept's potential vagueness. Then it looks at how tayyib has recently taken on new meanings and has come to constitute a core building block within halal's modern definition: a novel "tayyib-halal" ethos has developed in response to dubious slaughterhouse procedures, to fisheries or farms implicated in labor abuses or human slavery, to the reliance on biochemical additives. Activists who demand better food production and consumption practices; easier access to organic food; healthier halal products; the adoption of a quasi-vegetarian, vegetarian, or vegan diet; and the promotion of a non-market-oriented halal approach have related these demands to a Quran-based ethic. Finally, the chapter looks at how the overall tayyib-halal ethos has been received by different actors within the Muslim community, including its critics, and how various segments of global halal business have tried to take advantage of the economic opportunities it generates.

Tayyib Is Halal and Halal Is Tayyib

Ancient Near Eastern and Mediterranean civilizations were interested in the concept of eating good food. Both Greeks and Romans developed a keen appreciation for fine cuisine and expended much effort in acquiring high-quality ingredients and producing tasty dishes.[1] In the Hebrew Bible, the Israelites were told to "eat what is good, and your soul shall delight in fatness" (Isaiah 55:2), while Paul reminded his followers that "everything God created is good, and nothing is to be rejected if it is received with thanksgiving" (1 Timothy 4:4).[2] Compared to other Abrahamic traditions, however, it is possible to argue that the Islamic scripture makes the most emphatic case for eating good food and for linking that mandate to the religion's dietary rules. The Quran gives the imperative to "eat" (*kulu*) twenty-eight times; terms associated with the root of this word (*a-k-l*) appear 108 times, and they are often linked to al-tayyibat (the good things).[3] Indeed, mention of the adjective tayyib occurs thirteen times in the holy text, and tayyibat (the nominal plural) appears twenty-one times. However, even though tayyib is often translated simply as "good" and "wholesome," its Quranic usage incorporates a range of meanings. In his book about such concepts in the Quran, scholar of Islam Toshihiko Izutsu defines tayyib as "very delightful, pleasant, and sweet." The term is commonly applied to fragrances, drinks, and foods, but it can also be used to describe winds as "favorable" or soil as "fertile."[4] In various parts of the scripture, the term and its derivatives can take on additional connotations, including pious and chaste (when used for humans), clean, fair, favorable, amenable, healthy, and mature.[5]

Although tayyib is not strictly a legal category, the Islamic exegetical tradition repeatedly stresses its connection to halal and haram food rules.[6] In evaluating verses that mention tayyib, such as 2:57, 2:168, 2:172–173, 5:4–5, 87–88, 7:157, 16:72, and 16:114, medieval scholars define the term as that which is mubah (permissible) and/or halal.[7] In some discussions, tayyibat are also things that pre-Islamic Arabs (jahilis) as well as Jews and Christians may have forbidden but that God made halal for Muslims, thus indicating the divine being's benevolence toward believers.[8] Jurists also point out that tayyib food must be purchased with tayyib or halal earnings/money.[9] In other sources, tayyib is defined as the opposite of khabith (foul, bad, filthy, impure, abominable) and najis (impure, soiled), which Muslims should avoid.[10] Khaba'ith foods are those explicitly prohibited, such as pig, blood, and carrion. Tayyib is also that which is tahir, or pure, against what is najis.[11] In the Quran, the terms tahir and najis usually appear in the context of ritual purity, and invoking this broad vocabulary suggests, at least in modern readings, that consuming tayyib-halal food is good for the body and for the religion.[12]

Overall, classical discussions have a sense of circularity and vagueness. The crucial terms are defined through reference to each other: tayyib is halal and halal is tayyib; and tayyib and tahir are the opposite of khabith or najis. But jurists have been hesitant to tie the term tayyib to specific foods (within the canonical limits), and because they have not listed exactly what food items can be considered tayyib, it appears as if Muslims can fill in the blank with the dishes, recipes, diets, and eating practices they prefer (so long as they use well-defined halal substances).[13] In fact, scholars maintained that the Quran enjoins believers not to restrict themselves, as Jews, Christian monks, and ascetics have done, from eating all of the tayyibat that God made available to them (5:87–88).[14] Non-prescribed fasting and abstention from tayyib food is frowned upon.

Finally, several medieval writers simply defined tayyib as "tasty," without listing the criteria for tastiness.[15] The medieval Persian scholar Ibn Jarir al-Tabari suggests in his commentary on 5:87–88 that tayyibat are those "delicious things which people crave and over which the hearts swoon."[16] Also, in interpreting 16:114, he describes food which God had made "halalan tayyiban" as delicious (mudhakatan).[17] This terminology was put to practical use in medieval culinary texts, as in a tenth-century cookbook from Abbasid Baghdad, where references abound to "milh tayyib" ("pleasant-tasting salt") or "duhn tayyib" (a "high-quality fine-tasting fat free of acridity"), critical ingredients for ensuring flavorsome recipes.[18] The traveler Ibn Battuta described the apricots and quinces he ate in the Iraqi town of Basra as "tayyibat al mat'am" (delicious foods).[19] And documents drawn from charitable endowments in Mamluk Cairo show concern for serving tayyib food, even to the lowliest social groups; daily rations to the poor, some texts stipulated, should include "high-quality wheat bread" (khubz burr tayyib).[20] Everyone, it seems, should have equal access to tayyib foodstuffs, regardless of their social standing.

The lexicological flexibility of tayyib, as outlined in historical and exegetical discussions, has allowed many modern Muslims, particularly in the West, to utilize it within their advocacy for animal rights, environmental ethics, and a healthful lifestyle.

Ethical Halal

Islamic traditions hold that animals, like humans, are sentient creations of Allah and that harming animals without justification is contrary to Allah's will. In recent years, Muslim activists, especially in Western countries, have used the ethical connotations of tayyib to encourage people to be kind to animals, become vegetarians or vegans, and eat organic, locally produced food. By doing so, they have attempted to incorporate these values into halal considerations, via the tayyib-halal ethos. These advocates see the mistreatment of farm animals and the manipulation of their foods by chemical or biological means as troublesome, abhorrent, and thus anything but tayyib. In constructing a moral worldview that is simultaneously conscious of a distant past and alert to current concerns, many couch the ethical treatment of animals as the critical and missing link in prevalent halal discourses.

On humanely sourced food, they invoke Islamic traditions that highlight the Prophet Muhammad's mercy: how he forbade the cruel treatment of animals and how he prescribed painless slaughter. For example, the Prophet forbade striking and branding the face of animals and cursed those who did so. He prohibited his followers from instigating fights among animals and warned Muslims who neglected to feed their animals that they would be punished in the afterlife. He also stated that acts of charity to animals (including, remarkably, to dogs), just like to humans, would be rewarded by God.[21] It is therefore a duty, many Muslim activists argue, for good Muslims to alleviate the suffering of all animals.[22] They emphasize how halal and tayyib were fixtures in premodern farming practices that should inform modern Muslim food ethics, discourses, and customs.[23]

In the United States, one of the more mainstream voices in articulating this ethical script is Ibrahim Abdul-Matin, a New York–based writer, activist, and political consultant whose 2010 book *Green Deen: What Islam Teaches about Protecting the Planet* outlines the key principles for Muslims seeking to live "in balance with nature" and to be "protectors of the planet" as well as "steward[s] (*khalifah*) of the Earth."[24] "Green," the author notes, was the Prophet Muhammad's favorite color and also happens to be "the color of life on all corners of the planet."[25] To protect the lush forests, verdant fields, and the environment, therefore, Abdul-Matin cautions against overconsumption and suggests that environmental regulation, protection, and conservation are critical aspects of practicing a green Islamic life.[26] On food, he tells readers, "We need to make better choices."[27] For a start, this means opposing industrialized farming and the inhumane treatment of animals. Muslims must instead embrace "green zabiha" and tayyib meat: the latter "comes from animals that were raised properly, fed properly, allowed to graze freely, and permitted to act in the most natural way—the way God intended."[28] Factory farming and animal abuse, in this ethical narrative of Islamic history, simply did not exist in the religion's earliest days, and a return to this preindustrial age would be the only way to meet Islamic guidelines.

Environmentally responsible cultivation and animal husbandry projects are indeed gaining traction in Europe and North America, where eco-consciousness and ethical farming ideals are growing in popularity. In Britain, for example, Abraham Natural Produce and Willowbrook Organic Farm provide, according to the former, "ethically sourced halal meat through a business model that supports localisation and contributes to charitable causes through a fixed percentage donation from profits."[29] Willowbrook's stewards, Lutfi and Ruby Radwan, strive to "raise animals as the Qur'an and the Prophet Muhammad intended." In contrast to factory-farmed and industrially slaughtered animals, their chickens graze under wild cherry trees and their sheep and goats freely consume unadulterated grass. The animals are then slaughtered following the strictest Islamic prescriptions, meaning they are not stunned but are hand-slaughtered at a local abattoir where their slaughter is overseen by the Radwans. The Radwans believe that this approach enables them to realize the ethical spirit within both the lawful (halal) and the wholesome (tayyib).[30] Some Muslim farmers in North America follow a similar approach. Norwich Meadows Farm in upstate New York, Whole Earth Meats outside Chicago, Nature's Bounty in California, and BlossomPure Organic in Toronto all promote their halal products through a "faith-based approach to sustainable agriculture."[31] At Norwich Meadows, halal farmer Zaid Kurdieh extends his ethics beyond animal welfare and the consumption of unadulterated foods, noting that produce harvested by "poorly paid migrant workers, would not be tayyib" and, therefore, would not be halal.[32] How Muslim farmers treat other human beings also matters in this renewed tayyib-halal scheme.

These producers and merchants are now responding to Muslims who want to know not just how animals were slaughtered—a preoccupation of many halal standards, certifiers, and state agencies—but also how well they lived. They reject industrial practices like drugging, penning, fettering, confinement, stunning, cloning, and mutilation. They promote "green zabiha" and call for treating animals with kindness, allowing them to live free-range lives, feeding them organic and vegetarian foods, and not subjecting them to any harm or torture, in life and death.[33] If Muslims choose to eat halal meat, some argue, then it should be "organic, free-range *halal* meat"[34] even if that product's more prohibitive cost limits its consumption. Selling meat derived from humanely treated animals, under the halal label, is indeed an expensive but potentially profitable endeavor that attracts Muslim consumers and an increasing numbers of non-Muslim consumers as well. Some businesses, like the US-based Saffron Road Food, sell their frozen meat meals in mainstream supermarkets and organic food stores, like Whole Foods, and tout themselves not only as halal and "natural" but also as practicing an "ethical consumerism" that "strives to be inclusive and celebrate all faiths."[35] That company generated $40 million in revenue in 2016, with estimates that 80 percent of its consumers "aren't trying to follow Islamic law."[36] Another profitable but in this case "local" business is Honest Chops, a downtown Manhattan artisanal butcher that sources its meat from eco-conscious halal farmers but also takes pride in the fact that 60 percent of its customers are "secular." The owners offer an "Honest to God" guarantee, and they believe they provide a needed service and a high-quality product not just to fellow Muslims but to the broader community.[37] Businesses that appeal to Muslim and non-Muslim constituents are on the rise and are good indicators of how tayyib-halal food purveyors have positioned their products within a booming global market.

Likewise, some Muslim organizations are using tayyib to promote ecological and environmental consciousness. In living that ethical and utopian script, groups like Green Muslims, Eco-Halal, and Green Ramadan in the United States embrace a new halal conception that endorses mindful eating practices, green farming, composting, recycling, and awareness of one's carbon footprint.[38] Inspired by sustainable, organic, and locavore models and by global food activism, the Belgian-based Green Halal enjoins members to resist the profit-oriented, industrial model of halal production. Green Halal began in 2010, after its founders became horrified about commercial breeding and slaughter practices. As anthropologist Manon Istasse has pointed out, the group's leaders focus on several aspects of the food they offer: fair trade, ecologically responsible sourcing, high quality, and overall halal authenticity. They argue explicitly that "halal and tayyib (pure and healthy) go hand in hand."[39]

Fig. 8.1. Saffron Road frozen meals at an American supermarket. Authors' photograph.

Good Muslims must know where their food comes from, they maintain, and should persist in advocating ethical breeding and correct (i.e., "humane") halal slaughter practices. Green Halal also advocates minimizing, if not eliminating, one's overall meat consumption. Its leaders argue, for instance, that Muslims should consider following a fully vegan diet during the month of Ramadan.[40] This stance makes sense considering that animal husbandry, especially cattle breeding, has been implicated in some of the worst global greenhouse offenses in recent years.

Muslim quasi- or full vegetarianism has also emerged as a diverse if diffuse movement that challenges the production and consumption of any meat, halal or otherwise. To be clear, Islam—like other Abrahamic religions and unlike several South Asian traditions—is "not a vegetarian religion."[41] However, the Islamic tradition offers different models of vegetarianism. Many Sufis, especially in South Asia, adopted a vegetarian diet to intensify their spiritual discipline and reject worldly goods.[42] Contemporary activists note, moreover, that the Prophet Muhammad himself ate little meat and that his son-in-law and cousin Ali, the fourth Sunni Caliph and first Shiite Imam, may have discouraged regular meat eating. Some textual and legal sources suggest provegetarian interpretations, calling for moderation in food habits, gratitude for basic and simple foodstuffs, and prolonged abstention from meat.[43] Historically, this semivegetarian lifestyle has been exemplified by the Druzes, an offshoot of Shiite Islam. Druze farmers predominate in Lebanon's mountains, and many of them consume meat only on special occasions.[44]

Across sectarian orientations—Sunni or Shiite—some Muslims today have begun following and promoting a vegetarian or vegan diet. Many in the West choose to eat a more meatless diet because they are unable to acquire authentically halal meat. Others are more ethically deliberate in their decisions: they explain their dietary views by citing Quranic verses that support animal welfare (if not animal rights). One of the first to articulate this position in modern parlance was British-Indian thinker Basheer Ahmad Masri, whose book *Animal Welfare in Islam* invokes tayyib in outlining different models of a vegetarian ethic that continue to be widely cited today.[45] Scholar of Islam Kecia Ali reads Masri's treatise as advocating semivegetarianism for the glorification of the divine. As she observes, while Masri is clear that "Islam has left the option of eating meat to one's discretion," a vegetarian diet nurtures desirable virtues, discipline, and piety and should thus be encouraged.[46] While not directly promoting vegetarianism, in 2008, Islamic legal expert Kristen Stilt worked closely with scholars at Egypt's Al Azhar University to draft *Animal Welfare in Islamic Law*, a booklet documenting the scriptural, legal, and historical traditions of compassion, mercy, and justice toward animals. Such texts could be used by ethically motivated vegetarian activists seeking better application of Islamic injunctions to eat tayyib food.[47] More directly, a well-known opinion comes from one of Islamic vegetarianism's most visible proponents: American scholar Shaykh Hamza Yusuf, who has repeatedly reminded his followers in writings and speeches that "the meat and dairy today is not the meat and dairy that grandma and grandpa ate." All of Allah's creation—even ants—must be treated with kindness, respect, and tenderness, he notes. These injunctions are mostly ignored, he argues, in today's market-driven economy: the mass manufacture of food relies on efficiency and high levels of productivity, and for this reason meat and its derivative products have been implicated in disease, illness, and death. "I'm not here to tell you what to do," he once declared to audiences, but healthy food means "locally grown" and preferably vegetable-based.[48]

A more uncompromising, and to many animal rights activists the only ethical stance moves beyond occasional or semivegetarianism and renounces consumption of all animal-derived products (veganism). Beyond emphasizing animals' prized place in the Quran (24:41, 6:38), an ostensibly Muslim website affiliated with animal rights group People for the Ethical Treatment of Animals (PETA) rejects industrialized breeding and slaughter practices, citing animal cruelty, suffering, and disease as deterrents for eating meat or animal products. If Muslims are enjoined to eat halal and tayyib, and if tayyib means goodness defined ethically, then the only way to follow this injunction, the site maintains, is to stop eating meat. The website also pushes for a boycott of all animal-derived shoes, bags, and clothing (such as wool, silk, and cashmere).[49] A true vegan tayyib-halal lifestyle involves conscientious eating and lifestyle choices; veganism, the argument goes, is the position most unquestionably consistent with the Prophet Muhammad's mandate to treat animals with kindness and mercy.

Canadian-Saudi blogger Mohamed Ghilan similarly argues that veganism represents the true Islamic path and laments that current "dietary habits of Muslims reflect a belief that a 'Certified Halal' stamp removes us from the great chain of production." In a profound critique of "green Muslims," Ghilan notes that those who take comfort in "humane" discourses proposed by ethical farming proponents are living in denial: these people must open their eyes and acknowledge that "there is no such thing as humane treatment, happy animals, or a calming recitation of God's name prior to slaughter. Rather there is an industrial monstrosity taking place to support mass consumption, in which animals are abused and the Divine balance set in nature is not only transgressed but also trampled on." Ghilan argues that to stave off damage to suffering animals, rainforests, freshwater supplies, farmlands, and the atmosphere—to say nothing of human health—Muslims who are devotedly following the Prophet Muhammad's custom (sunna) must adopt a vegan diet.[50]

The debate about ethics and the propensity of human actions to violate God's will has further extended to questions about the use of GMOs in food production. In 2010, at the International Workshop for Islamic Scholars on Agribiotechnology held in Malaysia, genetically modified crops were declared halal so long as they were derived from halal sources.[51] In response to the 2010 decision sanctioning GMOs, environmentalist groups like the UK-based Islamic Foundation for Ecology and Environmental Sciences accused the decree of being myopic—of failing to see nature "as an organic whole" and to recognize that biotechnology undermines "the integrity of God's creation."[52] The GMO issue continues to be disputed in various religious and activist circles.

In Europe, a far more encompassing critique of the global halal business has been emerging since the 1990s. Formulated by Muslim-European intellectuals such as the Oxford-based Swiss philosopher Tariq Ramadan and the Geneva-based Imam Mostafa Brahimi, and increasingly popularized by organizations such as the French Union of Muslim Consumers and the Shatibi Center in Lyon, this critique represents an "alter-globalist" and anti-capitalist evaluation of wider trends in the halal world, based on the claim that its "for market" and "for profit" tendencies represent major threats to believers' faith, their relationship to fellow Muslims, to the environment, and to God. Very much influenced by secular critiques of capitalism, this position insists that Islam can be and should act as a force against global capitalism, which has hurt Muslims considerably in modern history. Ramadan, in particular, had long denounced the global halal market for its abject materialism and its exploitation of both people and natural resources. He and others promote an alternative consumption model for Muslims, one that imagines market conformity with Sharia prescripts (including its halal mandates) as possible only through a deliberately conscientious approach. An interpretation of halal that's in line with the Quranic ethics and prophetic examples requires Muslims to resist the consumerist stimuli that have come to govern the Islamic world through halal schemes and marketing. Muslims must not allow halal to be used as a means to Islamize capitalism. Rather, they should appropriate an array of consumption strategies ranging from resistance to overcodification and excessive normativity in halal regulation, which have recently functioned as marketing strategies; moderation in food consumption; attention to issues pertaining to healthfulness, food justice, and waste reduction; and the promotion of ecological responsibility. In this way, as anthropologist Florence Bergeaud-Blackler argues, this approach proposes to supplant the market-driven "Muslim consumer" with the more ethically oriented "consuming Muslim."[53]

Healthy Halal

For those unconvinced by pro-animal, environmental, or alter-globalist arguments in themselves, the health benefits associated with consuming tayyib food—which not only enables one to abide by religious injunctions but also results in better nourishment and physical well-being—might be more persuasive. The halal-should-be-healthy discourse provides even greater incentive to abandon or restrict meat consumption. Food's healing properties were commonly discussed in medieval Islamic medical texts and in numerous culinary treatises. Although tayyib is broadly tied to what's good for the body, medieval jurists, if not early modern ones, scarcely engaged with discourses of medical welfare when it came to defining the term. But in recent expositions, the idea of tayyib-halal food as health-giving, nutritious, and nourishing is presented with greater certainty, as an established concept with deep historical roots. Today several writers note that tayyib means "wholesome and safe to consume" and that "halal is not only a religious motive, but it conveys the idea of hygiene, wholesomeness and being friendly to the society, the environment and the animals."[54]

This sentiment becomes more apparent within specific attempts to link organic food with halal considerations via tayyib. In addition to questioning the ethical bases of nonorganic food production,[55] for instance, many modern Muslims reject food contaminated with pesticides, antibiotics, or additives; they seek to avoid the adverse health effects of such substances by buying organic produce and meat. Since the protection of the believer's physical well-being is a religious obligation, they opine, Muslims are duty-bound to avoid substances that might harm them. From this perspective, halal food has to be organic. Indeed, in a recent market study, one Muslim American family expressed this preference in no uncertain terms, arguing that halal "is not really Halal, in this country. We don't think [nonorganic] factory farming is able to produce a Halal product, although the final slaughter technique may be technically Halal." Organic food, they noted by explicitly associating their ethical and health-based concerns in dietary practices, respects "the health of the individual and the planet. Those should be qualities of Halal as well."[56] Although organic food is unaffordable for many, the demand for it is on the rise, with more Muslims in the West as well as in Indonesia, Saudi Arabia, Malaysia, Bulgaria, Turkey, and Kyrgyzstan expressing their preferences for high-quality organic ingredients that also meet halal standards.[57]

Beyond attempts to define halal as organic, some consumers and advocates also seek better labeling of halal food products: labeling with more detail and a greater emphasis on food items' healthfulness and nutritious qualities. Although technically sugar, fats, candies, and chocolates might be halal, more Muslims are consciously searching for foods that meet dietary, medical, and halal standards. For example, a 2011 study clearly revealed that Emirati shoppers expect their halal food to be "healthy and natural" and not to cause harmful diseases like cancer, diabetes, or obesity.[58] Recently various GCC countries, including the Emirates, have become disproportionately afflicted with obesity-related illnesses and have begun considering the reduction of processed foods and hydrogenated oils. The GCC is also exploring the overuse of chemical preservatives and GMOs as well as the correct labeling of organic food, due to concern for consumers' "health and safety."[59] This focus on customers' needs and wants, and on the market appeal of "healthful" tayyib-halal food products, will likely preoccupy producers and governments in the coming years. As one Dutch halal auditing company puts it, "a healthy lifestyle forms the basis of Halal. Apart from more exercise through sports and leisure, eating more consciously is the main path toward living a healthy life. Eating consciously means eating Halal food."[60]

Although Malaysia's *MS1500:2009* and the OIC-issued *SMIIC 1* do not overtly use the term tayyib, many of their provisions are concerned with the healthfulness of halal food and its cross-contamination not only with known najis substances (e.g., pork, dog, alcohol) but also with undesirable chemicals and excessive additives. Many international standards require, moreover, that halal foods be produced under hygienic conditions. *MS1500:2009* states that processed foods and their constituent ingredients "shall be safe for consumption, non-poisonous, non-intoxicating or non-hazardous to health."[61] *SMIIC 1* insists that "hygiene, sanitation, and food safety are prerequisites in the preparation of halal food."[62] It is unclear whether meat derived from animals injected with antibiotics or fed with potentially toxic chemicals would be deemed, under these guidelines, as hazardous to health. However, one policy recommendation has urged the Malaysian government and relevant agencies to more actively invoke health discourses when they market halal foodstuffs, in order to encourage greater sales and brand loyalty.[63]

On the other hand, Malaysia-based scholar Marco Tieman interprets modern halal injunctions as effective and healthful only if coupled with strict enforcement of tayyib ethics. Tieman says consumers cannot presume that current halal logos indicate a "healthy lifestyle choice."[64] To meet Islamic prescriptions, the halal certification system must also promote a strict diet that discourages eating processed foods, sugar, and antibiotic-laden meat and fish and instead promotes eating olives, nuts, and fruits, foods that are understood to be both tayyib and healthful in Islamic and modern medicine.

Extending this idea further, Tieman suggests a color-coded, "nutrient-profiling" halal system that warns consumers against high-fat, high-sugar, high-salt foods, which are linked to major health concerns. He points out that such a system would help fight global epidemics of heart disease, obesity, and diabetes:

> Under a traffic light system, the halal logo would have different colours: red, orange, or green. The colour would indicate if a product is a key building block of a healthy diet (green); a product with low levels of salt, sugar and/or fat (orange); or a product with high levels of salt, sugar, and/or fat (red). According to extensive research, the key building blocks of a healthy diet, or those things worthy of a "green" certification, would include such products as plain oats, vegetables, fruits, beans, seeds, fish, white meats, healthy oils, water, tea, coffee, plant-based milk and yoghurts, sugar replacers, and very dark chocolates (beyond 70% cocoa). Foods with high levels of salt, sugar and fat, on the other hand, would earn "red" certification, as these ingredients have been related to many of today's most serious diseases.[65]

Tieman does not tie his "traffic light" system to organic foods per se, but he favors the exclusion of "red meat" in favor of healthier "white meat" and fish, as well as nondairy milks and yogurts in place of dairy products. He also proposes that processed foods, even if technically categorized as halal, must be labeled with red warning signs to caution buyers of their potentially negative health repercussions.

Muslim advocates linked with the "ethical halal" movement have also taken to adopting the healthfulness discourse. On their blog, activists from the aforementioned Green Halal group recommend that each person consume no more than 400 grams of meat per week. Like Tieman, meat consumption, they argue, has been implicated in the epidemic of modern diseases and the rise of antibiotic-resistant bacteria. One activist blames these developments on Westernization and notes that "the abundance of food in Western society goes hand in hand with the bad quality of food products sold in supermarkets."[66] For "green halal" advocates, moreover, "cooking healthily" and "eating healthily" best embody the tayyib-halal intersection.[67] This new Islamic ethic directly links respect for animals and their well-being to human concerns with medical welfare: a suffering and diseased (and overmedicated) animal, no doubt, will lead to human suffering and illness.[68] Often, discussions of "healthy halal" are related to questions of ethics and provoke greater consciousness about questionable food practices, inorganic farming, cruel treatment of animals, and their links to overall human health.

More practically, some have begun to consider the concept of "willpower" (irada) in Islamic teachings as commensurate with halal eating. In addition to exploring herbal cures "in the fight against obesity," at an October 2015 conference titled "Halal and Healthy" held in Istanbul, presenters focused on "willpower training" in relation to food habits, and explored irada in the Quran, hadiths, and Sufi teachings.[69] Gluttony must be combated with a strong education program that focuses on moderation and self-control. Also, a comprehensive Islamic approach to dietary practice should entail using more rigorous halal certification guidelines in food production and teaching Muslim consumers that eating tayyib-halal food means following medical recommendations: in particular, limiting one's intake of fat, sugar, meat, and processed foods.

Resistance to Ethical and Healthy Halal

Despite high-profile artisanal organic halal butchers in downtown Manhattan and ethically oriented halal farms in the United Kingdom, food and ecological consciousness are still a novelty among the majority of Muslims, especially outside Western settings, but also in North America and Europe. According to Shireen Pishdadi, a former director at Taqwa, a Muslim food cooperative in

Chicago, many Muslims, including those in the West, resist the inclination to redefine tayyib in their dietary considerations in ethical and health-focused fashions because they "have a myopic view of halal, concerning themselves only with 'no alcohol' and 'no pork.'" Specifically, they continue to eat industrially produced meat, even though it is derived from animals that lived unsanitary and inhumane existences.[70] Moreover, to date, most Muslims still regard the idea of abandoning all consumption of meat—humanely slaughtered or not—as suspect and fringe.[71]

In fact, some scholars also oppose attempts to expand on the meaning of halal, precisely because interpretations of tayyib as ethical and healthy make it difficult for most Muslims to make halal choices. For example, in 2008, Islamic legal scholar Mohammad Hashim Kamali maintained that Muslims must "ensure that what they do, eat or drink is permissible in Shari'ah, even if it is not pure, tayyib, or best quality." It would be sufficient, Kamali argued, for those "who live, for instance, in non-Muslim majority countries to observe the rules of halal without being asked to go a step beyond halal to that of tayyib."[72] Shortly after, Kamali also offered a critique of the "more green" use of tayyib by suggesting that this "demanding position" was elitist and inflicted too many "hardships on ordinary consumers who are not sufficiently informed about the food varieties they buy in the marketplace." When it came to diet, he argued, the Islamic jurisprudential tradition was careful not to exceed the "basic" halal expectations, which made it flexible, open, and, by implication, conscientious toward ordinary people's financial abilities.[73] For Kamali and others, calls to follow a greener and more organic lifestyle, or a vegetarian philosophy, are unreasonably onerous and thus challenge Islam's core egalitarian spirit. Aside from the prohibitive cost of most organic foods, the logic follows, Muslims should have the equal opportunity to eat meat, a foodstuff that has been historically regarded—by the Prophet himself—as prized and tayyib.

Critics have also turned to religiously based attacks against animal welfare advocates, attacks that highlight humankind's absolute dominance over all living creatures in the Islamic cosmological order. Meat, some maintain, fits into the category of "what God made lawful," so abstaining from it violates basic Quranic injunctions.[74] On cattle, the Quran tells Muslims, "Eat of their [flesh], and feed the poor and unfortunate" (22:28). Animal slaughter, bloodletting, and meat consumption are enshrined in the ritual celebration of Eid al-Adha (Feast of the Sacrifice), held to mark the end of the annual hajj (pilgrimage) to Mecca. During the feast, Muslims slaughter a sheep, lamb, goat, cow, or even camel in commemoration of the Prophet Abraham's animal sacrifice given to save the life of his son Ismail.[75]

In some contexts, meat eating has been intrinsically tied to a local Muslim identity. In South Asia, for example, consumption of meat (particularly of beef) demarcated and often intensified communal boundaries between the majority Hindus, who view the cow as sacred, and the minority Muslims who ate beef because it was cheap, nutritious, and more readily available than other domestic animals. Historically, Muslims in India have viewed any attempts to ban cow slaughter, whether by British colonial rulers in the nineteenth and twentieth centuries or by Hindu nationalist governments, as an attack on their faith and cultural norms.[76] Most recently, the Indian government has issued a ban on the slaughter of cattle under the rubric of a new law against animal cruelty. Many have viewed the move as an attempt to appease conservative Hindus: among the latter, respect for living creatures is a basic religious principle and a vegetarian lifestyle is considered the ideal. For Muslims, Christians, and Dalits (lower-caste Hindus), however, the law eliminates a critical protein source.[77] In this setting, any calls for a vegetarian lifestyle can evoke a sense of discrimination and bigotry among India's minorities, particularly Muslims.

In all, while vegetarianism might be tolerated in some Muslim communities, many have suggested that it should never be presented as a fundamental Muslim way of life. This stance can be seen in relation to emerging debates in Jewish denominations in the United States: several Jewish activists have argued that an ethical approach toward food, its sourcing, and its certification must prevail in order to meet their religion's fundamental moral codes. Some have also advocated a kashrut-vegetarian lifestyle. On the other hand, as food historian Roger Horowitz notes, more Orthodox Jewish organizations have "pushed back, arguing that ethics were distinct from the requirements governing *kashrus*" and that classical kashrut concerns are solely focused on how an animal has been slaughtered, not on whether factory workers or livestock were well treated or whether a sugar- and preservative-laden processed cookie was "healthy."[78]

However, in the Islamic context, a critique of the conventional industrial meat complex and of the meat-centric position—at least in the West—has persisted despite facing robust challenges and even if it is not (yet) widely adopted. Recently, Kecia Ali observed that arguments for a Muslim vegetarian lifestyle provoke the most virulent reactions when based in discourses of animal welfare. Advocates for vegetarianism have more success, generally speaking, when they argue for improved environmental stewardship or healthfulness.[79] It is true, Ali notes, that the Muslim ethical tradition—like its Abrahamic correlates—generally privileges human welfare above animal welfare. Yet she suggests that for Muslims today, eating less or no meat might be "part of constructing a habitually virtuous self, and a more just society," and that vegetarianism can be easily situated within Islamic teachings that support moderation in eating if not extreme self-denial.[80]

Marketplace Reactions to Ethical and Healthy Halal

Notwithstanding the resistance to modern tayyib-halal formulations, as Muslim countries export more halal food products, particularly to Europe and the United States, concerns over both the ethics and healthfulness of their products have gained a higher profile.[81] A 2014–2015 Thomson Reuters report commissioned by the Dubai government declared that "a broader Halal market dynamic relates to its wider humane ethos relating to fair-treatment of animals, organic/pure (Tayyab) food and environment friendliness. While this aspect has not taken hold[,] it is a growing trend in select markets."[82] Another study produced by the International Trade Center—a joint agency with the World Trade Center and the United Nations—indicated that opportunities for growth in the halal food market will likely depend, in part, on successful "marketing based on 'tayyib' and eco-ethical values."[83] The convergence between growth in the halal food sector and eco- and health-conscious movements has become more explicit in recent years: interest in organic foods and veganism continues to rise. In May 2016, the Global Market Research Company Euromonitor International announced that "halal" and "vegan" are the fastest-growing food labels in the world, predicted to grow at a 5 percent annual rate between 2015 and 2020.[84] Some major halal producers have embraced these profitable and popular trends, exemplifying how the food industry is, as theologian and ethicist Andrew Linzey has argued, one of the most susceptible to rapidly changing consumer tastes.[85]

At a 2015 food fair in Cologne, Germany, Malaysian food businesses were not only eager to showcase the variety of their halal products but also demonstrated an awareness that "health and environmental concerns" carry more and more weight within their target European markets. Retailers offered a selection of organic and vegetarian products intended to highlight the responsiveness of Malaysian companies to customer demands in Germany and the

EU.[86] The most significant annual trade fair for all things halal, MIHAS (the Malaysia International Halal Showcase), has been billed as the largest global congregation of halal purveyors, from food and pharmaceuticals to travel and tourism.[87] Increasingly, many of MIHAS's purveyors focus on selling foods labeled halal, organic, vegetarian, and/or vegan.

But not all certifiers, producers, and their supporters have exhibited favorable responses to these market trends. Fearing that ethically minded Muslims may circumvent their halal-labeled products altogether, certain organizations warn consumers that seemingly vegan or vegetarian super-market breads, jams, cereals, and juices are not necessarily halal. The Muslim Food Board, a nonprofit certifying body in the United Kingdom, cautions that vegetarian products are often mislabeled and that the labels can be deceptive because the "subingredients" may contain animal products. More important, they claim that Muslims may never be able to trust veg-etarian products because many contain alcohol, which can be disguised as various flavor enhancers. They maintain that "halal consumers must insist that manufacturers have their products halal certified."[88] Competition with nonhalal-certified vegan and vegetarian food producers has intensified as both labels become more globally desirable and their backers stand to profit from greater product sales.

Fig. 8.2. Montreal halal restaurant. Restaurant name references tayyib in Arabic and French. Also note the halal signs in different scripts. Authors' photograph.

On the other hand, the concept of tayyib has gained the attention of commercial food producers who believe that they can expand their market by peddling foods that embody the tayyib-halal or even a tayyib-halal-organic ethos. For instance, a Hague-based private group called Stichting Halal Voeding en Voedsel (Foundation for Halal Food and Nutrition) inspects halal food production and certifies goods with a "Halal Tayyib Certificate."[89] In 2012, Othman Mohd Yusoff, president of the Nestlé Halal Committee on Regulatory Affairs in Malaysia, predicted that "halal alone won't take you far. Food must also be '*tayyib*,' which encompasses quality. In other words, food must be nutritious and hygienic, and manufacturers must ethically deliver what a consumer wants."[90] Yusoff's position illustrates how sensitive halal food purveyors and certifiers are to the demands of their more conscientious and, in some cases, more affluent consumers. Nestlé has been active in calling for consistent global halal regulations that appeal not only to Muslims but also to non-Muslims. By demanding more streamlined and universal standards, Nestlé and the food business community at large are focused on making and marketing products that elevate halal to "a global standard for safe and wholesome food."[91]

Large retailers have become more involved in producing halal food that is also ethical and healthy. Nema Food Company, based in Pittsburgh, Pennsylvania, targets consumers seeking "healthy and high-quality products" and celebrates its "adherence to environmental issues."[92] In Turkey, where a majority of food products are ostensibly halal, there is growing demand for organic foods. Large corporations like Pınar, for instance, have been producing organic dairy products since 2005.[93] Some Turkish organic producers are keen to advertise their products as halal and organic, recognizing the cachet that both labels would have for knowledgeable consumers. Others have begun labeling their products *doğal*, or natural, although Turkish consumer organizations have called these labels confusing as they can misguide consumers into thinking that products are fully free of GMOs, pesticides, hormones, chemicals, and antibiotics. As with the halal market, consumer advocates have asked for greater farmer education, better standardization, and more government administration in the tayyib-halal-organic food sector.[94]

A few providers have tailored their products to address specific concerns about disease. To combat childhood obesity, in 2007 the notable halal food purveyor and Dubai-based Al Islami Foods launched "Aladdin," a halal and mostly meat-based line of products targeted at children (e.g., chicken nuggets, mini burgers) that promised to be more nutritious, lower in fat, and higher in protein. The company argues that the focus on high-protein and low-fat products—if animal-based—was grounded in conventional scientific studies that concluded children should eat more protein.[95] The GCC region seems particularly poised to take advantage of trends tied to organic, ethical, and eco-conscious production of foods. In GCC countries, expenditure for organic produce alone, for instance, is expected to reach $1.5 billion by 2018, and there is growing desire for "sustainable and responsibly sourced" products, including cage-free eggs, free-range chickens, and eco-responsible meats. Although limited water resources and scarce grazing lands hinder the locavore sector in those countries, one study suggests that the market for seasonal local produce, meat, and seafood has been expanding. Consumer interest correlates with growing desires for a healthful lifestyle combined with the GCC countries' higher purchasing power.[96] Against these trends, however, some in the halal food industry suggest that most Muslims have lower purchasing power than other consumers and that for now, particularly in non-Muslim countries, tayyib-halal-organic products should be marketed for more "mainstream" (i.e. non-Muslim) customers.[97]

Across the world, more and more consumers are paying attention to how farm animals are treated or slaughtered, whether their vegetables were sprayed with toxic chemicals, or if their cereal is really healthy. At the grocery store, they peruse food labels to help them make sound purchasing decisions. From the American to Iranian markets, young couples, busy household heads, and working parents seek to buy food that is free of additives and antibiotics as well as ethically oriented products that are delicious, healthy, and halal.[98] In the process, and as discussed in an earlier chapter, many have acquired a sort of halal savviness, learning to decipher labels, closely read ingredients, or even scan product barcodes with their smartphones. In this context, "vegan," "vegetarian," "organic," "GMO-free," and "halal" all represent additional coded messages for shoppers eager to buy what's best for themselves and their families.

Among Muslim consumers, however, a growing number question whether a halal marker implies quality or healthfulness or guarantees that their meat came from well-treated animals. Despite some pushback, farmers, butchers, activists, and intellectuals have imagined a new tayyib-halal ethos, one that variably calls for animal and workers' rights, environmental protection, and healthful eating. At times, their use of "tayyib" can mean humane, unadulterated, and, quite often, organic; these values, many argue, ensure that halal's core but hitherto ignored legal requirements are truly met. Others call for more healthful halal consumption; they hold accountable slaughterers and manufacturers of packaged foods who fill their products with salt, sugar, unhealthy fats, artificial flavorings, and GMOs, ingredients that might be "halal" by the strictest definition but are also implicated in obesity, heart disease, hypertension, and diabetes. Outside of activist circles, these redefinitions have also been shaped by and have appealed to small businesses, multinational corporations, and state actors who might be eager to sell halal to non-Muslims by marketing it as healthy, pure, ethical, and as a "universal standard for a quality brand."[99]

The gradual move away from industrially produced halal meat to organic halal (i.e., healthy and drug-free animals), to humanely raised "green zabiha," to semivegetarianism, and finally toward adopting a fully vegetarian, vegan, and/or GMO-free lifestyle should be situated in the context of the global industrialization of halal food. Activists have taken to the Internet, blogs, and social media to raise consciousness and attract young, savvy, and better-educated followers. Protesting a profit-seeking model that overlooks ecological mindfulness or animal welfare, they argue that food produced by the modern halal industry is dubious (mashbuh) if not altogether haram. A new plurality of voices challenges hegemonic discourses, rules, and laws. It may be impossible to remain completely untouched by global capitalism and its instrumentalization of halal. Yet this sort of political engagement offers some representation in a conversation long dominated by ulama, states, corporations, and certifying bodies and generates opportunities to develop anti-establishment alternatives to mainstream trends. Although tayyib-halal is often seen as too onerous and financially burdensome, activists argue that it captures Islam's true egalitarian and ethical spirit. To what extent these trends will continue shaping the halal sector remains to be seen.

CHAPTER 9

n recent years, many Muslims have embraced halal food as a mark of their religious and cultural identity—and have imbued halal with new gastronomic cachet. For some, halal cooking and eating are being reimagined as part of a "cuisine," something akin to Italian, French, Chinese, or Indian food. Halal cooking connoisseurs and foodies (the latter often nicknamed "halalis" or, in one now-trademarked iteration, "haloodies") are diverse and scattered, but collectively they have ushered in a way of seeing halal not just as a form of pious practice or religious way of life but as a label that can apply to anything from kebab, biryani, and tandoori to "Coq without the Vin," wagyu steak, and foie gras.[1] New self-styled experts have been transforming any recipe from any repertoire into an appealing and religiously sanctioned dish.

This chapter uses the phrase "halal cuisine" (versus simply "halal food") to describe an ongoing phenomenon or—more accurately perhaps—an aspiration that has emerged since the early 2000s alongside the global obsession with all things culinary. To be clear, Muslim and non-Muslim usage of the phrase "halal cuisine" is still nascent and tentative, and its meanings are often vague, broad, and even conflicting.[2] But the halal cooks, chefs, and foodies discussed here have consciously imagined a cuisine. In the process, they have considered how halal food relates to and overlaps with established culinary repertoires.

Within popular media, halal cuisine is commonly but not exclusively made by Muslims, from recipes that are often but not strictly inspired by dishes from Muslim regions. Halal cooking experts point out that with the proper substitutions, even a recipe like risotto with parmesan cheese (questionable rennet) and white wine (alcohol) can be tweaked into a delectable and halal dish. Also, consistent with global consumption trends discussed in earlier chapters, many experts relish and highlight meat-centric dishes. For many Muslims, the creative and deliberate halalification of recipes allows them to fully enjoy and participate in the global food revolution—in the "fetishization of food, of cooking and eating, of watching other people cooking and eating that has become omnipresent across all platforms, all media, all screens and all palates."[3] And they can do so as Muslims who are proud of and unapologetic about their food customs and habits. Here the banner of cuisine and the idea of a common cooking style have not only, in a sense, helped unify Muslims all over the world but have also assured diaspora Muslims that they can integrate into various national and global culinary landscapes in good conscience, by eating halal versions of burgers, pizzas, or renowned gourmet dishes.[4]

The term "cuisine" is usually associated today with a country or nation. Following anthropologist Arjun Appadurai's work on cuisine creation in India, food historian Alison Smith defines national or ethnic cuisines as "collections of prepared dishes, created out of agricultural, trade, regional, local, family, and religious differences and traditions, and presented to a public—sometimes to introduce a nation to its own members, sometimes to introduce that nation to the outside world, and sometimes to preserve the memory of a nation in an immigrant population—through cookbooks, other media, restaurants, and specific goods."[5] In today's world, national cuisines are often a source of cultural pride and foster feelings of ethnocentrism; they can also allow for a greater degree of marketability and for the development of profitable products that could range from instructive cookbooks to smartphone apps replete with appropriate recipes.[6]

On the whole, though, "halal cuisine" evades this nationalist definition. "Halal has no territory or nation," writes religion scholar Romi Mukherjee. It can be "consumed anywhere" and is detached "from histories of recipes, of modes of cooking, of cultivations of national taste and cuisine." For this reason, contemporary notions of a halal cuisine are both adaptable and "vaporous."[7] Political scientist Olivier Roy has suggested that for Muslim "neofundamentalists" who seek—through ethical or lifestyle changes—to create a non-nationalist, globalized, and universal form of Islam, "cuisine" is irrelevant: "Anything that is halal is good, whatever the basic ingredients and the recipe."[8] Roy concludes that for these pious devotees, "halal is a way to kill an animal, not a way to cook it."[9] While this may be the case for some Muslims, for others, the evocation and usage of "halal cuisine" today (over a decade after Roy initially offered this analysis) helps to cultivate culinary recognition, consumer loyalty, and an arguably discriminating palate. For many culinary connoisseurs discussed here, "halal cuisine" is evidence of their individual gastronomic expertise in religious rules and in creating a sophisticated and refined cooking style. Attempts to define halal cuisine might reflect the idea that cooking halal-tayyib, tasty, and satisfying food is also "doing God's work."

As with more established cuisines, popular media—written, visual, and virtual—have played a critical role in shaping halal cooking and eating. In these media, many Muslim cooks and foodies have envisioned halal cuisine as a set of choices and preferences, based on the avoidance of certain ingredients and the purchase of specific halal products, rather than a collection of culinary techniques and skills. Some explicitly work toward this cuisine creation, while others avoid such terminology and simply hold that halal cooking—much like other culinary trends—represents what is delicious, global, and marketable. In either case, these culinary entrepreneurs are determining how halal food is crafted, consumed, and recognized throughout the world. They include television personalities, cookbook authors, blog writers, and social media celebrities, along with restaurateurs, chefs, and business owners.

The final two chapters of the book look at evolving conceptions of halal cuisine and the eating culture that accompanies them. Chapter 9 begins by exploring the varied endeavors to create and define cuisine, as well as the tensions and contradictions embedded in this process. This discussion is followed by media discourses shaping halal cuisine that run the gamut and further obscure a clear definition as they display an eclectic repertoire of recipes, ingredients, and cooking styles, sometimes mixed with religious edification and instruction.

"No Bacon Here!": Magazines and Blogs

"Cuisine" can be defined as a style of cooking and eating but also as the reliance on a creative toolbox of techniques, specific ingredients, and recipes as well as an awareness about food's place within certain cultural or geographic boundaries.[10] Food historians have noted, in the context of nineteenth-century France, that cuisine became articulated and defined through the expansion of print media by way of journalists, novelists, and philosophers.[11] That is, it was constructed primarily through a vast textual discourse, wherein culinary "writings extended the gastronomic public or 'taste community,'" as French food scholar Priscilla Ferguson writes, "well beyond immediate producers and consumers." Those texts helped transform a fundamentally "culinary product"—food— "into a cultural one," much like art or music.[12]

Halal cuisine evokes a cooking "style" in the sense that it uses or avoids specific ingredients, but it is not necessarily tied to a certain region or set of dishes.[13] "Cuisine," in that sense, could evoke an aspiration, a way for Muslim food connoisseurs to elevate "Muslim cooking" or "Muslims' cooking" to the level of other bona fide cuisines and, by doing so, to attain international recognition and affirmation. While it's difficult to pinpoint when this phenomenon emerged, the remarkable proliferation of websites, blogs, newsletters, cookbooks, and visual forms since the late 1990s and early 2000s reflects the demands of a young and more affluent generation of Muslims—most of them based in non-Muslim countries—who are eager to participate and take pleasure in the international "food rave" and to profit from global food trends.[14] Increased attention to halal cooking and eating also coincides with the numerous developments of the 1990s and 2000s discussed in previous chapters: the rise of halal-oriented consumerist and market-driven trends as well as the increasing numbers of Muslims culturally adapting to varied diasporic settings.

So what might one find in a halal cookbook, blog, newsletter, Facebook page, or TV show? What do Muslims' visions of a halal cuisine look like? A quick look at *Halal Consumer*, a print and online newsletter issued by the American halal certification agency IFANCA, provides some initial clues. Since the mid-2000s, this publication has included a regular section showcasing dishes and recipes drawn from different parts of the Muslim world in order to educate its (mostly American) readers about a sophisticated and perhaps unfamiliar palate. A typical collection of recipes might include a sweet Arabian pancake called *qatayef*; an Iranian-Iraqi date-filled pastry called *klaicha*; Beef Rendang, a Malaysian dish of spicy beef; and South African Curried Lamb Meatloaf. IFANCA presents these dishes as illustrating "an abundance of diverse tastes and culinary traditions" from Islamic lands rather than showcasing specific flavors or techniques.[15] That is, IFANCA associates traditional recipes from the Islamic world—foods that Muslims have made, dishes that Muslims have historically innovated—with the essence of halal cooking culture. A later issue of *Halal*

Consumer, however, goes further, offering a recipe for "halal top sirloin with avocado sauce" and specifying that readers should use an IFANCA-certified halal beef product. Here it's not the spices or the geographic origins of a recipe that matter but the presentation of an appetizing, easy-to-prepare dish based on an authentically halal product that makes for "great grilling," as the article suggests.[16] Similarly, since 2004 Britain's Halal Monitoring Committee (HMC) has issued newsletters with recipes that describe, for example, the use of "HMC approved" meat as yielding "Tantalising HMC Chops."[17] Thus there are two distinct elements of a halal "cuisine": the use of recipes from Islamic lands ("Muslim food") and the incorporation of products—mostly of meat—sanctioned as halal by modern certification bodies.

Highlighting similar themes, other media have shown Muslims how to convert popular recipes drawn from trendy global cuisines into halal fare. A 2005 article in *Azizah*, a magazine tailored to Muslim American women, attempts to bridge Italian and Middle Eastern cuisines and, in the process, devises halal-appropriate recipes. First the author, Amy El-Tanbedawy, reminds readers that Muslim Arabs played an important role in shaping Italian cookery.[18] Next she lists recipes for delicious and halal pasta sauces, ranging from simple vegan fare and shrimp ragouts (which may not be halal for all Muslims; see chapter 2) to sauces relying on "grated halal or organic rennetless parmigiano reggiano or pecorino romano cheese."[19] It is difficult to discern major differences in technique or flavor within these recipes and their original inspirations. But through them El-Tanbedawy achieves her goal of proving that trendy dishes are easily halal-adaptable. She encourages Muslims to lay claim to many Italian foods, presenting them as "originally Arab" and then "reverting" to the use of appropriate halal ingredients (e.g., rennetless cheese).

These approaches toward halal cooking carry over into dozens of food blogs. Following the newsletter and magazine model, blogs craft a convenient, eye-appealing ideal of halal home cooking; by teaching readers how to prepare, innovate, and modify recipes, they simultaneously embody a cuisine and a lifestyle. One such resource for Canadian Muslims is the Toronto-based site Halal Foodie. Replete with recipes, photographs, local restaurant recommendations, and even an eponymous magazine, the site also reports on the latest halal restaurant openings; offers religious clarifications on specific food additives ("Pectin is vegetarian and therefore halal"); and posts provocative pieces like "Confessions of a Muslim Vegetarian." Halal Foodie readers can try out its recipes for homemade treats such as halal marshmallows and "Watermelon

Granita," which is billed as a "cool dessert/drink/mocktail." The author of the former recipe, Hafsa, recounts how she struggled, as a child, to integrate with her Canadian peers, envious as she was of their marshmallow snacks. "Whether it was s'mores, Rice Krispie squares, or even just marshmallows straight out of the package," she notes, "I was always left out."[20] But with access to halal gelatin, Hafsa can create homemade delectable treats that recapture lost pleasures from her childhood and satisfy her taste buds, all while complying with religious mandates and expectations.

Other websites follow the same multicontributor model. Halal Recipes Japan is that country's first (self-declared) halal recipe website. Like Halal Foodie, it guides readers on how to choose halal supermarket products (a challenging endeavor in Japan, where many processed foods include pork derivatives or alcohol); offers information about "Muslim cooking events"; and lists a rich array of Japanese recipes that re-create noodle, rice, fish, and meat dishes using exclusively halal ingredients. Developed by a nutrition professor at Bunkyo University and his students, the site serves an educational purpose for non-Muslim Japanese who are curious about "how to cook dishes for Muslims," implying that there is a distinct cooking style to be mastered. The website also offers valuable information for the growing Japanese halal restaurant sector.[21]

Some blogs embrace halal's gastronomic globalization while at the same time highlighting one (celebrity) cook's talents. An American site titled Amanda's Plate is the brainchild of Amanda Saab, who in 2015 famously became the first woman to wear a head scarf (a hijab) on an American cooking show, in this case the FOX network's *Masterchef*. Before an audience of millions, Saab was able to participate in global food trends (including televised cooking shows) while proudly displaying her Muslim identity. On her blog, Saab shares her passion for cooking and eating, which began at the age of five. She strives to integrate her Muslim beliefs with her American heritage: most of her recipes have a clear North American flavor profile, and her guacamole, spaghetti squash, cinnamon rolls, and brownies win rave reviews from readers. Without using the term "halal," she warmly invites everyone to try her recipes, noting that they "will find the yummy treats, the savory bites and everything else that is created in my kitchen." But Saab also asserts her halal-based identity with the following caveat: "I am Muslim, so no bacon here!"[22]

Arguably one of the most important and popular English-language sites in this genre is My Halal Kitchen. Launched in 2008 by Yvonne Maffei, this blog includes an array of recipes from different ethnic traditions and captures yet another perspective on halal as cuisine. Maffei notes that she came up with the idea for her blog after seeing "a gap in the discussion about halal food in the culinary world and in the newly emerging food blogs at the time," adding, "I figure that I can't be the only one searching for answers."[23] Maffei—a Sicilian–Puerto Rican, Ohio-born, Chicago-based writer who converted from Catholicism to Islam[24]—promises to inform readers about "food and products that are natural, organic, pure, halal, raised humanely, sourced ethically and brought to market without poisonous toxins and chemicals." She presents an honest, warm, and welcoming openness: one of her mottos is "You'll always get the very best of what's cooking in my halal kitchen."[25] Before she began blogging, Maffei spent several years as IFANCA's "resident chef" and wrote a regular column for *Halal Consumer* titled "Cooking with Yvonne." That column, her blog, and her highly popular Facebook page (which has over 1.2 million likes, as of 2017) made her a celebrity within the English-speaking halal foodie community.

Notably, Maffei is one of the few bloggers who has attempted to define the phrase "halal cuisine." She suggests that this gastronomic concept is born out of a process of "conversion" and "reversion": when people—like her—convert to Islam or "'revert' to their natural religion . . . they must adapt the tastes and dishes they were raised with to halal guidelines." That is, one fully adheres to the religion by strictly following its food customs and, in this case, by adapting the familiar foods of one's national or ethnic heritage—Italian or Mexican, French or American—into halal meals made with halal ingredients, a process that requires some "creativity" and guidance from food experts like Maffei herself.[26] This, for her, is cuisine creation. In various interviews and on her website, Maffei serves as a critical interlocutor for interpreting halal cuisine. Her goal is to teach "the home cook how to make any dish from any global cuisine halal . . . without sacrificing flavor," and she insists that "it's really important to keep the integrity of the dish. It must be delicious. Otherwise, what's the point?"[27] Her website is notable for the helpful charts it offers to home cooks who are eager to try cuisines (e.g., French) known for using haram products in copious quantities. She suggests alternatives for everything from chorizo, pancetta, and prosciutto (replaced with *sucuk* or Turkish sausage, Merguez or North African sausage, and duck prosciutto respectively) to liquors like Calvados, Cointreau, and Tequila (replaced with apple juice, orange-flavored sugar syrup, and aloe juice respectively).[28] Affirming her own and her audience's domestic authority, Maffei guides readers toward appropriate and certified replacements.

Some substitutions are slightly more rigorous than IFANCA's. For instance, Maffei recommends omitting any vanilla extract that contains alcohol, even though IFANCA and other Muslim certifying bodies have permitted this product.[29] This suggestion stems from the argument that cooking with any form of alcohol still leaves residual traces in the final dish and must therefore be avoided. On the other hand, Maffei appears pragmatic and even flexible in her other creations. For example, while some might object to the idea of eating "turkey bacon," a product that (like nonalcoholic beer) might too closely emulate its haram lookalike, Maffei has no problem proposing this substitute in recipes calling for the real thing.[30] Maffei's suggestions may reflect her desire to create a repertoire of "signature recipes," to highlight her own inventive and, at times, discriminating cooking vision which takes advantage and promotes the halal marketplace and all of its offerings. Her cooking style, in a sense, reflects that impulse of conservative dynamism discussed in earlier chapters: the aspiration, by some Muslims today, to remain faithful to their Islamic heritage while also being adaptive to new products and opportunities.

Importantly, like Saab and many other first- and second-generation halal foodies living in non-Muslim countries, Maffei does not define halal cooking as (just) traditional Muslim recipes from the Middle East or South Asia. Halal cooking, for her, includes a boundless array of delicious dishes for the home cook to choose from. In that sense, halal cuisine represents the desire to elevate ordinary meals into something that is cosmopolitan and that allows individuals to participate, as Mukherjee notes, "in the greater brotherhood" and sisterhood of Muslims "through dietary choices."[31]

With regard to sisterhoods, halal blogs (and other media) are dominated by women and often function as "prescriptive household texts" that offer useful and timesaving information about nutrition, taste, and religious compliance. As these "texts" rise in popularity, female culinary celebrities and entrepreneurs help introduce new generations of Muslims to suitable, modern, and cosmopolitan halal eating; in the process, it seems, they are creating new forms of "domestic authority" for women.[32] In the Muslim world and especially among the Muslim diaspora, as anthropologist Florence Bergeaud-Blackler has noted, women have been at the forefront of developing the "art of [halal] cooking" and redrawing halal "food spaces." It is up to mothers, as household managers and home cooks, to police everything from supermarket purchases and Ramadan fasting to overall food purity; they are the guardians of a "domestic religious economy."[33] Halal-oriented media are now celebrating these contributions and highlighting a particular culinary and business mindset.[34] They reflect global trends in which women's influences on cooking and food writing have been more publicly celebrated: on television, on the web, and in print.[35] They also capture the entry of a new group of Muslim women entrepreneurs who are more actively partaking in and shaping the halal marketplace, often through the promotion of specific halal products. Today the public face of halal food— and by extension of halal "cuisine"—is arguably that of women like Maffei, figures who are becoming more recognizable, and perhaps trusted more as experts, than the (predominantly male) butchers, slaughterhouse operators, certifiers, and businessmen.

Cookbooks

Like blogs, cookbooks are emerging as a small but important arena for the formulation of a halal cuisine. In past centuries, cookbooks played a critical role in royal Islamic kitchens, from Abbasid caliphs to Mughal and Ottoman sultans. In the premodern world, as Appadurai has noted, such texts were part of an haute cuisine produced in societies where the wealthy could access the most sophisticated and expensive of ingredients and, more important, where they had "the special resources required for the production and consumption of written texts."[36] Food that Muslims have historically eaten (and cookbooks that Muslims have traditionally written) represents the epitome of gastronomic cosmopolitanism in their day. Many traditional dishes were lost; others became integrated into regional and national cuisines and have thus indirectly shaped contemporary halal cooking. Although today's halal cookbooks mix some of these recipes with modern fare, they are more democratic than their precursors; they are often written by ordinary Muslims, home cooks, blogosphere celebrities, and women. Especially for Muslims living in the West, they reflect a culinary ethos that responds to globalization, migration, and assimilation (or resistance to it) and is closely aware of what ingredients, recipes, and cooking styles might best suit busy lifestyles as well as current tastes and mores.

For decades, cookbooks about ethnic cuisines from Muslim-populated regions like the Middle East or Southeast and South Asia have been both plentiful and popular. But books devoted solely to halal or even to "Muslim food" are just starting to make their mark. By all indications they will find scores of devoted followers—particularly in North America, where the cookbook market is fairly expansive: here cookbooks reign as "objects of desire," and lavish, beautiful, well-styled offerings sell particularly well.[37] The emergence of halal cookbooks in the United States shares some commonalities with the proliferation of American kosher cookbooks, from the 1950s onward. In early days, the latter scarcely discussed food in relation to kosher labels or kosher-certified food.[38] By the 1990s, however, kosher cookbooks—focused on kosher ingredients and kosher-certified products—became newly popular at a time when American Jews faced increased challenges of assimilation, intermarriage, and denominational diversity. They helped develop a "national transnational cuisine" that advocated belonging to a Jewish community and integrating within broader American culture.[39]

Similarly, halal cookbooks with a transnational orientation can link readers to broader Muslim histories, customs, and habits as well as to those of their adopted homelands.[40] Electronic and self-published "Muslim cookbooks" have become more prevalent over the past few years. From its different global sites, Amazon.com offers readers downloadable cookbooks in English, French, Urdu, and Arabic covering diverse topics, from "foods of Ramadan" to "eco-halal Sufi vegan/vegetarian" fare. But even prior to the electronic book revolution, a few printed English-language cookbooks focused on "Muslim food." The *Muslim World Cook Book,* published in 1973 by the Women's Committee of the Muslim Students' Association in the United States and Canada, follows a more traditional model and offers basic culinary recommendations for diaspora Muslims. It lists halal rules and "recommended foods" and guides readers on Muslim eating etiquette. "Muslims are advised," as the introduction cautions against gluttony, "not to eat more than two-thirds of their normal capacity, and sharing of food is recommended." The book also points out that to avoid putting non-Muslims in awkward situations of serving pork or alcohol to Muslim guests, more widespread education about halal rules is needed for the American public.[41] As to recipes, the book embodies that transnational ideal and includes dishes from throughout the Muslim world but also from the United States (e.g., "Southern Yam Cauliflower Bake" and "Baked Tuna Fish with Noodles").[42] With its basic suggestions and instructions, the book likely appealed to students and home cooks alike. Halal cooking, for its authors, can bring together diaspora Muslims or converts through a shared (if newly imagined) food heritage.

Following the *Muslim World Cook Book*'s publication, a seemingly long lull ensued in the English-language halal cookbook market. In 2005, Linda Delgado released *Halal Food, Fun, and Laughter*, a brief primer that combines "good food, some fun and laughter but most importantly, remembrances of Allah" with the aim of creating "a happier and healthier recipe for your life."[43] Delgado's approach is to intersperse recipes with Quranic verses and hadiths and to use the cookbook as a form of religious edification.[44] A more current offering is Yvonne Maffei's *My Halal Kitchen: Global Recipes, Cooking Tips, Lifestyle Inspiration*, published in the summer of 2016. With its lustrous photographs, easy instructions, and colloquial appeal, it will likely be seen as a pioneer in this genre. In anticipation of its release and likely for the first time that a "Muslim cookbook" received such prominent accolades, the popular food website epicurious.com listed *My Halal Kitchen* as one of the most anticipated summer offerings, describing Maffei's cooking style as inclusive of "pretty much everything that can be made Halal."[45] Like the *Muslim World Cook Book*, the book offers basic advice on how to eat halal. But the book goes further, capturing how halal cuisine in the early twenty-first century is a broader matter that encompasses recipes, religious prescriptions, and a modern and cosmopolitan way of life.[46]

Expanding on material from her blog, Maffei provides useful sections for how to set up a halal kitchen (e.g., stock up on alcohol-free extracts, use agar-agar instead of gelatin) as well as several "tips for buying halal." In this list, Maffei suggests that readers ask their meat suppliers about how farmers treat and feed their animals; try to purchase organic milk, cheese, and produce; find out whether the cheese was washed with wine or (pork) lard; familiarize themselves with "quality" halal brands; grow their own food, when feasible; and, importantly, "study the Sunnah foods, those that the Prophet Muhammed ate. It was the practice of Prophet Muhammed to eat nutrient-dense foods, and he ate everything in moderation."[47] In one brief page, Maffei captures much of the discussion in previous chapters: for a conscientious, discriminating, and well-informed Muslim consumer, halal today is about the legal permissibility of food, but it is also healthy eating, sourced from ethically treated animals and reliable halal certifiers (IFANCA, in this case), and always eaten in moderation. The cookbook allows Maffei to cast a bright light on her culinary skills and her expert knowledge of legal codes and modern certification processes. Although she offers an early disclaimer—"I am not a scholar of Islam by any means"—she quickly adds, "I study food science and Islamic jurisprudence (*fiqh*) whenever I can—speaking to scholars, studying texts, listening to lectures, and attending courses."[48] She thus establishes her authority as Muslim chef, culinary expert, and interpreter of religious dictums. Her status as an American convert, moreover, allows her to mediate between the mainstream and the halal by translating American food to an array of Muslims, particularly those of immigrant background, who may otherwise be daunted by the foreignness of their new culinary environment.

Maffei's recipes are decidedly global in their taste profile, reflecting her target North American readers' interest in Asian, French, Italian, Latin, and American cooking. On first glance, many seem ordinary, such as homemade yogurt, crème fraiche, and ricotta cheese but several commercial versions of those might contain questionable ingredients like gelatin or rennet, and while suitable alternatives can be found in some markets, Maffei points out, they can be prohibitively expensive. Making such foods at home—rather than relying on suspect supermarket labels—guarantees their tastiness, freshness, and halalness. She also calls attention to more conspicuous haram products. Readers can use her recipes for mayonnaise and breads, for example, instead of buying store-bought correlates that can include questionable emulsifiers or dough conditioners. She warns that Dijon mustard, a French product, is traditionally made with wine, which may leave traces in the commercial product.[49] Other recipes focus on re-creating stand-bys: she offers alternatives to soy sauce (which may contain "remnants of alcohol")[50] and Béarnaise sauce (replace the white wine with white balsamic vinegar), and dishes such as asparagus wrapped in turkey (instead of bacon), beef pepperoni pizza, and "Coq without the Vin," Maffei's signature playful twist on a classic Julia Child recipe.[51] The book, incidentally, caters to omnivores and is decidedly meat-centric; few recipes target vegans or vegetarians.

Visual and Online Media

Aspirations of a coherent halal cuisine have also emerged within visual and online media. Turkey offers a good example of this growing genre on television. In the mid-twentieth century, Turkish cuisine, as broadcast on the radio or in print, promoted "modern" Western food and customs.[52] The Western culinary trend predominated until the 1990s, when more pious Islamic sensibilities became apparent in Turkey and elsewhere. At that time, the commercialization

Recipe Box 9.1   Yvonne Maffei's Recipe for *Coq without the Vin*

In this recipe, Maffei transforms Julia Child's famous recipe into a halal-compliant dish by incorporating substitutes like grape juice instead of red wine and cognac, and breakfast strips instead of lardons or thickly sliced bacon.

3 ounces beef breakfast strips
1 whole chicken, cut up, skin removed, and patted dry
1 ½ teaspoons sea salt, plus more to taste if desired
½ teaspoon freshly ground pepper, plus more to taste if desired
2 cups Concord grape juice (not from concentrate)
2 tablespoons minced garlic
1 tablespoons tomato paste
2 sprigs fresh or 2 teaspoons dried thyme
2 bay leaves
4 tablespoons unsalted butter, divided
1 pound crimini or button mushrooms, roughly chopped
½ yellow onion, thinly sliced
3 tablespoons all-purpose flour
1 (1-pound) package pappardelle or egg noodles, cooked
2 tablespoons chopped fresh flat leaf parsley, for garnish

1. In a large, deep-bottomed saucepan or Dutch oven over medium heat, sauté the beef strips in their own fat for 3 minutes, until they are nicely browned and somewhat crisp. Remove the strips to a paper towel-lined plate to drain any excess fat.
2. Season each of the chicken pieces with the salt and black pepper. Add the chicken pieces to the saucepan and cook on 1 side for 5 minutes, until browned. Turn and repeat until all sides are browned.
3. Return the beef strips to the saucepan. Add the grape juice, garlic, tomato paste, thyme, and bay leaves. Cover and cook over medium heat for 25 minutes.
4. While the chicken is cooking, in a large sauté pan over medium-high heat, melt 2 tablespoons of the butter. Add the mushrooms and onion. Season to taste with the salt and pepper and sauté for 10 minutes, until the mushrooms are browned and the onion is translucent and browned.
5. Create a roux by combining the remaining 2 tablespoons of butter and the flour in a small mixing bowl. Mix them together with your fingers until the butter and flour are fully incorporated.

6. Remove the cover from the saucepan. Using a slotted spoon, remove the chicken pieces from the saucepan and set them aside on a plate. Remove and discard the bay leaves. Add the roux to the saucepan and whisk vigorously until the roux has completely integrated into the liquid, the mixture has thickened, and there are no lumps. Return the chicken to the saucepan and gently stir in the sautéed mushrooms and onion.

7. Raise the heat to medium-high and bring the mixture to a boil.

8. Reduce the heat to medium, cover, and simmer for 20 minutes. The liquid in the saucepan should be thick enough to slightly stick to the back of a spoon. (If not, raise the heat to high and cook, uncovered, for 2 to 3 minutes, until the sauce cooks down.) Remove from the heat.

9. Remove the chicken with a slotted spoon and transfer to a serving platter lined with the cooked pappardelle or egg noodles. Ladle the sauce, including the mushrooms and onion, over the chicken and pasta. Garnish with parsley and serve hot.

From Yvonne Maffei, *My Halal Kitchen: Global Recipes, Cooking Tips, Lifestyle Inspiration*, 133–134.

of the food industry was also booming, with the greater production of prepackaged foods and the rise of the halal certification industry.

Changing trends eventually allowed television food celebrity Emine Beder to become a household name via a repertoire of cooking programs, including the recent *Kitchen Love* (*Mutfak Aşkı*). Beder's show on the religiously oriented channel Beyaz TV introduces Islamic principles to the Turkish kitchen.[53] With her modest head covering and her cooking savvy, Beder uses *Kitchen Love* to offer a primer on good Turkish cooking, while also referencing culinary traditions drawn from Islamic history, the Quran, and the hadiths. Overall, as scholar of Turkish television Emre Çetin writes, the show paints "a broad canvas on which the history and the culture of food are located."[54] Beder offers creative alternatives to gelatin and cautions viewers to use halal-only nonalcoholic products, suggesting that they replace wine with apple vinegar, ostensibly since alcohol—as noted—does not fully evaporate during the cooking process. Like Maffei, she embraces Western recipes that call for nonhalal ingredients by devising appropriate substitutes and techniques that merge a modern Islamic lifestyle with an "authentic" but also cosmopolitan Turkish halal cuisine.[55] The latter is now (re)purposed as part of a new global and transnational culinary culture.

Other TV shows reveal that Muslim desires to assimilate their halal food consciousness and their conceptualization of halal cooking to more dominant culinary frameworks may elicit conflicting reactions, both within and outside the community. On Australia's food competition program *MasterChef*, a controversy arose when two Muslim contestants who wore head scarves, Amina Elshafei in 2012 and Samira El Khafir in 2013, were asked to cook pork. Although both women said they had no objections to cooking it, they were criticized by some Muslim groups for touching and handling the prohibited meat. In her defense, Elshafei noted that after consulting with her father and with Muslim religious scholars, she decided to embrace the challenge by wearing gloves and staying free from directly contacting or tasting the haram product.[56] On the other hand, accusations emerged from Australia's Left of cultural intolerance, discrimination, and culinary xenophobia.[57] Should the show request that a Muslim or Jewish contestant cook pork even though other meats would have been less offensive and contentious? Small accommodations, an editorial in the *Sydney Morning Herald* argued, would go a long way toward showing that Australia "welcomes new communities." Food, the writer continued, is an arena where tolerance and accommodation can easily be made and to good effect.[58] By implication, halal cooking and dietary restrictions should be integrated as part of Australia's culinary fabric.

Globally, several programs over the past decade have exhibited Muslim, and inadvertently halal, "culinary skills." In 2015, mother of three and homemaker Nadiya Hussain was named winner of that season's *The Great British Bake Off*. Following her win, Hussain received several anti-Islamic threats on social media, to the point that she required police protection. The baker, who won the judges over with her "Rose Pistachio and Mocha Hazelnut Horns" and "Three-Tiered Lemon Drizzle Wedding Cake," displayed her faith by donning a modest head scarf. Although the issue of halal ingredients did not arise on the show, in later interviews with Muslim news outlets, Hussain was careful to clarify that she had used only halal ingredients (e.g., powdered halal gelatin). Importantly, some episodes were filmed during the month of Ramadan, and Hussain admitted that she "didn't even get to taste her bakes," although this had been her standard practice in her own home kitchen before the holiday. One of the show's biggest fans was Queen Elizabeth, and in April 2016 Hussain was invited to make the cake for the queen's ninetieth birthday. She has since released a cookbook called *Nadiya's Kitchen*. The book is not marketed as a "halal cookbook," however: Hussain seems content to share her love of cooking and baking with the broader British public.[59]

Riding the wave of popular cooking shows and the rise in viewership of Internet television, instructional videos have also popped up on various platforms such as YouTube. The Spanish-language site *Cocina Halal* (with roughly 13,000 subscribers and 1.9 million viewers as of 2017) is headlined by Ibrahim Romero, a young, charismatic self-described "halal chef." Spain is home to roughly 1.5 million Muslims, but on YouTube the show has the potential to reach millions more Spanish speakers. *Cocina Halal*, like other media by halal connoisseurs, highlights recipes ranging from apple pie, pancakes, and hamburgers to tajines, falafel, fettuccini alfredo, and gazpacho. Few of the dishes have Spanish roots, and each video is presented by an eclectic array of male and female chefs, including Romero. Since it is unclear how some of the recipes might otherwise be haram, it is mostly their redaction, editing, and preparation by Muslim cooks that help create a "cocina halal." In this context, "cocina" can be translated as not only "kitchen" or "cooking" but also "cuisine."[60]

Other videos may not be part of a culinary series but offer hints and appeal to viewers looking to make both basic and exotic foods. One of the most-watched halal cooking clips is from celebrity chef Gordon Ramsay's show *The F Word*. The episode was shot in Scotland, and the YouTube clip is titled "Halal Venison Masala" after the recipe prepared in it. The self-identified Muslim hunter who accompanies Ramsay cuts the deer's throat postmortem in "halal fashion."[61] Perhaps the clip is popular because it responds to commonly posed questions about halal and hunting, or perhaps because it portrays an international food celebrity, known for his gruff and abrasive style, partaking in (and respectful of) the preparation of halal food. Regardless, experts and jurists might disagree about whether that postmortem throat-slitting of a deer would be considered halal. In hunting, the meat would be deemed halal so long as the hunter used any piercing tool that caused bleeding and uttered Allah's name before the tool's release. In classical understandings, if the animal remained alive after it was shot, the hunter must slit its throat but if it was dead, there is no need to do so and it would still be considered halal.

Film is another medium where cuisine has been molded and debated. In French cinema, halal food has clashed head-on with traditional French culinary values, which are historically more nationalist and exclusive than in the United States or the United Kingdom. Because France has a significant Muslim community—Western Europe's largest, estimated at roughly 7.5 percent (4.71 million) by the Pew Research Center[62]—this food-centered political battle has drawn increasing attention. Over the past decade or so, French comedies and dramas have invoked culinary polarization by treating pork consumption as a signifier. French promotion of pork consumption represents the dominant nationalist cuisine and order, while halal eating and food culture embody the Muslim or Arab other. In this popular media, eating and cooking pork is represented as "an inescapable aspect of participating in the French economy"—a sort of partaking in "pork capitalism," as scholar of French film Nicole Beth Wallenbrock suggests. These images have proliferated despite the popularity of "Muslim food" in France; the North African dish couscous was recently found to be the country's third most popular dish, beating *boeuf bourgignon* and *moules et frites*.[63] Against a strong assimilationist current and the rise in right-wing political discourses, French Muslims have crafted their own halal cooking style, evidenced by the emergence of numerous eateries, a halal culinary school, and even "haute halal" dining establishments.

Finally, smartphone apps with convenient lists of permissible foods and recipes (some marketed by celebrities like Maffei) have flourished in multiple languages on iTunes and Google Play. Most are simply billed as recipes for "Islamic food" or "Muslim food," while others focus less on recipes and more on helping consumers make sound purchasing decisions in their grocery stores. The majority target Muslims living in non-Muslim countries, who may have anxieties about products sold in their local supermarkets. Perhaps more widespread, however, are apps that recommend and rate dining options for Muslims living in or visiting metropolitan centers.

Muslim writers, bloggers, home cooks, and television chefs have begun to reimagine modern halal food as a "cuisine" that merges religious prescriptions with an array of transregional recipes representing diverse culinary heritages and a commitment to a halal lifestyle. Even corporations have begun to appropriate this phrase: the American-based Saffron Road brightly displays the label "Certified Halal Cuisine" on the front of its products, from "Thai basil stir fry" to "chicken nuggets" to "chicken tikka masala." In this context, cuisine may have little to do with specific cooking techniques or dishes. In many non-Muslim countries, halal cooking and eating follows prescribed religious rules, but halal cooking can also stand in for Middle Eastern, North African, and South and Southeast Asian culinary traditions, often combined in quite arbitrary ways. Alternative visions of halal cuisine are proliferating: Muslims who choose to eat halalified versions of Western mainstays such as pizza, pasta, or burgers can feel good about consuming mainstream dishes while simultaneously laying ownership to their "own" cuisine. The halal cuisine ideal—fragmented and "under construction" as it may be—can thus offer a sense of belonging, and can also help create a (sophisticated) culinary culture centered around specific religious markers that blur or even supplant ethnic, regional, or nationalist identities. On the other hand, in some places—for example, France and Australia—conflict between local versus "immigrant" cuisines (halal or otherwise) can lead to tension and separation. Such struggles may also (perhaps inadvertently) further cement the boundaries of a halal cooking culture.

Here, media play a critical role. They reflect culinary discourses that outline not only a gastronomic repertoire (food from Muslim lands, food using halal-certified products, innovative recipes by Muslims) but also a cuisine that embodies shared feelings of belonging, adaptation, and integration, and one that subsumes ethno-national identities under the "halal" umbrella. Maffei's blog and cookbook are particularly representative of these sentiments, and specifically of the Muslim American experience. In the years after the September 11 attacks, American Muslims craved more signs of inclusion, as some felt

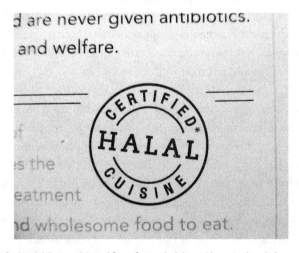

Fig. 9.1. "Certified Halal Cuisine." Detail from frozen halal meal box. Authors' photograph.

targeted and isolated by growing anti-Islamic sentiments.[64] During that time, news stories often highlighted Muslim Americans' religious piety, specifically their regimented prayer habits or how they preferred halal food to American fare like burgers and fries. Scholars of American Islam Suad Joseph and Benjamin D'Harlingue have suggested that these images marginalized Muslims and painted them as less patriotic.[65] Despite the restrictions embedded within traditional halal prescriptions, food-oriented publications and media increasingly help an often-disenfranchised community shape a halal cuisine while showcasing familiar and conventional foods like steak and burgers. They can help diminish feelings of alienation and ostracism. Alternatively, for some diaspora Muslims, halal cuisine—perhaps like the head scarf—might also symbolize a proud and defiant mark of their religious (rather than American or French) identity, a bold declaration of their faith and of all that entails. Regardless, a new generation of Muslim culinary entrepreneurs, through blogs, magazines, cookbooks, or other media, are actively (re)defining halal cooking as they guide fellow believers toward achieving a more complete halal lifestyle.

CHAPTER 10

When a friend recently visited New York City—Queens, to be exact—he asked his dinner companion where they should grab their meal: Thai, Chinese, Middle Eastern? The friend replied, "Let's have halal tonight!" In numerous New York and global dining establishments, halal is what's on the menu. There "halal" often signifies a Middle Eastern, North African, or South Asian–inspired food. More broadly, halal meals in many non-Muslim countries showcase a repertoire of transnational or "fusion" foods that is expanding in tandem with the development of a halal cuisine. The greater presence of halal in the culinary world means that these dishes can be enjoyed not just by Muslims at home but by anyone, at food carts and other fast-food places or in stylish and trendy restaurants, where they might be prepared by Muslim chefs trained in the high culinary arts—in haute halal cuisine.

Today halal meals are also served on airplanes, in college dining halls, and in prisons and school cafeterias, where they have been welcomed by some and vilified by others. Countries eager to attract Muslim travelers encourage halal food tourism and support the development of more halal-friendly eateries. On the other hand, in places like France, Germany, and Denmark, where Muslims are struggling to fully integrate within the national fabric, culinary wars are erupting between epicurean purists, animal rights activists opposed to religious slaughter, right-wing nationalists, and those advocating minority rights. Halal meals, the naysayers argue, belong in the sphere of home cooking or in a private restaurant or school, but not in public schools, government cafeterias, or daycare facilities. Oscillating trends of resistance and accommodation are also palpable in European and American prisons, as more and more inmates demand dietary religious accommodations, and specifically the right to consume halal meat, as their legal entitlement.

This chapter explores the complexities of halal dining and eating in public venues, especially during the first two decades of the twenty-first century. Outside the home, a halal meal is often much more than the sum of its ingredients: it could be a promise of cross-cultural reconciliation; a visible marker of otherness; and, for some, a basic human right. The chapter surveys a variety of halal restaurant dishes, highlights the entrepreneurial spirit driving halal dining's global rise, and considers how eating halal food can be a political act that draws both praise and criticism. It is less concerned with how and whether dining establishments receive their halal certification—a vast topic worthy of a separate study. Instead it looks at how eating halal cuisine outside the home has further transformed halal food—culturally, politically, and gastronomically.

Halal Fast Food

A recent feature in the *New Yorker* told the story of an Afghan immigrant named Zarif Khan or "Hot Tamale Louie." In 1915 Khan set up a Mexican restaurant in Sheridan, Wyoming, where few Muslims lived. Khan's famously delicious tamales were made from backyard-raised chickens, which he hand-slaughtered following halal prescriptions.[1] This might have been one of the country's first halal (or halal-Mexican-American fusion) restaurants. Halal eateries have likely existed wherever diaspora Muslims have settled—not just to serve their community but also as broader business ventures that facilitated connections between new immigrants and locals. However, the new positioning of halal restaurants as part of a distinct gastronomic trend, especially in non-Muslim countries, parallels the wider availability of halal products (particularly meat), the growth of the halal certification sector, and the overall demand for more dining options that reflect a Muslim cuisine, heritage, and tradition.

Eating out generally requires a disposable income, so for Muslims living in non-Muslim countries—especially for new immigrants or students—restaurant dining can be a challenge. Moreover, eating out without compromising one's religious beliefs entails some measure of confidence and trust in restaurant purveyors: diners might get to know their local halal butcher or trust the authenticity of a halal-certified packaged soup, but can they really know what goes on behind the closed kitchen doors of a halal dining establishment? In a 2005 study, Malay Muslims in London indicated that they preferred home cooking because it was cheaper and they had more control over the ingredients, making halal choices easier. When eating out, many opted for vegetarian meals even at halal-proclaimed restaurants that served meat.[2] Likewise, Muslim diners in Singapore practice "defensive dining": many mistrust food purveyors, especially small businesses, that claim to be halal. Some prefer not to eat out, while others choose to eat at fast-food chains like McDonald's, whose global brand possibly evokes more trustworthiness. A few diners stick to places where food is cooked only by Muslims.[3] Defensive dining is also on the rise in China, as many Muslims suspect or know that halal-labeled eateries or street stalls serve pork, its derivatives, and/or alcohol.[4]

Despite these reservations, the number of halal food outlets around the world is rapidly growing. Restaurants in majority Muslim nations—including Turkey, Morocco, and Indonesia—serve halal dishes that are usually associated with the favorite cuisine in that country. But in places with less homogeneous or minority Muslim populations, like Canada, the United Kingdom, or the United States, halal eateries reflect the transregional phenomenon of menus with a range of local and international flavors, including sushi, barbeque, chicken and waffles, soul food, Chinese, East African, South and Southeast Asian, and Middle Eastern. Throughout the world, moreover, fast-food restaurants are on the rise and rapidly making their mark with halal versions of popular foods, from fish and chips in London and kebab meats in Germany to the delectable hand-pulled noodle dishes served by Hui Muslims in the streets of Lanzhou, in the Gansu province of northwestern China.[5]

Perhaps the most prominent examples of the halal fast-food phenomenon are the food carts that populate the street corners of one of the world's culinary capitals: New York City. The history of halal food carts dates to the late 1980s, when Muslim cab drivers started to demand a halal alternative to burgers and hot dogs. Today the carts (and some trucks) are among the city's most popular eateries. As food journalist Tove Danovich points out, while the term "halal" usually evokes Islamic dietary rules as pertaining to animal slaughter or the avoidance of alcohol, these food carts bring to mind an eclectic, vaguely

Middle Eastern–inspired fare captured in one or two dishes that are "entirely native to New York."[6] Most of the city's halal food carts nowadays are run by Egyptian immigrants, and they typically serve a generous dish of halal chicken and rice topped with white and red sauce, or similar protein-rice-sauce combos. That red sauce may have derived from the North African spicy harissa, while the white may be a variation on the tzatziki (yogurt-garlic) sauce used by New York's Greek food cart vendors in the 1970s and 1980s.[7]

Thanks mostly to the chain known as Halal Guys, versions of this dish and its accompanying "halal food cart" brand have spread from New York all over the world. The story of this franchise truly exemplifies the growth of the American-halal culinary phenomenon and its global reach. Halal Guys began in 1990 as a hot dog pushcart in Midtown Manhattan owned by Egyptian partners Mohamed Abouelenein, Ahmed Elsaka, and Abdelbaset Elsayed. Heeding Muslim taxi drivers' demand for satiating and religiously approved fare, in 1992, they switched to halal meat and began selling a hot, quick, and affordable "complete" meal.[8] That truck's most famous dish became the now-ubiquitous chicken and rice with spicy red and cool white sauce. At Halal Guys, variations of this signature meal include lamb gyro or falafel, wraps instead of platters, and sides of fries or hummus. With their flashy yellow and red logo, their reliable, cheap, and plentiful food, and a strategic location (West Fifty-Third and Sixth Avenue), the Halal Guys garnered much media attention and became the most renowned and successful in a crowded field. They were the first halal cart owners to trademark their name, and they have cast their eatery as pivotal in shaping Muslim culinary culture, dubbing themselves the "first American Halal Food Chain." That is, Halal Guys take pride in having pioneered what they have characterized as a sort of American-halal fusion, represented in a single dish.[9]

In 2014, Halal Guys opened their first brick-and-mortar restaurant in New York and signed a deal with Fransmart, a restaurant franchising firm, to further expand their brand.[10] They have since opened branches in Washington, DC, Chicago, Boston, Philadelphia, New Jersey, southern California, Texas, Montreal, Toronto, and the Philippines and will soon be in Malaysia and Indonesia. More locations will open all over the world, including Europe. That Halal Guys restaurants are emerging even in American cities with small Muslim populations speaks to the fact that 95 percent of their customers are non-Muslims who have come to associate this brand with a particular taste profile (in this case, "Middle Eastern").[11] The American franchise will soon be

Fig. 10.1. Halal Guys food cart in Midtown Manhattan. Note the slogan "We are Different" used to distinguish this brand from other halal vendors. Photograph courtesy of Martin Naunov.

found in Muslim-majority countries where state-regulated halal food is widely available and where many restaurants are already halal certified, which illustrates the branding of halal as a culinary category with gastronomic variations. In Muslim countries, moreover, Halal Guys may come to represent—within the restaurant business—a desirable Western-style commodification of halal food, one that has parallels in the manufactured food sector (e.g., in the non-alcoholic beer industry).

Beyond being an entrepreneurial success story, the New York halal food cart also embodies American Muslims' aspirations to be acknowledged and respected for their religious identity. Halal Guys' accomplishments, if not their actual food, have intrigued and even mystified many observers. At a website called Muslim Eater that reviews halal dining establishments, blogger Saqib Shafi described the meal at his hometown Chicago location as "basic," "underwhelming," "one-dimensional," but good "in a, 'I'm eating salty, fatty, meaty food,' kind of way." Where the restaurant wins isn't in its taste or culinary inventiveness, argues Shafi; rather, it's in the American Dream success story and sheer resilience of its Muslim founders. "Think about the concept of The Halal Guys in post-Islamophobic America," Shafi writes. "These guys openly called themselves Halal 11 years before 9/11. And they never changed their name in the very city it took place. Business only kept growing. In a world where Islamophobia very much exists, it's pretty amazing to see a place whose very name has the word Halal packed with 20-somethings in downtown Chicago just like the long lines at the carts in New York City."[12] For immigrant, first-generation, and

Fig. 10.2. Halal food truck with Manhattan skyline. Photograph courtesy of Ayda Erbal.

second-generation Muslims, Halal Guys and other halal food eateries represent a pivotal culinary and cultural triumph at a time when American Muslims are increasingly vilified and shunned for their faith. Halal food, in this case, has allowed for an acceptable (if tentative) declaration of their identity and, thus far, this venture has been mostly received without prejudice.

The fast-food landscape in Germany contrasts sharply with the New York story. With nearly 6 million Muslims, Germany has become home to a thriving street food scene dominated by the Turkish *döner kebab* stand, which sells sandwiches of spiced and roasted thin slices of meat, made of lamb, beef, and sometimes chicken. The dish is likely a nineteenth-century Ottoman invention that was introduced and reinvented by Turkish immigrants in Berlin during the early 1970s.[13] Turks make up the bulk of the country's Muslim population, and döner kebabs are, today, Germany's unofficial street food.[14] Because of their long presence and ubiquity, kebab stands tended to signify not necessarily "halal" eating but just ethnically Turkish or Middle Eastern food. Today kebabs are almost wholly a German-Turkish fusion food. While New Yorkers and other Americans have mostly embraced the Halal Guys' Middle Eastern–American offerings, the rise of right-wing politics in various parts of Europe over the last several years have sparked new tensions, here between proponents of "German" foods and those advocating "immigrant" dishes. For a time, throughout Germany, neo-Nazis were spotted wearing sweatshirts with the slogan "Bockwurst statt Döner" (Bockwurst [a traditional pork sausage] instead of Döner), even as some of them debated whether they could still occasionally indulge in eating döner (the answer was mostly yes).[15] In a somber reminder of how food politics can become implicated in nationalist and religious violence, in 2011 several neo-Nazi youths were charged with the murder of nine (mostly Turkish) immigrants. Two of the victims owned döner kebab stalls, and the murder spree became widely known as the "döner killings."[16]

These tragic events aside, the culinary question on some customers' minds is whether all döner kebab vendors rely exclusively on halal meat, especially given that many of their customers are non-Muslims.[17] To clarify his credentials, one Turkish restaurant in Stuttgart that serves döner kebab, *pide*, *lahmacun*, and other Turkish dishes posted explicit halal signs in Arabic and Turkish. At first the restaurant owner decided not to serve alcohol, but in order to attract more customers, he began offering beer, which soon prompted rumors that his döner meat contained pork. It is a challenge, the owner later reflected, to serve halal meals and to earn a steady income without making any compromises.[18]

Fig. 10.3. Döner kebab shop in Hamburg, Germany with halal sign. Authors' photograph.

To protect itself from similar rumors, the first global franchise of this street food, the German "Döner Kebab," advertises itself as healthier, "free from additives and preservatives," and "100% halal." Both in Germany and at its locations in Pakistan and Arab Gulf countries, this Berlin-originated brand has made sure to distinguish its products as religiously compliant (in contrast to potential competitors), and it serves no alcohol.[19] These cases illustrate how an iconic food from a Muslim-majority country transformed into a hybrid German-Turkish dish but continues to draw suspicion about its German and/ or its halal authenticity. Understanding such nuances can be critical for both culinary and economic reasons: in 2012, the European döner kebab industry was estimated to generate €3.5 billion (roughly $3.7 billion) in annual revenue and to employ 200,000 people across Europe.[20]

In France too, halal dining culture is well represented in the country's fast-food scene. Muslims in France have worked hard, in recent years, to negotiate their religious, national, and culinary identities. But controversy broke out in 2009 when a Belgian-owned French chain called Quick (Burger)—second in popularity only to McDonald's—decided to serve a halal-only menu at some of its locations in order to appeal to a wider array of consumers. French nationalists objected that eliminating the bacon cheeseburger or "forcing" non-Muslims to eat halal beef whether they liked it or not undermined fundamental French values. Quick's decision, according to Romi Mukherjee, provoked a certain fear of "a larger annexation of French territory and the Republic itself."[21] This example also captures how halal eating can become implicated in global culinary wars: a food highly symbolic of American culinary might—the hamburger—became the battleground between proponents of French culinary nationalism and a then Belgian-owned business venture looking to profit from Muslim consumers.[22] Regardless, the financial success of Quick's experiment reportedly motivated Burger King to purchase the franchise in 2015; the burger giant plans to convert most of Quick's locations into its namesake brand but also to preserve, at least for now, twenty-one Quick eateries (out of a total of 401) that serve only halal food. To calm anxieties, in 2016 CEO Cédric Dugardin explained that Quick "will never be a 100 percent halal brand restaurant," but French halal eating wars have persisted in other dining venues.[23]

Haute Halal

Beyond street or fast food, halal eating in France has also transformed into a gourmet style dubbed "French-halal fusion" or "haute halal." Some young Muslims born and raised in France grew up unable—but yearning—to taste some of France's most iconic dishes, like foie gras and *magret de canard*, and several of them have long blogged about these frustrating barriers. The barriers began to fall in 2007, when two brothers of Algerian origin—Kamel and Sofiane Saidi—opened Paris's (and possibly that country's) first gourmet French-halal fusion restaurant, Les Enfants Terribles. "I love French cuisine," Kamel recalled, "but like all practicing Muslims I had to eat only fish or vegetarian when I went to a restaurant." [24] At their haute halal restaurant, however, the Saidis serve French classics using halal meat, and the flavors are "fused" with halal in the sense of combining French and North African influences; an upscale Franco-Arab food fusion has become emblematic of halal cuisine and eating in this particular context. The restaurant, moreover, serves no wine or alcohol, which the owners admitted was a "turnoff" for some French customers.[25]

Responding to this drive to make halal food more chic, gourmet, and even decadent, in 2015 the first halal cooking school, L'École de Cuisine Halal, opened in Paris. Led by a team of Muslim chefs, the school's aim is to teach "traditional" (i.e., mostly North African) and "gourmet" (i.e., French) cooking styles to professional chefs working in halal restaurants and to offer classes on butchery, pastry making, and bakery to any food lover.[26] Not all is so harmonious between French gastronomic nationalists and halal eaters and purveyors, however. French cuisine—which relies heavily on pork and alcohol—was named a UNESCO "Intangible Cultural Heritage of Humanity," and French nationalists have aggressively challenged any attempts to reinterpret this tradition. While some view the latter as a sign of "dietary apartheid,"[27] others see Muslim attempts to craft a halal haute cuisine as indications that they are becoming "more integrated," evidence that French Muslims recognize France as their home country and "want to eat like the rest of France. But at the same time they want to hold on to part of their heritage."[28] French chefs, eaters, and politicians alike are struggling over questions of how "Muslim cuisine" might harmonize or clash with a long-established and idealized national culinary tradition.

Halal Dining: A Globalizing Market

Halal dining and restaurant culture have developed in tandem with another global phenomenon: halal tourism. Some non-Muslim countries, including Japan and South Korea, have recently recognized that Muslim tourists from Europe, the Middle East, and South and Southeast Asia comprise a lucrative market and that, for many Muslims, "easy-to-find halal food" is an important variable in determining vacation destinations.[29] To attract those tourists, these countries have worked to create an "authentic" halal dining experience for their visitors and to erase any perception that their own national cuisines are exclusively or predominantly made with haram ingredients. Businesses and even governments have intervened to halalify national dishes to meet the expectations of Muslim visitors.

For Muslims living in or visiting non-Muslim countries, fish and seafood (like vegan and vegetarian) are usually seen as less risky menu items among the questionable or haram dishes. Lately Muslims have become more concerned about popular fish dishes associated with culinary globalization, and many wonder whether it is really permissible to eat these foods. With its omnipresence in cosmopolitan epicenters like New York, Kuala Lumpur, and Singapore, sushi has gained more scrutiny than other dishes. Sushi rice recipes often include vinegar, and occasionally *mirin*, a Japanese cooking wine, or *sake* (rice wine). Mirin and sake contain roughly 14 percent alcohol, and although only a relatively small amount is added to sushi rice, many popular blogs caution Muslims against consumption of alcohol (and therefore sushi rice) in any quantity.[30] Alerted to these concerns, Japanese restaurants all over the world, eager to attract Muslim diners, have worked to produce "halal sushi" and Islamically compliant versions of other Japanese dishes. In Singapore, several Japanese restaurants, chains, and food outlets have requested halal certifications from MUIS, the nation's highest religious authority. To meet its criteria, they have created pork-free ramen noodle dishes and have completely eliminated mirin or rice wine from their sushi preparations.[31] The rise of this Japanese-halal hybrid cuisine recalls the development of French-halal fusion.

In Japan, restaurateurs, chefs, politicians, and business leaders have been busy fashioning and marketing a similar repertoire. Their efforts to reap money from Muslim tourists have intensified even as Japan continues to view its own Muslim population—which constitutes roughly 100,000 residents—with deep suspicion.[32] As one news story put it, "Japan would like to entice the world's Muslim population to come visit, stay for a while, and eat." [33] Various government agencies are helping to promote the development of halal restaurants. In the Taito district of Tokyo, the local city government has offered subsidies to eateries that earned a halal certification.[34] In other prefectures, the Japan Tourism Agency has provided support, including halal cooking classes and instructions on building prayer rooms, with the goal of helping local businesses understand how to cater to Muslim tourists. But re-creating some special dishes that usually rely on haram seasoning blends can be difficult, laborious, and expensive; one Japanese halal chef traveled to Malaysia and spent two years learning how to craft *washoku* (or traditional Japanese cuisine) with strictly halal seasonings. Making dishes like rice bowls with chicken and egg is straightforward, but ramen noodles—whose broth traditionally includes pork—has proved more challenging.[35] To craft a tasty and authentic Japanese-halal meal, it turns out, one must train for an extensive period and possess a particular set of culinary skills, techniques, and ingredients. Even so, in anticipation of tens of thousands of athletes and foreign tourists for the Tokyo 2020 Olympics, the country is trying to make haste in expanding this sector. And, jumping on the profitable Olympics bandwagon, the Malaysian government has offered its advisory services. In a press interview, Prime Minister Datuk Seri Najib Razak declared that with his country's guidance, Japan's "halal products . . . will be easily accepted."[36]

Similar trends are evident in South Korea, which received 740,000 tourists from Muslim countries in 2015 and now showcases its 200 halal

Fig. 10.4. Halal restaurant in Tokyo, Japan. Photograph courtesy of Hiroko Miyokawa.

restaurants in a halal food guide published for tourist distribution. Most of these restaurants are affiliated with a traditional "Muslim cuisine," like Turkish, Pakistani, or Malay. But restaurateurs have also recognized that Muslim tourists would like to taste and enjoy authentic South Korean dishes free of pork or dog meat and served with nonalcoholic beverages. South Korean cuisine depends a good deal on these haram ingredients, particularly on pork, and halal restaurant purveyors are working to market their eateries as clean, hygienic, pure, and legitimate.[37] This latent "sensitivity to the eating habits of others"[38] reflects halal's central and profitable place within the global marketplace.[39]

To meet the demand for easy-to-find halal food and to popularize various restaurants, websites or downloadable phone apps have outpaced printed guidebooks in helping diners locate a fully halal dining experience in Seoul, London, or New York. In 2013, a specialized rating system called the Islamic Quality Standard for Hotels (IQS) was developed in Malaysia to evaluate "how well a hotel conforms to Islamic principles." The system's most basic requirements are met if a hotel has no alcohol on its premises and serves halal-only foods. Additional features such as segregated swimming pools, Muslim prayer rooms, and a Quran in each room increases an IQS score.[40] In China, these complex standards have yet to make their mark, but diners usually rely on various social media networks to choose their halal restaurants, including BBS (Bulletin Board System) and Weipo (a sort of Chinese Twitter).[41]

For English speakers, perhaps the more popular site is the marketing-oriented Zabihah.com, one of the oldest in the halal restaurant guide genre. Established in 1998 by a Silicon Valley engineer named Shahed Amanullah, the site/phone app offers thousands of user reviews of restaurants serving halal food, mostly in North America but also in South Africa, India, Singapore, New Zealand, Indonesia, Thailand, China, and Australia (there are over 1,300 listings in Australia alone). Aiming to be the halal version of Yelp or TripAdvisor, the site reportedly boasts 20 million annual users. The site's owner is proud of its place within the halal marketplace: "Over a decade of precise market data from our global user base has provided Zabihah with unprecedented consumer demographic information and marketing opportunities," writes Amanullah, ones "that will benefit the worldwide Halal industry as it continues to develop."[42] Halal dining sells and Muslim entrepreneurs are devising diverse technologies to link consumers to these services.

Eating Halal "On Demand"

Beyond fast-food carts, high cuisine, and tourist-oriented eateries, halal has also become more widely available on airplanes and in airports, in school cafeterias, and college campuses. What these locations have in common is that they are "restricted dining venues," where eaters often have limited (if any) food and drink choices. Someone else—a local school board official, an airline marketing specialist, or a college administrator—must determine, within the boundaries of a particular budget, policy, and/or political ideology, what meals to serve in order to accommodate a variety of religious and dietary concerns. Consequently, the greatest friction is found in this sector. Restaurants and urban eateries in New York, Tokyo, or Seoul are happy to cater to Muslim diners and to offer their customers an array of choices because this strategy reaps profit. The restricted dining sector tends to be less concerned with quality, choice, or even profitability, and within it Muslims—as citizens, or as tuition- or tax-paying consumers—often have to "fight for their right" to eat halal meals, a demand that frequently breeds tension with non-Muslims.

Airlines have been the most amenable in this arena, and many began to offer more varied dining options in the 1970s. Up to that point they had simply served their Muslim customers pork-free meals, but the steady rise in Muslim travelers prompted the establishment of halal kitchens at several international airports. With this development, airline chefs began to source meat that was specifically butchered along halal norms. Also, to avoid cross-contamination with nonhalal products, separate cooking facilities and utensils were used and accredited by appropriate certifying bodies.[43] As with the restaurant market, many airports have worked to accommodate Muslim travelers by building separate prayer rooms and offering halal meals at airport terminals.

Like other profit-seeking dining establishments, airlines want to make sure that food limitations do not deter customers from buying tickets on their flights. Consumers today can specify their dietary restrictions to most airlines, and in general these requests can be met. Especially during long international flights, airlines can now serve vegan, vegetarian, kosher, halal, gluten-free, dairy-free, nut-free, low-sodium, low-fat, and even certain "ethnic meal" options. In 2016, the demand for frozen halal airline meals grew by double digits, reaching over 40 million meals.[44] Whether these halal accommodations are enough to satisfy customers' demands remains to be seen. In one survey, some Muslim travelers suggested that halal meals were a good start but that airlines should really consider designating "non-drinking sections" in airplanes, both to respect travelers' personal sense of piety and to protect their children from potentially offensive or even dangerous inebriated drinkers.[45] However, even the consumption of halal airline food may decline in the coming years. Some experts have warned that a halal-food-based profiling system might be instituted if governments, police, and security authorities require information about passengers' dining preferences from airlines.[46]

Requests for halal dining have also become widespread among Muslim students enrolled in American universities. Limited to eating vegan and vegetarian meals, and occasionally fish, leaders of some Muslim student associations have called for greater options and specifically for halal meat. In 2001, by instituting a shared kosher/halal dining hall, the small liberal arts college of Mount Holyoke in Massachusetts was one of the first higher education institutions to address these concerns, albeit incompletely. To help the college save money, Muslim students agreed to a compromise with their Jewish colleagues and college administrators: they would eat kosher meat if halal meat was unavailable. This plan allowed the college to cut costs in terms of keeping separate suppliers, refrigerators, and utensils.[47] On the other hand, in 2002, officials at Dartmouth College in New Hampshire boasted that their cafeteria was the only college establishment that "observes the dietary laws outlined by the Old Testament (kashrut), the Quran (halal), and the Vedas and Upanishads (sakahara) [Hindu vegetarian diet]."[48] To keep cross-contamination in check, equipment and utensils were color-coded to correspond to each religious preference. In managing this complex undertaking, Dartmouth's dining director and his staff felt compelled to become proficient in diverse religious dietary laws and to find purveyors, such as a halal butcher in Vermont, who could supply them with appropriate products.[49]

Some universities, like Princeton, provided students with "occasional" halal meals on a rotational schedule or frozen (and often unappetizing) preparations. However, when Princeton students began meeting with dining officials in 2014 to discuss the possibility of adding more fresh varieties to the halal meal rotations, there was concern among the cooking staff that students had requested an unfamiliar and therefore difficult-to-prepare ethnic food. This conflation of "halal" with "ethnic cuisine" underscores how halal eating had become (mis) branded, in some circles, as a "cultural" food. Regardless, as Princeton Muslim chaplain Imam Sohaib Sultan noted, "Once we clarified to [dining managers] that [halal food] can be whatever food you already make, just with halal meat, the process became so much easier. That was our opening." Soon after, and to the students' appreciation, the chefs began serving "halal beef lasagna" and "halal beef roast," dishes that Muslim students felt could be enjoyed and "eaten by anyone."[50] The emphasis on halal eating as connoting meat consumption is important here. On some college campuses, accommodations for halal dining, and specifically for meat-based meals, have allowed students to feel less restricted, to consume what they viewed as a critical food group, and even to share some of "their" food with others.

By contrast, halal eating at public primary and high school cafeterias is more divisive in places like Denmark, the United Kingdom, France, and Germany. Whether to serve halal meat or even broadly halal-compliant meals in public schools has been linked to questions of freedom, animal rights, and nationalist identity—and to anti-Semitic and anti-Islamic sentiments. The subject has come to the fore as several European countries negotiate how to integrate their already-substantial population of immigrant, first-generation, and second-generation Muslims as well as the flood of refugees from places like Syria, Afghanistan, Somalia, and Iraq. Sourcing halal meals might be affordable for Ivy League universities, but specialized meals can be unbearably costly for public schools. Some venues have dealt with this question by instituting a form of "dietary equality" by always serving only halal meals, a decision that has led to considerable outcry and pushback.

In 2004, few schools in the United Kingdom served halal food, even though at the time demands for special meals (kosher, halal, allergy-free) were on the rise. Debates on facilitating the availability of these meals centered around issues of minority rights: Muslims constitute about 5 percent of the UK's population (roughly 3 million),[51] and many British Muslims argued that their specialized dietary choices must be respected, along with those of other religious communities, including Jews and Hindus. Opponents suggested that this was a matter of separation between religion and the (secular) schools and that schools therefore need not concern themselves with the issue. As one naysayer argued, dietary equality should reign and "everyone at schools should be treated the same,"[52] but they should be served identical non-religiously-sanctioned meals. The discussions over accommodating Muslim religious rules became more heated, so some schools in the UK began to serve only halal meat, even in places where Muslim students represented a fraction of the total number; this decision was likely implemented as a cost-saving strategy. Buying halal meat in bulk to feed all students made more economic sense.

Again, several non-Muslim parents objected to such policies, this time citing ethical concerns over religious slaughter. These parents argued, following animal rights activists, that stunning facilitates a more humane and less painful death. They stood against the argument, made by Jewish and some Muslim authorities, that animals should not be stunned prior to slaughter. They also maintained that the (religious and presumed non-stunned) "way the animals are killed for this meat is barbaric and cruel" and that their "Christian children should be given an equal chance to have non-halal meat."[53] Their description of these practices as "barbaric and cruel" led some Jews and Muslims to accuse them of anti-Semitism and Islamophobia. These debates belied the fact that many Muslims approve of pre-slaughter stunning and, indeed, nearly a decade after these controversies erupted, it was reported that 88 percent of "animals in the UK killed by halal methods were stunned beforehand in a way that many Muslims find religiously acceptable."[54] But animal rights discourses and meat-consumption habits are often instrumentalized in these ways, on behalf of xenophobic or anti-minoritarian interests, and this rhetoric can be found throughout the world. Similar vitriol has arisen, for instance, with reference to the types of meat consumed by Christian minorities living in Islamic countries.[55]

The trends seem to be shifting in Britain and some reports suggest that "hundreds" of British schools have switched to using halal meat exclusively.[56] On the other hand, recent policies implemented in France and Denmark reflect the rise of culinary nationalism and the growing strength of "pork-centric politics." After years of unofficially offering non-pork meal options for Jewish and Muslim students in French public schools, the mayor of one small town in eastern France, Chalon-sur-Saône, announced that his schools would no longer abide by these policies. This "secular mode of national cohesion"[57] was inspired by Marine Le Pen, leader of France's far-right-wing party the National Front, who in 2014 called for French leaders "to save secularism" by serving pork. The country's schools, she argued, "should not pander to Jewish and Muslim children by offering non-pork alternatives." Hoping to win votes from Le Pen supporters during his (failed) 2017 presidential bid, former president Nicolas Sarkozy also joined calls for "pork or nothing," telling (presumably) French Muslims and Jews, "If you want your children to have eating habits based on religion, go to a private faith school." For several years, nearly all schools had offered some alternative to a pork meal. A court ruling in 2015 upheld Chalon-sur-Saône's decision, and since then other mayors have made similar declarations and even implied that soon any given meal would likely include some pork product. This "pork or nothing" menu (save, perhaps, a small serving of side vegetables) would restrict food choices for hundreds of thousands of students.[58]

Pork wars in Denmark have also become enshrined within official policies. In the city of Randers, and after a proposal put forth by the far-right Danish People's Party, local politicians required that municipal menus must include pork. This decision, seen by many as a backlash to an earlier ruling to serve halal-only meat at some hospitals and nurseries, was extended to the town's public schools and daycare facilities.[59] The Danish People's Party was adamant that such measures were necessary "to uphold Danish culture in the face of potential threats from Islam." The party appealed to Denmark's agricultural, nationalist, and culinary identity, which are all tied to pork; in 2014, crispy pork with parsley sauce was named Denmark's national dish, and the relatively small country is one of the world's most important pork exporters.[60] Similarly, in Germany, "pork hysteria" has taken hold. Germany is the only European country to have accepted over 1 million mostly Muslim refugees since 2014. At that time, news outlets reported that—so as not to offend new refugees— some canteens and cafeterias in state schools and daycares had begun to purge their menus of any pork products, including sausages, bacon, and chops. In reaction, politicians from Chancellor Angela Merkel's Christian Democratic Union campaigned to mandate the sale of pork in these venues. Unlike in Denmark and France, there were no suggestions of a "pork only" policy, but Merkel backed her party's position, noting that tolerance for new immigrants "also means that we do not now need to change our eating habits" and that the country's culinary diversity must be preserved.[61]

Europe is not the only place where such tensions have been brewing. In multicultural and multireligious Singapore, similar questions arose about whether all "haram food" should be banned from school canteens and cafeterias. At one school where the ban was to take effect, only 20 percent of the students were Muslim. In reaction to this decision, several of Singapore's Muslim leaders argued that this policy would be "a step backwards for the Muslim community." They maintained that Muslim and non-Muslim students should learn to eat together, each with his or her own meal. One imam pointed out that he taught his own daughter that "it is not a sin if she sits next to her non-Muslim friend who might be eating pork. Even if she touches the food accidentally, it is not wrong." With such an outpouring of "racial harmoniousness," the school quickly admitted to making a mistake and withdrew its policy. In Singapore, the compromise over questions of food restrictions and religious prohibitions was championed by Muslim leaders, whose calls for bonding, mutual respect, and better education about different dietary customs helped defuse tensions.[62]

Halal (Meat) Eating as a Right

Some of these issues are tied to how dietary equality might be interpreted by various groups and whether minority religious communities have the "right" to demand religiously sanctioned meals, especially in publicly funded venues. But what happens when the dining establishment in question is a prison cafeteria? Is eating halal food—as couched in the framework of "freedom of religion"—a basic human right? These questions have been hotly debated (and litigated) in both the United States and Europe, and there seems to be no clear resolution, though some prisons are becoming more accommodating. Today Muslim prisoners in many Western settings demand access not just to any halal food (i.e., vegetarian meals) but specifically to zabiha meat. This stance can be read in light of broader arguments outlined throughout the book: halal food has been and still is mostly focused on meat consumption, its sourcing, and its slaughter. In fact, a 2016 survey conducted on behalf of the French think tank l'Institut Montaigne revealed that 40 percent of the respondents thought that eating halal meat ("*la viande halal*") was a mandatory religious practice and that it was one of the five pillars of Islam.[63] Meat has become an almost primal identity marker for Muslims, and prison canteens and cafeterias are not immune to these developments.

Beginning in the 1970s, several lawsuits were filed on behalf of US (mostly Jewish) inmates requesting special accommodations for their religious diets,[64] to the point that the US Congress passed the Religious Land Use and Institutionalized Persons Act of 2000, which was intended, in part, "to protect prisoners from religious discrimination."[65] But the legislation failed to benefit many Muslim prisoners, who continued to complain about limited access to meals with halal meat, especially in the years after 9/11. In 2003, Muslim inmates in the New Jersey State Prison sued the state for its failure to provide halal meat meals. They argued that Jewish inmates were served kosher meals and that the imbalance violated the Equal Protection Clause of the Fourteenth Amendment. A US circuit court dismissed their suit, however, citing that Muslims were given sufficient opportunities to practice their religion (through the provision, for example, of having an onsite imam) and that the kosher meals in question had not included meat.[66]

On closer examination, most legal actions and complaints filed by American Muslim prisoners have been prompted by the denial of zabiha meat.[67] For a time the situation seemed to be improving as the availability of American halal meat grew. In 2007 and 2008, Muslim inmates in New York prisons could eat more meat meals, particularly after the state signed cost-effective contracts with local halal vendors.[68] On the other hand, in 2011, an Ohio death row inmate, Abdul Awkal, sued for his right to meals with halal meat. Awkal's request stemmed from a stated desire to more closely "follow the requirements of [his] faith as [he] approach[ed] death."[69] It was insufficient, the plaintiff noted, to eat vegetarian or non-pork meals. Here access to and consumption of halal meat meals could be viewed as a fulfillment of a preferred Islamic practice (after all, meat was favored by the Prophet) but also as part of a process of atonement, an end-of-life repentance. To address these questions and to avoid costly lawsuits, Ohio stopped serving pork altogether. The state's logic, perhaps, was that even in the absence of zabiha or kosher meat, religiously observant inmates would prefer another type of meat over pork.[70] Perhaps following Ohio's policy—and to the dismay of the country's pork producers—in 2015 the federal government decided to ban pork products from its prisons, a decision that affected roughly 200,000 inmates. However, after vigorous pushback from "Big Pork" and possibly in response to conservatives who claimed the move was motivated by Muslim demands, the Bureau of Prisons reversed the ban within days of announcing it.[71]

In Europe, where some Muslims have struggled to access halal food in public schools, a wide range of prison policies exists. Halal food became more contested in the 1990s and 2000s, when inmates realized that Jewish inmates received kosher meals while Muslims received no such accommodations. Despite EU provisions forbidding discrimination based on religion or belief, as enshrined in the Charter of Fundamental Rights of the European Union,[72] countries have approached this issue quite differently. In Britain, prisons are now legally required to serve halal food to their Muslim inmates. These dietary policies have been generally well implemented, even if suspicion lingers that the food is "not authentically halal."[73] Britain's prisons have been inventive in their halal menu offerings, particularly the meat-based meals. The dishes served include "halal roasted chicken," the halal-British fusion "halal beef and Yorkshire pudding," and halal spicy curries and kebabs.[74]

The situation is more unsettled in France. In the mid-2000s, prisoners in that country began demanding equal rights offered to other religious communities: rights to prayer spaces, having their own prayer leader, and halal food.[75] While some prisons obliged, inmates complained that they had no access to zabiha meat and that eating vegetarian meals left them hungry.[76] In a case filed against the Saint-Quentin-Fallavier prison in Grenoble in 2013, a Muslim inmate argued that it was his right to eat meat meals, but in February 2016, the courts ruled in the prison's favor. In its verdict, France's highest legal body, the Council of State, argued that the prison had offered sufficient pork-free and vegetarian options. The council clarified that the French Republic's principle of laïcité (secularism) requires a respect for "freedom of worship" but that this does not translate into a mandate to serve inmates zabiha meat.[77] Other European countries are struggling with similar questions, particularly as religious slaughter facilities—for reasons related to the protection of animal rights—are banned in places like Norway, Switzerland, and Sweden. Over a decade ago, some European experts linked the issue of halal food accommodations to the potential growth in religious extremism. In 2004, they warned "that neglecting the needs of Muslim prisoners breeds resentment and leaves them open for more radical interpretations of Islam."[78]

The term "haloodie," which refers to a foodie who happens to follow halal prescriptions, was first coined by two British entrepreneurs, Imran Kausar and Norman Khawaja in 2013, the year they also organized London's first halal food fair. The two business partners have since trademarked the word and begun using it as the brand name for their food products, which can be found in some British supermarkets.[79] This terminology, its trademarking and branding, and the organization of a "halal food fair" reveal how a new generation of Muslims is driving transformations within the halal culinary scene. At the London festival, one young attendee articulated this generational divide, explaining that Muslims "who are older eat traditional Pakistani food. We are more diverse, we like fish and chips but we want to see halal fish and chips. We're always querying, 'is this halal?'"[80] The Economist, in 2014, described this development—this desire by younger and more affluent Muslims (at least in Britain) to eat something beyond "curry"—as a sign that "haute halal is on the up."[81]

Much of this new generation lives in majority non-Muslim countries, where they are effecting changes in dining habits and public discussions about the place and taste of halal food. As Florence Bergaud-Blackler has

Fig. 10.5. Haloodies chicken at a London supermarket. Note this company's slogan: "Haloodies . . . for Halal Foodies." Authors' photograph.

argued, they believe "that respect for the Islamic religion and its values was not only compatible with the liberal entrepreneurial system, but that it could foster it."[82] They tend to view halal eating, dining, and indeed "cuisine" as symbols of free enterprise, social integration, modernization, and assimilation with a halal twist. Most of them identify halal dining as eating zabiha meat: halal menus must extend beyond vegetarian, pork-, or alcohol-free offerings. Halal can also be presented (if vaguely) as an ethnic or fusion meal capturing one or two taste profiles. Thanks to outlets like the Halal Guys, it may even represent a single recognizable dish, a culinary fad, and a way for Muslims to wear their halal food label proudly—not just as a tiny logo issued by a sterile certifying body, but as the keyword in a restaurant name branded on T-shirts and baseball caps, and at eateries in Kuala Lumpur, London, and the American Midwest.

On the other hand, halal dining has met its share of struggles outside the restaurant sector, particularly in facilities offering limited food options. Among these venues, airlines have been the most obliging. As a gateway to the profitable halal travel sector growing especially in Southeast and East Asia, the airline industry has reformed itself to accommodate most dietary needs. With some nudging from diners, other restricted dining establishments, like American universities with student meal plans, have shown a similar willingness to self-educate about religious dietary needs, tweak their menus, and source kosher or halal meat. Others have not only scoffed at the idea of religious dietary accommodations but have even enforced an absolutist "pork or nothing" regime.

Halal eating is inevitably linked to a religious identity that can carry a stigma, and in countries where scrutiny and suspicion of Muslims is on the rise, discussions of religious dietary preferences sometimes devolve into heated debates about nationalism, acculturation, assimilation, and tolerance. Many Muslims hope that something like a popular plate of chicken and rice with red or white sauce, emblazoned with a halal brand, might help to ease these tensions.

CONCLUSION

At its foundations, halal eating is a divinely sanctioned injunction. Dietary laws in Islam belong to the realm of *'ibadat*, rules that govern acts of worship and service owed to God. For many Muslims, therefore, eating correct and prescribed foods is akin to fasting during Ramadan or paying obligatory alms. But this command need not be onerous, according to the Muslim scripture and many of its earliest interpretations. On food, the Quran shows affinity with Jewish and Christian customs, but its tenets are more lenient and accommodating than kashrut rules or ascetic Christian fasting traditions. Muslims must abstain from only a few key foods and drinks, and eating (in moderation) has been widely celebrated in Islamic scripture, poetry, literature, and art.

In the premodern period, whether in Baghdad or Timbuktu or Mostar or Isfahan, eating halal was a local affair, and qualms about halalness were more academic and doctrinal than routine. The majority of Muslims lived within modest means; meat was on the menu infrequently, and on those rare occasions families could slaughter their own animals or turn to trusted local farmers and butchers. Alcohol consumption was understood to be haram, even as it remained one of society's (especially the elite's) more blatant vices. In the case of intoxicants, the main concern, historically speaking, was policing unruly behavior among those who abused them. Recurring questions about halal compliance, when and if they existed, centered on a few suspicious or newly introduced products like coffee or tobacco. In most parts of the Islamic world, that food items might be contaminated with porcine derivatives was, in all likelihood, difficult to imagine.

A central thread running through this history is that Islamic food traditions exhibit a significant (and often overlooked) plurality. Since the time of the Prophet, legal scholars have produced a vast literature revealing a diversity of positions on all matters related to food, drink, and psychoactive substances. In their interpretations, different legal schools appear to be sensitive to regional, cultural, and even culinary variations. Muslims have never been monolithic, of course, in their search to understand divinely sanctioned food rules. But today many are considering how earlier interpretive traditions can meet new challenges specific to their own communities: in Europe and the United States, for example, they ponder how abiding by particular dietary rules can reinforce their Muslim identity in the face of growing marginalization. In Muslim-majority countries, believers might respect or challenge the state's authority to dictate their consumption habits according to top-down, often more restrictive interpretations.

Over the past few decades, Muslims have also faced an increasingly omnipresent monitoring system. Numerous bodies strive to control halal's legalistic formulations: jurists, certification agencies, governments, and international organizations all vie to administer food rules and to become halal's final arbiters. Market sensitivity, industrialized food production, and modern consumerist trends have played important roles in shaping these developments, as has the popularity of Islamist political orientations. On the one hand, in a world where the supermarket meat counter or freezer aisle has replaced the local butcher and where dinner might also be served from a can filled with unknown additives, Muslim consumers demand expert guidance. For this reason their persistent pursuit to eat what is good and right empowers halal's interlocutors in business, law, religion, science, and politics. On the other hand, as more diverse global actors become involved in halal food's production, legislation, and certification, the market must contend with the lack of uniform rules. There is no universal halal logo, no universal halal brand, no universal halal standard. This status quo and the existence of hundreds of halal certifiers and accreditors may suggest a multifarious ecology of halal, reflecting the plurality in the global umma. But the myriad criteria and labels also confuse customers, can stifle the growth of new businesses, and may even discourage multinational companies from fully participating in the halal food economy.[1]

Despite the challenges associated with monitoring halal standards in modern times, the future of the global halal economy seems bright. The world's Muslim population is growing and has become younger and more affluent. The economies of the OIC countries, particularly those of nations like Bangladesh, Indonesia, Malaysia, and Pakistan, are expected to expand at a rate of around 4.2 percent between 2015 and 2021 (vs. 3.6 percent for other global GDPs).[2] The demand for halal products has been increasing not only because Muslims today have a greater overall and per capita purchasing power than previous generations but also because most of them, according to recent surveys, faithfully adhere to Islamic rules and expectations in their daily lives,[3] indicating (at least in part) strong pietistic and identitarian tendencies in various Islamic settings.

This growth of the modern halal market reveals an alignment and convergence of religious values with a capitalist global economy.[4] The present book highlights how Muslim entrepreneurs have tapped into thousands of lucrative business opportunities and, in the process, reshaped and reinterpreted halal food provisions. Through the introduction of boundless halal products—from colas, chocolates, and nonalcoholic beers to cookbooks and food carts—business leaders have helped craft a new Market Islam that is arguably "situated in a bourgeois universe where piety, wealth, and cosmopolitanism" supplant ancient Islamic ideals of social justice and frugality.[5] This orientation plays out particularly well in supermarkets, whether in Abu Dhabi or Jakarta or Los Angeles. There Muslim customers walk the aisles seeking halal-labeled products that are attractively packaged and clearly marked with the most up-to-date and trendiest labels: nutritious, healthy, hygienic, organic, GMO-free. As demand for such products rises, this sector will likely grow: analysts predict that the halal market will see more investment in frozen meals, baby food, prepackaged snacks, and "protein-rich processed foods," as well as varied components of manufactured substances, such as halal gelatin and food colorants.[6]

Efforts to turn halal food into a product for the global capitalist market have accompanied corresponding developments in related arenas. For example, the bureaucratization of halal in Muslim-majority countries—prompted by the need for better regulation and administration of halal rules—reflects the ever-increasing intrusiveness of the modern state in believers' daily lives. In states' hands, halal codification essentially demands compliance with guidelines devised by religio-bureaucratic officials responsible for developing and enforcing halal prescriptions. This bureaucratization epitomizes the modern state's burgeoning authority over religion and the marginalization of unofficial, conflicting interpretations. The state, in many cases, is the final arbiter of a new halal ethos, one that some polities—like Malaysia—have sought to imprint, albeit not entirely successfully, as the normative and universal standard. Through these channels, the governments of Muslim-majority nations assert their hegemonic claims, often in the most intimate ways and with the help of the most sophisticated technologies.

In tandem with greater government control, the "scientization" or "scientification" of halal has become particularly noticeable in recent years. Muslims today consume more and more manufactured foodstuffs and beverages, filled with unknown additives and fillers. The proliferation of thousands of new products, each of which must be checked, verified, and approved, means that halal regulations (and the states invested in controlling them) now have to cover a remarkably wide domain. In contrast to premodern practices, halal questions nowadays extend beyond the type of meat or its correct slaughter and include concerns over animal- and alcohol-based substances found in industrial additives, medications, and foodstuffs. Muslims are also inquiring about the halal status of "cultured foods," most recently of laboratory-created chicken and duck meat cultivated from the stem cells of those animals.[7] Navigating these new and unfamiliar items requires the continuous involvement of religiously trained scientists: to determine the halalness of any given product, these experts use research laboratories equipped with spectrometers, alcohol analyzers, titrators, and refractometers to test compliance with ancient legal rulings. This is science in the service of religion: consumers likely feel reassured knowing that a "0.0%" APV nonalcoholic beer has been exhaustively scrutinized and stamped with scientific approval. An emphasis on precision and utility correlates with a growing quest to confirm halal authenticity, hence religious purity.

One consequence of the expanding government hegemony and its accompanying technical and scientific supervision is that halal monitoring has become increasingly pervasive and intrusive. Every layer of life, every act of consumption can now be checked, regulated, and policed. Simultaneously, more restrictive definitions of halal have been formulated to meet the demands of expediency and practicality desired by food manufacturers and bureaucratic authorities. Interestingly, the search for a common halal denominator—one that can be applied in a variety of transnational settings—encourages regulators, codifiers, and capitalists to opt for readings and interpretations that are more conservative rather than lenient: the desire to satisfy the greatest number of Muslim consumers in the cheapest way possible has chipped away at that pluralistic historical canon.[8]

More convenient and straightforward halal formulations are quite appealing to the global umma, to Muslims seeking a readily available connection to their religious heritage and with fellow believers. Imprinted on mass-produced and mass-labeled products, the new, narrower halal standards serve as an anchoring and unifying mechanism. They signify a "universal brotherhood of Muslims," as political scientist Olivier Roy has put it, and give individual Muslims a fixed and "portable kit of norms, adaptable to any social context."[9] Halal thus acts as a uniform set of instructions and guidelines devoid of any nonreligious (ethnic, cultural, geographic) markers: it has been deterritorialized, decontextualized, and divorced from specific cultural tendencies and inclinations. Consequently, the geographic locus of halal today is nowhere and everywhere. For some, this development may symbolize the most authentic reimagining of a greater Muslim community unencumbered by national borders or cultural distinctions, of that revolutionary umma preached by the Prophet Muhammad in seventh-century Arabia.

For others, however, modern trends deviate considerably from the religion's foundational teachings against materialism and avarice. Beyond enabling Muslims to follow Islamic law to the letter, eating halal has always served as a conduit for cultivating modest and ethical virtues. Historically, among Sufi dervishes, for instance, the daily functions of eating, sleeping, working, and praying promoted humility and forged the true mystical path.[10] The pious could follow the saints' example in using food and nourishment to foster a more intentional practice of key religious instructions. Through abstinence from najis foods and gluttonous eating, believers could avoid sinful acts; likewise, abiding by proper eating protocols enabled them to embrace their true moral selves.[11]

Perhaps recalling these pietistic goals, some Muslims today view the capitalistic orientation of the halal industry and the growing commodification of food as neglect of Islam's spiritual teachings and disregard for its call to live a moralistic and godly life. Focusing on mundane matters, the argument goes, may detract from a believer's more transcendent ambitions. That is, modern halal's preoccupation with precise rules, guidelines, measurements, and genetic components, in addition to its market orientation, transforms halal eating into a "secular," this-worldly pursuit, one far more fixated on factory efficiency, sanitation, and profits than on appreciating a "prayer's timbre."[12] Of course, halal rules and regulations have always been religiously sanctioned prescriptions with practical considerations, but the increasing micro-focus on their regulation, policing, and enforcement in all matters—or at least in matters pertaining to halal's commercial appeal—could, according to the spiritually inclined, lead believers away from the religion's otherworldly aims.

Other critical conceptualizations of halal emerge from a small but vocal group of Muslims who struggle with concerns that go beyond simple Sharia-compliance. Emphasizing that haram and najis invoke not just what is prohibitive or harmful but also what could damage a believing Muslim's soul and body, they attempt to recast tayyib as a signifier of a more ethical and healthful halal lifestyle. Such believers are keen to explore halal's layered meanings: in their activism, they might demand merciful treatment of animals, embrace their role as environmental stewards, resist capitalism under Islamic garb, or simply promote a health-conscious cooking style. Some may even embrace halal eating as a pleasurable act, as a fulfillment of the Quranic mandate to eat what is good (and tasty and, nowadays, even gourmet). These orientations form a small but potentially growing trend in the twenty-first century, one that is often promoted by a vocal and younger population.

If eating the right foods is the most legal and righteous stance, then meat may still be the prime locus of this effort. The halal rules pertaining to meat and slaughter may not have had a major impact on premodern people's everyday lives, but Muslims today—especially those in the West—are fully preoccupied with meat sourcing, the technicalities of animal slaughter, meat-derived food additives, and even the ethics of animal treatment. For those who condone modern factory slaughter, the debate might center on whether killing a prestunned animal violates fundamental legal codes. For many, it does. For others, also many, it does not. But for a smaller group of Muslims, human kindness to animals represents Quranic and hadith-based principles, so no form of factory farming or industrialized animal slaughter (with or without prestunning) could ever yield authentic ritual slaughter. For fewer others still, best practice requires total abstinence from meat. Looking ahead, discussions over omnivorous, vegetarian, or vegan eating, as well as animal rights and ethics, may form one increasingly mainstream framework within which Muslims debate halal food rules. Although these trends are currently promoted by a tiny group of Muslims with antiestablishment inclinations, some studies suggest that the market will effectively monetize them just as it did with organic and non-GMO foods, which have become much more widespread.[13] Such tendencies may hark back to some of halal's more flexible aspects, which may be increasingly lacking in modern halal standards: the desire to accept novel practices (e.g., animal-friendly husbandry, vegan eating, or organic farming) and adapt to a diverse marketplace. Freed from the model of industrial efficiency, a boutique butcher in Midtown Manhattan whose customers are primarily non-Muslim can be open to marketing his meat not just as halal-slaughtered but also as grass-fed, pasture-grazed, humanely treated, and organic.

Halal holds complex and divergent currents: the movements toward universal certification and increasing purity may encourage isolation and exclusion, while the efforts to bring halal into modern and diasporic settings—haute halal, healthy halal, and so on—may pursue a more integrative and individualistic course. As governments, halal certifiers, and large-scale manufacturers push for uniformity, the diversity of halal food customs and legal interpretations might dissipate, and Muslims' food practices may become more insular, as they often did in various historical settings. The persistent quest for halal authenticity may lead some to adopt exclusionary attitudes, rejecting any potential pollutant or disallowing any encounters with non-Muslims and their food. The growing suspicion of airplane meals and of food served in school cafeterias, prison dining halls, or even the halal sections of food courts is emblematic of these trends, as is the increased desire for purity and halalness at each stage of industrial food processing.[14]

On the other hand, contemporary Muslims' avid engagement with food and eating can be seen as an appreciative (and sometimes inventive) nod toward colorful historical culinary practices from all over the Islamic world, and halal might increasingly act as a conduit to a broader non-Muslim culture, especially in diasporic contexts. By eating a halal hamburger in New York City, for example, a Muslim can simultaneously claim membership in both her surrounding culture and a specific religious community. In short, the expansion of all matters related to halal food—its marketing, cooking, and even its conceptualization as "cuisine"—have reinvigorated a global Muslim cultural identity. Modern articulations of halal food reflect not only prevalent political, economic, and religious trends but also the vivid, particular visions and interpretations of countless individual Muslims.

Appendix A   A Comparison of Kosher, Christian, and Islamic Dietary Regulations

	Kosher food laws	Christian food laws	Halal food laws
Prohibition of animals for food	Animals that do not chew their cud (non-ruminants) and animals that do not have cloven hooves: pig, hare, camel, carnivores, and birds with talons. Also prohibited are sharks, dogfish, catfish, monkfish and similar species, shellfish and other animals from the sea with no scales or fins, insects (except for a rare locust), ostrich, emu, reptiles, and amphibians. (Leviticus and Deuteronomy) No carrion.	A few evangelical, fundamentalist, charismatic, and Orthodox Christian groups (e.g., Ethiopian) still practice some of the Torah (Old Testament, Leviticus 11) prohibitions against pigs, sea creatures with no fins or scales, hare, etc., but most Christians have no such prohibitions.	In the Quran, no pig. Muslims view wild animals with canine teeth and, generally, any bird with talons as prohibited. There are minor variations among legal schools about the permissibility of specific animals. In Shiite traditions, shrimp and only seafood that has fins and scales are permitted. In the Sunni Hanafi legal school, only seafood that "looks like fish" (including shark but not shrimp or crustaceans) is permitted. All other Sunni schools vary in their permissibility of various sea creatures, amphibians, and reptiles (e.g., turtles). No carrion.
Prohibition of Blood	Prohibited and must be fully drained during and after slaughter.	Prohibited in Old Testament (Genesis 9:3–4) and in New Testament (Acts 15:28–29). Prohibition continues among some early Christians but then generally dissipates.	Prohibited in the Quran. During and after slaughter, blood must be fully drained.

Appendix A Continued

	Kosher food laws	Christian food laws	Halal food laws
Prohibition of Alcohol	Not prohibited but strict production requirements on grape-derived products, including grape juice, vinegar, and wine (*yayin*). To be considered kosher, the latter cannot be prepared by non-Jews nor intended for use in idolatry. Passover wine must be kept away from leavening agents (yeast, bread, dough, etc.).	Not prohibited by most Christian sects. However, modern temperance movements persist among certain groups including Southern Baptists as well as some Pentecostal and charismatic believers (particularly in Latin America and Africa) who view alcohol consumption as a sin.	Prohibition of grape (and perhaps date) wine (al-khamr) in Quran and in hadith. Most jurists extend this prescription to all intoxicants.
Fasting	A significant and encouraged practice, as in the case of Yom Kippur.	A rich fasting tradition that includes Lent, Advent, and saints' feasts that continues among Catholic and Orthodox Christians. Fasting often includes abstinence from food for a few hours to prolonged abstinence from meat or adopting a vegan diet in the cases of some Christian denominations (e.g., Coptic and Ethiopian Orthodox).	Fasting, from sunrise to sunset, is an obligatory ritual for Muslims during the month of Ramadan.
Animal Welfare	Many believe that kindness to animals has a strong foundation in the Torah.	Old Testament and early Christian texts praising ascetic life offer important guidelines for animal welfare.	Ahadith call for kindness to animals and outline rules that govern the relationship between man and Allah.
Slaughter requirements for livestock and poultry	Strictly defined. Swift cut with sharp knife to the throat so that animal does not suffer pain. Pre-slaughter stunning of animals is prohibited.	Undefined.	Strictly defined. Swift cut with sharp knife to the throat so that animal does not suffer pain. Procedures like stunning and machine slaughter debated.

Appendix A Continued

	Kosher food laws	Christian food laws	Halal food laws
In case of doubt	Consult rabbi.	Romans 14:23 advises not eating in case of doubt but this is not followed by most Christians as the food laws are generally more flexible.	Different tendencies among Islamic legal schools, based on individual cases. Most jurists suggest avoidance.
Separation of food products in food supply chain	Separation of meat, dairy, and neutral products.	Undefined.	Separation between halal and haram, depending on product characteristics and market requirements.

Sources: Table adapted from Marco Tieman, "Convergence of Food Systems: Kosher, Christian, and Halal," *British Food Journal* 117, no. 9 (2015): 2320. See also Tilahun Bejitual Zellelew, "The Semiotics of the 'Christian/Muslim Knife': Meat and Knife as Markers of Religious Identity in Ethiopia," *Signs and Society* 3, no. 1 (2015): 44–70; Odelia E. Alroy, "Kosher Wine," *Judaism* 39, no. 4 (1990): 452–460; and Ken Albala, "Historical Background to Food and Christianity," in *Food and Faith in Christian Culture*, ed. Ken Albala and Trudy Eden (New York: Columbia University Press, 2011), 7–20.

Appendix B Medieval Opinions on Jewish and Christian Meat According to Legal Schools

Hanafis	The meat slaughtered by Jews and Christians (i.e., kitabis) is halal. This is the case even when the Muslim does not hear tasmiyya from the slaughterer at the time of slaughter. Only in those circumstances when Muslims hear an explicit invocation of the name of any entity other than Allah should they avoid kitabi meat. The same rule applies to hunted meat.
Shafi'is	The general opinion is that the meat slaughtered by kitabis is halal, although diverging formulations exist. In the case of slaughter "in the name of Jesus Christ," some Shafi'is find this practice objectionable (makruh) but consider the meat allowable because the real intent in the invocation of Christ's name is to honor Allah. Other Shafi'is consider this meat nonhalal. Shafi'is consider the meat hunted by kitabis permissible.
Imam Malik	The meat slaughtered by kitabis is halal as long as they slaughter animals according to their own religious rules and the names of deities other than Allah are not invoked. However, if Muslim meat is available, consuming non-Muslim meat is makruh.
Malikis	Malikis consider animals hunted by kitabis nonhalal. This interpretation is based on the Quran 5:95, which speaks of hunting but does not explicitly refer to kitabis.
Hanbalis	Hanbalis require the slaughterer, whether kitabi or Muslim, to pronounce tasmiyya before slaughter. Nevertheless, if it is not known that tasmiyya was pronounced, the kitabi or Muslim meat is still permissible. As in the case of Malikis, it is preferable to eat Muslim meat when possible.

Sources: Çayırlıoğlu, *Helal Gıda*, 419–423. Cf "Dhaba'ih," *Al-Mawsu'a al-Fiqhiyya*, 21:187–192.

INTRODUCTION

1. Emma Glanfield, "Muslim Family Sends Children to School with 'Halal Only' Stickers Taped across Their Chest after Daughter Is Served Up Non-Halal Food," *Daily Mail Online*, September 24, 2014, http://www.dailymail.co.uk/news/article-2768649/Muslim-family-sends-children-school-Halal-stickers-taped-chest-daughter-served-non-Halal-food.html.

2. Below the article about the Khan-Hussein family, in the comments from online readers, many anti-Islamic responses underscored Britain's troubled relationship with its Muslim minority; indeed, one commentator wrote, "A multicultural society is everything that's wrong with this country." Another reader, presumably referring to halal slaughter rules, commented that "halal meat is bloody barbaric." One post suggested that the parents send their children to school "with their own 'special' lunch!" Yet another comment remarked that the children in the photos "look[ed] really miserable. What terrible parents they must have." For more on long-standing "dietary wars" in British society, see "Bangers Ban in Hundreds of Schools," *Telegraph*, June 17, 2012, http://www.telegraph.co.uk/education/educationnews/9335831/Bangers-ban-in-hundreds-of-schools.html.

3. *State of the Global Islamic Economy 2016/2017 Report*, developed and prepared by Thomson Reuters, 25, http://www.iedcdubai.ae/assets/uploads/files/SGIE%20Report_f1_DIGITAL_1477897639.pdf (accessed January 14, 2017).

4. See H. E. Chehabi, "How Caviar Turned Out to Be Halal," *Gastronomica: The Journal of Food and Culture* 7, no. 2 (2007): 17–23.

5. Lucy Taylor, "The Halal Revolution," *Arabian Business.com*, July 10, 2009, https://www.arabianbusiness.com/561277 (accessed January 13, 2017); M. S. Nor-Zafir, "Establishing

Newspaper articles and non-official/academic online publications (such as blog entries) are cited in full in the footnotes and are not included in the Bibliography.

Shariah-Compliance [*sic*] Hotel Characteristics from a Muslim Needs Perspective," in *Theory and Practice in Hospitality and Tourism Research*, ed. Salleh Mohd Radzi et al. (Croydon, UK: CRC Press, 2015), 525.

6. *State of the Global Islamic Economy 2016/2017 Report*, 25–26. This figure presumably excludes the relevant numbers from non-OIC countries.

7. *State of the Global Islamic Economy 2016/2017 Report*, 7.

8. Faegheh Shirazi, *Brand Islam: The Marketing and Commodification of Piety* (Austin: University of Texas Press, 2016), 1–17.

9. Johan Fischer, "Manufacturing Halal in Malaysia," *Contemporary Islam* 10, no. 1 (2016): 40.

CHAPTER 1

1. See Ibn Ishaq, *The Life of Muhammad: A Translation of Ibn Ishaq's Sirat Rasul Allah*, trans. A. Guillaume (Oxford: Oxford University Press, 1955), 151–152, as related in Omid Safi, *Memories of Muhammad: Why the Prophet Matters* (New York: HarperOne, 2010), 48–49.

2. Tilahun Bejitual Zellelew, "The Semiotics of the 'Christian/Muslim Knife': Meat and Knife as Markers of Religious Identity in Ethiopia," *Signs and Society* 3, no. 1 (2015): 50–51.

3. Joseph Lowry, "Lawful and Unlawful," *Encyclopaedia of the Qurʾān*, Brill Online, http://referenceworks.brillonline.com/ (accessed May 2, 2016). In the Quran, words derived from the root ḥ-l-l (ل/ل/ح) in Arabic carry a range of meanings. These include words for "locale, residing area, township; stopping place, way station; to unpack, to come down, to take up residence, to terminate one's travelling; to become permissible, to become free, spouse; to untie, to solve; to dissolve; to deserve"; see "ل/ل/ح ḥ-l-l," *Dictionary of Qur'anic Usage*, ed. Elsaid M. Badawi and Muhammad Abdel Haleem, Brill Online, 2013, http://referenceworks.brillonline.com/ (accessed May 2, 2016).

4. The term could also mean "sacred," "sanctified," or "inviolable," as in "*al-bayt al-haram*," or the "sacred house," which in the Quran refers to Kaʿba in Mecca; see "م/ر/ح ḥ-r-m." Badawi and Haleem, *Dictionary of Qur'anic Usage*, Brill Online, 2013, http://referenceworks.brillonline.com/ (accessed May 2, 2016).

5. In other words, a "deceased man's heirs have no rights of marriage or otherwise over his widow." See A. B. al-Mehri, ed., *The Qur'an with Surah Introductions and Appendices* (Birmingham, UK: Maktabah, 2010), 81n149.

6. Lowry, "Lawful and Unlawful."

7. David Waines, "Food and Drink," *Encyclopaedia of the Qurʾān*, Brill Online, http://referenceworks.brillonline.com/ (accessed May 2, 2016). "O you who have believed, eat from the good things which We have provided for you and be grateful to Allah if it is [indeed] Him that you worship"; see Quran 2:172; cf. 20:81.

8. See Quran 6:145, 16:115, 2:173, and 5:3.

9. Cf. Mian N. Riaz and Muhammad M. Chaudry, *Halal Food Production* (Boca Raton, FL: CRC Press, 2004), 7.

10. The Quran uses multiple terms to refer to alcoholic beverages, including *sakar*, often translated as "strong drink"; *rahiq*, or "wine served in paradise"; and, most commonly, *al-khamr*, used six times in various contexts. See Enes Karic, "Intoxicants," *Encyclopaedia of the Qurʾān*, Brill Online, http://referenceworks.brillonline.com/ (accessed May 2, 2016).

11. Cf. Kathryn Kueny, *The Rhetoric of Sobriety: Wine in Early Islam* (New York: State University of New York Press, 2001), ch. 1.

12. See 56:16–21, 37:43–48. On the concept of najis food or that which is impure, see "Aṭʿima," *Al-Mawsuʿa al-Fiqhiyya*, 2nd ed. (Kuwait: Wizarat al-Awqaf waʾl Shuʾun al-Islamiyya, 1983), 5:126.

13. On how the Quran treats intoxication separate from wine and similar beverages, see Kueny, *The Rhetoric of Sobriety*, 14–19.

14. For a slightly different take on 4:43, see Kueny, *The Rhetoric of Sobriety*, 9.

15. Some (though not many) Muslim interpreters claimed that 5:90–91 "did not explicitly forbid khamr, but merely suggested, admittedly with some force, that one should desist from using it. God, they said, made this as a suggestion for proper behavior, just as he suggested, without making it a strict obligation, that one make a contract for the manumission of a slave if one believes there to be any good in him"; see Ralph Hattox, *Coffee and Coffeehouses: The Origins of a Social Beverage in the Medieval Near East* (Seattle: University of Washington Press, 1985), 50.

16. Maxime Rodinson, "Ghidhāʾ," *Encyclopaedia of Islam*, 2nd ed., Brill Online, http://referenceworks.brillonline.com/ (accessed May 2, 2016). For more on eating customs in early Islamic Arabia, see in general H. D. Miller, "The Pleasures of Consumption: The Birth of Medieval Islamic Cuisine," in *Food: A History of Taste*, ed. Paul Freedman (Berkeley: University of California Press, 2007), 135–162.

17. Nawal Nasrallah, ed. and trans., *Annals of the Caliphs' Kitchens: Ibn Sayyar al-Warraq's Tenth-Century Baghdadi Cookbook* (Leiden: Brill, 2010), 569.

18. Rodinson, "Ghidhāʾ."

19. These are identified as *bahira, saiba, wasila*, and *ham*. Bahira refers to a camel that gave birth to five calves, the last of which is a male. Saiba refers to a camel that was released to roam free due to a vow. Ham is a male camel that produced at least one second generation offspring that is strong enough to carry a rider. Wasila could be a female camel that gave birth to several female offspring or one that birthed both male and female offspring. See al-Qaradawi, *The Lawful and the Prohibited* (Indianapolis: American Trust Publications, 1999), 21–22; and Seyyed Hossein Nasr, ed., *The Study Quran: A New Translation and Commentary* (New York: HarperOne, 2015), 329 n.103.

20. Rodinson, "Ghidhāʾ." Mohammed Hocine Benkheira observes a strong connection between Islamic dietary prescriptions and the pastoral culture into which Islam was born: "Indeed, Islam was not born among fishermen but among pastoralists . . . . The fact that Islam emerged in a pastoralist culture has considerable implications, especially concerning food. It is striking that pastoralists today, for instance, are reluctant to eat poultry, including eggs, fish, and even game. It is known that Islam does not forbid hunting nor does it prohibit game, but a wild beast cannot be ritually sacrificed. There is no tax on hunting activity. The same can be said about fish—which is lacking in the Hijaz—as well as poultry" (translation is ours). See Benkheira, *Islâm et interdits alimentaires – Juguler l'animalité (Paris: Presses Universitaires de France, 2000)*, 66.

21. Unless otherwise noted, references to and quotations from the Bible are from the New International Version.

22. David Freidenreich, *Foreigners and Their Food: Constructing Otherness in Jewish, Christian, and Islamic Law* (Berkeley: University of California Press, 2011), 133. See also Jordan Rosenblum, *The Jewish Dietary Laws in the Ancient World* (New York: Cambridge University Press, 2016), 19–20, 25–26.

23. The intent behind and interpretations of these Pauline verses have been heavily debated in exegetical discussions. See Gordon D. Fee, "Εἰδωλόθυτα Once Again: An Interpretation of 1 Corinthians 8–10," *Biblica* 61, no. 2 (1980): 172–197; and, in general, Veronika E. Grimm, *From Feasting to Fasting: The Evolution of a Sin. Attitudes to Food in Late Antiquity* (London: Routledge, 1996), 60–73. See also Freidenreich, *Foreigners and Their Food*, 133.

24. For a parallel, yet earlier, take on the differences between the Quranic dietary restrictions and pre-Islamic Arab and Jewish tendencies, see Benkheira, *Islâm et interdits alimentaires*, ch. 2. We should mention that the Islamic and pre-Islamic distinctions in the Quran pertain primarily to food practices, in particular slaughter, rather than the types of food.

25. This is consistent with how Islam considers its ties to earlier Abrahamic traditions. Islam, Christianity, and Judaism are all monotheistic traditions that worship the same God and share a common belief in the prophets, divine revelation, angels, Satan, and the Day of Judgment. Muslims regard the Christian and Jewish prophets as the messengers of the same religion that Muhammad taught to his people. These prophets are to Muslims as sacred as Muhammad, but it is believed that the teachings of these prophets were misinterpreted and corrupted by their followers. This is why God sent one final prophet ("seal of the prophets"), Muhammad, to instruct humans about the divine truth. Thus Islam supersedes earlier Abrahamic religions not because it is ontologically different from them but because it has been protected from the corruption that the earlier religious traditions have experienced.

26. Later, Muslims would come to insist that "the [lawful] food of those who were given the Scripture" did not include pork or blood and could be subject to other restrictions. Also although Muslims would interpret verse 5:5 as permitting Muslim men to marry wives who were Jews and Christians, Muslim women were not allowed to marry Jewish or Christian men.

27. In fact, the Quran's comments about the severity of Jewish dietary prescriptions recall anti-Jewish polemic perpetuated by late antique Roman writers and early Christian commentators. Dennis E. Smith, "Food and Dining in Early Christianity," in *A Companion to Food in the Ancient World*, ed. John Wilkins and Robin Nadequ (West Sussex, UK: John Wiley, 2015), 358; Peter J. Tomson, "Jewish Food Laws in Early Christian Community Discourse," *Semeia* 86 (1999): 193–211. Here, it is important to note that verse 5:5 was revealed at a time when Muhammad's main concern was to build a stable polity in Medina, which comprised both Muslim and Jewish populations. Thus, the verse is consistent with Muhammad's attempts to support a relatively integrated and cosmopolitan social order.

28. Richard A. Lobban, "Pigs and Their Prohibition," *International Journal of Middle East Studies* 26, no. 1 (1994): 59–61. See also Warren R. Dawson, "The Pig in Ancient Egypt: A Commentary on Two Passages of Herodotus," *Journal of the Royal Asiatic Society of Great Britain and Ireland*, no. 3 (1928): 597–608.

29. All cited in Robert M. Grant, *Early Christians and Animals* (London: Routledge, 1999), 6–7.

30. Frederick Simoons, *Eat Not This Flesh: Food Avoidances from Prehistory to the Present* (Madison: University of Wisconsin Press, 1994), 65 and *passim*.

31. Simoons, *Eat Not This Flesh*, 64–71.

32. Marvin Harris, "The Abominable Pig," in *Food and Culture: A Reader*, ed. Carole Counihan and Penny Van Esterik (New York: Routledge, 1997), 67–79.

33. Simoons, *Eat Not This Flesh*, 71.

34. Walter D. Ward, *Mirage of the Saracen: Christians and Nomads in the Sinai Peninsula in Late Antiquity* (Berkeley: University of California Press, 2014), 22–23.

35. Simoons, *Eat Not This Flesh*, 71.

36. Mary Douglas, *Purity and Danger: An Analysis of Concepts of Pollution and Taboo* (New York: Routledge, 2002), ch. 3. For a recent critique of Douglas, see Rosenblum, *The Jewish Dietary Laws in the Ancient World*, 16–18.

37. Peter H. Görg, *The Desert Fathers: Anthony and the Beginnings of Monasticism* (San Francisco: Ignatius Press, 2011), 72–73; Elizabeth S. Bolman, *Shaping Monasticism in Early*

Byzantine Egypt: Selected Studies in Visual and Material Culture (Princeton, NJ: Princeton University Press, forthcoming).

38. Grant, *Early Christians and Animals*, 6–7.

39. Tito Orlandi, "A Catechesis against Apocryphal Texts by Shenute and the Gnostic Texts of Nag Hammadi," *Harvard Theological Review* 75, no. 1 (1982): 92; Allan Heaton Anderson, *An Introduction to Pentecostalism: Global Charismatic Christianity*, 2nd ed. (Cambridge: Cambridge University Press, 2013), 119.

40. Abu Hamid al-Ghazali, *On the Lawful and the Unlawful*, trans., intro., notes Yusuf T. DeLorenzo (Cambridge, UK: Islamic Texts Society, 2014), 13–15; al-Qaradawi, *The Lawful and the Prohibited*, 44, 123.

41. Yüksel Çayırlıoğlu, *Helal Gıda* (Istanbul: Işık Yayıncılık, 2014), 139; Riaz and Chaudry, *Halal Food Production*, 12.

42. Muhammad 'Ali al-Bar, *Al-Asrar al-Tibbiyya wa'l Ahkam al-Fiqhiyya fi Tahrim al-Khinzir* (Jeddah: Dar al-Su'udiyya li'l Nashr wa'l Tawzi', 1986), esp. 8–10.

43. For more, see "At'ima," *Al-Mawsu'a al-Fiqhiyya*, 5:140–141.

44. Indeed, Benkheira holds the scripture responsible for later Muslim attitudes toward the pig: "By confusing the inedible with the forbidden, the Quran allows [later] jurists to give religious legitimacy to non-Quranic prohibitions; it would also privilege the relationship between prohibition and repulsion. The khaba'ith are essentially disgusting and sickening foods. If the pig is included in this category, then there emerges a tendency to explain its prohibition by the repulsion it would provoke" (translation is ours). Benkheira, *Islâm et interdits alimentaires*, 47–48.

45. Mujahidul Islam Qasmi, *The Islamic Concept of Animal Slaughter* (Beirut: Dar al-Kotob al-Ilmiyyah, 2009), 8.

46. Çayırlıoğlu, *Helal Gıda*, 138.

47. Çayırlıoğlu, *Helal Gıda*, 138. Parallel characterizations of the pig also exist in much older sources. For example, Shihab al-Din al-Nuwayri, a scholar and civil servant in fourteenth-century Egypt, wrote in his encyclopedia that the swine "is characterized by lust and constant copulation, such that the female may be mounted by the male even as she is defecating . . . . They say that the males suffer from sodomy. Sometimes one sees a male [swine] cornered by twenty others, and they take turns mounting him until they have all done so." Shihab al-Din al-Nuwayri, *The Ultimate Ambition in the Arts of Euriditon: A Compendium of Knowledge from the Classical Islam*, ed., trans., intro., notes Elias Muhanna (New York: Penguin, 2016), 145–146.

48. Filial piety is a "quintessential Confucian virtue and the foundation of the traditional Chinese family system . . . . Pigs' lack of filiality was demonstrated by the way piglets climb all over their mothers when they suckle; lambs and calves, by contrast, kneel when they drink their mothers' milk"; see Maris B. Gillette, *Between Mecca and Beijing: Modernization and Consumption among Urban Chinese Muslims* (Stanford, CA: Stanford University Press, 2000), 119–120.

49. In sixteenth-century Ottoman Jerusalem, the pig generated such a level of disgust that the insult "pork-eater," if directed at Muslims (and presumably Jews), was punishable by law. See Amnon Cohen, *Economic Life in Ottoman Jerusalem* (Cambridge: Cambridge University Press, 1989), 38. For a fascinating critique of the negative Muslim and Jewish attitudes toward the pig composed by a group of medieval Muslim intellectuals in the late tenth century, see *The Case of the Animals versus Man Before the King of the Jinn: A Translation from the* Epistles of the Brethren of Purity, trans. Lenn E. Goodman and Richard McGregor (Oxford: Oxford University Press, 2012), 119–121.

50. While root explanations may be few, Muslim jurists extensively discussed whether eggs, milk, rennet, or a living offspring derived from carrion (e.g., an egg from a deceased chicken or a

calf from a cow) were edible. For more, see "At'ima," *Al-Mawsu'a al-Fiqhiyya*, 5:153–158, as well as our discussion of cheese in chapter 7.

51. Jacob Milgrom, "Food and Faith: The Ethical Foundations of the Biblical Diet Laws," *Bible Review* 8 (1992): 5–10. According to Milgrom, kashrut is a system that forces humans to consume animal flesh in an ethical manner. He states that the children of Noah were the first humans allowed to eat meat. When God realized that humans were carnivorous and could not resist the temptation of meat, he enforced a dietary system with the help of which humans satisfied their craving in an ethical manner (ibid.). For more on rabbinic rules regarding blood, see Rosenblum, *The Jewish Dietary Laws in the Ancient World*, 19–20, 97–99.

52. Simoons, *Eat Not This Flesh*, 87–88.

53. Cf. Qasmi, *Animal Slaughter*, 8; Riaz and Chaudry, *Halal Food Production*, 12.

54. Riaz and Chaudry, *Halal Food Production*, 12. Having said that, the Islamic medieval juristic tradition generally allowed for the consumption of organs, like liver or heart, and any offal that contained residual traces of blood. Even if cooked red meat showed traces of blood, that residual blood was not deemed impure or haram; see "At'ima," *Al-Mawsu'a al-Fiqhiyya*, 5:152. For more on the topic see chapter 2.

55. Riaz and Chaudry, *Halal Food Production*, 6, 12.

56. This phrase is taken from Jordan Rosenblum, who makes a similar argument for the context of kashrut rules: he notes that modern scholars may wish to parse the ecological, medical, or ethical logic behind these ancient rules, but according to the Bible, "the Israelites must follow these rules *because God says so*" (emphasis ours). See Rosenblum, *The Jewish Dietary Laws in the Ancient World*, 14.

57. Approximately one century after Muhammad's death, the Muslim polity witnessed a remarkable expansion. Muslim armies conquered the entire Arabian Peninsula, captured the Syrian province of Byzantium and penetrated into Anatolia, overcame the Sassanian Empire and subjugated Iran, occupied Egypt and North Africa, and seized most of the Iberian Peninsula. These regions were (and are) inhabited by peoples of significantly diverse ethnic, cultural, and linguistics characteristics, including the Kurds, Persians, Greeks, Copts, Jews, Armenians, Berbers, Nubians, and others.

58. "ط/ي/ب ṭ-y-b," Badawi and Haleem, *Dictionary of Qur'anic Usage*, Brill Online, http://referenceworks.brillonline.com/ (accessed May 2, 2016).

59. "خ/ب/ث kh-b-th," Badawi and Haleem, *Dictionary of Qur'anic Usage*, Brill Online, http://referenceworks.brillonline.com/ (accessed May 2, 2016).

60. Michael Cook, "Early Islamic Dietary Law," *Jerusalem Studies in Arabic and Islam* 7 (1986): 218–219.

61. See the following verses for comparison: 4:13, 4:59, 4:64, 5:92, and 33:71.

62. There are six sound hadith collections universally recognized by Sunni Muslims, each is a compilation of thousands of ahadith with overlaps. The collection by Muhammad al-Bukhari (d. 870), perhaps the most authoritative in the Sunni world, contains on its own 7,275 hadith reports with full chains of transmission (*isnad*) and 2,602 individual accounts excluding repeats; see Christopher Melchert, "al-Bukhari," *Encyclopaedia of Islam*, 3rd ed., Brill Online, http://referenceworks.brillonline.com/ (accessed May 2, 2016).

63. Ahmad ibn Shu'ayb al-Nasa'i, *Kitab al-Sunan al-Kubra*, ed. Hasan al-Mun'im Shalabi (Beirut: Mu'assasat al-Risala, 2001), 4:464–465; Ahmad ibn Shu'ayb al-Nasa'i, *English Translation of Sunan an-Nasa'i*, ed. Hafiz Abu Tahir Zubair 'Ali Za'i, Huda Khattab, and Abu Khaliyl; trans. Nasiruddin al-Khattab (Riyadh: Darussalam, 2007), 5:174–175.

64. Muhammad ibn 'Isa al-Tirmidhi, *Al-Jami' al-Kabir*, ed. Bashshar 'Awwad Ma'ruf, 2nd ed. (Beirut: Dar al-Gharb al-Islami, 1998), 1:134–136.

65. Al-Tirmidhi, *Al-Jami' al-Kabir*, 1:134–136. Also according to a less reliable hadith transmitted by Aisha, one of Muhammad's wives, "I and the Messenger of Allah used to perform ablutions from one vessel, from which the cat had previously drunk." See Muhammad ibn Yazid ibn Majah, *Sunan Ibn Majah*, ed. Bashshar 'Awwad Ma'ruf (Beirut: Dar al-Jil li'l-Tab' wa'l-Nashr wa'l-Tawzi', 1998), 1:318.

66. Ijma' could be a useful legal tool even when the Quran and/or ahadith contained information or statements about a substance or conduct and if these were difficult to interpret. In such cases, the consensus interpretation among jurists in a specific period, region, or legal school might constitute the preferred and binding legal interpretation, at least for the communities they represented.

67. Most Muslims use the terms "fard" and "wajib" as synonyms. Others, primarily the members of the Hanafi school (see below), define the first term as duties established by the Quran, the Prophet's custom, and the general consensus of Muslim scholars (ijma'). According to this opinion, wajib represents a less stringent obligation because it is based on deductive reasoning based on these sources, including "analogical reasoning"; see Theodor W. Juynboll, "Fard," *Encyclopaedia of Islam*, 2nd ed., Brill Online, http://referenceworks.brillonline.com/ (accessed May 2, 2016).

68. "At'ima," *Al-Mawsu'a al-Fiqhiyya*, 5:127; for some of these hadiths, see Muhammad ibn Isma'il al-Bukhari, *Sahih al-Bukhari*, ed. Mustafa Dib al-Bugha (Damascus: Dar ibn Kathir, 1987), 5:2076–2077.

69. Joseph Schacht, "Ibāḥa," *Encyclopaedia of Islam*, 2nd ed., Brill Online, http://referenceworks.brillonline.com/ (accessed May 2, 2016).

70. For example, according to numerous Hanafi and Shiite authorities, while the Prophet refused to eat lizard when he was offered, he also did not forbid it when he had an opportunity to do so and allowed people around him to consume it, which is why these authorities considered it makruh but not haram. Cook, "Early Islamic Dietary Laws," 226.

71. Mohammad Hashim Kamali, "The *Ḥalāl* Industry from a Sharī'ah Perspective," *Islam and Civilisational Renewal* 1, no. 4 (2010): 601–602; Riaz and Chaudry, *Halal Food Production*, 6–7.

72. Less popular Shiite schools of law include the Zaydi and the Ismailis.

73. This being said, all four Sunni legal schools recognize the other three as their equally legitimate counterparts and consider their differing opinions as based on acceptable divergence. The same is also true for the Shiite legal schools.

CHAPTER 2

1. David Waines, "Food in Antiquity: Islamic Dimension," in *A Companion to Food in the Ancient World*, ed. John Wilkins and Robin Nadeau (West Sussex: Wiley Blackwell, 2015), 383–384.

2. Waines, "Food in Antiquity," 383.

3. Waines, "Food in Antiquity," 383–384.

4. Rodinson, "Ghidhā'."

5. Waines, "Food in Antiquity," 384.

6. Waines, "Food in Antiquity," 384.

7. Sarra Tlili, *Animals in the Qur'an* (Cambridge: Cambridge University Press, 2012), 67; Rodinson, "Ghidhā'."

8. Rodinson, "Ghidhā'."

9. Shaikh Hamza Yusuf Hanson, "The Sunnah and Health" at http://behalal.org/health/islam-and-health/the-sunnah-and-health-by-shaykh-hamza-yusuf-hanson/ (accessed May 5, 2016).

10. Nizam al-Din ibn Abi al-Hadid, *Sharh Nahj al-Balagha*, ed. Muhammad Ibrahim (Baghdad: Dar al-Kitab al-'Arabi, 2007), 1:17.

11. On Ali, see Ibn Abi al-Hadid, *Sharh Nahj al-Balagha*, 49.11. For the original text of the report by Umar, see Malik ibn Anas, *Al-Muwatta'*, ed. Muhammad Fu'ad 'Abd al-Baqi (Beirut: Dar Ihya' al-Turath al-'Arabi, 1985), 2:935.

12. Paulina B. Lewicka, *Food and Foodways of Medieval Cairenes* (Boston: Brill, 2011), 173–174. Mutton was the most popular and expensive meat in medieval Cairo. Also consumed were beef, goat, and camel meat. The poorest groups also ate organ meat and sheep's heads and trotters (ibid., 174–175).

13. Quoted in Fernand Braudel, *Civilization and Capitalism, 15th–18th Century: The Structure of Everyday Life* (Berkeley: University of California Press, 1992), 201.

14. M. Carsten Niebuhr, *Travels through Arabia and Other Countries in the East . . .*, trans. Robert Heron (Edinburgh: Morison & Son, 1797), 2:231. Niebuhr also observed that "Arabians" had an aversion for hunting wild game because if their prey were killed improperly—that is, not according to halal slaughter prescriptions—their labor would be wasted (ibid., 2:327). The annual per capita meat consumption in mid-sixteenth-century Jerusalem was about 30 kilograms. The figure calculated for the early seventeenth-century Rome, supposed to be representative for the Italian peninsula, is 38.3 kilograms. The averages calculated for several French locales throughout the nineteenth century range between 40 and 77 kilograms. See Cohen, *Economic Life*, 56.

15. James Grehan, *Everyday Life and Consumer Culture in Eighteenth-Century Damascus* (Seattle: University of Washington Press, 2007), 95. Grehan indicates that in eighteenth-century Damascus, meat was an expensive food item "typically fetching five to six times the price of white bread (let alone humbler varieties)" (ibid.).

16. Grehan, *Everyday Life and Consumer Culture*, 96–97. Mutton was more popular than beef. Water buffalo, goats, and camel were butchered at times of economic difficulties (ibid., 97).

17. Grehan, *Everyday Life and Consumer Culture*, 96–97. Braudel suggests that "apart from the enormous consumption of mutton in Seraglio, the average in Istanbul from sixteenth to the eighteenth century was about one sheep or a third of a sheep per person per year. And Istanbul was well off"; see *Civilization and Capitalism*, 201.

18. During the sixteenth century, per capita meat consumption in Jerusalem, which was an important provincial city in the Ottoman Empire, was about one-third to one-quarter of the levels in Istanbul. See Cohen, *Economic Life*, 56.

19. Grehan, *Everyday Life and Consumer Culture*, 94–95.

20. Unfortunately, even rough estimates of average per-capita meat consumption are lacking before the twentieth century. There seems to be a consensus among scholars, however, that meat consumption remained quite low in the West until the second half of the nineteenth century and perhaps until World War II in many non-Western settings. See Amy J. Fitzgerald, *Animals as Food: (Re)connecting Production, Processing, Consumption, and Impacts* (East Lansing: Michigan University Press, 2015), ch. 4; Braudel, *Civilization and Capitalism*, 187–203. For more on this issue, see chapter 5.

21. See Richard Foltz, *Animals in Islamic Traditions and Muslim Cultures* (London: Oneworld, 2014), 31, for his take on "Cosmic Hierarchy in the Qur'an."

22. Foltz, *Animals*, 34.

23. See 2:30, 22:34, and 22:37; see also Foltz, *Animals*, 31–32. But see below for disagreements on how to interpret khalifa in the Quran.

24. Tlili, *Animals in the Qur'an*, 8.

25. Not every exegete agrees on the implications of this transformation. For example, in her attempt to offer a non-anthropocentric interpretation of this Quranic punishment, Sarra Tlili argues that the human-to-animal metamorphosis (*maskh*), rather than indicative of the lower status of the apes and pigs compared to humans, might have intended to cause human souls "utter confusion, frustration, and possibly also physical pain" in the strange, alien bodies of apes and pigs; see Tlili, *Animals in the Qur'an*, 117. For a secular critique of such animal-friendly exegetical efforts in Islamic and other religious traditions, see Kim Socha, *Animal Liberation and Atheism: Dismantling the Procrustean Bed* (Minneapolis-St. Paul: Freethought House, 2014), introduction and ch. 1.

26. Foltz, *Animals*, 38.

27. Foltz, *Animals*, 38–39.

28. Foltz, *Animals*, 57.

29. Influenced by earlier Muslim feminist interpretations of the revelation, these efforts challenge narratives of human domination over the environment and its nonhuman components. According to Kecia Ali, for instance, "Muslim feminist criticism has pointed out the ways that hierarchical cosmologies are used to naturalize and justify male dominance and female submission." Following this logic, Ali further argues that "meat eating supports patriarchy. The use(s) of female and animal bodies—and female animals' bodies in the case of milk and egg production—depend on and sustain relations of unjust dominance." See Ali, "Muslims and Meat-Eating: Vegetarianism, Gender, and Identity," *Journal of Religious Ethics* 43, no. 2 (2015): 276–277.

30. Foltz, *Animals*, 58–59.

31. Foltz, *Animals*, 59.

32. Tlili, *Animals in the Qur'an*, 253.

33. Tlili, *Animals in the Qur'an*, 115–123 and 254. However, Tlili is less forthcoming about how the term *khalifa* in the Quran should be interpreted. The closest that she comes to accomplishing this task is where she states that "previous research . . . shows that the earliest known meaning of the word *khalifa* is only 'successor' and 'follower' (of a previous nation, party, or ruler)"; ibid., 253–254. Also, Tlili takes no issue with the notion that human killing of animals for consumption is sanctioned by God and she overlooks the problematic status of the pig in the Quran. See *The Case of the Animals versus Man*, 119–121, for a medieval Muslim critique of the negative attitudes toward the pig.

34. See, in general, *The Case of the Animals versus Man*. According to the epistle, humans are different from animals only because they have immortal souls and because God sent to them prophets, saints, and imams; ibid., 311–313.

35. Interestingly, a great majority of Muslims consider elephant flesh as non-halal; see Table 2.1.

36. Kerry S. Walters and Lisa Portmess, *Religious Vegetarianism: From Hesiod to the Dalai Lama* (Albany: State University of New York Press, 2001), 173–174. Folk-tales from various Islamic settings characterize harming animals as contrary to Sufism. One popular story from Turkey tells of a bird with a broken wing who complained to the mythical prophet-king Suleiman that a dervish had injured him. Suleiman sent for the dervish, informed him of the bird's accusation, and demanded an explanation. The dervish replied that he had approached the bird, intending to capture it, and the bird had not fled. Thinking that the bird had surrendered, the dervish moved to grab it. At that point the bird attempted to escape, but in the process, the dervish snatched and injured its wing. When Suleiman asked the bird why he hadn't flown away when the dervish

first approached him, the bird said he had refused to believe that a dervish would hurt a soul. Suleiman ruled in the bird's favor and ordered that the dervish be punished by having one of his arms broken. The bird intervened, however, requesting that the king instead simply force the man to discard his dervish cloak. After all, the bird reasoned, the dervish might continue hunting after his arm heals, but no bird would allow a human to get close if he is not wearing dervish garments. See "Hz. Süleyman ve Kanadı Kırık Kuş," Bilgece Hikayeler at http://www.bilgecehikayeler.com/hz-suleyman-ve-kanadi-kirik-kus/ (accessed February 14, 2017).

37. Pasha M. Khan, "Nothing but Animals: The Hierarchy of Creatures in the Ringstones of Wisdom," *Journal of the Muhyiddin Ibn 'Arabi Society* 43 (2008), http://www.ibnarabisociety.org/articles/nothing-but-animals.html (accessed May 6, 2016). Our discussion should not be interpreted to suggest that all Sufi traditions are as explicitly non-anthropocentric. In fact, various Neoplatonic formulations, which place human beings between God and nonhuman creation in the cosmological hierarchy, are known to have influenced many Sufi masters. On Islamic Neoplatonism, see Sarra Tlili, "All Animals Are Equal, or Are They? The Ikhwān al-Ṣafā"s Animal Epistle and its Unhappy End," *Journal of Qur'anic Studies* 16, no. 2 (2014): 42–88; Lenn E. Goodman, "Introduction," in *The Case of the Animals versus Man*, 34–37 and *passim*; and Parviz Morewedge ed., *Neoplatonism and Islamic Thought* (Albany: State University of New York Press, 1992).

38. "At'ima," *Al-Mawsu'a al-Fiqhiyya*, 5:152–153. Unlike kashrut rules, however, halal traditions do not require the removal of the sciatic nerve and adjoining blood vessels, a difficult and labor-intensive process. For more on this kashrut rule, see Rosenblum, *The Jewish Dietary Laws in the Ancient World*, 20–21, 112–115.

39. Intraschool disagreements are quite common. Jurists affiliated with particular school can subscribe to opinions that conflict with majority interpretations. For this reason, information provided in the table should be taken as approximate.

40. Jurists have also agreed that the flesh of animals otherwise considered to be permissible cease to be so if they were fed food from haram sources. Indeed, modern halal expectations require that poultry intended for Muslim consumption should not be given feed that contains animal by-products or substances that may be contaminated by impure materials. See Shirazi, *Brand Islam*, 43 and also chapter 6. For more extensive information on various types and species of animals that are fit (or not) for eating, see in general Benkheira, *Islâm et interdits alimentaires*.

41. See, for example, Muhammad ibn 'Isa al-Tirmidhi, *Al-Jami' al-Kabir*, ed. Bashshar 'Awwad Ma'ruf, 2nd ed. (Beirut: Dar al-Gharb al-Islami, 1998), 3:144.

42. See Muhammad ibn Isma'il al-Bukhari, *Sahih al-Bukhari*, ed. Mustafa Dib al-Bugha (Damascus: Dar ibn Kathir, 1987), 5:2102.

43. The mechanics of adopting and defending specific positions pertaining to the status of individual species were often not straightforward. Legal scholar Mohammed Benkheira has suggested that most medieval jurists (just like most medieval scientists and intellectuals) differentiated among various animal groups with reference to a five-part classification system: domesticated animals; wild animals; birds; vermin; and aquatic animals. Within this system, specific categories could be composed of multiple subgroups based on a number of considerations, including the physical attributes of individual species, their behavioral tendencies, diets, relationships to humans, divine/demonic qualities, and even what they were called (see the discussion on isomorphs later in this chapter). For example, among domesticated animals, cattle and sheep were differentiated from species used for transportation, such as equines. Among wild animals, herbivores were distinguished from carnivores. Among carnivores, predators were

sometimes separated from animals that do not kill for meat. And while dogs were regarded to have demonic qualities, cats were not. This system, largely based on inherited cultural, philosophical, and cosmological attitudes qualified by canonical criteria, influenced juristic opinions, often in gradations of certainty, regarding human-animal relations and, more important for our concerns, which species were fit for human consumption and how they should be killed. For example, among land animals, while species domesticated primarily for food were universally considered acceptable for both consumption and ritual sacrifice, many jurists objected to putting equines to such uses. Although wild herbivores were deemed appropriate for consumption (but not for ritual sacrifice), jurists objected to eating carnivores, especially predators, lest their physical and behavioral qualities contaminate the humans. Among aquatic animals, all jurists considered fish with scales as suitable for human consumption but they conflicted on the statuses of species with different qualities. While this system of categorization remained broadly influential across generations, jurists often disagreed on whether a particular species should be included into one or another (sub-)category, based on the jurists' personal or "vernacular" preferences, which also influenced the choice of particular ahadith that they privileged in their opinions or how they interpreted ahadith that other jurists also acknowledged. For more on Benkheira's brilliant, long-neglected, yet often speculative analysis of this classification system and how various groups of jurists reached diverging opinions about different species, see *Islam et interdits alimentaires*.

44. Cook, "Early Islamic Dietary Law," 250–251.

45. "At'ima," *Al-Mawsu'a al-Fiqhiyya*, 5:135–137. The Ja'fari Shiite position on birds of prey tends to be more complex and is based on three major criteria: (1) whether a bird "hovers" or "beats its wings" (the latter is halal); (2) only birds that are not meat eaters are lawful (i.e., those that have a gizzard or a jabot); and (3) birds with no ergot are illegal. It is not necessary that a bird possess all three criteria in order to be lawful; just one is sufficient. See Benkheira, *Islam et interdits alimentaires*, 119–121.

46. Cook, "Early Islamic Dietary Law," 248–250; on "beasts of prey" and "birds of prey," see also "At'ima," *Al-Mawsu'a al-Fiqhiyya*, 5:134–135.

47. Cook, "Early Islamic Dietary Law," 254n334. Also, "At'ima," *Al-Mawsu'a al-Fiqhiyya*, 5:138–140. Most schools approve the consumption of domesticated donkey because there are multiple strands of Prophetic hadith to this effect. See Abu al-Husayn Muslim ibn al-Hajjaj al-Qushayri al-Naysaburi, *Sahih Muslim*, ed. Ahmad Shams al-Din (Beirut: Dar al-Kutub al-'Ilmiyya, 1998), 2:204. The latter is commonly known as "Muslim."

48. Waines, "Food in Antiquity," 384.

49. Cook, "Early Islamic Dietary Law," 237.

50. Cook, "Early Islamic Dietary Law," 239–240.

51. On locusts in the Sunni tradition, see "At'ima," *Al-Mawsu'a al-Fiqhiyya*, 5:142.

52. Chehabi, "How Caviar Turned Out to Be Halal," 18.

53. R. H. Barnes, "Lamakera, Solor. Ethnographic Notes on a Muslim Whaling Village of Eastern Indonesia," *Anthropos* 91, nos. 1/3 (1996): 75–88.

54. Cook, "Early Islamic Dietary Law," 240.

55. "At'ima," *Al-Mawsu'a al-Fiqhiyya*, 5:129.

56. Cook, "Early Islamic Dietary Law," 238–239. A good overview of the Sunni schools' different positions on sea life can be found in Muhammad ibn 'Abd al-Rahman ibn 'Abd al-Rahim al-Mubarakfuri, *Tuhfat al-Ahwadhi bi Sharh Jami' al-Tirmidhi*, 10 vols., ed. and ann. 'Abd al-Wahab 'Abd al-Latif (Cairo: Dar al-Fikr li'l-Tiba'a wa'l-Nashr wa'l-Tawzi', 1967), 1:224–231, at http://waqfeya.com/book.php?bid=905.

57. Snakes are makruh or haram in most Sunni traditions, except for Malikis; see Cook, "Early Islamic Dietary Law," 237–246; "At'ima," *Al-Mawsu'a al-Fiqhiyya*, 5:131.

58. Çayırlıoğlu, *Helal Gıda*, 164–165; Walid Khaled al-Rabi', *Ahkam al-At'ima fi'l-Fiqh al-Islami: Dirasa Muqarna* (Amman: Dar al-Nafa'is, 2008), 19–21; Benkheira, *Islam et interdits alimentaires*, 69–70; Ch. Pellat et al., "Ḥayawān," *Encyclopaedia of Islam*, 2nd ed., Brill Online, http://referenceworks.brillonline.com/ (accessed May 2, 2016).

59. Cook, "Early Islamic Dietary Law," 246–247; Al-Sayyid 'Ali al-Husseini al-Sistani, "Eating and Drinking: General Rules," http://www.sistani.org/english/book/46/2044/ (accessed November 5, 2016).

60. Anita Bagchi and Prithwiraj Jha, "Fish and Fisheries in Indian Heritage and Development of Pisciculture in India," *Reviews in Fisheries Science* 19, no. 2 (2011): 98.

61. Ståle Knudsen, "Between Life Giver and Leisure: Identity Negotiation through Seafood in Turkey," *International Journal of Middle East Studies* 38, no. 3 (2006): 403.

62. For a thorough and insightful discussion of this topic, see in general Chehabi, "How Caviar Turned Out to Be Halal"; Christian Bromberger, "Et l'esturgeon devin *halâl* en islam chiite duodécimain," in *Les sens du Halal: Une norme dans un marché mondial*, ed. Florence Bergaud-Blackler (Paris: CNRS Éditions, 2015), 25–30. For centuries, the status of sturgeon had been debated with reference to Jewish law: in the medieval period, rabbinic rulings from Egypt and France allowed its consumption, while the fish was deemed suspect by and remained off limits for most Ashkenazi Jews (i.e., those from Christian Europe). See Roger Horowitz, *Kosher USA: How Coke Became Kosher and Other Tales of Modern Food* (New York: Columbia University Press, 2016), 10–12.

63. "At'ima," *Al-Mawsu'a al-Fiqhiyya*, 5:132.

64. Ahmad Ya'qub and Maher 'Abd al-Wahab, "'Ulama' al-Din: Fatwa Tahrim 'Akl al-Fasikh Sahiha bi-Sabab Ra'ihatihi al-Kariha," *Youm7.com*, April 20, 2009, www.youm7.com/story/2009/4/20/علماء-دين-فتوى-تحريم-أكل-الفسيخ-الفسيحة-صحيحة-بسبب-رائحته-رائحة-الكريهة/91041.

65. Cook, "Early Islamic Dietary Law," 218–219. Despite these periodic prohibitions, one can still find a black market for this product during Egypt's annual springtime celebrations, when it is especially coveted by the country's Coptic Christian community.

CHAPTER 3

1. Al-Tirmidhi, *Al-Jami' al-Kabir*, 3:78.

2. Al-Bukhari, *Sahih al-Bukhari*, 5:2113.

3. "Dhaba'ih," *Al-Mawsu'a al-Fiqhiyya*, 21:183–189.

4. Another common formulation, "Bismillah al-Rahman al-Rahim" ("In the name of God, who is merciful and compassionate"), is often, though not universally, avoided, since the emphasis on God's compassion is considered inappropriate for the occasion. For more, see "Dhaba'ih," *Al-Mawsu'a al-Fiqhiyya*, 21:191–194. Jurists have disagreed on whether kitabi slaughterers should observe the tasmiyya requirement.

5. J. M. Regenstein et al., "The Kosher and Halal Food Laws," *Comprehensive Reviews in Food Science and Food Safety* 2 (2003): 120–121. This is consistent with the classical Hanafi prescription according to Mujahidul Islam Qasmi. The Malikis require all four passages to be severed. For the Shafi'is and Hanbalis, severing the respiratory and food pipes should be adequate; see Qasmi, *Animal Slaughter*, 31–32. For more on juridical disputes over the precise throat-slitting methods, see "Dhaba'ih," *Al-Mawsu'a al-Fiqhiyya*, 21:175–179, and our discussion in chapter 5.

6. See, for example, a hadith narrated by Rafi' ibn Khadij: The Prophet said, "Listen! If you slaughter the animal with anything that causes its blood to flow out, and if Allah's Name is mentioned on slaughtering it, eat of it, provided that the slaughtering instrument is not a tooth or a nail, as the tooth is a bone and the nail is the knife of Ethiopians." See Muhammad ibn Isma'il al-Bukhari, *The Translation of the Meanings of Sahih al-Bukhari: Arabic-English*, ed. Muhammad Muhsin Khan (1979; rpt., Riyadh: Darussalam, 1997), 7:265; Al-Bukhari, *Sahih al-Bukhari*, 5:2107. See also "Dhaba'ih," *Al-Mawsu'a al-Fiqhiyya*, 21:195–196. Incidentally, Imam Malik regarded slaughter with sharpened bones (but not teeth) as acceptable; see Qasmi, *Animal Slaughter*, 39–40.

7. Conventional wisdom suggests that most legal schools view "best practice" as a single horizontal cut to the animal's throat with the goal of achieving a speedy and painless death. However, only the Malikis explicitly specify this method, preferring that the slaughterer's hand be not lifted during slaughter. Both Malikis and Shafi'is indicate that if a slaughterer lifted his hand, the meat would be halal so long as the animal was not cut post-mortem. That is, if the slaughterer confuses post-mortem twitches and movements ("*harakat madhbuh*") with signs of life and continues to cut the animal, it renders his slaughter haram. See "Dhaba'ih," *Al-Mawsu'a al-Fiqhiyya*, 21:194.

8. Regenstein et al., "Kosher and Halal," 110–127. There are also major differences, however. For example, according to the shechita requirements, the person who performs the slaughter (*shohet*) should be Jewish (usually male) who is licensed by rabbinic authorities based on his knowledge of shechita requirements. Shechita also requires the blade used in the slaughter to be free from even a single nick. After the slaughter, the internal organs of the animals (particularly the lungs) are inspected. In order for the flesh of the slaughtered animal to be considered suitable for consumption, its organs should be without blemish and, if applicable, the sciatic nerve must be removed. For these reasons, halal meat is not kosher.

9. Regenstein et al., "Kosher and Halal," 110–127.

10. Al-Nasa'i, *Kitab al-Sunan al-Kubra*, 4:489. See also "Dhaba'ih," *Al-Mawsu'a al-Fiqhiyya*, 21:174.

11. Çayırlıoğlu, *Helal Gıda*, 166.

12. Some Shafi'is are also against torturing locusts before eating them: that is, cooking them while they are still alive. "At'ima," *Al-Mawsu'a al-Fiqhiyya*, 5:130–131; 5:142.

13. Taylor Kate Brown, "Hunting Whales with Rowing Boats and Spears," *BBC News Magazine*, April 26, 2015, http://www.bbc.com/news/magazine-32429447.

14. Narrated Ka'b ibn Malik: "A woman slaughtered a sheep with a stone and then the Prophet was asked about it and he permitted it to be eaten." Al-Bukhari, *Sahih al-Bukhari*, 7:249–250; 5:2096. Riaz and Chaudry agree with this interpretation; see *Halal Food Production*, 18. On the general consensus across the four Sunni madhhabs that support women's slaughter, see "Dhaba'ih," *Al-Mawsu'a al-Fiqhiyya*, 21:184.

15. G.-H. Bousquet, "Dhabiha," *Encyclopaedia of Islam*, 2nd ed., Brill Online, http://referenceworks.brillonline.com/ (accessed May 6, 2016).

16. Pınar Kasapoğlu Akyol, "Çorum'un Sungurlu İlçesinde 1895–1947 Yılları Arasında Kasapoğlu Ailesi Üzerinden Kasaplık Kültürüne Bir Bakış," *Acta Turcica: Online Thematic Journal of Turkic Studies* 3, no. 2 (2011): 10, http://actaturcica.com/_media/2011-07/iii_2_1.pdf.

17. Freidenreich, *Foreigners and Their Food*, 144–147. See also "Dhaba'ih," *Al-Mawsu'a al-Fiqhiyya*, 21:183–189.

18. Freidenreich, *Foreigners and Their Food*, 147–149.

19. 5:3: "Prohibited to you are dead animals, blood, the flesh of swine, and that which has been dedicated to other than Allah"; 6:121: "And do not eat of that upon which the name of Allah has not been mentioned, for indeed, it is grave disobedience. And indeed do the devils inspire their allies [among men] to dispute with you. And if you were to obey them, indeed, you would be associators [of others with Him]."

20. The term "abrogation" is used in Quranic exegesis to explain seemingly inconsistent statements in the scripture, whereby later revelations are considered to "abrogate" or supersede the earlier ones that they appear to contradict; see Andrew Rippin, "Abrogation," *Encyclopaedia of Islam*, 3rd ed., Brill Online, http://referenceworks.brillonline.com/ (accessed May 10, 2016).

21. Appendix B provides minor differences in the opinions of jurists who belonged to the four Sunni legal schools.

22. Freidenreich, *Foreigners and Their Food*, ch. 11.

23. Freidenreich, *Foreigners and Their Food*, 161.

24. Freidenreich, *Foreigners and Their Food*, 157. According to Freidenreich, there may be a few reasons for the Shiite inclination to define halal food in a more restrictive fashion; one of the more convincing ones is related to the Shiite attempts to distinguish themselves from Sunnis, at least until the modern period.

25. Abd al-Rahman b. Nasr al-Shayzari, *The Book of the Islamic Market Inspector*, trans., intro., notes R. P. Buckley (Oxford: Oxford University Press, 1999), 52.

26. Lewicka, *Food and Foodways*, 110.

27. Minna Rozen, "A Pound of Flesh: The Meat Trade and Social Struggle in the Jewish Istanbul, 1700–1923," in *Crafts and Craftsmen of the Middle East: Fashioning the Individual in the Muslim Mediterranean*, ed. Suraiya Faroqhi and Randi Deguilhem (London: I. B. Tauris, 2005), 197. The separation of animals into separate spaces within abattoirs, according to Orthodox Christian, Muslim, or European custom, is common practice in contemporary Ethiopia. Since ancient times, Ethiopian Orthodox Christians have valued the purity of their slaughter utensils (and by extension facilities) and require that the slaughterer be Orthodox Christian. See Zellelew, "The Semiotics of the 'Christian/Muslim Knife,'" 61–62.

28. Edward W. Lane, *An Account of the Manners and Customs of the Modern Egyptians . . .*, 5th ed. (London: John Murray, 1830), 291–292. In this anecdote, one religious scholar complains to the governor about Jewish butchers selling meat to Muslims but other scholars testify that this is acceptable according to the Quran, provided that the meat was butchered according to Islamic requirements. Afterward, the chief of the Jewish butchers is interrogated about how they slaughter their meat. In his testimony he states that they not only slaughter according to Islamic expectations but even say "In the name of God, God is Great" at the time of slaughter. Consequently, the authorities dismiss the complaint, thereby sanctioning the sale of Jewish-slaughtered meat to Muslims.

29. Jeff Welty, "Humane Slaughter Laws," *Law and Contemporary Problems* 70 (2007): 176–177; J. K. Shearer and Alejandro Ramirez, "Procedures for Humane Euthanasia," http://www.neacha.org/resources/Humane.livestock.Euthanasia.pdf (accessed May 9, 2016).

30. Gerhard Van der Schyff, "Ritual Slaughter and Religious Freedom in a Multilevel Europe: The Wider Importance of the Dutch Case," *Oxford Journal of Law and Religion* 3, no. 1 (2014): 78.

31. Humane Slaughter Association, "History of the HSA," http://www.hsa.org.uk/about/history-of-the-hsa (accessed May 9, 2016). The Slaughter of Animals Act of 1933 contained exemptions to preslaughter stunning on religious grounds; see "Halal Meat Row: Myths and Reality of Religious

Slaughter," *Telegraph*, May 7, 2014, http://www.telegraph.co.uk/foodanddrink/foodanddrinknews/10814716/Halal-meat-row-myths-and-reality-of-religious-slaughter.html.

32. Audun Lunga, "Butchery Law with Anti-Semitic Roots," *ScienceNordic*, November 6, 2013, http://sciencenordic.com/butchery-law-anti-semitic-roots.

33. Van der Schyff, "Ritual Slaughter," 78–79; "The Ban on Shechita in Switzerland," http://old.swissjews.ch/en/religioeses/koscherfleisch/schaechtverbot.php (accessed May 9, 2016). For more on the historical discussions about kosher slaughter and stunning in Germany, see Robin Judd, *Contested Rituals: Circumcision, Kosher Butchering, and Jewish Political Life in Germany, 1843–1933* (Ithaca, NY: Cornell University Press, 2007).

34. Florence Bergeaud-Blackler, "New Challenges for Islamic Ritual Slaughter: A European Perspective," *Journal of Ethnic and Migration Studies* 33, no. 6 (2007): 967.

35. References to Muslim ritual slaughter in Europe go back to the 1920s in relation to the dietary demands and expectations of Britain's Muslim soldiers and workers of Indian origin. See Florence Bergeaud-Blackler, *Le marché halal ou l'invention d'une tradition* (Paris: Seuil, 2017), 27–28.

36. Bergeaud-Blackler, "New Challenges," 967.

37. See Article 17 at https://rm.coe.int/CoERMPublicCommonSearchServices/DisplayDCTMContent?documentId=0900001680077da5 (accessed May 9, 2016).

38. See Article 5 at http://ec.europa.eu/food/fs/aw/aw_legislation/slaughter/93-119-ec_en.pdf (accessed May 9, 2016).

39. Bergeaud-Blackler, "New Challenges," 966.

40. Bergeaud-Blackler, "New Challenges," 965–999.

41. The requirement of keeping the trachea and the esophagus intact during slaughter had been instituted by *European Regulation No. 853* in 2004 in order to prevent the gastric and pulmonary contents of the animal from spilling over and soiling other parts of the carcass. This is an issue relevant to Muslims because most interpretations of halal slaughter involve severing these passages. See Bergeaud-Blackler, *Le marché halal*, 70–71.

42. See *Council Regulation (EC) No 1099/2009 on the Protection of Animals at the Time of Killing*. http://eur-lex.europa.eu/eli/reg/2009/1099/oj (accessed June 12, 2017); and Bergeaud-Blackler, *Le marché halal*, 69–71.

43. See Pablo Lerner and Alfredo Mordechai Rabello, "The Prohibition of Ritual Slaughtering (Kosher Shechita and Halal) and Freedom of Religion of Minorities," *Journal of Law and Religion* 22, no. 1 (2006-2007): 1–62; and Zachary Heier, "In Concern of Animal Welfare, or with Xenophobic Intent? An Analysis of State-Decreed Bans on Non-Stun Halal Slaughter in Europe and the Threat to Religious Freedom" (unpublished paper, University of Vermont, 2017).

44. Clare Speak, "Slaughter Ban Harms Halal Butchery Industry in Poland," *Prague Post*, May 24, 2013, http://halalfocus.net/eu-slaughter-ban-harms-halal-butchery-industry-in-poland/; "Polish Ban on Kosher Slaughter of Animals Is Overturned," *BBC News*, December 10, 2014; http://www.bbc.com/news/world-europe-30412551.

45. Line Elise Svanevik, "Denmark Bans Non-Stun Slaughter," *Global Meat News*, February 20, 2014, http://www.globalmeatnews.com/Industry-Markets/Denmark-bans-non-stun-slaughter.

46. "BVA Calls on Government to End Non-Stun Slaughter following Parliamentary Debate," February 26, 2015, http://www.bva.co.uk/News-campaigns-and-policy/Newsroom/News-releases/BVA-calls-on-Government-to-end-non-stun-slaughter-following-Parliamentary-debate/.

47. Samuel Osborne, "Belgium Votes to Ban Kosher and Halal Slaughter in Its Biggest Territory," *Independent*, May, 8, 2017, http://www.independent.co.uk/news/world/europe/

belgian-region-walloon-bans-kosher-halal-meat-islam-jewish-a7723451.html (accessed May 14, 2017).

48. Concerns for and restrictions to non-stun slaughter in some European countries have also been generating opportunities for others. For example, when ritual slaughter was banned for a short period of time in Poland, which is a major exporter of meat to the Middle East, meat exports were picked up by the Czech Republic, Latvia, Hungary, and France. The situation also provided a brief opportunity for Bosnia and Herzegovina, a Muslim-majority nation in Europe that "aims to become a hub for the halal industry" in Europe, to become a major exporter of halal and kosher meat; see Speak, "Slaughter Ban."

49. Welty, "Humane Slaughter Laws," 183. See also Bruce Friedrich, "Ritual Slaughter in the 'Ritual Bubble': Restoring the Wall of Separation between Church and State," *Vermont Journal of Environmental Law* 17 (2015): 224–225.

50. Friedrich, "Ritual Slaughter," 225.

51. Welty, "Humane Slaughter Laws," 186.

52. The text of the HMSA states that it covers "cattle, calves, horses, mules, sheep, swine, and other livestock"; Welty, "Humane Slaughter Laws," 198.

53. Welty, "Humane Slaughter Laws," 198.

54. Welty, "Humane Slaughter Laws," 199–201.

55. Welty, "Humane Slaughter Laws," 190–191.

56. See "Meat Industry Association of New Zealand: FAQs," http://www.mia.co.nz/industry_ information/FAQ-halal/index.htm (accessed May 9, 2016).

57. See Temple Grandin's influential research on how various forms of ritual slaughter can be performed in ways that minimize animal suffering, http://www.grandin.com/ritual/rec.ritual. slaughter.html (accessed May 7, 2017). In particular, see Temple Grandin and Joe Regenstein, "Religious Slaughter and Animal Welfare: A Discussion for Meat Scientists," *Meat Focus International* (1994): 115–123, http://www.grandin.com/ritual/kosher.slaugh.html (accessed May 7, 2017). We thank one of our referees for bringing Grandin's research to our attention.

58. Welty, "Humane Slaughter Laws," 192.

59. *Opinion of the Scientific Panel on Animal Health and Welfare*, 5, http://www.efsa.europa.eu/ sites/default/files/scientific_output/files/main_documents/45.pdf (accessed May 9, 2016.)

60. "Dhaba'ih," *Al-Mawsu'a al-Fiqhiyya*, 21:196–198.

61. Al-Qaradawi, *The Lawful and the Prohibited*, 59. Another well-known modern justification for this position can be found in a fatwa issued by Muhammad Abduh (d. 1905), a famous Egyptian Islamic modernist, in 1903 to the Muslims of Transvaal in South Africa. The fatwa, which would later be known as the "Transvaal Fatwa," allowed Muslims to eat animals slaughtered by the People of the Book, "so long as the slaughter has taken place according to the custom which has been approved by the chiefs of their religion." See Jakob Skovgaard-Petersen, *Defining Islam for the Egyptian State: Muftis and Fatwas of the* Dār Al-Iftā (Leiden: Brill, 1997), 123–125; also see Bergeaud-Blackler, *Le marché halal*, 30–31.

62. A well-known hadith attributes to the Prophet the following statement: "Leave that which makes you doubt for that which does not make you doubt, for certainty is peace of mind, and falsehoods are suspicious." Al-Tirmidhi, *Al-Jami' al-Kabir*, 4:286. Also relevant here is the Shiite jurists' doubt that 5:5 is applicable to meat and meat products. As discussed in chapter 2, Shiites believe that "food of those who were given Scripture" in the verse refers only to cereals and other dry foods. Given the exceptional nature of meat as a food source of during Muhammad's times, this may not be an outlandish claim.

63. Shaykh Taqi Usmani, *Legal Rulings on Slaughtered Animals*, trans. Mufti Abdullah Nana (Karachi: Maktaba-e-Darul-'Uloom, 2005), 64, 66, 110, 118, 123. Interestingly, the author did not raise the same concern for butchers with Muslim names or ancestry. As we discuss later (chapter 5), major Muslim markets now rely on foreign meat to meet their constantly expanding demand. The majority of this supply is transported in frozen or chilled form. But the aforementioned concerns about the status of non-Muslim-slaughtered meat have also contributed to the rise of live animal exports since the 1970s. For example, in 2014, Australia's live animal exports to the Middle East was valued about AU$281 million (US$210 million) and constituted about one-quarter of all meat sold to the region in value. https://www.rspca.org.au/sites/default/files/website/Campaigns/Live-export/RSPCA-live_export_vs_meat_export_infographics.pdf (accessed July 6, 2016). See also *Inquiry into Australia's Trade and Investment Relationships with Countries of the Middle East*, http://www.aph.gov.au/Parliamentary_Business/Committees/Joint/Foreign_Affairs_Defence_and_Trade/Middle_East_trade_and_investment/Report (accessed July 6, 2016).

64. See also the following verses in the Quran: 6:145, 16:115, 2:173. Muslims have made efforts in the past to explain the apparent conflicts among various Quranic statements pertaining to food. As stated, Shiites believe that 5:5 concerns dry foodstuff and is not applicable to animal flesh. Others have suggested that since 5:5 was revealed later than the verses instructing how animals intended for consumption should not be killed, including 5:3, it "abrogated" them, at least with respect to animals killed by Jews and Christians.

65. Çayırlıoğlu, *Helal Gıda*, 394–397; "Dhaba'ih," *Al-Mawsu'a al-Fiqhiyya*, 21:180–183.

66. Qasmi, *Animal Slaughter*, 56.

67. Bergeaud-Blackler, "New Challenges," 968.

68. Lauren Rothman. "Halal Slaughter Is More Complicated Than You Realize," *Munchies*, October 30, 2014, https://munchies.vice.com/en/articles/halal-slaughter-is-more-complicated-than-you-realize.

69. K. Nakyinsige et al., "Stunning and Animal Welfare from Islamic and Scientific Perspectives," *Meat Science* 95 (2013): 352–361. In industrial slaughterhouses, cattle are often stunned in stun boxes and then slaughtered either on the spot or after their bodies are hoisted by their hind-legs to carcass conveyor lines. Smaller animals can be electrocuted by hand-held devices in their holding enclosures or, in some facilities, while they are on v-shaped chutes which transfer them to slaughter spots or conveyor lines.

70. Qasmi, *Animal Slaughter*, 57–58.

71. Rothman, "Halal Slaughter."

72. Usmani, *Legal Rulings*, 87.

73. Usmani, *Legal Rulings*, 115.

74. Usmani, *Legal Rulings*, 153.

75. Usmani, *Legal Rulings*, 153–154.

76. Al-Tirmidhi, *Al-Jami' al-Kabir*, 3:78.

77. Romi Mukherjee eloquently expresses the doubts about industrialized slaughter in the following fashion:

> Industrial Halal plants have been, moreover, reproached for their usage of the "Halal track." Stereotypically associated with Belgian abattoirs, the Halal track is the continuous playing of prayers over an industrial conveyor belt where the slaughterman sacrifices en masse. The digitalization of Halal is notorious for its imperfect sacrifices, error, and easy slippage

into Haram. The digitalization of Halal is alternately deemed forbidden or scorned as a cheap means of performing a ritual, which hitherto was embodied, visceral, and "authentic." As with Kosher slaughter, the logic underlying anti-digital-Halal invective rests upon the question of intentionality. In other words, if God commanded it, it must be done with intention, which machines and compact discs cannot possess. While the machine may be driven by a human and reproduce the human voice, it still mediates and thus dilutes, if not destroys, the non-mediated line of command[ment] coming from God to believer to believer's spirit to his hand that wields the knife.

See Romi Mukherjee, "Global Halal: Meat, Money and Religion," *Religions* 5 (2014): 40.

78. Çayırlıoğlu, *Helal Gıda*, 407–413. In comparison, the religious identity of the person who stuns the animal is not a concern in disagreements concerning the legality of stunning.

79. Çayırlıoğlu, *Helal Gıda*, 410–411.

80. Çayırlıoğlu, *Helal Gıda*, 412–413.

81. Most legal experts, including those who are lenient about mechanized slaughter, reject audio-recorded tasmiyyas. The quote by Mukherjee in note 77 reflects the general sentiment on the issue.

82. Usmani, *Legal Rulings*, 70–82. Disagreements over the status of mechanically slaughtered and stunned poultry have recently generated disputes among Muslims regarding the permissibility of the products sold by the giant fast-food chain KFC, which announced in 2010 that a number of its stores in Britain would serve halal chicken. Although the Halal Food Authority (HFA), a leading regulatory organization in Britain, approved of the halal status of KFC's chicken, other organizations, including the Halal Monitoring Committee (HMC), another major regulator, challenged this position by claiming that poultry slaughter should be done by hand and without prior stunning. See Shirazi, *Brand Islam*, 44, 81. Objections to the halal status of mechanically slaughtered and stunned poultry is common in many Muslim-majority countries, which is why their poultry imports have been relatively low. For inconsistent attitudes toward stunned and mechanically slaughtered poultry in modern halal standards, see chapter 6. For more on HFA and HMC, see chapter 5.

83. Beyond the ritualistic nuances involving the very act of slaughter, lateral (rather than vertical) bleeding of the neck of the animal, and specific stunning procedures, skinning, portioning, and preserving processes in halal- and nonhalal- compliant industrial facilities for nonpoultry are generally similar.

84. See Ahmad ibn Shu'ayb al-Nasa'i, *English Translation of Sunan an-Nasa'i*, ed. Hafiz Abu Tahir Zubair 'Ali Za'i, Huda Khattab, and Abu Khaliyl; trans. Nasiruddin al-Khattab (Riyadh: Darussalam, 2007), 5:247; al-Nasa'i, *Kitab al-Sunan al-Kubra*, 4:363.

85. Jon Stone, "Halal Slaughter: Large Increase Reported in Number of Animals Not Being Stunned at Abattoirs," *Independent*, January 30, 2015, http://www.independent.co.uk/news/uk/home-news/increase-in-animals-not-being-stunned-before-they-are-halal-slaughtered-10012559.html. A majority of animals in the United Kingdom are still stunned before halal slaughter (ibid.).

86. Lorna Edwards, "Non-Stun Killing Hurts Industry: Halal Exporter," *The Age*, August 13, 2007. Jordan may be an exception, according to Kristen Stilt. Outside the Middle East, and under Australian pressure, Indonesia has also become more willing to stun animals before slaughter in its slaughterhouses following a 2011 exposé that led Australia to temporarily suspend the shipment of cattle to that country. Private communication with Kristen Stilt (May 19, 2017).

87. For a discussion of intensifying competition among European countries over the market for non-stun halal meat see Speak, "Halal Butchery Industry in Poland," and

Vladislav Vorotnikov, "Lithuania Eyes Increase in Meat Exports to Muslim Countries," *Global Meat News*, February 3, 2015, http://www.globalmeatnews.com/Industry-Markets/ Lithuania-eyes-increase-in-meat-exports-to-Muslim-countries.

CHAPTER 4

1. Martin Lings, *Muhammad: His Life Based on the Earliest Sources* (New York: Inner Traditions International, 1983), 101. For an alternative narrative in which the Prophet was offered three vessels that contained milk, honey, and wine, see Kueny, *The Rhetoric of Sobriety*, 55-58. In that narrative as well, the Prophet chooses milk.

2. Safi, *Memories of Muhammad*, 173.

3. Similar debates about wine have arisen in the context of Christianity. The Christian Bible makes frequent references to the vine and wine as central to the sacrament of the Eucharist. The latter may have indicated Jesus's tolerance of moderate drinking, or at least of a sacred and holy form of wine. Indeed, according to Rod Phillips, with his miraculous conversion of water into wine at Cana (John 2:1–11), Christian scripture portrayed Christ as a "new wine god" along the lines of ancient Greco-Roman deities. At the same time, as Phillips notes, nineteenth-century European and American biblical commentators prescribed temperance and restraint. They suggested a "two-wine" theory: "The positive, approving references to 'wine' in the Bible referred not to wine—the beverage resulting from fermentation—but to unfermented grape juice, whereas the negative references referred to actual wine. For them, the miracle at the marriage at Cana was that Jesus turned water not into wine but into grape juice .... In contrast, they argued that negative examples of wine involved the real thing, as when Noah drank so much wine that he stripped naked, and when Lot's daughters so befuddled their father with wine that he was not aware he was having sex with them. In these and other cases, supporters of the two-wine theory argued, alcohol was clearly at work, erasing the line between moral and immoral behavior." For more, see Rod Phillips, *Alcohol: A History* (Chapel Hill: The University of North Carolina Press, 2014), 47 and 50.

4. Note here that Abu Hanifa and his early Hanafi followers make a distinction between khamr or grape (perhaps also date) wine, which the Quran specifically warns believers against, and other alcoholic beverages. While there is no question about the impure nature of the first, the latter's legal status is less clear. We return to this topic below. Additional impure things include dogs, excrement, and the milk of animals whose flesh is not eaten; see A. J. Wensinck, "Nadjis," *Encyclopaedia of Islam*, 2nd ed., Brill Online, http://referenceworks.brillonline.com/ (accessed May 14, 2016).

5. Arguably, the Quran's indictment of intoxication is more consistent than its treatment of wine. For example 22:2 warns humans that on the Day of Judgment "you see it every nursing mother will be distracted from that [child] she was nursing, and every pregnant woman will abort her pregnancy, and you will see the people [appearing] intoxicated while they are not intoxicated; but the punishment of Allah is severe." And the immoral people whom the Prophet Lot left behind and whom God would eventually punish "wandered blindly in their intoxication" (15:72). See Kueny, *The Rhetoric of Sobriety*, 14–19.

6. For example, one hadith from Abu Dawud's collection notes the following: "Narrated Daylam al-Himyari: I asked the Prophet: 'Messenger of Allah, I live in a cold region where we perform heavy labor. We consume a drink from wheat which gives us strength in our work and helps us withstand the cold in our lands.' He asked, 'Is it intoxicating?' I answered, 'Yes.' He said, 'Avoid it.' I replied, 'The people will not abandon it.' He said, 'If they do not give it up, then fight

them." Abu Dawud Sulayman ibn al-Ash'ath al-Sijistani, *Sunan Abi Dawud*, ed. Shu'ayb al-Arna'ut and Muhammad Kamil Qarah Balili (Beirut: Dar al-Risala al-'Alamiyya, 2009), 5:525. From here on, this author will be cited using the more common nomenclature "Abu Dawud."

7. Wine production might have been insignificant and probably limited to Yemen in the Arabian Peninsula. Most wine consumed in the area was likely imported from Syria and Iraq, and wine trade could be connected with Jewish and Christian peoples; see A. J. Wensinck and J. Sadan, "Khamr," *Encyclopaedia of Islam*, 2nd ed., Brill Online, http://referenceworks.brillonline.com/ (accessed May 14, 2016).

8. "Nabidh" was a general designation for a variety of drinks made by infusing dried fruits, barley, honey, or spelt in water, some of which could be slightly intoxicating; see P. Heine, "Nabidh," *Encyclopaedia of Islam*, 2nd ed., Brill Online, http://referenceworks.brillonline.com/ (accessed May 14, 2016; see also chapter 7). Not all Muslim sources agree that the nabidh that the Prophet consumed contained alcohol. See Nurdeen Deuraseh, "Is Drinking al-Khamr (Intoxicating Drink) for Medical Purposes Permissible by Islamic Law," *Arab Law Quarterly* 18 (2003): 355–364; and "Al-Ashriba," *Al-Mawsu'a al-Fiqhiyya*, 5:20.

9. Deuraseh, "al-Khamr," 356; "Al-Ashriba," *Al-Mawsu'a al-Fiqhiyya*, 5:12–14; "Al-Sukr," *Al-Mawsu'a al-Fiqhiyya*, 25:90–104. In quantities that can intoxicate, these jurists considered non-khamr alcoholic drinks also as haram. By implication, their objection was not to alcohol as a chemical substance, which they regarded as non-najis, but to beverages they identified as khamr and to intoxication. Although Abu Hanifa and many of his early followers may have hesitated to expand the boundaries of khamr, most legal authorities prefer to take the following hadith reports as prescriptive in their interpretations: "Every intoxicant is khamr and every intoxicant is haram" (al-Nasa'i, *English Translation of Sunan an-Nasa'i*, 6:359; *Kitab al-Sunan al-Kubra*, 6:282–283), and "whatever intoxicates in a large amount, a small amount is haram"; see Ibn Majah, *English Translation of Sunan Ibn Majah*, 4:387 and Ibn Majah, *Sunan Ibn Majah*, 5:90. Some Hanafis contend that these hadiths were weak, inauthentic, or abrogated by Muhammad's later actions and deeds; see Hattox, *Coffee and Coffeehouses*, 53. According to Najam Haider, the Hanafi position shifted toward a more general prohibition after the twelfth century; see Haider, "Contesting Intoxication: Early Juristic Debates over the Lawfulness of Alcoholic Beverages," *Islamic Law and Society* 20, nos. 1–2 (2013): 48–89. However, Ibn Battuta, the prominent fourteenth-century traveler and jurist, recognized the Hanafi inclination to regard as permissible the consumption of small amounts of alcoholic drinks other than grape wine; see Priscilla Mary Işın, "Boza, Innocuous and Less So," in *Cured, Fermented and Smoked Foods: Proceedings of Oxford Symposium on Food and Cookery 2010*, ed. Helen Saberi (London: Prospect Books, 2011), 155.

10. The status of khamr owned by non-Muslims has been debated by jurists. See "Al-Ashriba," *Al-Mawsu'a al-Fiqhiyya*, 5:24–25. One tradition suggests that Muslims should not be seated at a table where alcohol is being consumed (ibid., 5:26–27).

11. "Al-Ashriba," *Al-Mawsu'a al-Fiqhiyya*, 5:23–24.

12. According to one hadith tradition, "The Prophet said, if they drink wine [al-khamr], then flog them. If they drink it again, flog them. And if they drink again, kill them." See Abu Dawud, *Sunan Abi Dawud*, 6:530–532.

13. One hadith recounts the following: "This is what was reported from Muhammad ibn Ishaq, from Muhammad ibn al-Munkadir, from Jabir ibn 'Abdullah, from the Prophet who said: 'Lash whosoever drinks wine, and if he drinks again for a fourth time, then kill him.' He said: 'Then a man was brought to the Prophet who had been drinking a fourth time, and so he beat him but did not kill him.' The same was reported by al-Zuhri from Qabisa ibn Dhu'ayb

from the Prophet. He said 'the order to kill was lifted, and it was a favor [from the divine].'" Al-Tirmidhi, *Al-Jami' al-Kabir*, 3:114–115. According to Kueny, the types of corporal punishment prescribed in hadith traditions for repeat offenders include hitting, flogging, whipping, striking them in the neck, and execution; *The Rhetoric of Sobriety*, 42–48. Other ahadith also suggest that God doesn't accept the prayers of drunks for forty days and on the Day of Judgment habitual drunkards will be made to drink sweat or pus from the inhabitants of hell or "liquid from the pudendum of fornicators" (ibid.).

14. David Waines, "Abu Zayd al-Balkhi on the Nature of Forbidden Drink: A Medieval Islamic Controversy," in *La alimentación en las culturas islàmicas: Una colección de estudios*, ed. Manuela Marin and David Waines (Madrid: Espanola de Cooperacion Internacional, 1994), 118–119. The claim regarding the absence of ahadith on punishment is not entirely accurate, although it is possible to question the reliability of many ahadith on this issue.

15. Rudi Matthee, "Alcohol in the Islamic Middle East: Ambivalence and Ambiguity," *Past and Present* 222, supp. 9 (2014): 105.

16. Phillips, *Alcohol: A History*, 62.

17. Lewicka, *Food and Foodways*, 514.

18. Lewicka, *Food and Foodways*, 524. David Waines's treatment of attitudes toward wine in other medieval Muslim settings reveals a parallel process. While attitudes toward alcohol and wine were relatively accommodating until at least the tenth century, in particular in medical discussions among Muslim physicians, three centuries later even medical experts demonstrate a more restrictive demeanor regarding its use; see Waines, "Abu Zayd al-Balkhi."

19. Haider, "Contesting Intoxication."

20. According to one contemporary European source, Istanbul contained more than fifteen hundred taverns in the seventeenth century, serving both Muslim and non-Muslim customers; see Ercan Eren, *Geçmişten Günümüze Anadolu'da Bira* (Istanbul: Tarih Vakfı Yayınları, 2005), 55.

21. Shahab Ahmed, *What Is Islam? The Importance of Being Islamic* (Princeton, NJ: Princeton University Press, 2016), 67.

22. Eric R. Dursteler, "Bad Bread and the 'Outrageous Drunkenness of the Turks': Food and Identity in the Accounts of Early Modern European Travelers to the Ottoman Empire," *Journal of World History* 25, nos. 2–3 (2014): 212. Others noted their abstinence (ibid., 220).

23. Lady Mary Wortley Montagu, *The Letters and Works of Lady Mary Wortley Montagu*, ed. Lord Wharncliffe (Paris: A. and W. Galignani, 1837), 234–235.

24. Eren suggests that alcohol bans became frequent in the Ottoman Empire during and after the seventeenth-century; see Eren, *Anadolu'da Bira*, 51.

25. Dursteler, "Bad Bread," 212.

26. Ahmed, *What Is Islam?*, 66–67.

27. Rice, barley, maize, oats, wheat, and even pea-flour could also be used for boza-making. Analyses of a variety of boza samples indicate that the beverage's alcohol level could be as high as 7.1 percent, though lower in most types; see Işın, "Boza," 155–158. See also chapter 7.

28. Eren, *Anadolu'da Bira*, 54.

29. Oleksander Halenko, "Wine Production, Marketing and Consumption in the Ottoman Crimea, 1520–1542," *Journal of the Economic and Social History of the Orient* 47 (2004): 507–547. The production and trade of alcoholic drinks in the Empire was concentrated among non-Muslim communities—primarily among Greeks, Jews, and Armenians—who carried the brunt of the associated taxes.

30. Eren, *Anadolu'da Bira*, 51.

31. Işın, "Boza," 157.

32. See chapter 5 for a more detailed discussion of the historical evolution of Islamic states' attempts to govern religion.

33. Emine Ö. Evered and Kyle T. Evered, "From Rakı to Ayran: Regulating the Place and Practice of Drinking in Turkey," *Space and Polity* 26, no. 1 (2016): 39–58. See also Emine Ö. Evered and Kyle T. Evered, "A Geopolitics of Drinking: Debating the Place of Alcohol in Early Republican Turkey," *Political Geography* 50 (2016): 48–60.

34. For more on the history of temperance movements in modern Egypt, especially as related to Protestant missionaries and Islamist pietism, see Omar Foda, "Anna and Ahmad: Building Modern Temperance in Egypt (1884–1940)," *Social Sciences and Missions* 28 (2015): 116–149.

35. Matthee, "Alcohol in the Islamic Middle East," 120.

36. Laurence Michalak and Karen Trocki, "Alcohol and Islam: An Overview," *Contemporary Drug Problems* 33, no. 4 (2006): 534.

37. Rudi Matthee, *The Pursuit of Pleasure: Drugs and Stimulants in Iranian History, 1500–1900* (Princeton, NJ: Princeton University Press, 2005), 97.

38. Thus cannabis was popularly known among Arab scholars as "Indian hemp"; see Taha Baasher, "The Use of Drugs in the Islamic World," *British Journal of Addiction* 76 (1981): 238.

39. According to Matthee, references to the recreational use of opium appear only in the late tenth or early eleventh century, and the Muslims in Iran and elsewhere in the Middle East "became better acquainted with opium under the Mongols," after the thirteenth century; Matthee, *Pursuit of Pleasure*, 98. Franz Rosenthal has suggested that cannabis use might have been known "here and there for pleasure and enjoyment but we have no evidence to this effect from the first four or five centuries of Islam. Any speculation that the use of the drug for this purpose might have occurred only in the eastern portions of the Muslim world close to India could also not be verified"; see Rosenthal, *The Herb: Hashish versus Medieval Muslim Society* (Leiden: Brill, 1971), 41. Ibn Battuta, a fourteenth-century Moroccan traveler, reported hashish use in southern Anatolia; see Marinos Sariyannis, "Law and Morality in Ottoman Society: The Case of Narcotic Substances," in *The Ottoman Empire, The Balkans, The Greek Lands: Towards a Social and Economic History*, ed. Elias Kolovos et al. (Istanbul: Isis Press, 2007), 310.

40. A discussion on the issue of *banj* (hemp) in a thirteenth- to fourteenth-century market inspection (*ihtisab*) manual by Umar b. Muhammad al-Sunami demonstrates the interpretive difficulties Muslim legal authorities experienced in the medieval era. According to this source, when one eminent medieval jurist, Hamid al-Din al-Darir, was asked about the legal status of banj, he could not come up with an immediate answer. Afterward, he asked his colleagues to research the topic in jurisprudential treatises, where they subsequently located an anecdote attributed to Abu Hanifa that proclaimed it prohibited. The scholars who considered the legality of the substance also reached a consensus that banj should be prohibited on the basis of public interest. On the other hand, a popular medieval jurisprudential treatise, *Al-Hidaya fi Sharh Bidayat al-Mubtadi* by Burhan al-Din al-Marghinani (d. 1197) considered banj permissible (mubah). There are other legal works, too, that regard the medical use of banj as acceptable if its consumption does not lead to loss of reason; see Mawil Izzi Diene, *The Theory and the Practice of Market Law in Medieval Islam: A Study of Kitab Nisab al-Ihtisab of Umar b. Muhammad al-Sunami* (Warminster: E. J. W. Gibb Memorial Trust, 1997), 98–100. On addiction in general, see "Takhdir," *Al-Mawsu'a al-Fiqhiyya*, 11:33–38.

41. Rosenthal, *The Herb*, 107.

42. Rosenthal defines the meaning of "intoxication" according to the Quran as follows: "All the statements of jurists with respect to intoxication share the description of it as something leading to *n-sh-w*. This commonly used root is hardly anything but a synonym of the other term

for intoxication, *s-k-r*"; see Rosenthal, *The Herb*, 107–108. *Dictionary of Qur'anic Usage* gives the meaning of *s-k-r* as "intoxicating drinks, intoxication, drowsiness, un-consciousness; blocking a gap, corking a bottle"; see "س-ك-ر/ك/ر," Brill Online, http://referenceworks.brillonline.com/ (accessed May 14, 2016). "But," Rosenthal continues, "*n-sh-w* was also distinguished as indicating 'the beginning and preliminaries' of intoxication (*sukr*). In this way it was probably understood to denote in particular the exhilaration that was the initial emotional effect of fine" (Rosenthal, *The Herb*, 108). Later, Rosenthal adds "joy," "bravery," and "confidence" to the definition of the Quranic use of the term "intoxication" (ibid., 109). Ralph Hattox observes differences between how various legal schools defined intoxication: "To the Malikis and Shafi'is, . . . a person giddy and boisterous could be considered drunk, and any potion capable of putting one in such a state would be forbidden. According to the Hanafis, one would have to be almost dead-drunk and senseless before he would be considered *sakran* (drunk), and hence liable to punishment" (Hattox, *Coffee and Coffeehouses*, 57). According to Haider, Hattox's suggestion regarding the Hanafi position requires qualification: "Abu Hanifa and [Muhammad] al-Shaybani claimed that intoxication occurs when an individual cannot differentiate the ground from the sky and a man from a woman, while [another Hanafi jurist] Abu Yusuf lowered the bar to a simple slurring of speech." In fact, the latter definition was upheld by a majority of Hanafis according to one source, al-Tahawi, that Haider relies on in his discussion; see Haider, "Contesting Intoxication," 75.

43. Trisha Marie Myers, "*Kitabu Mesalihi'l Muslimin* and Counsel for Sultans: Text and Context in the Nasihatname Genre of the Ottoman Empire, 16th–17th c." (MA thesis, Ohio State University, 2011), 20, 57. Interestingly, Mustafa Ali's objections to opium use were not based on the claim that the practice challenged Quranic prescriptions (ibid., 57). According to Marinos Sariyannis, Ebussuud Efendi, the renowned Ottoman chief-mufti in the sixteenth century, issued contradictory fatwas concerning the legality of opium- and hashish-use, which is indicative of the jurisprudential uncertainty surrounding this issue at the time. See Sariyannis, "Law and Morality in Ottoman Society," 317–319.

44. Niebuhr, *Travels*, 2:224–225. On the popularity of opium in eighteenth-century Anatolia see Eren, *Anadolu'da Bira*, 57.

45. Lane, *An Account*, 96. The popularity of opium and cannabis in premodern Muslim settings is not dissimilar to what we observe in many Western societies, where medical and recreational drug use was popular and legally unrestricted before the twentieth century.

46. Quoted in Maziyar Ghiabi, "Drugs and Revolution in Iran: Islamic Devotion, Revolutionary Zeal and Republican Means," *Iranian Studies* 48, no. 2 (2015): 142.

47. Ghiabi, "Drugs and Revolution in Iran," 142. Agahi and Spencer estimate the opium addiction rate in Iran during the 1950s as 7 percent of the adult population; see Cyrus Agahi and Christopher P. Spencer, "Drug Abuse in Pre- and Post-Revolutionary Iran," *Journal of Psychoactive Drugs* 13, no. 1 (1981): 39–46.

48. See "Grand Mufti: Drugs More Dangerous than A-bombs," *Arab News*, September 13, 2014, http://www.arabnews.com/saudi-arabia/news/629456.

49. Patrick Gallahue and Rick Lines, *The Death Penalty for Drug Offences: Global Overview 2015: The Extreme Fringe of Global Drug Policy* (London: Harm Reduction International, 2015), 5, https://www.hri.global/files/2015/10/07/DeathPenaltyDrugs_Report_2015.pdf (accessed December 12, 2016).

50. Gallahue and Lines, *The Death Penalty for Drug Offences*, 5.

51. These include Bahrain, Bangladesh, Egypt, Iraq, Kuwait, Libya, Oman, Pakistan, the Palestinian Authority, Qatar, UAE, Syria, Sudan, and Yemen, in addition to the aforementioned

four. While in many of these countries the actual executions are rare, long prison sentences are not; Gallahue and Lines, *The Death Penalty for Drug Offences*, 5–8.

52. Gallahue and Lines, *The Death Penalty for Drug Offences*, 14. In Iran, there were an estimated 570 executions in the first six months of 2015, of which 394 were imposed on drug offenders. In comparison, China executed 430 drug offenders in 2012 and 2013, which constitutes less than 10 percent of all executions (5,400) in those years. Recently, however, Iranian authorities have begun considering the legalization of cannabis as an alternative measure to tackle the country's immense drug-addiction problem. Various estimates indicate that there are 2 to 6 million addicts in the country. Iran has also relatively progressive policies toward addiction including the distribution of clean needles to drug users, methadone substitution programs, and an established system of addiction treatment. See Mayizar Ghiabi, "Drug Laws: Iran Takes Steps towards Legalising Cannabis," *Independent*, October 26, 2015, http://www.independent.co.uk/news/world/middle-east/drugs-laws-iran-takes-steps-towards-legalising-cannabis-marijuana-a6709176.html (accessed July 7, 2016).

53. Gallahue and Lines, *The Death Penalty for Drug Offences*, 15.

54. Gallahue and Lines, *The Death Penalty for Drug Offences*, 15.

55. Joe Donatelli, "The World's Scariest Places to Be Busted for Drugs," *The Fix: Addiction and Recovery, Straight Up*, https://www.thefix.com/content/worst-places-be-caught-drugs?page=all (accessed July 7, 2016).

56. United Nations Office on Drugs and Crime, "World Drug Report 2014," http://www.unodc.org/wdr2014/en/interactive-map.html (accessed May 11, 2016).

57. Afghanistan, Pakistan, Iran, and Azerbaijan are also among the worst countries for numbers of opioid abusers according to the same report, with user rates ranging between 1.0 to 2.92 percent. Unfortunately, gender-specific statistics are not available.

58. Amphetamine-based stimulants (in particular Captagon and its knockoffs) have been popular in some Muslim-majority nations, including Saudi Arabia. See Cecily Hilleary, "Captagon: 'Breaking Bad' in Saudi Arabia," *VOA News*, November 6, 2015, http://www.voanews.com/a/captagon-breaking-bad-in-saudi-arabia/3044225.html (accessed May 8, 2017). We thank one of our referees for bringing this point to our attention.

59. James Grehan, "Smoking and 'Early Modern' Sociability: The Great Tobacco Debate in the Ottoman Middle East (Seventeenth to Eighteenth Centuries)," *American Historical Review* 111, no. 5 (2006): 1352–1377; Hattox, *Coffee and Coffeehouses*, ch. 2. Katip Çelebi, a seventeenth-century Ottoman intellectual, claimed that coffee and tobacco appeared in Ottoman lands in 1543 and 1601, respectively; see Katip Chelebi, *The Balance of Truth*, trans., intro., notes G. L. Lewis (London: George Allen and Unwin, 1957), 51, 60.

60. Grehan, "Smoking and 'Early Modern'"; Hattox, *Coffee and Coffeehouses*.

61. Relli Shechter, *Smoking, Culture and Economy in the Middle East: The Egyptian Tobacco Market 1850–2000* (London: I. B. Tauris, 2006), 17. See also Katip Chelebi, *The Balance of Truth*, 50–59.

62. Shechter, *Smoking*, 16–17; "Tabgh," *Al-Mawsu'a al-Fiqhiyya*, 10:108–109. See also Yahya Michot, *Against Smoking: An Ottoman Manifesto by Ahmad al-Aqhisari* (Oxford: Interface, 2010).

63. Coffee, cold and dry according to some physicians (and hot and dry, according to others) in the Galenic system of bodily humors, was said to cause melancholia and lethargy. It was also associated with insomnia and suppressed appetite for food and sex; other claims were that it caused hemorrhoids and headaches, and disturbed ingestion when consumed without food. "Yet despite these problems," Hattox writes, "Muslim physicians were far from unanimous in their condemnation of the drink"; see *Coffee and Coffeehouses*, 65–68. Rudi Matthee suggests that

"some Muslim physicians and pharmacologists considered tobacco to be dry and cold, though most followed European practice by placing tobacco in the category of dry and hot substances"; Rudi Matthee, "Tutun," *Encyclopaedia of Islam*, 2nd ed., Brill Online (accessed May 15, 2016). It was said to have weakened the brain and teeth and caused leprosy, coughing, and shortness of breath; Matthee, *Pursuit of Pleasure*, 137. Again, the claims about the adverse health effects of tobacco were not universally held; cf. Katip Chelebi, *The Balance of Truth*, 50–62.

64. One concern among Ottoman rulers was the coffeehouses, where much coffee and tobacco consumption took place and which they considered to be centers of political sedition and opposition. Concerns about fire were also used to limit coffee drinking and tobacco smoking; see Matthee, "Tutun"; Shechter, *Smoking*, 16–17; and "Tabgh," *Al-Mawsu'a al-Fiqhiyya*, 10:104.

65. The Quran says "Do not falsely declare: 'This is lawful and this is unlawful,' to invent falsehood about Allah. Indeed, those who invent falsehood about Allah will not succeed. Brief is their enjoyment of this life, and grievous the punishment that awaits them" (16:116–117).

66. For the wide range in these opinions during the premodern period, see "Tabgh," *Al-Mawsu'a al-Fiqhiyya*, 10:101–113.

67. Shechter, *Smoking*, 164.

68. Nazim Ghouri, Mohammed Atcha, and Aziz Sheikh, "Influence of Islam on Smoking among Muslims," *British Medical Journal* 332, no. 7536 (2006): 291–294. The prevalence of smoking among female populations is significantly lower (between 1 [UAE, Azerbaijan, Uzbekistan, Turkmenistan] and 65 percent [Algeria]) among females in Muslim communities (ibid.).

69. Ghouri et al., "Influence of Islam on Smoking among Muslims," 291.

70. Heba Nassar, "The Economics of Tobacco in Egypt: A New Analysis of Demand," World Bank HNP Discussion Paper (2003), 14, http://www-wds.worldbank.org/external/default/WDSContentServer/WDSP/IB/2004/05/19/000265513_20040519171838/Rendered/PDF/288920Nassar010The0Economics010whole.pdf (accessed May 15, 2016). Between 1990 and 1997, tobacco consumption decreased in South America and the Caribbean by 17 percent, in North America by 8 percent, in Western Europe by 6 percent, and in Eastern Europe by 5 percent. The only other region where consumption increased in the same period is Africa, by 4 percent (ibid.).

71. See, for example, M. H. Khayat, ed., *The Right Path to Health: Islamic Ruling on Smoking* (Alexandria, Egypt: World Health Organization, Office for the Eastern Mediterranean, 1988), http://applications.emro.who.int/dsaf/dsa46.pdf (accessed May 15, 2016).

72. M. Petticrew et al., "'Fighting a Hurricane': Tobacco Industry Efforts to Counter the Perceived Threat of Islam," *American Journal of Public Health* 105, no. 6 (2015): 1086–1093. These attempts included establishing contacts with Islamic studies faculty at McGill University in Canada in 1987 and also at prominent al-Azhar University in Egypt in 1995. The industry also attempted to frame the growing antitobacco sentiment among religious authorities as a consequence of the rise of Islamic fundamentalism and presented smoking as an act of personal freedom analogous to women's rights in the modern world (ibid.).

73. Abdullah Borek, "Smoking and Religion: The Position of Islam towards Smoking," transcript of presentation at the INFOTAB Workshop in Malaga, October 19, 1988, http://industry-documents.library.ucsf.edu/tobacco/docs/njyp0193 (accessed May 15, 2016).

74. British American Tobacco (BAT) Türkiye, which represents the industry position on a variety of issues related to tobacco in Turkey, insists that although recent epidemiological studies on tobacco consumption have indicated significant health risks in a large population, these studies are poor indicators of how specific individuals might be impacted by tobacco consumption. See "Sigaranın Sağlıkla İlgili Riskleri," http://www.bat.com.tr/group/sites/

BAT_7X7FK5.nsf/vwPagesWebLive/DO7X7K6R?opendocument, and "Sigara İçmenin Riskleri Azaltılabilir Mi?," http://www.bat.com.tr/group/sites/BAT_7X7FK5.nsf/vwPagesWebLive/ DO7X7K9C?opendocument (accessed May 15, 2016). BAT documentation has also suggested that the relative health risk estimates for tobacco consumption "vary considerably between different countries . . . . These differences in relative risks reported in different countries are not fully understood but, if accurate, indicate that factors in addition to smoking appear to be relevant"; see British American Tobacco, *Positions on Smoking and Health: Smoking and Lung Cancer*, 3, https://www.industrydocumentslibrary.ucsf.edu/tobacco/docs/gzgd0209 (accessed May 15, 2016).

75. One modern jurist who has refused to consider tobacco as haram is the prominent Egyptian scholar Sheikh Ali al-Tantawi, who declared in 1988 that he was "unable to equate the smoking of a cigarette with the drinking of a glass of alcohol. Alcohol is clearly forbidden and only God can forbid things. It may well be that it is better not to smoke and give it up, but it is not a sin in the sense as is drinking alcohol"; see Borek, "Smoking and Religion," 7.

76. Chewing qat leaves is popular in Southern Arabia, in particular Yemen, and among Muslim populations in Eastern Africa, especially in Somalia, Kenya, and Uganda. The qat plant, indigenous to Eastern Africa, was brought to southern Arabia in the fourteenth or early fifteenth centuries, possibly by Sufi mystics, who were said to have used it as a stimulant in order to stay awake during long periods of ritual practice. The first legal opinions on qat use come from this region during the sixteenth century; see Daniel M. Varisco, "The Elixir of Life or the Devil's Cud? The Debate over Qat (*Catha edulis*) in Yemeni Culture," in *Drug Use and Cultural Contexts "Beyond the West": Tradition, Change and Post-Colonialism*, ed. Ross Coomber and Nigel South (London: Free Association Books, 2004), 101–118; Daniel M. Varisco, "On the Meaning of Chewing: The Significance of Qat (*Catha edulis*) in the Yemen Arab Republic," *International Journal of Middle East Studies* 18, no. 1 (1986): 1–13. According to modern estimates, up to 90 percent of men and 60 percent of women in Yemen chew qat. Its popularity among East African Muslim communities is believed to be comparable; Susan Beckerleg, "What Harm? Kenyan and Ugandan Perspectives on Khat," *African Affairs* 104 (2006): 219–241. Generally speaking, jurists have disagreed on the permissibility of qat chewing. See in general "Takhdir," *Al-Mawsu'a al-Fiqhiyya*, 11:33–38.

77. Nutmeg is native to the Moluccas islands in modern-day Indonesia, although it is now grown in various tropical regions. The ground-walnut-colored spice has been used for medicinal and cosmetic purposes since ancient times but would become highly prized during the European spice trade, which peaked in the sixteenth and seventeenth centuries. As a medicinal plant, nutmeg was valued for its properties as a stimulant and was known to relieve indigestion, diarrhea, and minor pain. Some ubiquitous modern food products such as Coca-Cola and sweets or soups flavored with "pumpkin spice mix" also include nutmeg or its oils. See David W. Freeman, "'This American Life' Reveals Coca-Cola's Secret Recipe," *CBS News*, February 15, 2011, http://www.cbsnews.com/news/this-american-life-reveals-coca-colas-secret-recipe-full-ingredient-list/. Small amounts of nutmeg are harmless, but larger quantities have psychoactive and hallucinogenic properties. Thus most Muslim jurists have classified its use as haram, though some Hanafis allowed its use in small amounts in food or in medicines; see Heather Douglas and Abdi Hersi, "Khat and Islamic Legal Perspectives: Issues for Consideration," *Journal of Legal Pluralism and Unofficial Law* 62 (2010): 106; Muhammad Sa'id Muhammad al-Ramlawi, *Al-Halal wa'l-Haram wa'l-Mughlib Minhuma fi'l-Fiqh al-Islami: Dirasa Tatbiqiyya Mu'asira* (Cairo: Dar al-Jami'a al-Jadida, 2008), 413–416; and "Takhdir," *Al-Mawsu'a al-Fiqhiyya*, 11:33–38.

78. Muslim jurists have also recently condemned the use of qat and nutmeg for the same reasons that they object to the use of other psychoactive substances.

79. Kamali, "The Ḥalāl Industry." Riaz and Chaudry also claim that "doubtful things should be avoided. There is a gray area between clearly lawful and clearly unlawful. This is the area of 'what is doubtful.' Islam considers it an act of piety for Muslims to avoid doubtful things"; see *Halal Food Production*, 6–7.

80. According to one hadith tradition, "the Prophet said: 'What is halal is clear and so is what is haram. Between them are suspicious matters. He who avoids what he may suspect as sinful avoids sin. He who engages in what he suspects as sinful is likely to act sinful. Sins are [among] Allah's pastures and he who grazes [his sheep] around that pasture will likely encounter them.'" See al-Bukhari, *Sahih al-Bukhari*, 2:723–724.

81. For an elaborate discussion of this point, see Ahmed, *What Is Islam?*, ch. 1.

82. Ahmed, *What Is Islam?*, ch. 1. Cf. Benkheira, *Islâm et interdits alimentaires*, 37. For an alternative "culinary script," see chapter 9.

83. A few prominent medieval physicians, including al-Razi (Rhazes; d. 925) and Ibn Sina (Avicenna; d. 1037) suggested that beverages that contain alcohol could be used for medical purposes in small amounts. According to al-Razi, alcoholic drinks could heat the body, help digestion, quench thirst, and enhance fertility; Deuraseh, "al-Khamr," 364. The Hanafis, among all Sunni and Shiite legal schools, have been relatively sympathetic to this position. Unlike other legal schools, Hanafis allowed the use of alcoholic beverages other than wine for medicinal purposes and in circumstances "of immediate danger of death to keep one from perishing from dehydration and choking"; Hattox, *Coffee and Coffeehouses*, 50. This is consistent with the opinion that alcohol as a chemical substance is not najis in itself, though khamr might be and God certainly forbids intoxication.

84. Quoted in Ahmed, *What Is Islam?*, 58–59.

85. In early fourteenth century, al-Nuwayri wrote that opium "alleviates migraines and calms painful coughing. It stops diarrhea, soothes itching, and is effective against intestinal ulcers"; al-Nuwayri, *The Ultimate Ambition*, 187. Some medieval experts considered hashish good for treating flatulence and dandruff, and also effective in suppressing appetite. The welcome anesthetic effects of cannabis and opium have been also recognized by medical experts, especially in situations that required medical operation or amputation. Finally, narcotics have been sanctioned for use by individuals trying to taper down their addition to alcohol, as mentioned above; Rosenthal, *The Herb*, passim. See also "Takhdir," *Al-Mawsu'a al-Fiqhiyya*, 11:33–38.

86. Most jurists, premodern and modern, have objected to the use of alcohol as medicine because "God has never made remedies in things that He has prohibited"; Deuraseh, "al-Khamr," 361.

87. Walter G. Andrews and Mehmet Kalpaklı, *The Age of Beloveds: Love and the Beloved in Early-Modern Ottoman European Culture and Society* (Durham, NC: Duke University Press, 2006), ch. 3. See also Lisa Balabanlılar, "The Emperor Jahangir and the Pursuit of Pleasure," *Journal of the Royal Asiatic Society* 19, no. 2 (2009): 173–186.

88. Matthee, "Alcohol in the Islamic Middle East," 107–109.

89. Ahmed, *What Is Islam?*, 68.

90. Ahmed, *What Is Islam?*, 71–72. As is well-known, minting coins in a ruler's name was a universally recognized proclamation of legitimate rulership in premodern Islamic lands.

91. Jalal al-Din al-Rumi and William C. Chittick, *The Sufi Path of Love: The Spiritual Teachings of Rumi* (Binghamton: State University of New York Press, 1983), 318.

92. Sariyannis, "Law and Morality in Ottoman Society," 312.

93. Rodinson, "Tutun."

CHAPTER 5

1. Unless otherwise noted, all currency figures cited are in US dollars.

2. *State of the Global Islamic Economy 2016/2017 Report*, developed and produced by Thomson Reuters, 25–28, http://www.iedcdubai.ae/assets/uploads/files/SGIE%20Report_f1_DIGITAL_1477897639.pdf (accessed January 14, 2017). This figure may not include the size of the market in Muslim-minority nations. Also see "Iran to Launch International Halal Food Brand Soon," *PRESSTV*, September 15, 2015, http://www.presstv.ir/Detail/2015/09/14/429147/iranhalalindustryfoodtourismjalalpour. See also "The Fight for Islamic Economy Leadership Explained by Dr. Cedomir Nestorovic," *HQ Asia*, May 2, 2016, http://hqasia.org/insights/fight-islamic-economy-leadership-explained-dr-cedomir-nestorovic.

3. *State of the Global Islamic Economy Report 2016/2017*, 25–26.

4. *State of the Global Islamic Economy Report 2016/2017*, 25–26. Here we should mention that there is a significant incongruity between this report and its earlier version, *State of the Global Islamic Economy 2014–2015 Report*, in their respective estimates of the market's recent growth performance. While the most recent report estimates that between 2014 and 2015, Muslims' food and beverage expenditures grew by around 3.4 percent at the global scale, only slightly higher than the global market growth in food and beverage sector, which is 3.3 percent (30), the earlier report indicates that between 2012 and 2013, Muslim food and beverage expenditures grew by 10.8 percent (48). No other source indicates that the growth in the global demand for halal food and beverages has slowed down to this extent between 2012 and 2015, which is also inconsistent with the 2016/2017 report's own estimate of 8.5 percent compound annual growth rate between 2015 and 2021 (7, 30). See *State of the Global Islamic Economy 2014–2015 Report*, http://www.flandersinvestmentandtrade.com/export/sites/trade/files/news/342150121095027/342150121095027_1.pdf (accessed January 14, 2017). The two reports also diverge, if slightly so, on the overall size of the global halal market for food and beverage. The 2014–2015 report gives this figure as about $1.3 trillion for 2013 (48), which, if true, implies a market contraction. Again, no evidence exists for such a trend. The discrepancies between the reports are likely due to methodological and/or computational variations in their estimations.

5. This may also be true for some non-Muslims depending on how halal is defined, a topic discussed in chapter 8.

6. Johan Fischer, "Branding Halal: A Photographic Essay on Global Muslim Markets," *Anthropology Today* 28, no. 4 (2012): 21. As of 2010, which is the most recent year for which we have information, Nestlé's annual sales of halal foods exceeds $5 billion and accounts for about 5 percent of the company's global sales; see "Nestlé Expands Its Halal Presence with the Launch of Its 'Flavours of Ramadan' Range throughout the Islamic Fasting Period," August 23, 2010, http://www.nestle.com/Media/NewsAndFeatures/Nestle-expands-halal-presence-during-Ramadan.

7. Charles Rarick et al., "Marketing to Muslims: The Growing Importance of Halal Products," *Journal of the International Academy for Case Studies* 18, no. 2 (2012): 101–106; Besheer Mohamed, "A New Estimate of the U.S. Muslim Population," *Pew Research Center*, January 6, 2016, http://www.pewresearch.org/fact-tank/2016/01/06/a-new-estimate-of-the-u-s-muslim-population/?utm_source=Pew+Research+Center&utm_campaign=65c3bb5fd7-Religion_Weekly_Jan_7_2016&utm_medium=email&utm_term=0_3e953b9b70-65c3bb5fd7-400104481.

8. Authors' calculations based on World Development Indicators compiled by the World Bank, http://databank.worldbank.org/data/ (accessed May 17, 2016).

9. Research on Muslim consumption patterns indicate that Muslims in Western settings eat primarily according to Islamic sensitivities. Attempts to quantify this inclination indicate that as

many as three-quarters of Muslims in the United States and France follow halal prescriptions in their choices of food consumption. See Mohammad Mazhar Hussaini, "Halal Haram Lists: Why They Do Not Work" (1993), http://www.soundvision.com/article/why-halal-haram-lists-do-not-work (accessed May 29, 2016); Karijn Bonne et al., "Determinants of Halal Meat Consumption in France," *British Food Journal* 109, no. 5 (2007): 367–386. Unclear from this type of research, however, is how consumers define halal food or how these sensitivities might vary over time. One also wonders how halal sensitivities in food consumption, in different Western settings, might compare to those in Muslim-majority communities.

10. Elif İzberk-Bilgin, "Infidel Brands: Unveiling Alternative Meanings of Global Brands at the Nexus of Globalization, Consumer Culture, and Islamism," *Journal of Consumer Research* 39, no. 4 (2012): 664. A more insular approach toward a Western lifestyle and against cultural assimilation has also been palpable among American Orthodox Jews throughout the twentieth century. Some have advocated greater stringency in kashrut standards as a path to recovering ancient ideals and rules. See Horowitz, *Kosher USA*, 68.

11. Florence Bergeaud-Blackler, "The Halal Certification Market in Europe and the World: A First Panorama," in *Halal Matters: Islam, Politics and Markets in Global Perspective*, ed. Florence Bergeaud-Blackler, Johan Fischer, and John Lever (London: Routledge, 2015), ch. 7.

12. Hackett, "Muslim Population in Europe."

13. Catarina Kinnvall and Paul Nesbitt-Larking, *The Political Psychology of Globalization: Muslims in the West* (Oxford: Oxford University Press, 2011).

14. Olivier Roy argues that in the West, Muslim identity has acquired a "neo-ethnic" meaning in the sense that the immigrant's origin is no longer relevant for his or her identity and that Islam is "de-territorialized." Accordingly, in the West, "1. Every person of Muslim background is supposed to share a common Muslim culture, whatever his or her real culture of origin (Turk, Bosnian, Pakistani or Arab), which means that religion [as a singular entity] is seen as the main component of these cultures . . . . 2. This culture is attributed to everybody with Muslim origin, whatever his or her religious practice or level of faith (that is, without any link to religiosity). In this sense, one could speak of 'non-believing Muslims.' 3. This culture differentiates a 'Muslim' from an 'other,' who, in the West, is defined as a member never of religious community, but a pseudo-ethnic group." See Roy, *Globalized Islam: The Search for a New Ummah* (New York: Columbia University Press, 2004), 124 and 126.

15. Kinnvall and Nesbitt-Larking, *The Political Psychology of Globalization*, 65.

16. Kinnvall and Nesbitt-Larking, *The Political Psychology of Globalization*, 58.

17. Isiaka Abidoun Adams, "Globalization: Explaining the Dynamics and Challenges of the Ḥālal Food Surge," *Intellectual Discourse* 19, no. 1 (2011): 127. For a more personal and popular discussion of these developments, see Shelina Janmohamed, *Generation M: Young Muslims Changing the World* (London: I. B. Tauris, 2016).

18. Mukherjee, "Global Halal," 5; Roy, *Globalized Islam*, 144, 145.

19. Roger Finke and Laurence R. Iannaccone, "Supply-Side Explanations for Religious Change," *Annals of the American Academy, AAPSS*, 527 (1993): 27–39.

20. Mara Einstein, *Brands of Faith: Marketing Religion in a Commercial Age* (New York: Routledge, 2008), 20.

21. John Lever and Mara Miele, "The Growth of Halal Meat Markets in Europe: An Exploration of the Supply Side Theory of Religion," *Journal of Rural Studies* 28, no. 4 (2012): 528–537.

22. In the absence of halal-compliant alternatives, most Muslim legal experts would consent to the use of standard medications, especially in cases of serious medical need. However, there

have been recent attempts by a number of private companies to produce halal-compliant drugs and health products. See, for example, "Halal Vaccines 'To Be Ready in Three Years," *Euroenews*, April 10, 2014, http://www.euronews.com/2014/04/10/halal-vaccines-to-be-ready-in-three-years-/; and Shafaat Shahbandari, "Is Your Toothpaste Halal?," *Gulf News*, November 16, 2012; on file with the authors. For a more specific discussion about the development of halal-compliant food manufacturing, see chapter 7.

23. Vloreen Nity Mathew, Ardiana Mazwa Raudah binti Amir Abdullah, and Siti Nurazizah binti Mohamad Ismail, "Acceptance of Halal Food among Non-Muslim Consumers," *Procedia—Social and Behavioral Sciences* 121 (2014): 262–271. Also, see our discussion in chapter 8.

24. *State of Global Islamic Economy 2014–2015 Report*, 49. Unfortunately, the later version of the report, *State of Global Islamic Economy Report 2016/2017*, does not provide analogous estimates.

25. *State of Global Islamic Economy 2014–2015 Report*, 49.

26. *State of Global Islamic Economy 2014–2015 Report*, 49.

27. Bergeaud-Blackler, "New Challenges for Islamic Ritual Slaughter"; Abidoun Adams, "Globalization," 131.

28. *State of Global Islamic Economy 2014–2015 Report*, 50. However, a few pages later, the report gives the same figure as 91 percent (ibid., 60). Analogous figures are not provided in *State of Global Islamic Economy Report 2016/2017*.

29. In 2014, Turkey's animal and animal product exports was worth about $0.7 billion. *State of Global Islamic Economy Report 2016/2017*, 38.

30. *Global Islamic Finance Report, 2013*, Edbiz Consulting, 145, http://www.gifr.net/gifr2013/ch_13.PDF (accessed May 29, 2016). There is a lack of comprehensive information about global trade patterns in these items.

31. *State of Global Islamic Economy 2014–2015 Report*, 50.

32. *State of Global Islamic Economy 2014–2015 Report*, 52.

33. *State of Global Islamic Economy 2014–2015 Report*, 55; *State of Global Islamic Economy Report 2016/2017*, 36–37.

34. Frans van Waarden and Robin van Dalen, "Halal and the Moral Construction of Quality," in *Constructing Quality: The Classification of Goods in Markets*, ed. Jens Beckert and Christine Musselin (Oxford: Oxford University Press, 2013), 207–208.

35. See Horowitz, *Kosher USA*, ch. 4 to compare this development with the history of kosher certification in the United States.

36. Fischer, "Branding Halal," 18.

37. On medieval market regulators or *muhtasibs*, see Kristen Stilt, *Islamic Law in Action: Authority, Discretion, and Everyday Experiences in Mamluk Egypt* (Oxford: Oxford University Press, 2012).

38. Van Waarden and van Dalen, "Halal and Moral Construction of Quality," 209.

39. Cf. Horowitz, *Kosher USA*, ch. 4. Horowitz speaks of the rise—since the 1930s—of an "organized kashrus" and of the growing tensions between "lay scientific knowledge and rabbinic authority rooted in traditional Jewish law" (79).

40. The latter have been standard practice for international assessment agencies like the widely recognized Swiss-based International Organization for Standardization (or ISO), which evaluates not just food safety but also medical facilities, industrial services, and the healthcare sector. See http://www.iso.org/iso/home/about.htm (accessed August 4, 2016). The rise of the halal certification sector, particularly in Muslim diasporic settings, shares some important parallels with the development of the modern kosher food certification

sector in the United States. This topic has been closely studied by Roger Horowitz in *Kosher USA*.

41. Shirazi, *Brand Islam*, 52.

42. Van Waarden and van Dalen, "Halal and the Moral Construction of Quality," 213.

43. m-haditec, "Halal-Certification Worldwide," http://www.halal-zertifikat.de/englisch/worldwide/halal_certification_bodies.htm (accessed May 29, 2016).

44. m-haditec, "Halal-Certification Worldwide."

45. For example, Halal Monitoring Authority in Canada, one of the few certifiers that openly list their fees, charges meat stores and retailers a monthly fee starting at CA$150, depending on the size of the facility. "Abattoirs, slaughter plants [and] meat processing plants are charged for the salary of the hours of the inspectors at $14.50 per hour. A monthly administration cost of anywhere between $250 [*sic*] (depending on the size of the facility) per month [*sic*] is charged to cover costs related to equipment, labels, stamps and administration." And "non meat manufacturing facilities are charged anywhere between $300 [*sic*] per month (depending on the size of the facility) to cover cost of monitoring, supervision, travel and administration"; see http://hmacanada.org/certification-costs-fees/ (accessed July 1, 2016). For a comparable fee scheme in the United Kingdom, see http://www.halalhmc.org/CostsandFees.htm (accessed July 1, 2016).

46. Geoff Chambers, "Halal: Islamic Certifier Companies Are Making Millions in Accreditation Fees," *Daily Telegraph*, August 10, 2015, http://www.dailytelegraph.com.au/news/nsw/halal-islamic-certifier-companies-are-making-millions-in-accreditation-fees/news-story/7d0e7663ea7b3391c6ff510115c0acf9. Figures converted to US dollars.

47. "Halal Certification 'Creates More Value Than It Costs,' Says Peak Food Body," *The Guardian*, August 14, 2015, https://www.theguardian.com/australia-news/2015/aug/14/halal-certification-creates-more-value-than-it-costs-says-peak-food-body. Figures converted to US dollars.

48. Chambers, "Certifier Companies Making Millions."

49. Mukherjee, "Global Halal," 47.

50. See A votre service (AVS), "Home Page," http://avs.fr/ (accessed May 29, 2016). For more on AVS also see Bergeaud-Blackler, *Le marché halal*, 126–127.

51. Bergeaud-Blackler, "Halal Certification Market."

52. Bergeaud-Blackler, "Halal Certification Market."

53. According to Bergeaud-Blackler, the second-generation certifiers have done well against their first-generation competitors partly because of their reputations as incorrupt organizations and the zealous attention that they pay to detail, including to matters of stunning, which translates into their relatively higher fees. See Bergeaud-Blackler, "Halal Certification Market." Claims of corruption are common in the certification industry and organizations often allude to, if not explicitly assert, their rivals' abuse of trust either by acting less than vigilant in their authentication efforts or even deliberately making shady certificate-for-money arrangements with their clients. See Johan Fischer, "Feeding Secularism: Consuming Halal among the Malays in London," *Diaspora: A Journal of Transnational Studies* 14, nos. 2/3 (2005): 286; see also "Halal Certification: The Local Picture," http://www.soundvision.com/article/halal-certification-the-local-picture (accessed May 29, 2016).

54. IFANCA is perhaps the most established halal authority in the United States. The organization certifies halal products in more than fifty countries and has been recognized by official halal authorities in Malaysia, Thailand, Indonesia, Singapore, Saudi Arabia, and United Arab Emirates (among others). Inspired by the organization of the American kosher market, IFANCA's halal regulations were developed in the 1980s by a Kuwaiti-born, US-trained agricultural engineer named Hani Mansour al-Mazeedi who worked for several decades with American and

Australian manufacturers to institute halal monitoring systems. See Shirazi, *Brand Islam*, 56; and Bergeaud-Blackler, *Le marché halal*, 139.

55. See Islamic Food and Nutrition Council of America (IFANCA), "IFANCA® Develops a Unique Five Star Halal Identification System for Halal Certification of Meat Products," http://www.ifanca.org/PressKit/presskit07112015.html (accessed December 5, 2016).

56. "Whole Foods Market Meat Department Animal Welfare," August 2012, http://www.wholefoodsmarket.com/sites/default/files/media/Global/PDFs/5-step-meat-brochure.pdf (accessed December 4, 2016).

57. This is what IFANCA states to explain its slaughter criteria: "While IFANCA is committed to making sure that the major vessels of the neck are cut during slaughter, it is allowable in stunned red meat plants to have a multistep cut which involves opening the skin and then cutting the major vessels. In poultry plants, IFANCA allows mechanical slaughter if the machine is turned on by a Muslim reciting the Tasmiyyah and Takbir and a Muslim is standing on the line to recite a blessing, supervising the slaughter, and hand slaughtering animals that are missed by the mechanical knife while reciting the Tasmiyyah and Takbir." See http://china.ifanca.org/presskit/presskit07112015.html (accessed December 5, 2016).

58. These are the relevant statements on IFANCA's website on these criteria: "The shading of the third star indicates that the slaughter plant has a program in place to ensure that animals were fed an all natural vegetarian diet." Also, "the shading of the fourth star indicates the plant has at least two, third party animal welfare audits per year. Plants must pass both their yearly audits to retain this star. All audits must be conducted by Professional Animal Auditor Certification Organization (PAACO) certified auditors using the species appropriate audit tool." See http://www.ifanca.org/Pages/index.aspx# (accessed December 5, 2016).

59. See chapter 8 for recent justifications to associate halal with human health and animal welfare and critical responses to this tendency.

60. For a critique of IFANCA's increasingly market-oriented approach based on statements by Mohammad Mazhar Husseini, a cofounder and former executive director of the organization, see Shirazi, *Brand Islam*, 56–57.

61. Quran 3:104, 3:110.

62. Charles Tripp, *Islam and the Moral Economy: The Challenge of Capitalism* (Cambridge: Cambridge University Press, 2006), 77.

63. Tripp, *Islam and the Moral Economy*, 88.

64. Fischer, "Feeding Secularism."

65. *Global Islamic Finance Report, 2013*, 148.

66. *Global Islamic Finance Report, 2013*, 149–151; MIHAS, "About MIHAS," http://www.mihas.com.my/about-mihas/ (accessed May 29, 2016); and MIHAS 2017, "About Us," http://mihas2017.my/about/the-malaysia-halal-showcase (accessed February 13, 2017).

67. Lever and Miele, "The Growth of Halal Meat Markets."

68. *Global Islamic Finance Report, 2013*, 151.

69. *Global Islamic Finance Report, 2013*, 151; see also "LPPOM MUI Pioneer of Halal Standard and Founder of World Food Halal Council," http://www.halalmui.org/newMUI/index.php/main/go_to_section/2/31/page/2 (accessed May 29, 2016); and Riaz and Chaudry, *Halal Food Production*, 53–54.

70. In the new setup, the MUI's role is limited to setting standards for products to be considered halal, but not to certification, monitoring, or enforcement. See Chris Johnston, "Why Halal Certification Is in Turmoil," *Sun Herald*, December 28, 2014, http://www.smh.com.au/national/why-halal-certification-is-in-turmoil-20141222-12cmd3; and Pearl Liu, "Indonesian Law Aims

for One-Stop Shop for Halal Certification," *BioWorld*, September 11, 2015, http://www.bioworld. com/content/indonesian-law-aims-1-stop-shop-halal-certification.

71. See, for example, Adisti Sukma Sawitri, "Turkish Firms Lament RI's Halal Certification," *Jakarta Post*, November 4, 2016, http://www.thejakartapost.com/news/2015/11/04/turkish-firms-lament-ri-s-halal-certification.html.

72. Afterward, Malaysia's JAKIM also confirmed Ajinomoto's claim that no pig-based substances were used in its products. See "Ajinomoto: Haram or Halal?," *Tempo*, January 28, 2001, article on file with the authors.

73. Mohammad Yazid, "When Pork Is Found in Halal-Guaranteed Food," *Jakarta Post*, April 29, 2009, http://www2.thejakartapost.com/news/2009/04/29/when-pork-found-halalguaranteed-food.html.

74. Liu, "One-Stop Shop for Halal Certification." Islamic legal traditions make exceptions, as discussed in chapter 1, for consuming haram ingredients out of dire necessity, so IFANCA's stance makes legal sense only if halal-compliant alternatives to this vaccine were known to be available. See also Shirazi, *Brand Islam*, 65–66, 83–84, for recent controversies involving MUI.

75. Liu, "One-Stop Shop for Halal Certification."

76. Jun Suzuki, "Halal Push Hits a Snag in Indonesia," *Nikkei Asian Review*, November 17, 2016, http://asia.nikkei.com/Politics-Economy/Policy-Politics/Halal-push-hits-a-snag-in-Indonesia.

77. Riaz and Chaudry, *Halal Food Production*, 53.

78. Majlis Ugama Islam Singapura (MUIS), "Overview of MUIS," http://www.muis.gov.sg/ About/overview-of-muis.html (accessed May 29, 2016).

79. "MUIS eHalal System," http://www.acaps.sg/Content/Data/CMSImage/37/ACAPS%20 60000.04.02-MUISeHalalSystemDetails.pdf (accessed May 29, 2016).

80. Others may include the Philippines, Thailand, and Brunei. Of the 150 third-party halal certifiers we could identify at the time of writing this chapter, 67 claim to use the standards developed by JAKIM (Malaysia), 57 to use those of Halal Stock (Philippines), and 32 to use those of MUI (Indonesia). Many of these certifiers can utilize multiple different standards based on their clients' needs and desires.

81. World Halal Food Council (WHFC), "Who We Are," http://www.whfc-halal.com/about-us/who-we-are (accessed May 29, 2016). On the ways in which Indonesia has been accused of generating obstacles in issuing religious licenses to exporters for countries that do not recognize WHFC's authority in halal matters, see Sawitri, "Turkish Firms Lament RI's Halal Certification."

82. Bergeaud-Blackler, "Halal Certification Market."

83. IHI Alliance, "Background," http://www.ihialliance.org/background.php (accessed May 29, 2016).

84. Bergeaud-Blackler, "Halal Certification Market."

85. Bergeaud-Blackler, "Halal Certification Market."

86. Comparable to JAKIM in Malaysia, DİB is a bureaucratic body, whose responsibility is to govern Turkey's religious affairs. The directorate is responsible with fostering Islamic (Sunni) identity in the country, providing religious education and guidance, organizing annual pilgrimages to Mecca, and supporting research, translation, and publication efforts in religious sciences. The body also has bureaus and educational outreach programs in foreign countries with significant Turkish populations.

87. Haluk Dağ and Emel Erbaşı-Gönç, "SMIIC and Halal Food Standards," *Journal of Chemical Metrology* 7, no. 1 (2013): 1–6.

88. These figures are from the SMIIC website, https://www.smiic.org/en/members (accessed November 24, 2017). The SMIIC members are Afghanistan, Algeria, Azerbaijan, Benin, Burkina Faso, Cameroon, Djibouti, Egypt, Gabon, Gambia, Guinea, Iran, Iraq, Jordan, Kyrgyzstan, Lebanon, Libya, Malaysia, Mali, Mauritania, Morocco, Niger, Pakistan, Palestine, Saudi Arabia, Senegal, Somalia, Sudan, Suriname, Tunisia, Turkey, Uganda, and United Arab Emirates. The observers are Bosnia and Herzegovina, Thailand, and Turkish Cypriot State.

89. Murat Şimşek, "Helal Belgelendirme ve SMIIC Standardı," *İslam Hukuku Araştırmaları Dergisi* 22 (2013): 19–44.

90. European Committee for Standardization (CEN), "Who We Are," https://www.cen.eu/about/Pages/default.aspx (accessed May 29, 2016).

91. See Lever and Miele, "The Growth of Halal Meat Markets"; and John Lever, "Reimagining Malaysia: A Postliberal Halal Strategy," in Halal *Matters: Islam, Politics and Markets in Global Perspective*, ed. Florence Bergeaud-Blackler, Johan Fischer, and John Lever (London: Routledge, 2015), ch. 2.

92. "Muslims Get to Rise Up and Get Together against CEN Halal Standard Interference," http://www.worldhalalcouncil.com/muslims-get-to-rise-up-and-get-together-against-cen-halal-standard-interference.html (accessed May 29, 2016). This critique arose despite the fact that CEN, in its ongoing efforts, had been consulting and cooperating with prominent Muslim religious authorities in Europe and elsewhere. See CEN, "Creation of a New Project Committee on 'Halal Food,'" https://www.standard.no/Global/PDF/Standardisering%20-%20nye%20prosjek-ter/Halal%20food.pdf (accessed May 29, 2016).

93. The idea of the gradual decline and degeneration of the Islamic civilization since the time of the Prophet is not a recent one. In fact, it is also a general feature of Islamic revivalist movements in the medieval and early-modern eras. See Madeline Zilfi, *The Politics of Piety: The Ottoman Ulema in the Post Classical Age (1600–1800)* (Minneapolis: Bibliotheca Islamica, 1988), 134.

94. For an articulate take on the ironic nature of global halal business on which this interpretation is based, see İzberk-Bilgin, "Infidel Brands," and İzberk-Bilgin, "Theology Meets the Marketplace: The Discursive Formation of the Halal Market in Turkey," unpublished paper (n.d.), https://www.academia.edu/14459777/Theology_Meets_the_Marketplace_The_Discursive_Formation_of_the_Halal_Market_in_Turkey (accessed May 30, 2016).

CHAPTER 6

1. Based on the definitions in these documents, the Malaysian state proposed in 1979 a set of halal guidelines to be incorporated into the International Food Codex by FAO and WHO. The guidelines would be published in the Codex for the first time in 1997. See Bergeaud-Blackler, *Le marché halal*, 87–88.

2. *Trade Descriptions (Use of Expression "Halal") Order 1975*, http://www.wipo.int/wipolex/en/text.jsp?file_id=128857 (accessed June 1, 2016).

3. *Trade Descriptions (Marking of Food) Order 1975*, http://www.wipo.int/wipolex/en/text.jsp?file_id=128860 (accessed May 1, 2016).

4. See *Trade Description (Certification and Marketing of 'Halal') Order 2011*, http://www.punto-focal.gov.ar/notific_otros_miembros/mys27_t.pdf, 3–5 (accessed June 1, 2016).

5. Zalina Zakaria and Siti Zubaidah Ismail, "The Trade Description Act 2011: Regulating 'Halal' in Malaysia," paper presented at International Conference on Law, Management and Humanities, Bangkok, Thailand, June 21–24, 2014, http://icehm.org/upload/8779ED0614020.pdf (accessed June 1, 2016); and Mustafa 'Afifi Ab. Halim and Azlin Alisa Ahmad, "Enforcement

of Consumer Protection Laws on Halal Products: Malaysian Experience," *Asian Social Science* 10, no. 3 (2014): 9–14.

6. JAKIM is one of the many bodies in Malaysia through which the federal government defines and regulates Islamic affairs. The department became incorporated into the prime minister's office in 1997 and since then has been utilized effectively "for setting the trend in Sharia expansion and implementation"; see Maznah Mohamed, "The Ascendance of Bureaucratic Islam and the Secularization of the Sharia in Malaysia," *Pacific Affairs* 83, no. 3 (2010): 513.

7. The document is only two pages long.

8. According to Seyyed Vali Reza Nasr, however, Malaysia's attempts at Islamization since the 1980s represent more than a simple response to Islamic opposition in the country. Instead, Islamization, as a proactive rather than reactive process, helped the state to enhance its hegemonic position and expand its intrusive power, thus it constituted a basis for the state's progrowth, export-oriented economic policies. See Nasr, *Islamic Leviathan: Islam and the Making of State Power* (Oxford: Oxford University Press, 2001), 3–17.

9. For other factors that contributed to Malaysia's state-led Islamization policies, including intra-elite competition, see Kikue Hamayotsu, "Demobilization of Islam: Institutionalized Religion and the Politics of Co-optation in Malaysia" (PhD Dissertation, Australian National University, Canberra Act 0200, Australia, 2005). Nasr suggests that in Malaysia, state-led Islamization and export-led economic development in the 1980s and 1990s are related: the former process enhanced the state's hegemonic stature and, by doing so, gave it the ability to formulate the policies and establish the institutional framework required for international market-based economic orientation; see Nasr, *Islamic Leviathan*, ch. 5.

10. Consequently, the state banned many nongovernmental groups and organizations, including dozens of Sufi orders, because they did not conform with the official definition of Islam; see Maznah Mohamed, "Legal-Bureaucratic Islam in Malaysia: Homogenizing and Ring-Fencing the Muslim Subject," in *Encountering Islam: The Politics of Religious Identities in South Asia*, ed. Hui Yew Foong (Singapore: Institute of Southeast Asian Studies 2012), 103–132. See also Nasr, *Islamic Leviathan*, 118.

11. *Malaysian Standard (MS) 1500:2000 "General Guidelines on the Production, Preparation, Handling and Storage of* Halal *Food"* (Jakarta: Department of Standards Malaysia, 2000). This is a thirteen-page document (cover and back pages, pp. i–iii, and pp. 1–8), which is extremely difficult to find in Western libraries and on the Internet. This is why it has received almost no attention in the literature on modern halal standards; instead, the scholarship has focused on the document's later versions (2004 and 2009). In fact, many studies discuss *MS 1500* as if its original version does not exist, although *MS 1500:2004* (iii) explicitly indicates that it is "the first revision of MS 1500:2000." The authors are grateful to the Harvard Law Library staff for locating and providing a copy of the document, which is on file with them.

12. See Sirim BERHAD, "Portfolio of Services," http://www.sirim.my/document/corporate%20 profile/SIRIM%20Corporate%20Profile.pdf (accessed February 12, 2017). The corporation operates under the Ministry of Finance and is involved in product design, development, testing, and marketing services to companies specializing in the manufacture of industrial machinery, energy and economical sustainability, and healthcare and medical technology. The phrase "total solutions provider" refers to the corporation's orientation to offer a comprehensive set of services necessary to fully complete a project to which it is assigned. Sirim BERHAD also defines itself as the "national standards development agency" in Malaysia.

13. *MS 1500:2000*, back of the cover page (no page number).

14. *MS 1500:2000*, ii. The Working Group included SIRIM-Berhad, Ministries of Health and of Domestic Trade and Consumer Affairs, Departments of Islamic Development Malaysia (JAKIM) and Veterinary Services, Malaysian Agricultural Research and Development Institute, Universities of Putra Malaysia and Kebangsaan Malaysia, Ilham Daya, as well as Nestlé. Ilham Daya was a private company designated by the government in 1997 to carry out halal inspections; see Halal Malaysia Official Portal, "Halal History," http://www.halal.gov.my/v4/index.php/en/korporat-mobile/sejarah-halal-mobile (accessed June 1, 2016).

15. *MS 1500:2000*, ii. Specifically, they included the Ministries of Health and Agriculture, Federations of Malaysian Consumers' Association and Malaysian Manufacturers, Departments of Agriculture and Standards Malaysia, Federal Agricultural Marketing Authority, Malaysian Agricultural Research and Development Institute, Malaysian Oil Palm Grower's Council, and Universities of Putra Malaysia and Kebangsaan Malaysia.

16. *MS 1500:2000*, 1.

17. On Malaysia's attempts to "make various modern academic disciplines compatible with Islam," see Nasr, *Islamic Leviathan*, 124–125.

18. *MS 1500:2000*, 1.

19. *MS 1500:2000*, 1.

20. *MS 1500:2000*, 1.

21. *MS 1500:2000*, 1.

22. *MS 1500:2000*, 1–2.

23. *MS 1500:2000*, 2. The same circular logic is evident in the later editions of the standard as well.

24. *MS 1500:2000*, 2.

25. *MS 1500:2000*, 2.

26. Note here that the document is also not ascribed to some medieval Shafi'i jurists' negative inclinations against isomorphs.

27. In this sense, the document is representative of the tendencies in subsequent editions of *MS 1500* and the two other international standards that we examine below.

28. *MS 1500:2000*, 3.

29. Mukherjee, "Global Halal," 41. On "scientization" or "scientification," also see Fischer, "Manufacturing Halal in Malaysia." The latter is Fischer's preferred term.

30. For more on *istihala* and *istihlak*, see chapter 7. Interestingly, *MS 2393:2013: Islamic and Halal Principles—Definitions and Interpretations on Terminology*, 3, a state-issued document that provides brief definitions of the terminology directly relevant to halal considerations, contains short explanations of these terms. The document is on file with the authors. See Department of Standards Malaysia, "MS 2393:2013: Islamic and *halal* principles - Definitions and interpretations on terminology," http://www.msonline.gov.my/download_file.php?file=31707&source=production (accessed February 12, 2017).

31. The document states that halal foods "do not contain any components or products of animals that are non-halal as foods to Muslims by Shariah Law or products of animals which are not slaughtered according to Shariah Law"; see *MS 1500:2000*, 1.

32. *MS 1500:2000*, 3.

33. Malaysia's current self-sufficiency rates in beef, mutton, and dairy are all below 25 percent. See Nor Amna A'liah Mohammad Nor and Mohamad Hifzan Rosali, "The Development and Future Direction of Malaysia's Livestock Industry," FFTC Agricultural Policy Platform Articles, October 10, 2015, http://ap.fftc.agnet.org/ap_db.php?id=529&print=1.

34. Darren Zook, "Making Space for Islam: Religion, Science, and Politics in Contemporary Malaysia," *Journal of Asian Studies* 69, no. 4 (2010): 1151–1155. Cf. Bergeaud-Blackler, *Le marché halal*, 101.

35. *MS 1500:2000*, 3, 6.

36. *MS 1500:2000*, 3.

37. *MS 1500:2000*, 4.

38. *MS 1500:2000*, 4.

39. *MS 1500:2000*, 4.

40. See Hamayotsu, "Demobilization of Islam"; Patricia Martinez, "The Islamic State or the State of Islam in Malaysia," *Contemporary Southeast Asia* 23, no. 3 (2001): 474–503.

41. *Malaysian Standard (MS) 1500:2004: Halal Food—Production, Preparation, Handling, and Storage—General Guidelines* (Jakarta: Department of Standards Malaysia, 2004). The authors have a copy on file.

42. *MS 1500:2004*, ii.

43. *MS 1500:2004*, ii.

44. *MS 1500:2004*, ii. Other bodies that newly took part in the 2004 version include Royal Customs Malaysia and Universiti Teknologi Mara.

45. *MS 1500:2004*, 1.

46. *MS 1500:2004*, 2.

47. The 2004 edition of the standard also states that "halal food and its ingredients do not contain any human parts or its derivatives that are not permitted by the Shariah law," a clause that does not exist in the 2000 edition. *MS 1500:2004*, 2.

48. *MS 1500:2004*, 8–9.

49. *MS 1500:2004*, 4. The 2009 version retained the same wording.

50. *MS 1500:2004*, 2. On the classical Muslim juristic rulings regarding the consumption of (halal) animal organs, reproductive parts, offal, and eggs or fetuses, see "At'ima," *Al-Mawsu'a al-Fiqhiyya*, 5:151–157, and chapter 2.

51. Here are the examples of "severe" najis: "dogs and pigs (*khinzir*) including any liquid and objects discharged from their orifices, descendants and derivatives." "Light" najis can be "urine from a baby boy at the age of 2 years and below who has not consumed any other food except his mother's milk." "Medium" najis could be "vomit, pus, blood, alcoholic drinks (*khamar*), carrion, liquid and objects discharged from the orifices" (*MS 1500:2004*, 2–3).

52. Interestingly, some Muslims considered the use of this phrasing inappropriate for slaughter. For them, it is better to say "Bismillah. Allah al-akbar" ("In the name of Allah. Allah is great") or simply "Bismillah."

53. *MS 1500:2004*, 4.

54. *MS 1500:2004*, 14. The soil and water to be used for cleansing should be free from najis substances and other impurities and should be in adequate amounts (ibid.).

55. Some hadiths on this topic can be found in Abu Dawud, *Sunan Abi Dawud*, 1:53–55.

56. *MS 1500:2004*, 8.

57. *MS 1500:2004*, 5.

58. Cited in Gerhard Hoffstaedter, "Secular State, Religious Lives: Islam and the State in Malaysia," *Asian Ethnicity* 14, no. 4 (2013): 476.

59. *Malaysian Standard (MS) 1500:2009: Halal Food—Production, Preparation, Handling and Storage—General Guidelines (Second Revision)* (Jakarta: Department of Standards Malaysia, 2009). The authors have a copy on file.

60. *MS 1500:2009*, ii. The new additions included the Halal Industry Development Corporation and Malaysian Association of Standards Users in the Industry Standards Committee on Halal Standards. They included the Department of Fisheries, Federal Territory Mufti Office, Federation of Marketing Authority, and Halal Industry Development Corporation in the Technical Committee on Halal Food, which appears to be renamed Technical Committee on Halal Food and Islamic Consumer Goods in the 2009 version.

61. *MS 1500:2009*, 1. *MS 2564:2014* Halal *Packaging: General Guidelines*, issued five years later, gives the meaning of the obscure term "al wadh'u" as follows: "Al wadh'u is a requirement prior to the implementation of any Shariah law, e.g. adhering to the prayer time is the requirement for prayer to be valid" (p. 2n1). The text is on file with the authors.

62. *MS 1500:2009*, 7.

63. *MS 1500:2009*, 7.

64. *MS 1500:2009*, 7.

65. *MS 1500:2009*, 5.

66. *MS 1500:2009*, 3–4, 10–11.

67. In 2014, the Malaysian state issued an independent document, *MS 2565:2014: Halal Packaging—General Guidelines*, focused solely on halal packaging, which was included earlier in the successive versions of *MS 1500*. This development also demonstrates the trend of further specialization and bureaucratization of halal processes in Malaysia.

68. *OIC/SMIIC 1:2011: General Guidelines on Halal Food* (Ankara: Türk Standartlar Enstitüsü, 2011). On file with the authors. We are grateful to the staff at the Harvard Law Library for obtaining and sharing with us a copy of this document.

69. To our knowledge, the earlier 2009 guidelines were the first to be issued by the OIC. Incidentally, Malaysia is also not represented in any of the seven Technical Committees, including those on Cosmetics (TC2), Service Site Issues (TC3), and Tourism (TC5), which are directly related to halal matters. We discussed in chapter 5 the tense and competitive relationship between Malaysia and the OIC in global halal affairs.

70. SMIIC, "Technical Committees," http://www.smiic.org/tcs (accessed June 1, 2016). Just before this book was sent to the printer, the composition of TC1 was slightly altered and Malaysia appeared among its members (https://www.smiic.org/en/tc-member/1; accessed November 24, 2017).

71. *SMIIC 1*, 1.

72. The inconsistency between the Malaysian and OIC standards in the definition of Sharia is more obvious between *MS 1500:2004* and *SMIIC 1*. As we have seen, the 2004 version defines Islamic law as follows: "*Shariah* law means the laws of Islam in the *Mazhab* of Shafie or the laws of Islam in any other Mazhabs of Maliki, Hambali [*sic*] and Hanafi which are approved by the Yang di-Pertuan Agong to be in force in the state or fatwa approved by the Islamic Authority." In the 2009 version the following sentence is added to the definition: "*Shariah* law is the orders of Allah which relate to the action of the people who are being accountable (*mukallaf*) by obligation, option or al *wadh'u*." It is unclear who copied what from whom but the fact that the 2009 version of the Malaysian Standard and *SMIIC 1* both identify God's will as the basis of their authority is noteworthy.

73. *SMIIC 1* treats fish with scales (and their by-products) and aquatic animals without scales separately, perhaps reflecting the Hanafi and Shiite inclinations to distinguish them, before pronouncing them all halal, a choice more consistent with the traditions of other legal schools (ibid., 3–4).

74. The *SMIIC 1* document requires that the blades be made of steel. The Malaysian Standard does not.

75. *MS 1500:2009*, 6–7 *SMIIC 1*, 4.

76. *MS 1500:2009*, 7; *SMIIC 1*, 5

77. *SMIIC 1*, 5–7.

78. *SMIIC 1*, 4, 9. The document also lists the following international standards among its reference texts:

> CODEX STAN 1: General Standard for the Labeling of Prepacked Food
> CAC/RCP 58: Code of Hygienic Practice for Meat
> ISO 22000: Food Safety Management Systems-Requirements for Any Organization in the Food Chain
> ISO 22005: Traceability in the Feed and Food Chain-General Principles and Basic Requirements for System Design and Implementation

In regard to food safety and hygiene, *MS 1500:2009* states: "Halal food shall be processed, packed and distributed under hygienic condition in premises licensed in accordance with good hygiene practices (GHP), good manufacturing practices (GMP) or such as specified in the Garispanduan ama/an pengilangan yang baik, Ministry of Health Malaysia, MS 1514 or MS 1480 and public health legislation currently in force by the competent authority in Malaysia" (*MS 1500:2009*, 5). *MS 1480* is titled "Food Safety according to Hazard Analysis and Critical Control Point (HACCP) System." *MS 1514* is "Good Manufacturing Practice (GMP) for Food." Readers should note here the symbolism associated with citing national (read "Muslim"), rather than international ("non-Muslim"), standards as reference documents, especially in light of the recent conflicts among various certifying bodies over the right to determine halal. Also, while we should assume significant overlaps between the Malaysian Standards and the international regulations, the fact that the Malaysian state determined the former as compulsory and the latter as voluntary gives the impression that there are some variations among them. A formal comparison between *MS 1514* and *MS 1480* and their international counterparts awaits extended analysis. For more information on these two documents and their implementation, see Habibah Abdul Talib and Khairul Anuar Mohd Ali, "An Overview of Malaysian Food Industry: The Opportunity and Quality Aspects," *Pakistan Journal of Nutrition* 8 (2009): 507–517, http://scialert.net/fulltext/?doi=pjn.2009.507.517.

79. *SMIIC 1*, 4–5.

80. *SMIIC 1*, 4.

81. *SMIIC 1*, 4.

82. *SMIIC 1*, 5.

83. *MS 1500:2009*, 13.

84. *SMIIC 1*, 7–8. Honeybee parts in honey are halal.

85. *SMIIC 1*, 8. According to the document, those derived from nonhalal animals or animals considered carrion according to Islamic law are not acceptable. Neither document brings up isti-hala and istihlak in their discussions.

86. *SMIIC 1*, 8.

87. *SMIIC 1*, 7.

88. *SMIIC 1*, 6.

89. *SMIIC 1*, 6–7.

90. *SMIIC 1*, 3.

91. GCC Standardization Organization (GSO), "GSO 05/FDS/2055 1:2014: Halal products Part one: General Requirements for Halal Food," http://www.puntofocal.gov.ar/notific_otros_miembros/kwt282_t.pdf (accessed February 12, 2017)

92. *GSO 2055*, 1.r

93. The Ibadi legal school is a legal affiliation associated with the Khawarij (sing. Khariji), an early sectarian position in Islam, different from both Sunnism and Shiism. Although the Ibadi legal school still exists in locales such as Oman, Zanzibar, and North Africa, the Khawarij sect has largely died out since medieval times. See J. E. Peterson, "Oman's Diverse Society: Northern Oman," *Middle East Journal* 58, no. 1 (2004): 31.

94. *GSO 2055*, 2.

95. *GSO 2055*, 3.

96. *GSO 2055*, 4.

97. The Gulf code also states that when "transforming any appliances, tools or production lines that have been used or in touch with non-Halal foods, they shall be cleaned according to general cleaning rules to remove traces of non-Halal products completely" (*GSO 2055*, 3). It does not make clear, however, whether the "general cleaning rules" mentioned in the statement are different from the "Islamic Rules" of purification and, if so, how.

98. *GSO 2055*, 3.

99. *GSO 2055*, 1, 3. For example, clause 4.8 on page 3 states that "at the production of meat or its products, health requirements specified in item (2.4) shall be adhered to." The item identified as "2.4" is a separate GCC guideline, titled "GSO/CAC/RCP 58: Code of hygienic practice for meat." Later, *GSO 2055* states in clause 4.10, also on page 3, that "the general health requirements of foods as stated in the standard mentioned in item (2.5) shall be adhered to." The standard identified as "2.5" is the guideline titled "GSO 1694: General principles of food hygiene." The Malaysian and OIC/SMIIC Standards, too, cite additional guidelines that need to be observed when discussing hygiene and sanitation. But the documents, and especially the OIC guidelines, are much more inclined to directly tackle the health aspects of halal compliance.

100. *GSO 2055*, 6.

101. See *GS 993: Animal Slaughtering Requirements according to Islamic Law* (1999), 2, http://www.halalcertifiering.se/newwebsiteimages/Gulf_standard.pdf (accessed June 1, 2016). This being said, *GS 993* also requires that "the slaughter shall be carried out under the supervision of a rational equitable Muslim" who knows the rules of Islamic slaughter, which complicates the permissibility of animals slaughtered according to "kitabi" traditions that *GSO 2055* explicitly considers nonharam; see *GSO 2055*, 6.

102. *GS 993*, 2.

103. *GS 993*, 2.

104. *GS 993*, 2.

105. *GS 993*, 2.

106. *GS 993*, 2.

107. The Gulf Standard requires genetically modified food to be labeled as such; see *GSO 2055*, 5.

108. *GSO 2055*, 2, 5.

CHAPTER 7

1. "Packaged Food Market Is Expected to Reach $3.03 Trillion, Worldwide, by 2020—Allied Market Research," July 23, 2015, http://www.prnewswire.co.uk/news-releases/packaged-food-market-is-expected-to-reach-303-trillion-worldwide-by-2020---allied-market-research-518286401.html.

2. Soha Ghandou, "MENA Region Drives Food Packaging Demand," *Middle East Food* 31, no. 1 (2015): 10, http://www.mefmag.com/PDFFiles/MEF-January-2015.pdf.

3. Conversely, in 2015, the OIC countries exported $37 billion worth of processed and manu-factured food. *State of the Global Islamic Economy 2016/2017 Report*, 27.

4. Bergeaud-Blackler, *Le marché halal*, 98–99. The Swiss-based Nestlé makes hundreds of packaged halal foods, including chicken bouillon cubes, dried milk, and instant coffee, among others, and has 151 halal certified factories (out of 418) in countries like Iran, Pakistan, and Saudi Arabia. See Jeff Green and Craig Giammona, "How Halal Food Became a $20 Billion Hit in America," *Bloomberg*, September 14, 2016, https://www.bloomberg.com/news/articles/2016-09-14/america-loves-muslim-food-so-much-for-a-clash-of-civilizations; and Nestlé, "Annual Review 2016," 57, at http://www.nestle.com/asset-library/documents/library/documents/annual_reports/2016-annual-review-en.pdf (accessed June 22, 2017).

5. The same questions arose several decades ago among Orthodox and Conservative American Jews and, to some extent, they have yet to be fully resolved. See Horowitz, *Kosher USA*, passim.

6. Shirazi, *Brand Islam*, 15. On the issue of consumer trust in labels and in the manufacturing production process of so-called "credence goods" (i.e., halal, kosher, organic, fair trade, etc.), see Bergeaud-Blackler, *Le marché halal*, 79–80 and 155.

7. An alternative meaning to the word is impossibility or inconceivability. See "Istihala," *Al-Mawsu'a al-Fiqhiyya*, 3:213–214. Istihala in Malaysian Standard publications is defined as "the changes of the substances to become new substances with difference in taste, color and odour. It involves the transformation of a compound to other compound(s)." See Department of Standards Malaysia, "MS 2393:2013: Islamic and Halal Principles—Definitions and Interpretations on Terminology" (Selangor Darul Ehsan, 2013), 3.

8. Qadhafi 'Izzat al-Ghunanim, *Al-Istihala wa Ahkamiha fi'l-Fiqh al-Islami* (Amman: Dar al-Nafa'is, 2008), 85, 111–112, 192–195.

9. Çayırlıoğlu, *Helal Gıda*, 207, 212, 250–251.

10. Çayırlıoğlu, *Helal Gıda*, 218–219; al-Ghunanim, *Al-Istihala wa Ahkamiha fi'l-Fiqh al-Islami*, 139.

11. One hadith recounts the Prophet as saying, "What an excellent condiment vinegar is!" At-Tirmidhi, *English Translation of Jami' At-Tirmidhi*, 3:532; Al-Tirmidhi, *Al-Jami' al-Kabir*, 3:420; see also Çayırlıoğlu, *Helal Gıda*, 226–227.

12. Çayırlıoğlu, *Helal Gıda*, 219.

13. Some, possibly including Ahmad ibn Hanbal (d. 855), agree that the process is to be con-demned but the resulting vinegar can be consumed. Others within these two schools maintain that any substance made from haram sources, even if the process of istihala transformed it and changed its nature, is forbidden. Çayırlıoğlu, *Helal Gıda*, 220–222, 232–233, 238–239; al-Ghunanim, *Al-Istihala wa Ahkamiha fi'l-Fiqh al-Islami*, 141, 144–148. Examples of hadiths that prohibit consuming vinegar made from wine come from al-Tirmidhi, *Al-Jami' al-Kabir*, 2:567–568 and Abu Dawud, *Sunan Abi Dawud*, 5:518–519.

14. Muhammad Mahdi ibn Abi Zarr al-Naraqi, *Mu'tamad al-Shi'a fi Ahkam al-Shari'a* (Beirut: Mu'assasat al-Bayt li Ihya' al-Turath, 2008), 1:331–334, http://www.narjes-library.com/2014/08/blog-post_8.html; Abu al-Qasim al-Khaw'i and Mirza 'Ali al-Gharawi al-Tabrizi, *Al-Tanqih fi Sharh al-'Urwa al-Wuthqa*, 10 vols. (Qom: Dar al-Hadi li'l Matbu'at, 2000), 3:167, http://ar.lib.eshia.ir/10134/3/167/ (accessed December 21, 2016).

15. Çayırlıoğlu, *Helal Gıda*, 280–281. Jewish rabbinic traditions pertaining to kashrut employ a similar concept called *bitul b'shishim* (nullification by one-sixtieth) to address the contamina-tion of a kosher ingredient with a small amount of a non-kosher substance. The conventional wisdom is that "so long as the offending ingredient is no more than one-sixtieth of the mixture

and does not affect it materially," the substance can be consumed. This concept was applied in the modern period to a variety of manufactured foods, most famously in the case of animal-derived glycerin added to Coca-Cola in the 1930s. See Horowitz, *Kosher USA*, 23. For more on *bitul* or "nullification" in kosher law, see Zushe Yosef Belch, *Kosher Food Production* (Oxford: Blackwell, 2004), 40–43.

16. A *qulla* is a clay urn commonly found in Near Eastern cultures which was and still is used to hold water. On this dispute, see Ze'ev Maghen, "Ablution," in *Encyclopaedia of Islam*, 3rd ed., Brill Online, http://dx.doi.org/10.1163/1573-3912_ei3_COM_0150 (accessed December 4, 2015). On the modern measurements, see Çayırlıoğlu, *Helal Gıda*, 280–281; "Fatwa 16107," *Markaz al-Fatwa*, http://fatwa.islamweb.net/fatwa/index.php?page=showfatwa&Option=FatwaId&Id=16107 (accessed December 4, 2015).

17. See, for example, Al-Khaw'i, *Al-Tanqih fi Sharh al-'Urwa al-Wuthqa*, 1:71, 1:88, 1:257.

18. The majority opinion attributed to the school's founder, on the other hand, suggests that even if it is technically acceptable to use a clean substance contaminated with a tiny amount of impure material, one should avoid the contaminated substance and use a wholly uncontaminated material if the latter is available. Çayırlıoğlu, *Helal Gıda*, 282.

19. Abu Hanifa and the Hanbali jurist Ibn Taymiyya take this opinion. Çayırlıoğlu, *Helal Gıda*, 286–289.

20. J. Poppe, "Gelatin," in *Thickening and Gelling Agents for Food*, ed. Alan P. Imeson (London: Blackie, 1997), 144–145.

21. For an excellent discussion of gelatin's controversial place within Orthodox and Conservative American Jewish circles, see Horowitz, *Kosher USA*, ch. 3. To our knowledge, there has been no scholarly comparison done between ponim chadashos and istihala, nor between bitul b'shishim and istihlak.

22. "Gelatin Market Analysis- Size, Share, Growth, Trends and Segment Forecasts to 2020," *M2 Presswire*, August 5, 2015.

23. Çayırlıoğlu, *Helal Gıda*, 350–351.

24. "Recommendations of the 8th Fiqh-Medical Seminar," May 22–24, 1995 (Kuwait), at http://islamset.net/bioethics/8thfiqh.html (accessed December 20, 2016).

25. Ayatollah Sistani, "Al-Istifta'at: Jalatin," http://www.sistani.org/arabic/qa/02067/ (accessed December 20, 2016).

26. "May We Eat Gelatin," at http://www.ifanca.org/Pages/Faq.aspx (accessed June 13, 2016).

27. GİMDES is Turkey's oldest and possibly most recognized private halal certifier. The company was established in 2005 and has been issuing halal certificates and monitoring products since 2009. It is a founding member of the WHC, the World Halal Foundation, and the European Association of Halal Certifiers (AHC-Europe), among others. GİMDES is JAKIM-accredited and uses the Malaysian Standard as the basis of its certification. See, GİMDES, "Hakkımızda," http://www.gimdes.org/kurumsal (accessed May 29, 2016).

28. Mohammad Aizat Jamaludin et al, "Istihala: Analysis on the Utilization of Gelatin in Food Products," *IPEDR* 17 (2011): 174–178. See also "Gelatin Transformation (Istihala) in Science and Fiqh," http://www.halalcertificationturkey.com/en/2015/01/gelatin-transformation-istihala-in-science-and-fiqh/ (accessed February 8, 2017).

29. John Lever and Haluk Anil, "From an Implicit to an Explicit Understanding: New Definitions of Halal in Turkey," in Bergeaud-Blackler, Fischer, and Lever, *Halal Matters*, 44.

30. Until recently, insulin for treatment of diabetes was commonly derived from pigs. With few exceptions, most diabetes treatments today are biosynthesized to mimic human insulin.

Incidentally, concerned vegans and vegetarians, particularly in Western countries, have long made calls for clearer labeling of these products. "Many Drugs 'Non-vegetarian and Need Better Labelling,'" February 28, 2012, http://www.bbc.com/news/health-17182625.

31. Riaz and Chaudry, *Halal Food Production*, 100. See also Fahmi Mustafa Mahmud, *Al-I'jaz al-Tashri'i fi Tahrim al-Khinzir*, part 1 (Amman: Markaz Ibn al-Nafis li'l-Buhuth al-'Ilmiyya wa-Dirasat al-Mar'a, 2007), 116–117.

32. See "Malaysia Has Potential to Capture Slice of Halal Gelatin Market," *Organisation of Asia-Pacific News Agencies*, June 4, 2011; "HD IIU and King Saud University Collaborate to Produce Camel Gelatin," *Bernama Daily Malaysian News*, December 20, 2012.

33. Rousselot maintains a sales office in Kuala Lumpur to help oversee certification and marketing operations in South and Southeast Asia. "Rousselot Pharmaceutical Gelatines," http://www.parmentier.de/gpfneu/gelatine/pharmagelatines.pdf (accessed December 20, 2016).

34. The website of one Pakistani company, established in 2002, indicates that its current annual capacity for producing halal gelatin is only one kilo ton, a minuscule portion of the international output as discussed above. See "Vision and Mission," http://www.halalgelatin.org/company-profile/vision-mission/ (accessed February 8, 2017).

35. Until today, products containing industrially produced gelatin (not derived from kosher-slaughtered animals) might be labeled "kosher" by some American kosher certifying authorities who have used a more "lenient application" of ponim chadashos. Other kosher certifying agencies, however, have applied stricter rules in regulating gelatin. See Horowitz, *Kosher USA*, 72–74.

36. We thank one of our referees for bringing this point to our attention.

37. L-cysteine that can be proven to have derived from bird feathers is permissible.

38. "Additives and Ingredients," *Gulf Halal Center*, http://gulfhalal.com/additives-ingredients/ (accessed June 30, 2016). On enzymes and halal food, see Riaz and Chaudry, *Halal Food Production*, 107–112.

39. Similar concerns have arisen among Jewish kosher certifying agencies and rabbinical authorities about a variety of food additives in manufactured products deemed to violate kashrut standards. Compare Riaz and Chaudry, *Halal Food Production*, passim with Belch, *Kosher Food Production*, passim.

40. See in general "Consumer FAQ," at http://www.ifanca.org/Pages/Faq.aspx (accessed June 13, 2016). See also discussion of these additives in Shirazi, *Brand Islam*, 60–63.

41. "Halal Shopper's Quick Reference Guide," http://www.ifanca.org/Assets/PopularLinks/Halal%20Shoppers%20Guid.pdf (accessed July 12, 2017).

42. Syed Azhar, "App to Check Halal Food Status Launched," *Star Online*, May 26, 2017, http://www.thestar.com.my/news/nation/2017/05/26/app-to-check-halal-food-status-launched/. Also see Shirazi, *Brand Islam*, 85.

43. See "Scan Halal," https://itunes.apple.com/us/app/scan-halal/id589534185?mt=8, and "Halal Food SN," https://play.google.com/store/apps/details?id=com.appnotech.halalfoods (both accessed December 12, 2016).

44. "Confectionery in the Middle East and Africa," *Euromonitor International*, November 2016, http://www.euromonitor.com/confectionery-in-the-middle-east-and-africa/report; "Chocolate Confectionery in Indonesia," *Euromonitor International*, September 2016, http://www.euromonitor.com/chocolate-confectionery-in-indonesia/report (accessed December 22, 2016).

45. Anuradhu Raghu, "Halal Chocolate Takes Off as Sweet-Tooth Muslims Seek Fix," *Bloomberg*, June 16, 2017, https://www.bloomberg.com/news/articles/2017-06-16/halal-chocolate-takes-off-as-sweet-tooth-muslims-want-their-fix/.

46. See a list of these confections at "Halal Products," Cadbury, https://www.cadbury.com.au/products/halal-products.aspx (accessed June 14, 2016).

47. Yasmine Hafiz, "Cadbury Malaysia Upsets Muslims after Pork DNA Found in 'Halal' Chocolate," *HuffPost Religion*, May 28, 2014, http://www.huffingtonpost.com/2014/05/28/cadbury-malaysia-muslims-pork-halal_n_5404555.html. In 2010, a Japanese company developed a "pork detection kit" to sense pork DNA particles in and contaminants in the halal food supply. See Shirazi, *Brand Islam*, 86–86, and Bergeaud-Blackler, *Le marché halal*, 89–90.

48. "Are Guylian Products Halal?," http://www.guylian.com/hrf_faq/are-guylian-products-halal/ (accessed June 14, 2016).

49. "Chocolate Goes Halal," *Daily Record*, March 30, 2007.

50. "Is Chocolate Liquor Haram," http://www.ifanca.org/Pages/Faq.aspx (accessed June 14, 2016).

51. Whether one can consume milk from the udders of carrion, a naturally deceased animal, was disputed in the medieval Islamic literature. The Hanafi line proposes that milk from carrion's udder is clean, but other legal schools view that milk as suspicious (mashbuh) or even dirty (najis). Michael Cook, "Magian Cheese: An Archaic Problem in Islamic Law," *Bulletin of the School of Oriental and African Studies* 47, no. 3 (1984): 459–460.

52. 'Abd al-Karim al-Najaf, *Al-Halal wa'l-Haram fi'l Shari'a al-Islamiyya* (Tehran: al-Majma' al-'Alami li'l-Taqrib bayna al-Madhahib al-Islamiyya, 2008), 512; Abi Bakr ibn Hassan al-Kishnawi, *Ashal al-Madarik: Sharh Irshad al-Salik fi Fiqh Imam al-'Amm'atu Malik*, 2nd ed. (Beirut: Dar al-Fikr, 2000), 1:47, http://waqfeya.com/book.php?bid=10428. Until recently, with their introduction as novelty items, pig milk and derivative cheeses were almost nonexistent, since pig milk is physically difficult to extract, has a watery consistency, and tastes gamy. See "Are You Ready for Pig's Milk Cheese?," *Fox News*, August 26, 2015, http://www.foxnews.com/leisure/2015/08/26/ill-governor-demands-labeling-for-pig-milk-and-camel-milk/.

53. Viji Sundaram, "Got Milk, Halal or Haram?," *India-West*, June 9, 1995. The general halal status of most commercially available milk applies to any milk-containing manufactured product (e.g., chocolate, yogurt, etc.), so long as its other ingredients (e.g., emulsifiers, gelatin, etc.) have also been deemed halal.

54. Modern Orthodox Jewish interpretations follow similarly rigid rules. In the case of rennet, see Horowitz, *Kosher USA*, 37–42. David Freidenreich disputes the logic of restrictive rabbinic positions, since the contents of an animal's stomach were generally considered "outside" the animal's body and therefore not subject to the same legal rules as other parts of that body. See Freidenreich, *Foreigners and Their Food*, 64–65.

55. Salih al-'Awd, *Sina'at al-Ajban al-Haditha wa Hukm Akliha: bi-Adillat al-Kitab wa'l Sunna wa-Nuqul al-A'imma wa Aqwal 'Ulama' al-Umma* (Beirut: Dar al-Kutub al-'Ilmiyya, 2009), 85.

56. Cook, "Magian Cheese," 456–458; "Question and Answer: Cheese," http://www.sistani.org/english/qa/01159/ (accessed August 9, 2014). Freidenreich offers a different interpretation than Cook on the Shiite position toward Magian cheese. See his *Foreigners and Their Food*, 162–166.

57. For example, a 1982 Saudi fatwa advises that if a Muslim suspects that any pig by-products have come into contact with his food, medicine, or toothpaste, then they must be avoided. A similar 1992 Turkish fatwa notes that cheese should be eaten only when the rennet's source can be identified. Both fatwas are included in al-'Awd, *Sina'at al-Ajban*, 55–56, 62–63.

58. "Cheddar Cheese and Dairy Facts," Cabot Cheese, https://www.cabotcheese.coop/top-cheddar-facts (accessed June 3, 2016).

59. Çayırlıoğlu, *Helal Gıda*, 373–376. Iraq's Ayatollah Sistani has also ruled that in medications where alcohol is used as a solvent, its presence is "so minute" that the product is permissible. "Question and Answer: Eating and Drinking," http://www.sistani.org/english/qa/01178/ (accessed June 14, 2016).

60. *Halal Consumer Magazine: A Publication of the Islamic Food and Nutrition Council of America*, 24 (Spring 2013): 16, http://www.ifanca.org/HCM/Halal percent20Consumer percent20Issue percent2024/index.html#/I/zoomed.

61. The ruling by Yusuf al-Qaradawi applied only to products that go through a natural (not human-induced) fermentation process. The fatwa was originally published in the Qatari newspaper *Al 'Arab* but can also be found in Hilmy al-Asmar, "Kharij al-Nass: al-Qaradawi wa'l Khamr," April 14, 2008, http://www.addustour.com/ (accessed June 8, 2018). Also see Frances Harrison, "Alcohol Fatwa Sparks Controversy," *BBC News*, April 11, 2008, http://news.bbc.co.uk/2/hi/middle_east/7342425.stm.

62. See Bryan Miller, "Low-Alcohol Beer: Lighter Than Light," *New York Times*, April 18, 1984; Bernice Kanner, "Brew News," *New York Magazine*, August 13, 1984.

63. "Istishari Yatma'in: al-Bira al-Su'udiyya Khaliyya min al-Kuhul," *Al-Jazirah Online*, September 30, 2013, http://al-jazirahonline.com/2013/20130930/ec47532.htm.

64. The fatwa indicated that some nonalcoholic drinks naturally contain a small amount of alcohol ("such as 1 percent, 2 percent, or 3 percent") and that this level does not necessarily render these products haram, because it is intoxication (*sukr*) which is haram, an interpretation we have observed in some early Hanafi opinions. Some Muslims were unsure about how to understand the sheikh's comments; Internet blogs and discussion groups have debated the fatwa for years. An audio of the sheikh's fatwa ("Hukm Shurb ma Yusama bi-'l Bira" or "Ruling about What's Called Beer") can be heard here: http://binothaimeen.net/content/3222. The text's Arabic transcription can be accessed at "Hukm Shurb ma Yusamma bi'l Bira," at http://alnasiha.net/node/1280 (accessed June 8, 2016).

65. "Majlis Fatwa Kebangsaan: Koleksi Fatwa Berkaitan Alkohol Dalam Makanan Dll" [English and Malay], http://www.al-ahkam.net/home/content/majlis-fatwa-kebangsaan-koleksi-fatwa-berkaitan-alkohol-dalam-makanan-dll (accessed June 4, 2016).

66. These data were provided in W. A. Wan Nadiah et al., "Determination of *Halal* Limits for Alcohol Content in Foods by Simulated Fermentation," in Puziah Hashim et al., "Proceedings of the 3rd IMT-GT International Symposium on Halal Science and Management," December 21–22, 2009 (Selangor Dar Ehsan, Malaysia: Halal Products Research Institute, 2009), 62, http://www.academia.edu/1367215/Determination_of_Halal_Limits_for_Alcohol_Content_in_Foods_by_simulated_fermentation; and by Dzulkifly Mat Hashim, a Malaysian expert in food technology and halal affairs, in "Unraveling the Issue of Alcohol in the Halal Industry," http://www.hdcglobal.com/upload-web/cms-editor-files/b08c8a04-c946-4ebe-99b9-2492bd32fcfc/file/11%29%20En%20Dzulkifli%20Mat%20Hashim%20-%20WHR2010_Unraveling%20the%20Issue%20of%20Alcohol_Final.pdf (accessed June 4, 2016).

67. "Jadal Hawla Fatwa li'l-Qaradawi Tabih al-Mashrubat bi Nisab Kuhul Da'ila," April 11, 2008, *Al Arabiya,* http://www.alarabiya.net/articles/2008/04/11/48148.html.

68. Çayırlıoğlu, *Helal Gıda*, 377.

69. Heine, "Nabidh." In his tenth-century Baghdadi cookbook, medieval food authority Ibn Sayyar al-Warraq provided several recipes for nabidh. As Middle East food historian Nawal Nasrallah points out, however, nabidh was more or less thought of—in this period—as "wine" and was distinguished, by some medieval writers, from the drink consumed by the Prophet Muhammad and his companions which some called *al-naqi'* (meaning "soaked"). The latter was

consumed within three days. See Nasrallah, *Annals of the Caliphs' Kitchens*, 554. One recipe for date nabidh (*nabidh al-dibs*) captures this (medieval) differentiation between the two drinks. In it, al-Warraq instructs a cook to "take 50 *ratls* [50 pounds] date syrup [and put it in a vessel]. Pour on it a similar amount of water and put [the vessel] in a sunny place for 20 days." Next one should add some sweeteners, including honey, which have been boiled with water, and the date-sweetener mixture should be set aside for three days in vessels sealed with mud. "When two months have passed," al-Warraq enthuses, "the wine will be splendid." See Nasrallah, *Annals of the Caliphs' Kitchens*, 469.

70. A. Anis Najiha et al., "A Preliminary Study on *Halal* Limits for Ethanol Content in Food Products," *Middle East Journal of Scientific Research* 6, no. 1 (2010): 45–50.

71. Cited in Işın, "Boza," 157–158; Eren, *Anadolu'da Bira*, 45–48. Incidentally, and distinct from boza, medieval Islamic culinary texts speak of a malted barley drink called *fuqqa'*, whose simplest preparation involved boiling ground malted barley with water, waiting for the sediments to settle, and consuming the clear liquid ("barley water"). According to Nawal Nasrallah, this drink was considered a form of "alcohol-free beer" (*al-fuqqa' al-mukhtar*). See Nasrallah, *Annals of the Caliphs' Kitchens*, 453-459; and also, Lewicka, *Food and Foodways of Medieval Cairenes*, 465-482.

72. Y. Teramoto et al., "Characteristics of Egyptian Boza and a Fermentable Yeast Strain Isolated from the Wheat Bread," *World Journal of Microbiology and Biotechnology* 17, no. 3 (2001): 241–243. On the Egyptian fatwa, see "Dar al-Ifta': al-Buza min al-Musakirat wa Sharbiha 'Haram,'" *Al-Yawm al-Sabi'*, March 28, 2013, http://www.youm7.com/story/0000/0/0/-/997005.

73. Sirma Yeğin and Marcelo Fernández-Lahore, "Boza: A Traditional Cereal-Based, Fermented Turkish Beverage," in *Handbook of Plant-Based Fermented Food and Beverage Technology*, 2nd ed., ed. Y. H. Hui et al. (Boca Raton, FL: CRC Press, 2012), 539.

74. Ahmet C. Gören et al., "Halal Food and Metrology," *International Second Halal and Healthy Food Congress*, November 7–10, 2013, Konya, Turkey, 103, http://www.helalvesaglikli.org/docs/kongre2013/sozlu/4.pdf (accessed December 18, 2016).

75. "Akman Boza Hakkında Herşey," http://akmanboza.com/akman-boza-faydalari; and "Vefa Bozası," http://www.vefa.com.tr/index.php?dil=tr&sayfa=boza (both accessed July 15, 2017).

76. Esra Kaymak, "9,000-Year-Old Turkish 'Energy Drink' Still on [*sic*] High Demand," *Anadolu Ajansı*, December 26, 2013, http://aa.com.tr/en/archive/9-000-year-old-turkish-energy-drink-still-on-high-demand/194843 (accessed December 17, 2016).

77. R. K. Robinson, "Snack Food of Dairy Origin," in *Snack Food*, ed. R. Gordon Booth (New York: Van Nostrand Reinhold, 1990), 171.

78. M. Wszolek et al., "Production of Kefir, Koumiss and Other Related Products," in *Fermented Milks*, ed. Adnan Y. Tamime (Oxford: Blackwell Science, 2006), 175.

79. See "Frequently Asked Questions," http://lifewaykefir.com/faq/ (accessed June 9, 2016).

80. Alcohol content in Turkish kefir, according to one study, was at 0.3 percent. Özgül Özdestan and Ali Üren, "Biogenic Amine Content of Kefir: A Fermented Dairy Product," *European Food Research and Technology* 231, no. 1 (2010): 102. Other sources indicate that kefir's alcohol content can range between 0.5 percent and 1.0 percent. See Robinson, "Snack Food of Dairy Origin," 171. Incidentally, kombucha is another slightly fermented brew that's been deemed as a cure-all for everything from digestive ailments and cancer to arthritis. A carbonated, tangy, and sweet beverage made from tea, sugar, and a bacteria-yeast mix, the drink originated in China but has been commercially produced in other countries over the past two decades. US sales were reported to be $600 million in 2015. Levels of alcohol in kombucha range from slightly below

0.5 percent to 1 percent (or more), especially if the drink is left to age unrefrigerated. However, Kombucha Brewers International, the industry's trade association, insists that the drink "is considered halal because it is non-inebriating and the ethanol serves as a preservative." See Kristen Wyatt, "As Kombucha Sales Boom, Makers Ask Feds for New Alcohol Test," Associated Press, October 12, 2015, http://www.businessinsider.com/ap-as-kombucha-sales-boom-makers-ask-feds-for-new-alcohol-test-2015-10; and "Kombucha FAQ," https://kombuchabrewers.org/resources/kombucha-faqs/ (accessed June 10, 2016).

81. In the 1930s, American rabbinic authorities questioned Coca-Cola's kosher status because the manufacturer's recipe, at the time, included animal-derived glycerin; the company eventually acquiesced and agreed to substitute glycerin derived from cottonseed. Horowitz, *Kosher USA*, ch. 2.

82. Peter Hockaday, "Coke, Pepsi Contain Some Alcohol, Study Says," June 28, 2012, http://blog.seattlepi.com/hottopics/2012/06/28/coke-pepsi-contain-some-alcohol-study-says/.

83. "Is Coke Halal?," https://www.coca-colaanswers.co.uk/en/qtile.html/ingredients/is-coke-halal-/ (accessed December 7, 2015).

84. "Unleafed: Is Coca-Cola Halal?," Halal Hub, http://www.halalhubusa.com/unleafed-cocacola/ (accessed December 7, 2015).

85. See Nazlida Muhamad, "Fatwa Rulings in Islam: A Malaysian Perspective on Their Role in Muslim Consumer Behavior," in *Handbook of Islamic Marketing*, ed. Özlem Sandıkcı and Gillian Rice (Cheltenham, UK: Edward Elgar, 2011), 50–51. See also Sue Chan, "The Muslim Cola Wars," February 7, 2003, Associated Press, http://www.cbsnews.com/news/the-muslim-cola-wars/ (accessed December 7, 2015).

86. Zamzam is the name of a holy and sacred well in Mecca that the Prophet Muhammad's family (the Banu Hashim) was charged with guarding. It is an important visitation site for Muslims making the annual pilgrimage or *hajj* to Mecca.

87. For the alleged ingredients of Coca-Cola, which may include nutmeg—a haram substance by some Muslim standards—see David W. Freeman, "'This American Life' Reveals Coca-Cola's Secret Recipe (Full Ingredient List)," *CBS News*, February 15, 2011, http://www.cbsnews.com/news/this-american-life-reveals-coca-colas-secret-recipe-full-ingredient-list/. For questions on halal compliance of Coca-Cola, Pepsi Cola, and Cola Turka on Turkish websites, see "Kolada Alkol Alarmı!," http://www.gimdes.org/kolada-alkol-alarmi.html (accessed July 14, 2017) and "Teşekkürler Ülker & Cola Turka," *ergonomik.com*, June 27, 2011, http://www.egonomik.com/2011/06/tesekkurler-ulker-cola-turka/.

88. See Sec. 169.175 Vanilla extract, *Code of Federal Regulations*, Title 21, vol. 2 (revised April 1, 2015), http://www.accessdata.fda.gov/scripts/cdrh/cfdocs/cfcfr/CFRSearch.cfm?fr=169.175 (accessed June 4, 2015).

89. Haider Khattak, "Vanilla Flavoring," *Halal Consumer Magazine: A Publication of the Islamic Food and Nutrition Council of America* 15 (Winter 2008): 17, http://www.ifanca.org/HCM/Halal percent20Consumer percent20Issue percent2015/hc_15.pdf.

90. "Majlis Fatwa Kebangsaan: Koleksi Fatwa Berkaitan Alkohol Dalam Makanan Dll" [English and Malaysian], http://www.al-ahkam.net/home/content/majlis-fatwa-kebangsaan-koleksi-fatwa-berkaitan-alkohol-dalam-makanan-dll (accessed June 4, 2016); see also Dzulkifly Mat Hashim, "Unraveling the Issue of Alcohol for the Halal Industry," http://www.hdcglobal.com/upload-web/cms-editor-files/b08c8a04-c946-4ebe-99b9-2492bd32fcfc/file/11%29%20En%20 Dzulkifli%20Mat%20Hashim%20-%20WHR2010_Unraveling%20the%20Issue%20of%20 Alcohol_Final.pdf (accessed June 4, 2016).

91. Gina Hames, *Alcohol in World History* (London: Routledge, 2012), 103, 105, 117, 119.

92. For a more personal perspective on the popularity of faux libations and nonalcoholic beer in the Islamic world, see British Muslim blogger and writer Shelina Janmohamed's view in ch. 3 ("You Had Me at Halal") of *Generation M: Young Muslims Changing the World*.

93. During this period, beer powerhouses like Anheuser-Busch invested millions of dollars in developing alcohol-removal equipment and in producing new, alternative beverages, such as ginger ale. Tomaš Branyik, "A Review of Methods of Low Alcohol and Alcohol-Free Beer Production," *Journal of Food Engineering* 108 (2012): 494; Philip H. Howard, "Too Big to Ale? Globalization and Consolidation in the Beer Industry," in *The Geography of Beer*, ed. Mark Patterson and Nancy Hoalst-Pullen (New York: Springer, 2014), 156; Bernice Kanner, "Brew News," *New York Magazine*, August 13, 1984, 12.

94. Glenn W. Schultz, "No Alcohol, No Problem," *Modern Brewery Age*, January 21, 1991, http://www.thefreelibrary.com/No+alcohol,+no+problem.-a010342267.

95. A 1984 *New York Magazine* article described attraction to these "healthier" products as follows: "No beer bellies here. The near-beers are lower in carbohydrates, salt, and sugar than regular beer and contain far fewer calories." Kanner, "Brew News," 12.

96. Kanner, "Brew News," 12.

97. The decree banning alcohol sales came after a Saudi prince became "involved in an alcohol related shooting after leaving the British embassy, which infuriated the King." See Chad Parker, "Transports of Progress: The Arabian American Oil Company and American Modernization in Saudi Arabia, 1945–1973" (PhD diss., Indiana University, 2008), 86–87. For more on home brewing among ARAMCO employees, see Loring M. Danforth, *Crossing the Kingdom: Portraits of Saudi Arabia* (Berkeley: University of California Press, 2016), 45–46.

98. Eunice Fried, "The Best in Brews," *Black Enterprise* (July 1990), 77; Dan Hayoun and Fadila Bakkar-LeTurq, "La bière 'halal,' choc ou rencontre des cultures?," *EHED: L'École des Hautes Études de la Décision*, March 12, 2012, http://www.ehed.fr/article-2/.

99. Steve Hindy, "Ancient Ales: The Past, Present, and Future of Middle Eastern Beer Brewing," August 27, 2015, *Foreign Affairs*, https://www.foreignaffairs.com/articles/middle-east/2015-08-27/ancient-ales (accessed December 19, 2016).

100. Hayoun and Bakkar-LeTurq, "La bière 'halal.'"

101. "Near Beer a Hit in Middle East," Associated Press, February 12, 2003.

102. Megan Wycoff, "The Brewer, His Halal Beer and a Potential Fortune," *Financial Times*, July 26, 2005.

103. At the time, the drink was produced much like others in its class: its manufacturer made real beer and then stripped it of its alcohol through a "vacuum distillation" process. Dan Berger, "It Began with Vacuum Distillation: How the Brewmaster Makes Non-Alcoholic Beer," *LA Times*, August 19, 1988.

104. The company also added new flavors. Like Moussy and other malt beverages targeting Muslim customers, most of these drinks are sweet and fruity (peach, apple, raspberry, lemon, fusion, and pomegranate); in terms of taste, they are less likely to compete with a plain non-alcoholic beer than with commercial soft drinks. "Saudi Arabia: Non-alcoholic Malt Beverage Barbican to Be Issued to Abroad Channels," *e-malt.com*, August 2, 2006, http://www.e-malt.com/NewsSrv.asp?Command=ArticleShow&ArticleID=8564&Template=IndustryNewsTemplate.htm.

105. "About Us," http://www.barbicanworld.com/en/about-company/ (accessed June 9, 2016). Since the nineteenth century, in various colonial and postcolonial societies, developing local beers signified an important part of the modernization and nation-building process, one that was often replete with Western-style advertisements that connoted masculinity

and chivalry. For more on this point, see Jeffrey M. Pilcher, "'Tastes like Horse Piss': Asian Encounters with European Beer," *Gastronomica: The Journal of Critical Food Studies* 16, no. 1 (2016): 32–33. Within the context of the Islamic world, see a broader discussion of these trends in Janmohamed, *Generation M*, ch. 3.

106. Amin Alkhatib, "Middle East and Africa: An Optimistic Stance for Non-Alcoholic Beer," November 8, 2013, http://blog.euromonitor.com/2013/11/middle-east-and-africa-an-optimistic-stance-for-non-alcoholic-beer.html.

107. "Egypt's Alcohol-Free Beer Conquers Arab Markets," *Agence France-Presse*, May 26, 2000; Abeer Allam, "Making Near Beer Acceptable in Near East," *New York Times*, January 4, 2003.

108. Adam Teeter, "The Non-Alcoholic Beer That Fueled American Pharoah's Triple Crown Victory," June 8, 2015, http://vinepair.com/wine-blog/the-non-alcoholic-beer-that-fueled-american-pharoahs-triple-crown-victory/; Allam, "Making Near Beer Acceptable in Near East."

109. One recent report indicated that Egypt's overall beer market is dominated by Al-Ahram's alcoholic beer Stella, which captured 37 percent of sales in 2014, followed by Birell at 14 percent. "Beer in Egypt," *Euromonitor*, June 2015, http://www.euromonitor.com/beer-in-egypt/report (accessed June 12, 2016).

110. "Sin-Free Ale: Non-alcoholic Beer Is Taking Off among Muslim Consumers," *Economist*, August 3, 2013. On nonalcoholic beer in Iran, see Shirazi, *Brand Islam*, 50, and on Palestinian beer producer Taybeh, see Anne Meneley, "Resistance Is Fertile!," *Gastronomica: The Journal of Critical Food Studies* 14, no. 4 (2014): 69–78.

111. "Supplier: We Didn't Say It's 'Halal Beer,'" *New Straits Times*, June 1, 2011, http://news.asiaone.com/News/AsiaOne+News/Malaysia/Story/A1Story20110601-281805.html. See also Shirazi, *Brand Islam*, 53–54.

112. JAKIM authorities declared, "Malt soft drinks like Barbican are allowed to be consumed by Muslims," since their alcohol content is "very low and not intoxicating." See "Malaysia: Malt Soft Drinks Halal for Muslims, Says National Fatwa Council," *Halal Focus,* July 26, 2011, http://halalfocus.net/malaysia-malt-soft-drinks-halal-for-muslims-says-national-fatwa-council/.

113. Suzann Audi, "Chocolate Liquor, Root Beer, Cooking Wine and Non-Alcoholic Beer—Are They Halal?," *Halal Consumer* 12 (Summer 2007): 30–31.

114. Johari Yap, "Halal Beer—Is There Such a Thing?" December 10, 2015, http://www.malaysiandigest.com/features/583721-halal-beer-is-there-such-a-thing.html.

115. That country's biggest beer producer, Efes Pilsen, introduced a local nonalcoholic beer in 2000 and again in 2011, but neither was successful.

116. In 2013, echoing stances in many other Muslim-majority countries, the Turkish parliament passed a law banning the sale of "nonalcoholic beers" under that name (preferring instead, the label "fermented malt beverages"). Riada Ašimović Akyol, "'Halal Beer' Flops in Turkey," *Al Monitor*, http://www.al-monitor.com/pulse/originals/2014/04/halal-beer-no-sale-turkey.html (accessed June 11, 2016). Though the indigenous Turkish brand Maltana (produced by Ülker) is stocked in several grocery store chains throughout Turkey, in that country one is hard-pressed to find blockbuster malt brews common in other parts of the Muslim world, like Barbican, Moussy, or Fayrouz.

117. "GİMDES'ten Alkolsüz Şarap ve Bira Açıklaması: O da Haram," April 10, 2015, http://www.haberler.com/gimdes-ten-alkolsuz-sarap-ve-bira-aciklamasi-7176680-haberi/.

118. Fre's wine was proven to contain 0.2 percent ABV, which an Arab industry expert deemed acceptable since it falls below the 0.5 percent maximum. The beverage is made through the traditional dealcoholization process—the mulling of regular wine followed by the removal of alcohol—a method that is controversial in the context of nonalcoholic beers but that has

seemingly been disregarded in discussions of nonalcoholic wine. "Fre of Alcohol," *ITP.net*, June 1, 2006, http://www.itp.net/493206-fre-of-alcohol.

119. "Gallery," http://www.halal-wine.com/halal-wine/products.asp, and "Lussory Red," http://www.lussorywines.com/red (both accessed June 11, 2016).

120. Anthony Bond, "Alcohol-Free Wine 'Doesn't Taste Like Wine' and Is Too Expensive, Say Experts," *Daily Mail Online*, November 23, 2012, http://www.dailymail.co.uk/news/article-2237241/Alcohol-free-wine-doesnt-taste-like-wine-expensive-say-experts.html; Rachel Hennessey, "Lussory's 24-Karat-Gold, Alcohol-Free Wine Is All the Rage in Dubai," *Forbes.com*, September 19, 2014, http://www.forbes.com/sites/rachelhennessey/2014/09/18/lussory-gold-24-carat-alcohol-free-halal-wine-dubai-lootah/#22ea642f68a3.

121. Bergeaud-Blackler, *Le marché halal*, 88–89. On the religious verification of industrial foods in the Jewish context, see Horowitz, *Kosher USA*, ch. 5.

CHAPTER 8

1. See Veronika E. Grimm, "The Good Things That Lay at Hand," in *Food: A History of Taste*, ed. Paul H. Freedman (Berkeley: University of California Press, 2007), 80, 97.

2. In Hebrew, the word for "good" is *tov* (טוב), which is often translated—according to its biblical usage—into "good" or "pleasing." The word shares similar letter roots (*t-o-b, t-u-b*), in essence, as the Arabic word tayyib (*t-y-b, t-a-b*), although in Hebrew, the letter "bet" can be vocalized as a "b" or a "v" sound, depending on certain grammatical factors. The authors would like to thank Jordan Rosenblum for his guidance on this point.

3. Benkheira, *Islam et interdits alimentaires*, 45.

4. Toshihiko Izutsu, *Ethico-Religious Concepts in the Qur'an* (1966; rpt., Montreal: McGill-Queen's University Press, 2002), 235. Also see Benkheira, *Islam et interdits alimentaires*, 45–46. For a more popular and broader look at what tayyib might mean to Muslims today, see Janmohamed, *Generation M*, 61–64.

5. Elsaid M. Badawi and Muhammad Abdel Haleem, "ط/ي/ب t-y-b," in Badawi and Haleem, *Dictionary of Qur'anic Usage*, Brill Online, 2013. Also, Benkheira, *Islam et interdits alimentaires*, 45–46.

6. Mohammad Hashim Kamali, *The Parameters of Ḥalāl and Ḥaram in Shari'ah and the Ḥalāl Industry* (Kuala Lumpur: International Institute of Advanced Islamic Studies, Malaysia, 2013), 6, http://www.academia.edu/7121321/The_Parameters_of_Halal_and_Haram_in_Shari_ah_and_the_Halal_Industry_-_Mohammad_Hashim_Kamali (accessed December 22, 2016).

7. Muhammad ibn Jarir al-Tabari, *Tafsir al-Tabari min Kitabihi Jami' al-Bayan 'an Ta'wil Ayat al-Qur'an*, ed. Bashar 'Awad Ma'ruf and 'Isam Faris al-Hirshani (Beirut: Mu'assasat al-Risala, 1994), 1:216, 1:463–464, 3:21; Isma'il ibn 'Umar ibn Kathir, *Tafsir al-Qur'an al-'Azim*, ed. Sami ibn Muhammad al-Salama, 2nd ed. (Riyadh: Dar Tayyiba li'l Nashr wa'l Tawzi', 1999), 1:273, 3:31–33; Abi Bakr Muhammad ibn 'Abdallah ibn al-'Arabi, *Ahkam al-Qur'an*, ed. Muhammad 'Abd al-Qadir 'Ata (Beirut: Dar al-Kutub al-'Ilmiyya, 2013), 2:32, 2:143; Mulla Muhammad ibn Murtada ibn Mahmud al-Kashani, *Tafsir al-Safi*, ed. Husayn al-A'lami (Tehran: Maktabat al-Sadr, 2000), 2:79–80; Izutsu, *Ethico-Religious Concepts in the Qur'an*, 235.

8. Al-Tabari, *Tafsir al-Tabari*, 3:508.

9. Ibn Kathir, *Tafsir al-Qur'an al-'Azim*, 3:31–33.

10. Ibn al-'Arabi, *Ahkam al-Qur'an*, 2:32; Ibn Kathir, *Tafsir al-Qur'an al-'Azim*, 3:488; Izutsu, *Ethico-Religious Concepts in the Qur'an*, 236. Also see, Benkheira, *Islam et interdits alimentaires*, 47 and 57.

11. The phrase is "tayyiban fa inahu ya'ni bihi: tahiran ghayr najis wa la muharram." See Al-Tabari, *Tafsir al-Tabari*, 1:458; Ibn Kathir, *Tafsir al-Qur'an al-'Azim*, 1:480–483.

12. Ibn Kathir, *Tafsir al-Qur'an al-'Azim*, 3:488.

13. Tayyib's flexible meaning are also mentioned in the writings of the famous eleventh-century Shafi'i jurist and statesman Abu al-Hasan al-Mawardi (d. 1058), who suggests that what is considered tayyib for one person might be seen as khabith for another, depending on each person's material needs. See Abu al-Hasan 'Ali Ibn Muhammad ibn Habib al-Mawardi, *Al-Hawi al-Kabir*, ed. 'Ali Muhammad 'Awad and 'Adil Ahmad 'Abd al-Mawjud (Beirut: Dar al-Kutub al-'Ilmiyya, 1994), 15:132–133.

14. Al-Tabari, *Tafsir al-Tabari*, 3:151–152; Ibn Kathir, *Tafsir al-Qur'an al-'Azim*, 3:169; Ibn al-'Arabi, *Ahkam al-Qur'an*, 2:143; Al-Kashani, *Tafsir al-Safi*, 2:79–80.

15. Al-Tabari, *Tafsir al-Tabari*, 1:216, 5:51; Ibn al-'Arabi, *Ahkam al-Qur'an*, 2:32; Al-Kashani, *Tafsir al-Safi*, 2:79–80; Ibn Kathir, *Tafsir al-Qur'an al-'Azim*, 5:97. Also see Benkheira, *Islam et interdits alimentaires*, 46.

16. Al-Tabari, *Tafsir al-Tabari*, 3:151. The exact phrase is "al-tayyibat al-ladhidhat allati tashtahiha al-nufus wa tamil ilayha al-qulub."

17. Al-Tabari, *Tafsir al-Tabari*, 4:564–565.

18. Nasrallah, *Annals of the Caliphs' Kitchens*, 579, 621.

19. Ibn Battuta, *Rihlat Ibn Battuta*, as cited and discussed in Megan H. Reid, *Law and Piety in Medieval Islam* (Cambridge: Cambridge University Press, 2013), 99; also see Reid, 114.

20. Mark R. Cohen, "Feeding the Poor and Clothing the Naked: The Cairo Geniza," *Journal of Interdisciplinary History* 35, no. 3 (2005): 410–411.

21. See Abu Dawud, *Sunan Abi Dawud*, 4:208–212; al-Bukhari, *Sahih al-Bukhari*, 3:1205 and 5:2238–2239. For a discussion of painless slaughter, see chapter 3.

22. Ingrid Mattson, "Eating in the Name of God," *Islamic Horizons* 39, no. 2 (2010): 22–25.

23. Noor Fatima Kareema Iqbal, "From Permissible to Wholesome: Situating Ḥalāl Organic Farms within the Sustainability Discourse," *Islamic Sciences* 13, no. 1 (2015): 52. Eco-halal or ethical halal can be compared to other eco-religious movements that have arisen especially in Western contexts, including the American-established "eco-kosher" movement (a term coined by Rabbi Zalman Schachter-Shalomi in the late 1970s and popularized by activist Andrew Waskow), eco-Sikh (an organization established in 2009 by the United Nations Development Program), and a historically diverse array of Christian-based groups that combine theological and ecological activism. See Dana Evan Kaplan, *Contemporary American Judaism* (New York: Columbia University Press, 2010), 86–87; Arthur Waskow, "And the Earth Is Filled with a Breath of Life," *Cross Currents* 47, no. 3 (1997): 348–363; and Antonia Blumberg, "Religious, Interfaith Environmental Organizations Put the Faith Back in Green Activism," *Huffington Post*, April 22, 2014, http://www.huffingtonpost.com/2014/04/22/religious-environmental-organization_n_5185400.html.

24. Ibrahim Abdul-Matin, *Green Deen: What Islam Teaches about Protecting the Planet* (San Francisco: Berrett-Koehler, 2010), 5. On the complex meaning of the term khalifa, see chapter 2.

25. Abdul-Matin, *Green Deen*, 47.

26. Abdul-Matin, *Green Deen*, 33–45.

27. Abdul-Matin, *Green Deen*, 143.

28. Abdul-Matin, *Green Deen*, 174.

29. "Our Intentions, Roots and Plans," Abraham Organics, http://www.organic-halal-meat.com/about_us.php (accessed May 28, 2016).

30. Athar Ahmad, "Halal Meat Consumers Urged to Consider Animal Welfare," *BBC News*, February 4, 2014, http://www.bbc.com/news/uk-england-oxfordshire-26020090; Carla Power, "Ethical, Organic, Safe: The Other Side of Halal Food," *The Guardian*, May 18, 2014, http://www.theguardian.com/lifeandstyle/2014/may/18/halal-food-uk-ethical-organic-safe.

31. Iqbal, "From Permissible to Wholesome," 51. Also see the perspective of Muhammad Ridha Payne, co-founder of the UK's Abraham Organics, as cited in Janmohamed, *Generation M*, 64.

32. Leah Koenig, "Reaping the Faith," *Gastronomica: The Journal of Food and Culture* 8, no. 1 (2008): 81–82.

33. Nadirah Z. Sabír, "Healthy + Halal + Humane," *Azizah* 6, no. 2 (2010): 69–72. Green Zabihah was also the name of one of these organic halal meat producers based in Virginia, but the company has gone out of business.

34. Abdul-Matin, *Green Deen*, 149.

35. "Our Story," Saffron Road, http://saffronroadfood.com/our-story/ (accessed January 14, 2017).

36. *State of the Global Islamic Economy 2016/2017 Report*, 37; and Jeff Green and Craig Giammona, "How Halal Food Became a $20 Billion Hit in America," *Bloomberg*, September 14, 2016, https://www.bloomberg.com/news/articles/2016-09-14/america-loves-muslim-food-so-much-for-a-clash-of-civilizations.

37. "Halal Butcher Promises 'Honest to God' Burgers," *CNN Money*, May 30, 2014, http://money.cnn.com/2014/05/30/smallbusiness/halal-honest-chops-butcher/index.html.

38. A discussion of some of these groups can be found in Md Saidul Islam, "Old Philosophy, New Movement: The Rise of the Islamic Ecological Paradigm in the Discourse of Environmentalism," *Nature and Culture* 7, no. 1 (2012): 83.

39. Manon Istasse, "Green Halal: How Does Halal Production Face Animal Suffering?," in Bergeaud-Blackler, Fischer, and Lever, *Halal Matters*, 133.

40. Istasse, "Green Halal," 133.

41. Cf. Yael Shemesh, "Vegetarian Ideology in Talmudic Literature and Traditional Biblical Exegesis," *Review of Rabbinic Judaism* 9, no. 1 (2006): 141.

42. Foltz, *Animals*, 121–122.

43. Qamar ul-Huda, "Sufism and Sufis: South Asia," in *Medieval Islamic Civilizations: An Encyclopedia*, ed. Josef W. Meri (New York: Routledge, 2006), 774.

44. Robert Brenton Betts, *The Druze* (New Haven, CT: Yale University Press, 1990), 37.

45. Basheer Ahmad Masri, *Animal Welfare in Islam* (Markfield, UK: Islamic Foundation, 2007); his work and position is well discussed in Ali, "Muslims and Meat-Eating," 275–276.

46. Masri, *Animal Welfare in Islam*, 87; Ali, "Muslims and Meat-Eating," 275.

47. On matters of animal welfare, the treatise "invite[s] Muslims to be the example for everyone else to follow." See Kristen Stilt, *Animal Welfare in Islamic Law* (Clinton, WA: Animal People, 2008), 8, http://animalpeopleforum.org/wp-content/uploads/2016/09/Animal-Welfare-in-Islamic-Law-EN.pdf (accessed December 24, 2016).

48. Shaykh Hamza Yusuf, "Fair Trade Commerce for a Better World," transcribed at http://shaykhhamza.com/transcript/RIS-2013-The-Devil's-Traps (accessed December 24, 2016); see also Ali, "Muslims and Meat-Eating," 272.

49. "Halal and Tayyib in the Here and Now," http://www.animalsinislam.com/islam-animal-rights/bismillah/, and "Clothing," http://www.animalsinislam.com/islam-animal-rights/clothing/ (both accessed December 23, 2016).

50. Mohamed Ghilan, "The Halal Bubble and the Sunnah Imperative to Go Vegan," Al-Madina Institute, May 16, 2016, http://almadinainstitute.org/blog/vegan-sunnah/.

51. "Resolution on Halal Status of GM Crops and Foods Adopted at Agri-biotech Workshop for Islamic Scholars," *International Service for the Acquisition of Agri-Biotech Applications*, http://www.isaaa.org/kc/cropbiotechupdate/article/default.asp?ID=7064 (accessed October 8, 2015). While this decree is consistent with the 2011 *SMIIC 1* and 2014 *GSO 2055* standards, it contradicted the Malaysian guidelines outlined in *MS1500:2009*, which stated that "food and drinks containing products and/or by-products of Genetically [*sic*] modified organisms (GMOs) . . . are not halal." See *MS 1500:2009*, 6.

52. Mohideen Abdul Kader, "Shock as GM Declared 'Halal,'" *Eco Islam*, no. 8 (June 2011): 1–2, http://www.ifees.org.uk/wp-content/uploads/2015/04/newsletter_EcoIslam8.pdf/.

53. Bergeaud-Blackler, *Le marché halal*, 181–186.

54. Golnaz Rezai et al., "Can Halal Be Sustainable? Study on Malaysian Consumers' Perspective," *Journal of Food Products Marketing* 21, no. 6 (2016): 654–655.

55. For the proponents of organic agriculture and animal farming, these are ethically superior forms of food production because they preserve natural resources and biodiversity, support animal health and welfare by providing animals access to the outdoors, and receive frequent on-site inspections by third parties and federal authorities. See http://www.usda.gov/wps/portal/usda/usdahome?contentidonly=true&contentid=organic-agriculture.html (accessed August 2, 2016).

56. Interview with an American Muslim family as cited in *State of the Global Islamic Economy 2014–15 Report*, 30, http://www.flandersinvestmentandtrade.com/export/sites/trade/files/news/342150121095027/342150121095027_1.pdf (accessed May 28, 2016).

57. Cited in *State of the Global Islamic Economy 2014–15 Report*, 29, 33–35.

58. John Ireland and Soha Abdollah Rajabzadeh, "UAE Consumer Concerns about Halal Products," *Journal of Islamic Marketing* 2, no. 3 (2011): 279 [274–283].

59. "Qatar to Curb Use of Fat in Fast Food," *Peninsula*, June 1, 2015. The 2014 GCC halal guideline, *GSO 2055*, insists on correct labeling. The document requires that product labels should contain "sources of actual ingredients" and "products containing fats, oils, meat derivatives or extracts such as gelatin or rennet." Labels should also indicate whether products contain genetically modified substances, additives, and "all kinds of fish with scales, shrimp and fish egg of fish with scales including their byproducts" (6–7). The Malaysian and OIC/SMIIC Standards contain similar requirements.

60. "Halal Audit Company: Trends and Developments," http://www.halalaudit.nl/content.php?ID=31 (accessed May 27, 2016).

61. *MS1500:2009*, 7.

62. *SMIIC-1*, 9. As noted in chapter 6, the emphasis on hygiene and health is more explicit in *MS 1500:2009* and *SMIIC-1*, than in the Gulf Standard. But the latter document also contains references to food hygiene and safety.

63. Abdul Raufu Ambali and Ahmad Naqiyuddin Bakar, "Ḥalāl Food and Products in Malaysia: People's Awareness and Policy Implications," *Intellectual Discourse* 21, no. 1 (2013): 15.

64. Marco Tieman, "Halal Diets," *Islamic and Civilisational Renewal* 7, no. 1 (2016): 128.

65. Tieman, "Halal Diets," 130.

66. Istasse, "Green Halal," 133.

67. Istasse, "Green Halal," 133; cf. Shemesh, "Vegetarian Ideology in Talmudic Literature," 159–161.

68. Istasse, "Green Halal," 133–134.

69. "3rd International Halal and Healthy Food Congress," October 30–31, 2015, Istanbul, Turkey, program at http://ihhfc.helalvesaglikli.org/en/section/technicalprogram (accessed May 27, 2016).

70. Cited in Koenig, "Reaping the Faith," 82.

71. Ali, "Muslims and Meat-Eating," 273.

72. Kamali, *Parameters of* Halal *and* Haram, 6, http://www.academia.edu/7121321/The_ Parameters_of_Halal_and_Haram_in_Shari_ah_and_the_Halal_Industry_-_Mohammad_ Hashim_Kamali (accessed December 24, 2016).

73. Kamali, "The *Halal* Industry," 601.

74. Ali, "Muslims and Meat-Eating," 274, 279–280. Similarly, Aaron Gross writes in the context of rabbinic traditions, "the practice of eating animals according to the laws of kashrut symbolically orders the cosmos—particularly the human being's place in it in relation to human and nonhuman animals." See Gross, *The Question of the Animal and Religion: Theoretical Stakes, Practical Implications* (New York: Columbia University Press, 2015), 25.

75. For more, see Gerd Marie Ådna, *Muhammad and the Formation of Sacrifice* (Frankfurt: Peter Lang, 2014); see also Quran 37:102–110.

76. Ian Copland, "What to Do about Cows? Princely versus British Approaches to a South Asian Dilemma," *Bulletin of the School of Oriental and African Studies* 68, no. 1 (2005): 59–76.

77. Parth M. N., "India Bans Sale of Cows for Slaughter, a Move Designed to Appease Conservative Hindus," *Los Angeles Times*, May 26, 2017, http://www.latimes.com/world/la-fg-india-cow-slaughter-20170526-story.html/. We thank Andrew Amstutz for calling our attention to this point.

78. Horowitz, *Kosher USA*, 246, 248, and "Conclusion," passim.

79. Ali, "Muslims and Meat-Eating," 279–280.

80. Ali, "Muslims and Meat-Eating," 273, 282.

81. To be clear, these market responses to ethical concerns address the critiques made by the proponents of animal rights and environmental sustainability and not those raised by anti-capitalist Muslim advocates, such as Tariq Ramadan. In fact, such efforts to marketize the former bolster Ramadan and others' critique of capitalism's use of halal for profit.

82. *State of the Global Islamic Economy 2014–15 Report*, 52.

83. International Trade Center, "From Niche to Mainstream: Halal Goes Global" (Geneva: International Trade Center, 2015), 12, www.intracen.org (accessed December 24, 2016).

84. "Halal and Vegan Drive Ethical Label Market with Annual Growth of over 5 Percent by 2020," *Business Wire*, http://www.businesswire.com/news/home/20160523006045/en/Halal-Vegan-Drive-Ethical-Label-Market-Annual (accessed May 27, 2016).

85. Andrew Linzey, *Why Animal Suffering Matters: Philosophy, Theology, and Practical Ethics* (New York: Oxford University Press, 2009), 67.

86. "50 Malaysian Companies to Showcase Halal Food Products in Cologne," *Malaysian News Agency*, October 8, 2015.

87. See http://www.mihas.com.my/about-mihas/ (accessed December 24, 2016).

88. "Vegetarian Halal?," Muslim Food Board Consultancy, Research, and Authentication of Products for Halal Use, http://www.tmfb.net/component/tags/tag/20-vegetarian-halal (accessed December 24, 2016).

89. Frans van Waarden, "Taste, Traditions, Transactions, and Trust: The Public and Private Regulation of Food," in *Where's the Beef? The Contested Governance of European Food Safety*, ed. David Vogel (Cambridge, MA: MIT Press, 2006), 54. See also "Stichting Halal Voeding en Voedsel," http://www.halal.nl/ (accessed October 21, 2015).

90. Cited in Florence Bergeaud-Blackler, "'Islamiser l'Alimentation': Marchés halal et dynamiques normatives," *Genèses* 4, no. 89 (2012): 77; and Bergeaud-Blackler, *Le marché halal*, 99.

91. "Halal Food Standards Too Complex—Nestlé," *Daily News Egypt*, October 19, 2014, http://www.dailynewsegypt.com/2015/10/19/interview-halal-food-standards-too-complex-nestle/.

92. See Nema Halal Quality, "Who We Are," http://nemahalal.com/ (accessed May 28, 2016).

93. Pınar, "Organik Süt," http://www.pinar.com.tr/urunler/detay/Organik-Sut/596/100/0 (accessed May 28, 2016).

94. Işıl Eğrikavuk, "Inspections Next Hurdle for Turkey's Growing Organic Market," *Hürriyet Daily News*, January 30, 2010, http://www.hurriyetdailynews.com/default.aspx?pageid=438&n=organic-market-needs-its-own-inspector-gadget-2010-01-29.

95. "Al Islami Revitalizes Halal Food Range for Children," *Middle East Company News*, November 27, 2007.

96. "20 Global Food Trends for 2015 and Beyond," *Arabian Gazette*, January 12, 2015, http://www.arabiangazette.com/gulfood-20-global-food-trends-20150112/.

97. *State of the Global Islamic Economy 2014–15 Report*, 59.

98. Maryam Attar, Khalil Lohi, and John Lever, "Remembering the Spirit of Halal: An Iranian Perspective," in Bergeaud-Blackler, Fischer, and Lever, *Halal Matters*, 67; and Abdul-Matin, *Green Deen*.

99. Bergeaud-Blackler, *Le marché halal*, 100.

CHAPTER 9

1. Foodies, to use one definition, are "people with a long-standing passion for eating and learning about food but who are not food professionals." See Kate Cairns, Josée Johnston, and Shyon Baumann, "Caring about Food: Doing Gender in the Foodie Kitchen," *Gender and Society* 24, no. 5 (2010): 592.

2. In this chapter, we use the phrase "halal cuisine" (without quotations, on the whole) with these tentative and ambiguous meanings in mind.

3. Ron Rosenbaum, "Anthony Bourdain's Theory on the Foodie Revolution," *Smithsonian Magazine*, July 2014, http://www.smithsonianmag.com/arts-culture/anthony-bourdains-theory-foodie-revolution-180951848/?no-ist.

4. Mukherjee, "Global Halal," 28.

5. Alison K. Smith, "National Cuisines," in *The Oxford Handbook of Food History*, ed. Jeffrey M. Pilcher (Oxford: Oxford University Press, 2012), 446.

6. These products can also include specific foodstuffs. Recently, legal disputes over the nationalist trademarking of certain foods and dishes have proliferated, as in the cases of hummus and "Greek yogurt," as well as feta, parmesan, and gorgonzola cheeses. See Mary Clare Jalonick, "Trade Battle Ferments over European Labels," Associated Press, March 11, 2014, http://www.pbs.org/newshour/rundown/trade-battle-ferments-european-cheeses/; Kat Sieniuc, "Chobani Says Greek Yogurt Labeling Suit Has No Case," *Law 360*, July 5, 2016, http://www.law360.com/articles/813942/chobani-says-greek-yogurt-labeling-suit-has-no-case; Ari Ariel, "The Hummus Wars," *Gastronomica: The Journal of Food and Culture* 12, no. 1 (2012): 34–42.

7. Mukherjee, "Global Halal," 65. Likewise, one could argue that other cooking styles based in dietary choices and/or religious restrictions rather than national boundaries—not only halal but also vegan, organic, gluten-free, local, and kosher—have begun to function, like ethnic cuisines, as imagined gastronomic totalities. See Sidney W. Mintz and Christine M. Du Bois, "The Anthropology of Food and Eating," *Annual Review of Anthropology* 31 (2002): 109.

8. See Roy, *Globalized Islam*, 271. Olivier Roy uses the term "neofundamentalism" to describe a globalized and "de-territorialized" Islam that arose in the late twentieth century, which emphasizes "the individualization of religion" (9) and which looks to religious norms as the "lowest

common denominators in defining a Muslim culture" (131). For Roy, therefore, phenomena such as the proliferation of halal food (particularly of halal "fast food") as well as the adoption of the head scarf offer potent symbols of comradery for Muslims, particularly youth, who are seeking to create a transnational, normative, and modern Muslim lifestyle-culture.

9. Roy, *Globalized Islam*, 131.

10. Linda Civitello, *Cuisine and Culture: A History of Food and People* (Hoboken, NJ: Wiley, 2004), 3.

11. Sierra Clark Burnett and Krishnendu Ray, "Sociology of Food," in *The Oxford Handbook of Food History*, ed. Pilcher, 142.

12. Priscilla Parkhurst Ferguson, "A Cultural Field in the Making: Gastronomy in 19th-Century France," *American Journal of Sociology* 104, no. 3 (1998): 600–601.

13. In a way, halal cuisine subsumes other ethno-nationalist markers (e.g., Pakistani, Turkish, Arab, Somali) within a broader religious framework and allows Muslims to reimagine their local identities in a generalized fashion.

14. Speaking broadly about current food-centrism, one critic has described modern food "obsessiveness" as a safer and more socially acceptable fixation on the last licit substance. Steven Poole, "Let's Start the Foodie Backlash," *The Guardian*, September 28, 2012, https://www.theguardian.com/books/2012/sep/28/lets-start-foodie-backlash.

15. "Festive Dishes from around the Muslim World," *Halal Consumer: A Publication of the Islamic Food and Nutrition Council of America* 13 (Winter 2007): 24–27, http://www.ifanca.org/HCM/Halal%20Consumer%20Issue%2013/hc_13.pdf.

16. "Great Grilling," *Halal Consumer: A Publication of the Islamic Food and Nutrition Council of America* 14 (Summer 2008): 14, http://www.ifanca.org/HCM/Halal%20Consumer%20Issue%2014/hc_14.pdf.

17. "Tantalising HMC Chops," *Halal Monitoring Committee Newsletter*, no. 2 (May 2004): http://www.halalhmc.org/userfiles/file/NewsLetters/issue2.pdf.

18. Culinary historians have long debated the origins of different foods in Italy. Clifford A. Wright has made a convincing case for the likelihood that Arabs brought pasta to Sicily and to the Italian Peninsula. See Wright, "The History of Macaroni," *CliffordAWright.com*, http://www.cliffordawright.com/caw/food/entries/display.php/id/50/ (accessed June 19, 2017).

19. Amy Riolo El-Tanbedawy, "Authentic Halal Pasta Sauces," *Azizah*, August 31, 2005.

20. "Make Your Own Halal Marshmallows," *Halal Foodie*, November 16, 2014, http://halalfoodie.ca/recipes/make-your-own-halal-marshmallows/.

21. "About HRJ," *Halal Recipes Japan*, http://www.halalrecipes.jp/en/introduction/; see also Alex Swerdloff, "Why Japanese Chefs Are Embracing Halal Food," *Munchies*, January 7, 2016, https://munchies.vice.com/en/articles/why-japanese-chefs-are-embracing-halal-food. Less focused on a single ethnic cuisine, the Singapore-based Halaal Recipes is home to hundreds of recipes submitted by registered users and boasts tens of thousands of followers on Facebook. Most of the site's recipes have a Chinese, South Asian, Southeast Asian, or Middle Eastern flavor, with dishes like Meat Curry, Kung Pao Meatballs, and Chicken Bunny Chow (a South African recipe with Indian roots). See http://halaal.recipes/ (accessed June 26, 2016).

22. Lucas Peterson, "Masterchef's Amanda Saab Is the First Woman in a Hijab on an American Cooking Show," *Eater.com*, May 21, 2015, http://www.eater.com/2015/5/21/8640161/masterchefs-amanda-saab-is-the-first-woman-in-a-hijab-on-an-american; see also "About," Amanda's Plate, http://amandasplate.com/about/ (accessed June 26, 2016).

23. Syeda Hasan, "'My Halal Kitchen' Blog Offers Creative Twist on Islamic Cuisine," *India.com*, September 24, 2014, at http://www.india.com/food-2/

my-halal-kitchen-blog-offers-creative-twist-on-islamic-cuisine-531263/ (accessed on June 26, 2016).

24. Kim Mikus, "Des Plaines Blogger Helps Muslims Follow Halal without Giving Up Taste," *Daily Herald*, September 8, 2009, http://prev.dailyherald.com/story/?id=318705.

25. See the websites "About My Halal Kitchen," http://myhalalkitchen.com/homepage/, and "About Yvonne," http://myhalalkitchen.com/homepage/about-yvonne-2/ (both accessed October 22, 2015).

26. "What Is Halal Cuisine?," My Halal Kitchen, http://myhalalkitchen.com/what-is-halal-cuisine/ (accessed December 26, 2016).

27. "My Halal Kitchen—Yvonne Maffei," Mad Mamluks podcast interview, April 4, 2016, http://themadmamluks.libsyn.com/.

28. Yvonne Maffei, *myhalalkitchen.com*, "Substitutes for Pork in Cooking," at http://myhalal-kitchen.com/substitutes-for-pork-in-cooking/; "Substitutes for Alcohol in Baking," at http://myhalalkitchen.com/substitutes-for-alcohol-in-baking/; and "Substitutes for Alcohol in Cooking," at http://myhalalkitchen.com/substitutes-for-alcohol-in-cooking/ (all accessed on July 27, 2017).

29. Yvonne Maffei, "How to Make French Cuisine Halal," My Halal Kitchen, http://myhalal-kitchen.com/tips-making-french-cuisine-halal/ (accessed June 24, 2016).

30. Maffei's conservative-pragmatic approach toward halal cooking, particularly her promotion of newly-available halal products, came through in a recent interview. Before the wider availability of halal foods, Maffei welcomed the use of certain kosher products (like chicken) but then noted that nowadays "seeing beautifully packaged halal chicken in the supermarket makes me feel so normal." Cited in Leah Koenig, "The Rise of Halal-Certified Food," *Tablet*, February 27, 2017, http://www.tabletmag.com/jewish-life-and-religion/223595/the-rise-of-halal-certified-food.

31. Mukherjee, "Global Halal," 24.

32. Paula M. Salvio, "Dishing It Out: Food Blogs and Post-Feminist Domesticity," *Gastronomica: The Journal of Food and Culture* 12, no. 3 (2012): 33, 38.

33. Bergeaud-Blackler, *Le marché halal*, 44–46 and 206–209. Following the work of various anthropologists and sociologists, Bergeaud-Blackler also notes that food rituals, specifically under women's management and as passed down from mothers to their children, can be one of the most effective forms of domestic religious instruction (47–48).

34. Historically in most places, and certainly in Islamic lands, men were the "masters of the professional kitchen" and women of the domestic kitchen. Rebecca Swenson, "Domestic Divo?," in *Food and Culture: A Reader*, 3rd ed., ed. Carole Counihan and Penny Van Esterik (New York: Routledge, 2013), 141.

35. As Elizabeth Fleitz maintains, cooking has become "one area where women are allowed full rein to compose and produce, without the previous limitations imposed on them by men and patriarchal forces." Elizabeth Fleitz, "Cooking Codes: Cookbook Discourses as Women's Rhetorical Practices," *Present Tense: A Journal of Rhetoric in Society* 1, no. 1 (2010): 3, http://www.presenttensejournal.org/wp-content/uploads/2010/07/Fleitz.pdf.

36. Arjun Appadurai, "How to Make a National Cuisine: Cookbooks in Contemporary India," *Society for the Comparative Study of Society and History* 30, no. 1 (1988): 4. For more on medieval Islamic cooking, see in general Lilia Zaouali, *Medieval Cuisines of the Islamic World: A Concise History with 174 Recipes*, trans. M. B. DeBevoise (Berkeley: University of California Press, 2009).

37. Corie Brown, "Publishing Trend for 2014: A New Demand for Eye-Catching Cookbooks," *Entrepreneur*, November 19, 2013, https://www.entrepreneur.com/article/229842.

38. Horowitz, *Kosher USA*, 85.

39. Laurence Roth, "Toward a Kashrut Nation in American Jewish Cookbooks, 1990–2000," *Shofar: An Interdisciplinary Journal of Jewish Studies* 28, no. 2 (2010): 72, 75.

40. Dining establishments and restaurants function similarly, as will be discussed in chapter 10.

41. Muslim Students' Association of the United States and Canada, *Muslim World Cook Book* (Brentwood, MD: International Graphics, 1973), 10–11.

42. Muslim Students' Association of the United States and Canada, *Muslim World Cook Book*, 52, 75.

43. Linda D. Delgado, *Halal Food, Fun, and Laughter* (Tempe, AZ: Muslim Writers, 2005), 1, as discussed in Johan Fischer, *The Halal Frontier: Muslim Consumers in a Globalized World* (New York: Palgrave Macmillan, 2011), 17–18.

44. Similarly, see the self-published Chef Yusuf, *Cooking the Islamic Way: Food in the Holy Qur'an and the Blessed Sunnah* (Lexington, KY: CreateSpace, 2010).

45. Paula Forbes, "The 30 Most Exciting Cookbooks of the Summer," Epicurious.com, May 27, 2016, http://www.epicurious.com/expert-advice/cookbook-preview-summer-2016-article.

46. See also Fischer, *The Halal Frontier*, 17–18.

47. Yvonne Maffei, *My Halal Kitchen: Global Recipes, Cooking Tips, and Lifestyle Inspiration* (Chicago: Surrey Books, 2016), 24–25.

48. Maffei, *My Halal Kitchen*, xii.

49. Maffei, *My Halal Kitchen*, 46–47.

50. Maffei, *My Halal Kitchen*, 104.

51. Maffei, *My Halal Kitchen*, 133.

52. Defne Karaosmanoğlu, "Cooking the Past: The Revival of Ottoman Cuisine" (Ph.D. diss., McGill University, 2006), 83–84.

53. Emre Çetin, "Islamic Lifestyle and Emine Beder's TV Cookery Show Kitchen Love," *European Journal of Cultural Studies* 20, no. 4 (2015): 4–5.

54. Çetin, "Islamic Lifestyle and Emine Beder's TV Cookery Show Kitchen Love," 7.

55. Çetin, "Islamic Lifestyle and Emine Beder's TV Cookery Show Kitchen Love," 11.

56. Tahira Yaqoob, "When Muslims Are Faced with Haram Foods," *The National*, March 11, 2014, http://www.thenational.ae/lifestyle/food/when-muslims-are-faced-with-haram-foods.

57. Lara Anderson and Heather Benbow, "Are We 'Foodies' or Food Phobic?," *The Age*, November 20, 2014, http://www.theage.com.au/comment/are-we-foodies-or-food-phobic-20141119-11pmb6.html; and Tazin Abdullah, "Amina Elshafei: MasterChef of Halal Proportions," *Aquila Style: Modern Muslim Living*, August 22, 2013, http://www.aquila-style.com/focus-points/mightymuslimah/amina-elshafei-masterchef-of-halal-proportions/43933/.

58. Samantha Balaton-Chrimes, "Should MasterChef Have Asked a Muslim to Cook Pork?," *Sydney Morning Herald*, July 19, 2013, http://www.smh.com.au/entertainment/masterchef/should-masterchef-have-asked-a-muslim-to-cook-pork-20130718-2q74m.html.

59. Lisa Twang, "British Bake Off Champion Proud of Her Islam," *muslimvillage.com*, March 19, 2016, http://muslimvillage.com/2016/03/19/117442/british-bake-off-champion-proud-of-her-islam/; "The Queen's Orange Drizzle Birthday Cake Made by Bake Off's Nadiya Hussain," *Telegraph*, April 21, 2016, http://www.telegraph.co.uk/food-and-drink/news/the-queens-90th-birthday-cake-made-by-bake-offs-nadiya-hussain/.

60. "Cocina Halal TV," https://www.youtube.com/channel/UCzoA8gzYub0fJqz4BAs9RiQ (accessed November 24, 2017).

61. "Halal Wild Venison Hunting—Gordon Ramsay," *The F Word*, March 3, 2011, https://www.youtube.com/watch?v=q_Sdj_PK3I8.

62. Conrad Hackett, "5 Facts about the Muslim Population in Europe," Pew Research Center, July 19, 2016, http://www.pewresearch.org/fact-tank/2016/07/19/5-facts-about-the-muslim-population-in-europe/.

63. Nicole Beth Wallenbrock, "'Almost But Not Quite Eating Pork: Culinary Nationalism and Islamic Difference in Millennial French Comedies," *Performing Islam* 4, no. 2 (2015): 116–117.

64. Sarah E. Robinson, "Refreshing the Concept of Halal Meat: Resistance and Religiosity in Chicago's Taqwa Eco-Food Cooperative," in *Religion, Food, and Eating in North America*, ed. Benjamin E. Zeller et al. (New York: Columbia University Press, 2014), 275–276.

65. Suad Joseph and Benjamin D'Harlingue, "Arab Americans and Muslim Americans in the *New York Times*, before and after 9/11," in *Race and Arab Americans before and after 9/11: From Invisible Citizens to Visible Subjects*, ed. Amaney Jamal and Nadine Naber (Syracuse, NY: Syracuse University Press, 2008), 247.

CHAPTER 10

1. Kathryn Schulz, "Citizen Khan," *New Yorker*, June 6 and 13, 2016.

2. Johan Fischer, "Feeding Secularism: Consuming Halal among the Malays in London," *Diaspora: A Journal of Transnational Studies* 14, nos. 2/3 (2005): 292.

3. Kamaludeen Mohamed Nasir and Alexius A. Pereira, "Defensive Dining: Notes on Public Dining Experiences in Singapore," *Contemporary Islam* 2, no. 1 (2008): 68.

4. Several Chinese Muslim leaders have requested more rigorous government regulations for halal food and dining establishments, and in 2002 the Ethnic Affairs Committee of the National People's Congress was tasked to write new legislation addressing this "reasonable and necessary" matter. But in April 2016 the legislative project was dismissed, at least for now: it was said to violate "the principle of separation of State and religion." See "Halal Food Law Dropped from China's 2016 Legislation Plan," *Indo Asian News Service English*, April 18, 2016.

5. For a video survey of halal street food among the Hui in Lanzhou, see Food Ranger, "Muslim Chinese Street Food Tour in Islamic China," https://www.youtube.com/watch?v=ETkZpJcZhkI (accessed December 29, 2016). For more on halal food and the Chinese Hui identity, see Yukari Sai and Johan Fischer, "Muslim Food Consumption in China: Between Qingzhen and Halal," in Bergeaud-Blackler, Fischer, and Lever, *Halal Matters*, 160–174.

6. Tove Danovich, "Street Meat: The Rise of NYC's Halal Cart Culture," *Eater*, July 10, 2015, http://www.eater.com/2015/7/10/8924449/halal-cart-street-food-meat-nyc-cheap-eats.

7. Danovich, "Street Meat: The Rise of NYC's Halal Cart Culture."

8. Ina Yalof, *Food and the City* (New York: Putnam, 2016), 41; Danovich, "Street Meat: The Rise of NYC's Halal Cart Culture."

9. "What Is American Halal Food," Halal Guys, http://thehalalguys.com/american-halal/ (accessed July 4, 2016).

10. "How This Egyptian Food Cart Has Rocked New York City," *Daily News Egypt*, February 15, 2015, http://egyptianstreets.com/2015/02/15/how-this-egyptian-food-cart-has-rocked-new-york-city/.

11. Jason Daley, "How a NY Food Cart Is Becoming an International Brick-and-Mortar Chain," *Entrepreneur*, April 22, 2015, https://www.entrepreneur.com/article/244620.

12. Saqib Shafi, "Is The Halal Guys Really Halal and Is It Worth the Hype?," *Muslim Eater* (blog), November 9, 2015, http://muslimeater.com/2015/11/09/is-the-halal-guys-really-halal-is-it-worth-the-hype/.

13. Fred Searle, "From Berlin to the World—the Döner Kebab," *The Local*, October 31, 2013, https://www.thelocal.de/20131031/doner-kebab-inventor-kadir-nurman-dies;

Dan Gentile, "The Story of Doner Kebab: The World's Most Popular Spitted Meat," *Thrillist*, March 27, 2014, https://www.thrillist.com/eat/nation/the-history-of-donor-kebab-shwarma-gyros-and-more-thrillist-nation.

14. Spread by "transnational entrepreneurs," döner kebab is also quite popular throughout other parts of Europe, particularly in France. French scholar Pierre Raffard refers to its prominence in that country as a form of "cheap exoticism" and "fetishism" of Turkish/Oriental culture. As cited in Delphine Roucaute, "Au kebab, on mange turc sans manger turc," *LeMonde.fr*, October 11, 2012, at http://www.lemonde.fr/planete/article/2012/10/11/au-kebab-on-mange-turc-sans-manger-turc_1772518_3244.html#BEdg4Z4sJhosrS6r.99.

15. See Marin Möhring, "*Döner Kebab* and West German Consumer (Multi-)Cultures," in *Hybrid Cultures—Nervous States: Britain and Germany in a (Post) Colonial World*, ed. Ulrike Lindner, Marin Möhring, Mark Stein, and Silke Stroh (Amsterdam: Rodopi, 2010), 159–160.

16. David Crossland, "Neo-Nazis behind 'Doner Killings' as German Security Services under Fire," *The National*, November 16, 2011, http://www.thenational.ae/news/world/europe/neo-nazis-behind-doner-killings-as-german-security-services-under-fire. On "kebabaphobia" by right-wing groups in France, see Elaine Sciolino, "Kebabs as a Political Statement in France," *New York Times*, December 24, 2014.

17. In the United Kingdom, a 2009 study conducted of different döner meats revealed that some vendors were mixing in pork and chicken with lamb and beef. The study also pointed out that this new "staple of British takeaways" was laden with fat and salt, "enough to give you a heart attack." James Meikle, "Doner Kebabs Contain 'Shocking' Levels of Fat, Salt and Even Pork," *The Guardian*, January 27, 2009, https://www.theguardian.com/uk/2009/jan/27/doner-kebabs-fat-salt-pork.

18. Petra Kuppinger, "A Neighborhood Shopping Street and the Making of Urban Cultures and Economies in Germany," *City and Community* 13, no. 2 (2014), 151.

19. "World's First Döner Kebab Franchise Success Continues in Dubai," *UAE Government News*, May 27, 2013.

20. Germany has also become a major exporter of döner meat; the bulk of its sales go to France and Poland. James Angelos, "There's Nothing More German than a Big, Fat Juicy Döner Kebab," *Wall Street Journal*, April 18, 2012, http://www.wsj.com/articles/SB10001424052702304432704577350194262835880.

21. Mukherjee, "Global Halal," 58.

22. Olivier Roy suggests that for Muslim "neofundamentalists," the hamburger—one of the most iconic symbols of American "cultural hegemony"—can be deemed acceptable or "neutral" as long as it is halal. See Roy, *Globalized Islam*, 271.

23. "Quick. Le fast-food purement halal fait polémique," *Le Télégramme*, February 18, 2010, http://www.letelegramme.fr/ig/generales/france-monde/france/quick-le-fast-food-purement-halal-fait-polemique-18-02-2010-789015.php#r8sKU6Lf68ubCbrE.99; "Burger King France avale Quick, conversion des restaurants dès la fin du premier semestre 2016," *Nord Pas-de-Calais*, December 18, 2015, http://france3-regions.francetvinfo.fr/nord-pas-de-calais/burger-king-france-avale-quick-conversion-des-restaurants-des-la-fin-du-premier-semestre-2016-887753.html. In 2014, a similar controversy erupted in the United Kingdom when the global fast-food chain Subway decided to remove ham and bacon from its menus in two hundred stores and to serve "halal-only" meat in most of those branches. Subway clarified, however, that its halal meat comes from prestunned animals, a practice that's frowned upon by many Muslims. See Sean Poulter, "Subway Removes Ham and Bacon from Nearly 200 Stores and Offers Halal Meat Only after 'Strong Demand' from Muslims," *Daily Mail Online*, April 30, 2014, http://www.dailymail.

co.uk/news/article-2616576/Subway-removes-ham-pork-nearly-200-stores-strong-demand-Muslims-eat-Halal-meat.html#ixzz4EDgXFQ16.

24. Eleanor Beardsley, "French Muslims Ease Cultural Tensions with French-Halal Food," *The Salt* (NPR), April 2, 2012, http://www.npr.org/sections/thesalt/2012/03/30/149718871/french-muslims-ease-cultural-tensions-with-french-halal-food.

25. Beardsley, "French Muslims Ease Cultural Tensions with French-Halal Food."

26. "Qui sommes nous?," http://ecolecuisine-halal.com/content/4-a-propos (accessed July 5, 2016).

27. Mukherjee, "Global Halal," 25.

28. Anita Elash, "Halal Restaurants Spark a New Kind of French Revolution," *Globe and Mail*, July 26, 2010, http://www.theglobeandmail.com/life/halal-restaurants-spark-a-new-kind-of-french-revolution/article1376074/.

29. For more, see in general Nor-Zafir, "Establishing Shariah-Compliance [*sic*] Hotel Characteristics."

30. See "Sushi," *Spotlight Halal Magazine*, January 25, 2010, http://spotlighthalal.blogspot.com/2009/01/spotlight-halal-sushi.html.

31. "'Halal' Sushi Crops Up as Japanese Restaurants Woo Muslims," *Kyodo News*, February 7, 2006.

32. It recently became known that the state had long subjected all Japanese Muslims to an extensive form of profiling and surveillance and that monitoring halal restaurants was one way of shadowing this community. Jarni Blakkarly, "Shadow of Surveillance Looms over Japan's Muslims," *Japan Times*, July 13, 2016, http://www.japantimes.co.jp/community/2016/07/13/issues/shadow-surveillance-looms-japans-muslims/#.WGVMCHrGDaI.

33. Alex Swerdloff, "Why Japanese Chefs Are Embracing Halal Food," *Munchies*, January 7, 2016, https://munchies.vice.com/en/articles/why-japanese-chefs-are-embracing-halal-food.

34. Swerdloff, "Why Japanese Chefs Are Embracing Halal Food."

35. Masami Ito, "Learning to Embrace the Halal Industry," *Japan Times*, February 27, 2016.

36. "Malaysia Offers to Become Advisor to Japan's Halal Industry," *New Straits Times*, November 17, 2016, http://www.nst.com.my/news/2016/11/189340/malaysia-offers-become-advisor-japans-halal-industry.

37. "S. Korea Encourages Restaurants to Serve Halal Food to Boost Muslim Tourists," *Daily Sabah*, April 7, 2016, http://www.dailysabah.com/asia/2016/04/07/s-korea-encourages-restaurants-to-serve-halal-food-to-boost-muslim-tourists.

38. Mukherjee, "Global Halal," 27.

39. South Korea, incidentally, established a Korean Institute of Halal Industry in 2014 (with the help of Malaysia's JAKIM) in order to develop a Korean National Halal Food Standard and to supervise all processes of food certification. *State of the Global Islamic Economy 2016/2017 Report*, 39.

40. Dallen J. Timothy and Amos S. Ron, "Religious Heritage, Spiritual Ailment and Food for the Soul," in *Heritage Cuisines: Traditions, Identities and Tourism*, ed. Dallen J. Timothy (London: Routledge: 2016), 113–114.

41. Sai and Fischer, "Muslim Food Consumption in China," 169.

42. "Our Story," Zabihah, http://www.zabihah.com/com/about (accessed on July 7, 2016). In the United States, some sites are using video reviews to promote various restaurants. See, for instance, "Sameer's Eats" at http://www.sameerseats.com/. There is also a growing array of halal online meal and takeout delivery platforms particularly in non-Muslim majority settings. These

include HalalEat (the United Kingdom), Halalonclick (Singapore), and HalalEda.me (Russia). And some websites even help diners make meal reservations, such as the Halal Dining Club in the United Kingdom. See *State of the Global Islamic Economy 2016/2017 Report*, 24, 40.

43. Fazli Ibrahim, "Airline Caterers Learn Proper Way to Prepare," *Business Times*, October 4, 2002.

44. Tomohiro Osaki, "Airports Eager to Cater to Muslims' Needs," *Japan Times*, March 31, 2014; Charmaine Fernz, "Airlines Look to Boost Halal-Certified Food," May 15, 2016, *Travel Daily*, http://www.traveldailymedia.com/236394/airlines-look-to-boost-halal-certified-food/.

45. Mahomed Battour et al., "The Impact of Destination Attributes on Muslim Tourist's Choice," *International Journal of Tourism Research* 13, no. 6 (2011): 535.

46. Mary Atkinson, "'Muslim' Meals Could Be Used to Profile Passengers, Airline Tells Authorities," *Middle East Eye*, December 14, 2016, http://www.middleeasteye.net/news/use-muslim-meal-choices-screen-passengers-airlines-advise-border-agencies-162557171.

47. "Mount Holyoke College to Celebrate Opening of Kosher/Halal Dining Hall," *Mountholyoke. edu*, September 10, 2001, https://www.mtholyoke.edu/media/mount-holyoke-college-celebrate-opening-kosher/halal-dining-hall/.

48. Marialisa Calta, "Pleasing the Pious Palate at Dartmouth: A Cafeteria Caters to Specialized Religious Diets with Zeal; Purple Utensils for Halal," *Wall Street Journal*, March 19, 2002.

49. Calta, "Pleasing the Pious Palate at Dartmouth."

50. Katherine Oh, "Halal Food Now Available in Dining Halls," *Daily Princetonian*, October 14, 2014, http://dailyprincetonian.com/news/2014/10/halal-food-now-available-in-dining-halls/.

51. Conrad Hackett, "5 Facts about the Muslim Population in Europe," *Pew Research Center*, November 17, 2015, http://www.pewresearch.org/fact-tank/2015/11/17/5-facts-about-the-muslim-population-in-europe/.

52. Nick Sharpe, "Halal Food Remains off the Menus," *South Wales Echo*, July 30, 2004.

53. Andrew Buckwell, "Fury at Schools' Halal Meals for All," *Mail on Sunday*, December 17, 2006.

54. James Meikle, "What exactly does the halal method of animal slaughter involve?," *The Guardian*, May 8, 2014, https://www.theguardian.com/lifeandstyle/2014/may/08/what-does-halal-method-animal-slaughter-involve.

55. Mukherjee, "Global Halal," 32. In Egypt, for example, Muslim politicians, religious leaders, and media have long maligned and attacked Coptic Christians for raising and eating pork. See Mariz Tadros, "Scapepigging: H1N1 Influence in Egypt," in *Epidemics: Science, Governments, and Social Justice*, ed. Melissa Leach and Sarah Dry (London: Routledge, 2010), 213–238.

56. Sean Poulter, "One of Britain's Largest Halal Slaughterhouses Is under Investigation over Allegations of Animal Cruelty," *Daily Mail Online*, April 7, 2017, http://www.dailymail.co.uk/news/article-4391914/Halal-slaughterhouse-investigated-animal-cruelty.html/.

57. Mukherjee, "Global Halal," 50.

58. "France's Le Pen: Ban Non-pork Meals in Schools," *Telegraph*, April 5, 2014; Ian Jack, "The Row over Pork Comes as a Surprise in France, Where Couscous Is a Favourite Food," *The Guardian*, October 19, 2015; Elizabeth Bryant, "French Court Rules School Lunches May Include Pork; Muslims Alarmed," *Religion News Service*, August 13, 2015, http://religionnews.com/2015/08/13/french-court-rules-school-lunches-may-include-pork-muslims-alarmed/. For more discussion of the French context, see Bergeaud-Blackler, *Le marché halal*, 211–212 and 221–226.

59. Deena Shanker, "Politicians Insist That Making Pork Mandatory in Danish City's Schools Is Not 'Harassment of Muslims,'" *Quartz*, January 22, 2016, http://qz.com/600836/politicians-insist-that-making-pork-mandatory-in-danish-citys-schools-is-not-harassment-of-muslims/.

60. Dan Bilefsky, "Mandatory Pork: Menu Rule in Denmark Opens New Front in Immigration Debate," *New York Times*, January 21, 2016.

61. Stefan Voss, "Merkel: Germany Should Not Change Food Culture for Muslim Migrants," *DPA International*, July 9, 2016; Rebecca Perring, "Germany Bans Sausages: Pork Banned in Cafes and Schools to 'Not Offend Refugees,'" *Express* (Online), March 6, 2016, http://www.express. co.uk/news/world/650246/Germany-bans-pork-cafes-schools-offending-Muslim-migrants.

62. "Singapore Muslim Leaders Oppose School's Bid to Ban Non-halal Food," *BBC Monitoring Asia Pacific*, February 5, 2008.

63. See Bergeaud-Blackler, *Le marché halal*, 148. The five pillars of Islam are the testimony of faith, prayer, giving alms, fasting the month of Ramadan, and the pilgrimage to Mecca. For the original study which cites these figures, see Hakim El Karoui, *Un islam français est possible: Rapport septembre 2016*, developed and produced by Institut Montaigne, 32, http://www. institutmontaigne.org/res/files/publications/rapport-un-islam-francais-est_-possible.pdf (accessed September 29, 2017).

64. William J. Chambliss, *Key Issues in Crime and Punishment*, vol. 4 (Thousand Oaks, CA: Sage, 2011), 252.

65. Kenneth L. Marcus, "Jailhouse Islamophobia: Anti-Muslim Discrimination in American Prisons," *Race and Social Problems* 1, no. 1 (2009): 37.

66. "*Williams v. Morton*," *FindLaw*, September 9, 2003, http://caselaw.findlaw.com/us-3rd-circuit/1371033.html.

67. See Marcus, "Jailhouse Islamophobia," 37, especially n. 22, which lists many such cases.

68. Juli S. Charkes, "Muslim Prisoners Win Right to Diet Equality," *New York Times*, April 6, 2008.

69. "U.S. Muslim Inmates Sue over Meal Preparation," *CBS News*, October 3, 2011, http:// www.cbsnews.com/news/us-muslim-inmates-sue-over-meal-preparation/. Incidentally, Awkal's execution was reversed in 2013 by the Ohio Supreme Court, which ruled he was mentally incompetent.

70. Although Ohio had decided that pork meals would no longer be served in its prisons, the fact that the meat served was non-zabiha still concerned the plaintiffs. It also came to light that Ohio prisons accommodated kosher dietary provisions and spent—at that time—between $3.50 and $7 on each kosher meal (as compared to the regular cost of $1.70). For more, see "U.S. Muslim Inmates Sue over Meal Preparation." Also, while this observation invites further study, there are probably fewer Jewish inmates in US prisons than Muslims, and the question of cost-effectiveness continues to be cited as a deterrent for more fully modifying prison menus.

71. Andrew Welsh-Higgins, "Prisons' New Ban on Pork Draws Ire of Ohio Producers," *Columbus Dispatch*, October 5, 2011; Lisa Rein, "Finally, the Government Has Decided to Eliminate Pork—from the Menu in Federal Prisons," *Washington Post*, October 9, 2015, and "After Firestorm, Pork Roast Is Back on the Menu at Federal Prisons," *Washington Post*, October 16, 2015.

72. See "Charter of Fundamental Rights of the European Union," http://eur-lex.europa.eu/ legal-content/EN/TXT/?uri=CELEX:12012P/TXT (accessed December 31, 2016).

73. James A. Beckford, "Muslims in the Prisons of Britain and France," *Journal of Contemporary European Studies* 13, no. 3 (2005): 292. These suspicions came true when in 2013, pork DNA and other non-halal animal DNA were discovered in pies and pastries supplied to UK prisoners from a halal-certified caterer. The supplier was suspended, the UK Department of Justice issued an apology, and the Food Standards Agency conducted an investigation into the contamination. See Lucy Crossley, "Halal Pies and Pasties Given to Muslim Prisoners Found

to Contain Pork in Latest Meat Contamination Scandal," *Daily Mail Online*, February 2, 2013, http://www.dailymail.co.uk/news/article-2272304/Halal-pies-pasties-given-Muslim-prisoners-contain-PORK-latest-meat-contamination-scandal.html.

74. Judith Duffy, "Convicts Claim to Be Muslims in Prison Scam," *Scottish Express*, May 9, 2011; Lewis Pennock, "This Is Bristol Prison's Christmas Dinner Menu—Featuring Halal Chicken," *Bristol Post*, December 21, 2016, http://www.bristolpost.co.uk/this-is-bristol-prison-s-christmas-day-food-menu-8211-featuring-halal-chicken/story-29997808-detail/story.html#6c4HopI7LjrF3y4F.99.

75. Christopher de Bellaigue, "Are French Prisons 'Finishing Schools' for Terrorism?," *The Guardian*, March 18, 2016.

76. Craig S. Smith, "Islam in Jail: Europe's Neglect Breeds Angry Radicals," *New York Times*, December 8, 2004.

77. "Repas halal en prison: Le pourvoi d'un détenu rejeté par le Conseil d'État," *20 Minutes*, February 10, 2016, http://www.20minutes.fr/lyon/1784331-20160210-repas-halal-prison-pourvoi-detenu-rejete-conseil-etat. Also see Bergeaud-Blackler, *Le marché halal*, 229–232.

78. Smith, "Islam in Jail: Europe's Neglect Breeds Angry Radicals."

79. Natalie Whittle, "The Rise of Britain's Halal Foodies," *Financial Times*, March 12, 2014; Carina Perkins, "Haloodies Wins Sainsbury's and Tesco Listings for Halal Chicken," *Grocer*, November 21, 2016, http://www.thegrocer.co.uk/buying-and-supplying/categories/meat/haloodies-wins-sainsburys-and-tesco-listings-for-halal-chicken/545133.article. Kauser and Khawaja were prominently featured in a recent Islamic marketing report, where their Haloodie brand was touted as a major success story. See *State of the Global Islamic Economy 2016/2017 Report*, 46–48.

80. Haroon Siddique, "Haloodie Heaven: The Halal Food Festival Opens in London," *The Guardian*, September 27, 2013, http://www.theguardian.com/lifeandstyle/2013/sep/27/halal-food-festival-london.

81. "Halal La Carte," *Economist*, July 5, 2014.

82. Bergeaud-Blackler, *Le marché halal*, 92–93.

CONCLUSION

1. *State of the Global Islamic Economy 2016/2017 Report*, 4 and 22.

2. *State of the Global Islamic Economy 2016/2017 Report*, 12–13.

3. See the 2015 Pew Global Attitudes survey, which revealed that 83 percent of respondents from Muslim-majority countries considered religion "very important in their lives." Cited in *State of the Global Islamic Economy 2016/2017 Report*, 12–13, but see also 16–17. For more, refer to Hussaini, "Halal Haram Lists," and Bonne et al., "Determinants of Halal Meat Consumption in France."

4. Mukherjee, "Global Halal," 62–64.

5. Patrick Haenni, *L'Islam de marché: L'autre révolution conservatrice* (Paris: Seuil, 2005), 59–60, as cited in Mukherjee, "Global Halal," 54.

6. *State of the Global Islamic Economy 2016/2017 Report*, 37, 44, 46.

7. Susan Labadi, "'Clean Meat': Is Lab-Grown Chicken and Duck Halal?," *Salaam Gateway*, March 26, 2017, https://www.salaamgateway.com/en/food/story/clean_meat_is_labgrown_chicken_and_duck_halal-salaam26032017192911/.

8. One major exception to this trend might be the relative flexibility toward stunned slaughter, which is, as discussed in chapter 3, primarily based on market considerations.

9. Roy, *Globalized Islam*, 271.

10. Gabriel Said Reynolds, "The Sufi Approach to Food: A Case Study of Adab," *Muslim World* 90, nos. 1/2 (2000): 198.

11. Daniel Winchester, "Embodying the Faith: Religious Practice and the Making of a Muslim Moral Habitus," *Social Forces* 86, no. 4 (2008): 1769.

12. Mukherjee, "Global Halal," 40.

13. *State of the Global Islamic Economy 2016/2017 Report*, 15, 50, 170.

14. Frans van Waarden and Robin van Dalen, "Halal and the Moral Construction of Quality: How Religious Norms Turn a Mass Product in a Singularity," in *Constructing Quality: The Classification of Goods in Markets*, ed. Jens Beckert and Christine Musselin (Oxford: Oxford University Press, 2013), 204.

BIBLIOGRAPHY

PRIMARY SOURCES

Batmanglij, Najmieh. *Food of Life: Ancient Persian and Modern Iranian Cooking and Ceremonies.* 25th anniversary ed. London: Mage, 2011.

Borek, Abdullah. "Smoking and Religion: The Position of Islam towards Smoking." Transcript of Presentation at the INFOTAB Workshop in Malaga on October 19, 1988. http://industrydocuments.library.ucsf.edu/tobacco/docs/njyp0193.

British American Tobacco. *Positions on Smoking and Health: Smoking and Lung Cancer.* N.d. https://www.industrydocumentslibrary.ucsf.edu/tobacco/docs/gzgd0209.

British American Tobacco Türkiye. "Sigaranın Sağlıkla İlgili Riskleri." http://www.bat.com.tr/group/sites/BAT_7X7FK5.nsf/vwPagesWebLive/DO7X7K6R?opendocument.

al-Bukhari, Muhammad ibn Isma'il. *Sahih al-Bukhari.* 7 vols. Edited by Mustafa Dib al-Bugha. Damascus: Dar ibn Kathir, 1987.

al-Bukhari, Muhammad ibn Isma'il. *The Translation of the Meanings of Sahih al-Bukhari: Arabic-English.* 9 vols. Edited by Muhammad Muhsin Khan. 1979; rpt., Riyadh: Darussalam, 1997.

The Case of the Animals versus Man Before the King of the Jinn: A Translation from the Epistles of the Brethren of Purity. Translated by Lenn E. Goodman and Richard McGregor. Oxford: Oxford University Press, 2012.

Chef Yusuf. *Cooking the Islamic Way: Food in the Holy Qur'an and the Blessed Sunnah.* Lexington, KY: CreateSpace, 2010.

Delgado, Linda D. *Halal Food, Fun, and Laughter.* Tempe, AZ: Muslim Writers, 2005.

al-Ghazali, Abu Hamid. *Al-Ghazali on the Lawful and the Unlawful: Book XIV of the Revival of the Religious Sciences.* Translated with introduction and notes by Yusuf T. DeLorenzo. Cambridge: Islamic Texts Society, 2014.

Hafiz. *The Gift: Poems by the Great Sufi Master*. Translated by Daniel James Ladinsky. New York: Arkana, 1999.

ibn Abi al-Hadid, Nizam al-Din. *Sharh Nahj al-Balagha*. 10 vols. Edited by Muhammad Ibrahim. Baghdad: Dar al-Kitab al-'Arabi, 2007.

ibn Anas, Malik. *Al-Muwatta'*. 2 vols. Edited by Muhammad Fu'ad 'Abd al-Baqi. Beirut: Dar Ihya' al-Turath al-'Arabi, 1985.

ibn al-'Arabi, Abi Bakr Muhammad ibn 'Abdallah. *Ahkam al-Qur'an*. 4 vols. Edited by Muhammad 'Abd al-Qadir 'Ata. Beirut: Dar al-Kutub al-'Ilmiyya, 2013.

ibn Ishaq. *The Life of Muhammad: A Translation of Ibn Ishaq's Sirat Rasul Allah*. Translated by A. Guillaume. Oxford: Oxford University Press, 1955.

ibn Kathir, Isma'il ibn 'Umar. *Tafsir al-Qur'an al-'Azim*. 2nd ed. 8 vols. Edited by Sami ibn Muhammad al-Salama. Riyadh: Dar Tayyiba li'l Nashr wa'l Tawzi', 1999.

ibn Majah, Muhammad ibn Yazid. *English Translation of Sunan Ibn Majah*. 5 vols. Edited by Hafiz Abu Tahir Zubair 'Ali Za'i, Huda Khattab, and Abu Khaliyl. Translated by Nasiruddin Khattab. Riyadh: Darussalam, 2007.

ibn Majah, Muhammad ibn Yazid. *Sunan Ibn Majah*. 6 vols. Edited by Bashshar 'Awwad Ma'ruf. Beirut: Dar al-Jil li'l-Tab' wa'l-Nashr wa'l-Tawzi', 1998.

ibn Qudama, Muwafaq al-Din 'Abd Allah ibn Ahmad. *Al-Mughni*. 10 vols. Beirut: Dar Ihya' al-Turath al-'Arabi, 1985. http://library.islamweb.net/newlibrary/display_book.php?bk_no=15&ID=1699&idfrom=1753&idto=2226&bookid=15&startno=187.

International Trade Center. "From Niche to Mainstream: Halal goes Global." Geneva: International Trade Center, 2015. www.intracen.org.

Inquiry into Australia's Trade and Investment Relationships with Countries of the Middle East 2014. http://www.aph.gov.au/Parliamentary_Business/Committees/Joint/Foreign_Affairs_Defence_and_Trade/Middle_East_trade_and_investment/Report.

al-Kashani, Mulla Muhammad ibn Murtada ibn Mahmud. *Tafsir al-Safi*. 5 vols. Edited by Husayn al-A'lami. Tehran: Maktabat al-Sadr, 2000.

Katip Chelebi. *The Balance of Truth*. Translated with an introduction and notes by G. L. Lewis. London: George Allen and Unwin, 1957.

al-Khaw'i, Abu al-Qasim and Mirza 'Ali al-Gharawi al-Tabrizi. *Al-Tanqih fi Sharh al-'Urwa al-Wuthqa*. 10 vols. Qom: Dar al-Hadi li'l Matbu'at, 2000. http://ar.lib.eshia.ir.

al-Kishnawi, Abi Bakr ibn Hassan. *Ashal al-Madarik: Sharh Irshad al-Salik fi Fiqh Imam al-'Amm'atu Malik*. 2nd ed. 3 vols. Beirut: Dar al-Fikr, 2000. http://waqfeya.com/book.php?bid=10428.

Lane, Edward W. *An Account of the Manners and Customs of the Modern Egyptians . . .* 5th ed. London: John Murray, 1830.

Maffei, Yvonne. *My Halal Kitchen: Global Recipes, Cooking Tips, and Lifestyle Inspiration*. Chicago: Surrey Books, 2016.

al-Mawardi, Abu al-Hasan 'Ali ibn Muhammad ibn Habib. *Al-Hawi al-Kabir*. 20 vols. Edited by 'Ali Muhammad 'Awad and 'Adil Ahmad 'Abd al-Mawjud. Beirut: Dar al-Kutub al-'Ilmiyya, 1994.

al-Mehri, A. B., ed. *The Qur'an with Surah Introductions and Appendices*. Birmingham, UK: Maktabah, 2010.

Montagu, Lady Mary Wortley. *The Letters and Works of Lady Mary Wortley Montagu*. Edited by Lord Wharncliffe. Paris: A. and W. Galignani, 1837.

al-Mubarakfuri, Muhammad ibn 'Abd al-Rahman ibn 'Abd al-Rahim. *Tuhfat al-Ahwadhi bi Sharh Jami' al-Tirmidhi*. 10 vols. Edited and annotated by 'Abd al-Wahab 'Abd al-Latif. Cairo: Dar al-Fikr li'l-Tiba'a wa'l-Nashr wa'l-Tawzi', 1967.

Muslim Students' Association of the United States and Canada. *Muslim World Cook Book*. Brentwood, MD: International Graphics, 1973.

al-Naraqi, Muhammad Mahdi ibn Abi Zarr. *Mu'tamad al-Shi'a fi Ahkam al-Shari'a*. 19 vols. Beirut: Mu'assasat al-Bayt li Ihya' al-Turath, 2008. http://www.narjes-library.com.

al-Nasa'i, Ahmad ibn Shu'ayb. *English Translation of Sunan an-Nasa'i*. 6 vols. Edited by Hafiz Abu Tahir Zubair 'Ali Za'i, Huda Khattab, and Abu Khaliyl; translated by Nasiruddin al-Khattab. Riyadh: Darussalam, 2007.

al-Nasa'i, Ahmad ibn Shu'ayb. *Kitab al-Sunan al-Kubra*. 12 vols. Edited by Hasan 'Abd al-Mun'im Shalabi. Beirut: Mu'assasat al-Risala, 2001.

Nasr, Seyyed Hossein, ed. *The Study Quran: A New Translation and Commentary*. New York: HarperOne, 2015.

Nasrallah, Nawal, ed. and trans. *Annals of the Caliphs' Kitchens: Ibn Sayyar al-Warraq's Tenth-Century Baghdadi Cookbook*. Leiden: Brill, 2010.

al-Naysaburi, Abu al-Husayn Muslim ibn al-Hajjaj al-Qushayri. *Sahih Muslim*. 5 vols. Edited by Ahmad Shams al-Din. Beirut: Dar al-Kutub al-'Ilmiyya, 1998.

New Zealand Meat Industry Association. *2014 Annual Report*. http://www.mia.co.nz/docs/publications/AR2014.pdf.

Niebuhr, M. Carsten. *Travels through Arabia and Other Countries in the East . . .* 2 vols. Translated by Robert Heron. Edinburgh: Morison & Son, 1797.

al-Nuwayri, Shihab al-Din. *The Ultimate Ambition in the Arts of Euriditon: A Compendium of Knowledge from the Classical Islam*. Edited, translated, and with an introduction and notes by Elias Muhanna. New York: Penguin, 2016.

Opinion of the Scientific Panel on Animal Health and Welfare. July 6, 2004. http://www.efsa.europa.eu/sites/default/files/scientific_output/files/main_documents/45.pdf.

"Recommendations of the Eighth Fiqh-Medical Seminar." May 22–24, 1995, Kuwait, http://islamset.net/bioethics/8thfiqh.html.

Saheeh International. *The Qur'ān: Arabic Text with Corresponding English meanings = al-Qur'ān al-Karīm ma'a Tarjamat al-Ma'ānī bi-al-Lughah al-Injilizīyah*. Jeddah: Abul-Qasim Publishing House, 1997.

al-Shayzari, Abd al-Rahman b. Nasr. *The Book of the Islamic Market Inspector*. Translated and with an introduction and notes by R. P. Buckley. Oxford: Oxford University Press, 1999.

al-Sijistani, Abu Dawud Sulayman ibn al-Ash'ath. *Sunan Abi Dawud*. 7 vols. Edited by Shu'ayb al-Arna'ut and Muhammad Kamil Qarah Balili. Beirut: Dar al-Risala al-'Alamiyya 2009.

al-Sistani, al-Sayyid 'Ali al-Husseini. "Al-Istifta'at: Jalatin." http://www.sistani.org/arabic/qa/02067/.

al-Tabari, Muhammad ibn Jarir. *Tafsir al-Tabari min Kitabihi Jami' al-Bayan 'an Ta'wil Ayat al-Qur'an*. 7 vols. Edited by Bashshar 'Awad Ma'ruf and 'Isam Faris al-Hirshani. Beirut: Mu'assasat al-Risala, 1994.

al-Tirmidhi, Muhammad ibn 'Isa. *Al-Jami' al-Kabir*. 6 vols. 2nd ed. Edited by Bashshar 'Awwad Ma'ruf. Beirut: Dar al-Gharb al-Islami, 1998.

at-Tirmidhi, Hafiz Abu 'Eisa Mohammad ibn 'Eisa. *English Translation of Jami' At-Tirmidhi*. 6 vols. Compiled by Imam Hafiz Abu 'Eisa Mohammad Ibn 'Eisa At-Tirmidhi; translated by Abu Khaliyl; ahadith edited and referenced by Hafiz Abu Tahir Zubair 'Ali Za'i; final review by Islamic Research Section Darussalam. Riyadh: Darussalam, 2007.

Turabi Efendi. *Turkish Cookery Book: A Collection of Receipts*. London: William. H. Allen, 1865.

World Development Indicators Database. http://databank.worldbank.org/data/.

BIBLIOGRAPHY

OFFICIAL GUIDELINES, REGULATIONS, AND DESCRIPTIONS

Code of Federal Regulations. Title 21, vol. 2. Rev. April 1, 2015. http://www.accessdata.fda.gov.

Council Directive 93/119/EC of 22 December 1993 on the Protection of Animals at the Time of Slaughter or Killing. http://ec.europa.eu/food/fs/aw/aw_legislation/slaughter/93-119-ec_en.pdf.

Council Regulation (EC) No 1099/2009 2009 on the Protection of Animals at the Time of Killing. http://eur-lex.europa.eu/eli/reg/2009/1099/oj.

European Convention for the Protection of Animals for Slaughter. May 10, 1979. https://rm.coe.int/CoERMPublicCommonSearchServices/DisplayDCTMContent?documentId=0900001680077da5.

GS 993: Animal Slaughtering Requirements according to Islamic Law (1999). http://www.halalcertifiering.se/newwebsiteimages/Gulf_standard.pdf.

GSO 05/FDS/2055—1:2014: Halal Products—Part One: General Requirements for Halal Food. http://www.puntofocal.gov.ar/notific_otros_miembros/kwt282_t.pdf.

GSO 1931/2008: Halal Food. https://law.resource.org/pub/gso/ibr/gso.2055.e.ds.2008.pdf.

Malaysian Standard (MS) 1500:2000: General Guidelines on the Production, Preparation, Handling and Storage of Halal Food. Jakarta: Department of Standards Malaysia, 2000.

Malaysian Standard (MS) 1500:2004: Halal *Food—Production, Preparation, Handling, and Storage—General Guidelines.* Jakarta: Department of Standards Malaysia, 2004.

Malaysian Standard (MS) 1500:2009: Halal *Food—Production, Preparation, Handling and Storage—General Guidelines (Second Revision).* Jakarta: Department of Standards Malaysia, 2009.

Malaysian Standard (MS) 2393:2013: Islamic and Halal *Principles—Definitions and Interpretations on Terminology.* Jakarta: Department of Standards Malaysia, 2013. http://www.msonline.gov.my/download_file.php?file=31707&source=production.

Malaysian Standard (MS) 2564:2014 Halal *Packaging: General Guidelines.* Jakarta: Department of Standards Malaysia, 2014.

OIC/SMIIC 1:2011: General Guidelines on Halal Food. Ankara: Türk Standartlar Enstitüsü, 2011.

Trade Description (Certification and Marketing of 'Halal') Order 2011. http://www.puntofocal.gov.ar/notific_otros_miembros/mys27_t.pdf, 3–5.

Trade Descriptions (Marking of Food) Order 1975. http://www.wipo.int/wipolex/en/text.jsp?file_id=128857.

Trade Descriptions (Marking of Food) Order 1975. http://www.wipo.int/wipolex/en/text.jsp?file_id=128860.

SECONDARY SOURCES

Abdul-Matin, Ibrahim. *Green Deen: What Islam Teaches about Protecting the Planet.* San Francisco: Berrett-Koehler, 2010.

Abidoun Adams, Isiaka. "Globalization: Explaining the Dynamics and Challenges of the Ḥālal Food Surge." *Intellectual Discourse* 19, no. 1 (2011): 123–145.

Ådna, Gerd Marie. *Muhammad and the Formation of Sacrifice.* Frankfurt: Peter Lang, 2014.

Agahi, Cyrus, and Christopher P. Spencer. "Drug Abuse in Pre- and Post-Revolutionary Iran." *Journal of Psychoactive Drugs* 13, no. 1 (1981): 39–46.

Ahmed, Shahab. *What Is Islam? The Importance of Being Islamic.* Princeton, NJ: Princeton University Press, 2016.

Albala, Ken. "Historical Background to Food and Christianity." In *Food and Faith in Christian Culture,* edited by Ken Albala and Trudy Eden, 7–20. New York: Columbia University Press, 2011.

Ali, Kecia. "Muslims and Meat-Eating Vegetarianism, Gender, and Identity." *Journal of Religious Ethics* 43, no. 2 (2015): 268–288.

Alroy, Odelia E. "Kosher Wine." *Judaism* 39, no. 4 (1990): 452–460.

Ambali, Abdul Raufu, and Ahmad Naqiyuddin Bakar. "Ḥalāl Food and Products in Malaysia: People's Awareness and Policy Implications." *Intellectual Discourse* 21, no. 1 (2013): 7–32.

Anderson, Allan Heaton. *An Introduction to Pentecostalism: Global Charismatic Christianity.* 2nd ed. Cambridge: Cambridge University Press, 2013.

Andrews, Walter G., and Mehmet Kalpaklı. *The Age of Beloveds: Love and the Beloved in Early-Modern Ottoman and European Culture and Society.* Durham, NC: Duke University Press, 2006.

Appadurai, Arjun. "How to Make a National Cuisine: Cookbooks in Contemporary India." *Society for the Comparative Study of Society and History* 30, no. 1 (1988): 3–24.

Ariel, Ari. "The Hummus Wars." *Gastronomica: The Journal of Food and Culture* 12, no. 1 (2012): 34–42

"Al-Ashriba." *Al-Mawsu'a al-Fiqhiyya* 5:11–30.

"At'ima." *Al-Mawsu'a al-Fiqhiyya* 5:123–162.

Attar, Maryam, Khalil Lohi, and John Lever. "Remembering the Spirit of Halal: An Iranian Perspective." In *Halal Matters: Islam, Politics, and Markets*, edited by Florence Bergeaud-Blackler, Johan Fischer, and John Lever, 55–71. London: Routledge, 2015.

al-'Awd, Salih. *Sina'at al-Ajban al-Haditha wa Hukm Akliha: bi-Adillat al-Kitab wa'l Sunna wa-Nuqul al-A'imma wa Aqwal 'Ulama' al-Umma.* Beirut: Dar al-Kutub al-'Ilmiyya, 2009.

Baasher, Taha. "The Use of Drugs in the Islamic World." *British Journal of Addiction* 76 (1981): 233–243.

Badawi, Elsaid M., and Muhammad Abdel Haleem, eds. *Dictionary of Qur'anic Usage.* Brill Online. http://referenceworks.brillonline.com/.

Badawi, Elsaid M., and Muhammad Abdel Haleem. "ط/ي/ب ṭ–y–b." In *Dictionary of Qur'anic Usage*, edited by Elsaid M. Badawi and Muhammad Abdel Haleem. Brill Online. http://reference-works.brillonline.com/.

Bagchi, Anita, and Prithwiraj Jha. "Fish and Fisheries in Indian Heritage and Development of Pisciculture in India." *Reviews in Fisheries Science* 19, no. 2 (2011): 85–118.

Balabanlılar, Lisa. "The Emperor Jahangir and the Pursuit of Pleasure." *Journal of the Royal Asiatic Society* 19, no. 2 (2009): 173–186.

al-Bar, Muhammad 'Ali. *Al-Asrar al-Tibbiyya wa'l Ahkam al-Fiqhiyya fi Tahrim al-Khinzir.* Jeddah: Dar al-Su'udiyya li'l Nashr wa'l Tawzi', 1986.

Barnes, R. H. "Lamakera, Solor. Ethnographic Notes on a Muslim Whaling Village of Eastern Indonesia." *Anthropos* 91, nos. 1/3 (1996): 75–88.

Bartholomew, J. G. *Land Surface Features of Arabia.* Edinburgh: Edinburgh Geographical Institute, 1904.

Battour, Mahomed et al. "The Impact of Destination Attributes on Muslim Tourist's Choice." *International Journal of Tourism Research* 13, no. 6 (2011), 527–540.

Beckerleg, Susan. "What Harm? Kenyan and Ugandan Perspectives on Khat." *African Affairs* 104 (2006): 219–241.

Beckford, James A. "Muslims in the Prisons of Britain and France." *Journal of Contemporary European Studies* 13, no. 3 (2005): 287–297.

Belch, Zushe Yosef. *Kosher Food Production.* Oxford: Blackwell, 2004.

Benkheira, Mohammed Hocine. *Islâm et interdits alimentaires—Juguler l'animalité.* Paris: Presses Universitaires de France, 2000.

Bergeaud-Blackler, Florence. "New Challenges for Islamic Ritual Slaughter: A European Perspective." *Journal of Ethnic and Migration Studies* 33, no. 6 (2007): 965–980.

Bergeaud-Blackler, Florence. "'Islamiser l'Alimentation': Marchés halal et dynamiques normatives." *Genèses* 4, no. 89 (2012): 61–87.

Bergeaud-Blackler, Florence. "The Halal Certification Market in Europe and the World: A First Panorama." In *Halal Matters: Islam, Politics, and Markets*, edited by Florence Bergeaud-Blackler, Johan Fischer, and John Lever, 105–126. London: Routledge, 2015.

Bergeaud-Blackler, Florence, ed. *Les sens du halal: Une norme dans un marché mondial.* Paris: CNRS Éditions, 2015.

Bergeaud-Blackler, Florence. *Le marché halal ou l'invention d'une tradition.* Paris: Seuil, 2017.

Bergeaud-Blackler, Florence, Johan Fischer, and John Lever, eds. *Halal Matters: Islam, Politics, and Markets.* London: Routledge, 2015.

Betts, Robert Brenton. *The Druze.* New Haven, CT: Yale University Press, 1990.

Bolman, Elizabeth S. *Shaping Monasticism in Early Byzantine Egypt: Selected Studies in Visual and Material Culture.* Princeton, NJ: Princeton University Press, forthcoming.

Bonne, Karijn, Iris Vermeir, Florence Bergeaud-Blackler, and Wim Verbeke. "Determinants of Halal Meat Consumption in France." *British Food Journal* 109, no. 5 (2007): 367–386.

Bousquet, G.-H. "Ḏhabiḥa." *Encyclopaedia of Islam.* 2nd ed. Brill Online. http://referenceworks. brillonline.com/.

Branyik, Tomaš. "A Review of Methods of Low Alcohol and Alcohol-Free Beer Production." *Journal of Food Engineering* 108 (2012): 493–506.

Braudel, Fernand. *Civilization and Capitalism, 15th–18th Century: The Structure of Everyday Life.* Berkeley: University of California Press, 1992.

Bromberger, Christian. "Et l'esturgeon devin *halâl* en islam chiite duodécimain." In *Les sens du halal: Une norme dans un marché mondial*, edited by Florence Bergeaud-Blackler, 25–30. Paris: CNRS Éditions, 2015.

Burnett, Sierra Clark, and Krishnendu Ray. "Sociology of Food." In *The Oxford Handbook of Food History*, edited by Jeffrey M. Pilcher, 135–153. New York: Oxford University Press, 2012.

Cairns, Kate, Josée Johnston, and Shyon Baumann. "Caring about Food: Doing Gender in the Foodie Kitchen." *Gender and Society* 24, no. 5 (2010): 591–615.

Cesari, Jocelyne. "The Securitisation of Islam in Europe." Challenge Research Paper No. 14 (2009). http://aei.pitt.edu/10763/1/1826.pdf.

Chambliss, William J. *Key Issues in Crime and Punishment.* Vol. 4. Thousand Oaks, CA: Sage, 2011.

Chehabi, H. E. "How Caviar Turned Out to Be *Halal.*" *Gastronomica: The Journal of Food and Culture* 7, no. 2 (2007): 17–23.

Civitello, Linda. *Cuisine and Culture: A History of Food and People.* Hoboken, NJ: Wiley, 2004.

Cohen, Amnon. *Economic Life in Ottoman Jerusalem.* Cambridge: Cambridge University Press, 1989.

Cohen, Mark R. "Feeding the Poor and Clothing the Naked: The Cairo Geniza." *Journal of Interdisciplinary History* 35, no. 3 (2005): 407–421.

Cook, Michael. "Early Islamic Dietary Law." *Jerusalem Studies in Arabic and Islam* 7 (1986): 218–277.

Cook, Michael. "Magian Cheese: An Archaic Problem in Islamic Law." *Bulletin of the School of Oriental and African Studies* 47, no. 3 (1984): 449–467.

Copland, Ian. "What to Do about Cows? Princely versus British Approaches to a South Asian Dilemma." *Bulletin of the School of Oriental and African Studies* 68, no. 1 (2005): 59–76.

Çayırlıoğlu, Yüksel. *Helal Gıda*. Istanbul: Işık Yayıncılık, 2014.

Çetin, Emre. "Islamic Lifestyle and Emine Beder's TV Cookery Show Kitchen Love." *European Journal of Cultural Studies* 20, no. 4 (2015): 1–14.

Dağ, Haluk, and Emel Erbaşı-Gönç. "SMIIC and Halal Food Standards." *Journal of Chemical Metrology* 7, no. 1 (2013): 1–6.

Danforth, Loring M. *Crossing the Kingdom: Portraits of Saudi Arabia*. Berkeley: University of California Press, 2016.

Dawson, Warren R. "The Pig in Ancient Egypt: A Commentary on Two Passages of Herodotus." *Journal of the Royal Asiatic Society of Great Britain and Ireland*, no. 3 (1928): 597–608.

Deuraseh, Nurdeen. "Is Drinking al-Khamr (Intoxicating Drink) for Medical Purposes Permissible by Islamic Law?" *Arab Law Quarterly* 18 (2003): 355–364.

"Dhaba'ih." *Al-Mawsu'a al-Fiqhiyya* 21:171–204.

Donner, Fred M. *The Early Islamic Conquests*. Princeton, NJ: Princeton University Press, 1981.

Douglas, Heather, and Abdi Hersi. "Khat and Islamic Legal Perspectives: Issues for Consideration." *Journal of Legal Pluralism and Unofficial Law* 62 (2010): 95–114.

Douglas, Mary. *Purity and Danger: An Analysis of Concepts of Pollution and Taboo*. New York: Routledge, 2002.

Dursteler, Eric R. "Bad Bread and the 'Outrageous Drunkenness of the Turks': Food and Identity in the Accounts of Early Modern European Travelers to the Ottoman Empire." *Journal of World History* 25, nos. 2–3 (2014): 203–228.

Einstein, Mara. *Brands of Faith: Marketing Religion in a Commercial Age*. New York: Routledge, 2008.

Encyclopaedia of Islam. Brill Online. 1st ed., 1913–1936; 2nd ed., 2012; 3rd ed., 2017. http://referenceworks.brillonline.com/.

Eren, Ercan. *Geçmişten Günümüze Anadolu'da Bira*. Istanbul: Tarih Vakfı Yayınları, 2005.

Evered, Emine Ö., and Kyle T. Evered. "From Rakı to Ayran: Regulating the Place and Practice of Drinking in Turkey." *Space and Polity* 26, no. 1 (2016): 39–58.

Evered, Emine Ö., and Kyle T. Evered. "A Geopolitics of Drinking: Debating the Place of Alcohol in Early Republican Turkey." *Political Geography* 50 (2016): 48–60.

Fee, Gordon D. "Εἰδωλόθυτα Once Again: An Interpretation of 1 Corinthians 8–10." *Biblica* 61, no. 2 (1980): 172–197.

Ferguson, Priscilla Parkhurst. "A Cultural Field in the Making: Gastronomy in 19th-Century France." *American Journal of Sociology* 104, no. 3 (1998): 597–641.

Finke, Roger, and Laurence R. Iannaccone. "Supply-Side Explanations for Religious Change." *Annals of the American Academy, AAPSS* 527 (1993): 27–39.

Fischer, Johan. "Feeding Secularism: Consuming Halal among the Malays in London." *Diaspora: A Journal of Transnational Studies* 14, nos. 2/3 (2005): 275–297.

Fischer, Johan. *The Halal Frontier: Muslim Consumers in a Globalized World*. New York: Palgrave Macmillan, 2011.

Fischer, Johan. "Branding Halal: A Photographic Essay on Global Muslim Markets." *Anthropology Today* 28, no. 4 (2012): 18–21.

Fischer, Johan. "Manufacturing Halal in Malaysia." *Contemporary Islam* 10, no. 1 (2016): 35–52.

Fitzgerald, Amy J. *Animals as Food: (Re)connecting Production, Processing, Consumption, and Impacts*. East Lansing: Michigan University Press, 2015.

Fleitz, Elizabeth. "Cooking Codes: Cookbook Discourses as Women's Rhetorical Practices." *Present Tense: A Journal of Rhetoric in Society* 1, no. 1 (2010): 1–8. http://www.presenttensejournal.org/wp-content/uploads/2010/07/Fleitz.pdf.

Foda, Omar. "Anna and Ahmad: Building Modern Temperance in Egypt (1884–1940)." *Social Sciences and Missions* 28 (2015): 116–149.

Foltz, Richard. *Animals in Islamic Traditions and Muslim Cultures*. London: Oneworld, 2014.

Freidenreich, David M. *Foreigners and Their Food: Constructing Otherness in Jewish, Christian, and Islamic Law*. Berkeley: University of California Press, 2011.

Friedrich, Bruce. "Ritual Slaughter in the 'Ritual Bubble': Restoring the Wall of Separation between Church and State." *Vermont Journal of Environmental Law* 17 (2015): 222–254.

Gallahue, Patrick, and Rick Lines. *The Death Penalty for Drug Offences: Global Overview 2015: The Extreme Fringe of Global Drug Policy*. London: Harm Reduction International, 2015. https://dl.dropboxusercontent.com/u/64663568/library/DeathPenaltyDrugs_Report_2015.pdf.

Ghandou, Soha. "MENA Region Drives Food Packaging Demand." *Middle East Food* 31, no. 1 (2015): 10.

Ghiabi, Mayizar. "Drugs and Revolution in Iran: Islamic Devotion, Revolutionary Zeal and Republican Means." *Iranian Studies* 48, no. 2 (2015): 139–163.

Ghouri, Nazim, Mohammed Atcha, and Aziz Sheikh. "Influence of Islam on Smoking among Muslims." *British Medical Journal* 332, no. 7536 (2006): 291–294.

al-Ghunanim, Qadhafi 'Izzat. *Al-Istihala wa Ahkamiha fi'l-Fiqh al-Islami*. Amman: Dar al-Nafa'is, 2008.

Gignoux, Phillip. "Dietary Laws in Pre-Islamic and Post-Sasanian Iran: A Comparative Survey." *Jerusalem Studies in Arabic and Islam* 17 (1994): 16–42.

Gillette, Maris B. *Between Mecca and Beijing: Modernization and Consumption among Urban Chinese Muslims*. Stanford, CA: Stanford University Press, 2000.

Global Islamic Finance Report, 2013. Edbiz Consulting. http://www.gifr.net/gifr2013/ch_13.PDF.

Goitein, S. D. *A Mediterranean Society: The Jewish Communities of the Arab World as Portrayed in the Documents of the Cairo Geniza*, vol. 4: *Daily Life*. 1967; rpt., Berkeley: University of California Press, 1999.

Gören, Ahmet C. et al. "Halal Food and Metrology." *International Second Halal and Healthy Food Congress*, November 7–10, 2013, Konya, Turkey. http://www.helalvesaglikli.org/docs/kon-gre2013/sozlu/4.pdf.

Görg, Peter H. *The Desert Fathers: Anthony and the Beginnings of Monasticism*. San Francisco: Ignatius Press, 2011.

Graf, Katharina. "Beldi Matters: Negotiating Proper Food in Urban Moroccan Food Consumption and Preparation." In *Halal Matters: Islam, Politics, and Markets*, edited by Florence Bergeaud-Blackler, Johan Fischer, and John Lever, 72–90. London: Routledge, 2015.

Grandin, Temple, and Joe Regenstein. "Religious Slaughter and Animal Welfare: A Discussion for Meat Scientists." *Meat Focus International* (1994): 115–123. http://www.grandin.com/ritual/kosher.slaugh.html.

Grant, Robert M. *Early Christians and Animals*. London: Routledge, 1999.

Grehan, James. "Smoking and 'Early Modern' Sociability: The Great Tobacco Debate in the Ottoman Middle East (Seventeenth to Eighteenth Centuries)." *American Historical Review* 111, no. 5 (2006): 1352–1377.

Grehan, James. *Everyday Life and Consumer Culture in Eighteenth-Century Damascus*. Seattle: University of Washington Press, 2007.

Grimm, Veronika E. *From Feasting to Fasting: The Evolution of a Sin. Attitudes to Food in Late Antiquity*. London: Routledge, 1996.

Grimm, Veronika E. "The Good Things That Lay at Hand." In *Food: A History of Taste*, edited by Paul H. Freedman, 63–98. Berkeley: University of California Press, 2007.

Gross, Aaron. *The Question of the Animal and Religion: Theoretical Stakes, Practical Implications.* New York: Columbia University Press, 2015.

Hackett, Conrad. "5 Facts about the Muslim Population in Europe." Pew Research Center, July 19, 2016. http://www.pewresearch.org/fact-tank/2016/07/19/5-facts-about-the-muslim-population-in-europe/.

Haider, Najam. "Contesting Intoxication: Early Juristic Debates over the Lawfulness of Alcoholic Beverages." *Islamic Law and Society* 20, nos. 1–2 (2013): 48–89.

Halenko, Oleksander. "Wine Production, Marketing and Consumption in the Ottoman Crimea, 1520–1542." *Journal of the Economic and Social History of the Orient* 47 (2004): 507–547.

Halim, Mustafa 'Afifi Ab., and Azlin Alisa Ahmad. "Enforcement of Consumer Protection Laws on Halal Products: Malaysian Experience." *Asian Social Science* 10, no. 3 (2014): 9–14.

Hamayotsu, Kikue. "Demobilization of Islam: Institutionalized Religion and the Politics of Co-optation in Malaysia." PhD diss., Australian National University, Canberra Act 0200, Australia, 2005.

Hames, Gina. *Alcohol in World History.* London: Routledge, 2012.

Harris, Marvin. "The Abominable Pig." In *Food and Culture: A Reader*, edited by Carole Counihan and Penny Van Esterik, 67–79. New York: Routledge, 1997.

Hashim, Puziah, et al., eds. "Proceedings of the Third IMT-GT International Symposium on Halal Science and Management." December 21–22, 2009 (Selangor Dar Ehsan, Malaysia: Halal Products Research Institute, 2009). http://www.academia.edu/1367215/Determination_of_Halal_Limits_for_Alcohol_Content_in_Foods_by_simulated_fermentation.

Hattox, Ralph. *Coffee and Coffeehouses: The Origins of a Social Beverage in the Medieval Near East.* Seattle: University of Washington Press, 1985.

Heier, Zachary. "In Concern of Animal Welfare, or with Xenophobic Intent? An Analysis of State-Decreed Bans on Non-Stun Halal Slaughter in Europe and the Threat to Religious Freedom." Unpublished Paper. University of Vermont, 2017.

Heine, P. "Nabidh." *Encyclopaedia of Islam.* 2nd ed. Brill Online. http://referenceworks.brillonline.com/.

Hitti, Phillip K. *History of the Arabs.* London: Palgrave, 2002.

Hoffstaedter, Gerhard. "Secular State, Religious Lives: Islam and the State in Malaysia." *Asian Ethnicity* 14, no. 4 (2013): 475–489.

Horowitz, Roger. *Kosher USA: How Coke Became Kosher and Other Tales of Modern Food.* New York: Columbia University Press, 2016.

Howard, Philip H. "Too Big to Ale? Globalization and Consolidation in the Beer Industry." In *The Geography of Beer*, edited by Mark Patterson and Nancy Hoalst-Pullen, 155–165. New York: Springer, 2014.

ul-Huda, Qamar. "Sufism and Sufis: South Asia." In *Medieval Islamic Civilization: An Encyclopedia*, vol. 2, edited by Josef W. Meri, 773–775. New York: Routledge, 2006.

Iqbal, Noor Fatima Kareema. "From Permissible to Wholesome: Situating Ḥalāl Organic Farms within the Sustainability Discourse." *Islamic Sciences* 13, no. 1 (2015): 49–56.

Ireland, John, and Soha Abdollah Rajabzadeh. "UAE Consumer Concerns about Halal Products." *Journal of Islamic Marketing* 2, no. 3 (2011): 274–283.

Işın, Priscilla May. "Boza, Innocuous and Less So." In *Cured, Fermented and Smoked Foods: Proceedings of Oxford Symposium on Food and Cookery 2010*, edited by Helen Saberi, 154–164. London: Prospect Books, 2011.

Islam, Md Saidul. "Old Philosophy, New Movement: The Rise of the Islamic Ecological Paradigm in the Discourse of Environmentalism." *Nature and Culture* 7, no. 1 (2012): 72–94.

Istasse, Manon. "Green Halal: How Does Halal Production Face Animal Suffering?" In *Halal Matters: Islam, Politics, and Markets*, edited by Florence Bergeaud-Blackler, Johan Fischer, and John Lever, 127–142. London: Routledge, 2015.

"Istihala." *Al-Mawsu'a al-Fiqhiyya* 3:213–214.

İzberk-Bilgin, Elif. "Infidel Brands: Unveiling Alternative Meanings of Global Brands at the Nexus of Globalization, Consumer Culture, and Islamism." *Journal of Consumer Research* 39, no. 4 (2012): 663–687.

İzberk-Bilgin, Elif. "Theology Meets the Marketplace: The Discursive Formation of the Halal Market in Turkey." Unpublished paper (n.d.). https://www.academia.edu/14459777/Theology_Meets_the_Marketplace_The_Discursive_Formation_of_the_Halal_Market_in_Turkey.

İzberk-Bilgin, Elif, and Cheryl C. Nakata. "A New Look at Faith-Based Marketing: The Global Halal Market." *Business Horizons* 59 (2016): 285–292.

Izutsu, Toshihiko. *Ethico-Religious Concepts in the Qur'an*. 1966; rpt., Montreal: McGill-Queen's University Press, 2002.

Izzi Diene, Mawil. *The Theory and the Practice of Market Law in Medieval Islam: A Study of Kitab Nisab al-Ihtisab of Umar b. Muhammad al-Sunami*. Warminster: E. J. W. Gibb Memorial Trust, 1997.

Jamaludin, Mohammad Aizat et al. "Istihala: Analysis on the Utilization of Gelatin in Food Products." *IPEDR* 17 (2011): 174–178.

Janmohamed, Shelina. *Generation M: Young Muslims Changing the World*. London: I. B. Tauris, 2016.

Joseph, Suad, and Benjamin D'Harlingue. "Arab Americans and Muslim Americans in the *New York Times*, before and after 9/11." In *Race and Arab Americans before and after 9/11: From Invisible Citizens to Visible Subjects*, edited by Amaney Jamal and Nadine Naber, 229–275. Syracuse, NY: Syracuse University Press, 2008.

Judd, Robin. *Contested Rituals: Circumcision, Kosher Butchering, and Jewish Political Life in Germany, 1843–1933*. Ithaca, NY: Cornell University Press, 2007.

Juynboll, Theodor W. "Fard." *Encyclopaedia of Islam*. 2nd ed. Brill Online. http://referenceworks.brillonline.com/.

Kamali, Mohammad Hashim. "The Ḥalāl Industry from a Sharī'ah Perspective." *Islam and Civilisational Renewal* 1, no. 4 (2010): 595–612.

Kamali, Mohammad Hashim. *The Parameters of Ḥalāl and Ḥaram in Shari'ah and the Ḥalāl Industry*. Kuala Lumpur: International Institute of Advanced Islamic Studies, Malaysia, 2013. http://www.academia.edu/7121321/The_Parameters_of_Halal_and_Haram_in_Shari_ah_and_the_Halal_Industry_-_Mohammad_Hashim_Kamali.

Kaplan, Dana Evan. *Contemporary American Judaism*. New York: Columbia University Press, 2010.

Karaosmanoğlu, Defne. "Cooking the Past: The Revival of Ottoman Cuisine." PhD diss., McGill University, 2006.

Karic, Enes. "Intoxicants." *Encyclopaedia of the Qur'ān*. Brill Online. http://referenceworks.brillonline.com/.

El Karoui, Hakim. *Un islam français est possible: Rapport septembre 2016*. Developed and produced by Institut Montaigne. http://www.institutmontaigne.org/res/files/publications/rapport-un-islam-francais-est_-possible.pdf.

Kasapoğlu Akyol, Pınar. "Çorum'un Sungurlu İlçesinde 1895–1947 Yılları Arasında Kasapoğlu Ailesi Üzerinden Kasaplık Kültürüne Bir Bakış." *Acta Turcica: Online Thematic Journal of Turkic Studies* 3, no. 2 (2011): 1–23. http://actaturcica.com/_media/2011-07/iii_2_1.pdf.

Khan, Pasha M. "Nothing but Animals: The Hierarchy of Creatures in the Ringstones of Wisdom." *Journal of the Muhyiddin Ibn 'Arabi Society* 43 (2008). http://www.ibnarabisociety.org/articles/nothing-but-animals.html.

Khayat, M. H., ed. *The Right Path to Health: Islamic Ruling on Smoking.* Alexandria, Egypt: World Health Organization, Office for the Eastern Mediterranean, 1988. http://applications.emro.who.int/dsaf/dsa46.pdf.

Kinnvall, Catarina, and Paul Nesbitt-Larking. *The Political Psychology of Globalization: Muslims in the West.* Oxford: Oxford University Press, 2011.

Knudsen, Ståle. "Between Life Giver and Leisure: Identity Negotiation through Seafood in Turkey." *International Journal of Middle East Studies* 38, no. 3 (2006): 395–415.

Koenig, Leah. "Reaping the Faith." *Gastronomica: The Journal of Food and Culture* 8, no. 1 (2008): 80–84.

Kueny, Kathryn. *The Rhetoric of Sobriety: Wine in Early Islam.* New York: State University of New York Press, 2001.

Kuppinger, Petra. "A Neighborhood Shopping Street and the Making of Urban Cultures and Economies in Germany." *City and Community* 13, no. 2 (2014): 140–157.

Lerner, Pablo, and Alfredo Mordechai Rabello. "The Prohibition of Ritual Slaughtering (Kosher Shechita and Halal) and Freedom of Religion of Minorities." *Journal of Law and Religion* 22, no. 1 (2006-2007): 1–62.

Lever, John. "Reimagining Malaysia: A Postliberal Halal Strategy." In *Halal Matters: Islam, Politics, and Markets*, edited by Florence Bergeaud-Blackler, Johan Fischer, and John Lever, 19–37. London: Routledge, 2015.

Lever, John, and Haluk Anıl. "From an Implicit to an Explicit Understanding: New Definitions of Halal in Turkey." In *Halal Matters: Islam, Politics, and Markets*, edited by Florence Bergeaud-Blackler, Johan Fischer, and John Lever, 38–54. London: Routledge, 2015.

Lever, John, and Mara Miele. "The Growth of Halal Meat Markets in Europe: An Exploration of the Supply Side Theory of Religion." *Journal of Rural Studies* 28, no. 4 (2012): 528–537.

Lewicka, Paulina B. *Food and Foodways of Medieval Cairenes.* Boston: Brill, 2011.

Lings, Martin. *Muhammad: His Life Based on the Earliest Sources.* New York: Inner Traditions International, 1983.

Linzey, Andrew. *Why Animal Suffering Matters: Philosophy, Theology, and Practical Ethics.* New York: Oxford University Press, 2009.

Lobban, Richard A. "Pigs and Their Prohibition." *International Journal of Middle East Studies* 26, no. 1 (1994): 57–75.

Logan, Kate. "The Time for Tea: How Tea Displaced Coffee as the Preferred Beverage of the Middle East." Unpublished Paper. Middlebury College, 2013.

Lowry, Joseph E. "Lawful and Unlawful." In *Encyclopaedia of the Qur'ān*, edited by Jane Dammen McAuliffe. Brill Online. http://referenceworks.brillonline.com/.

Lunga, Audun. "Butchery Law with Anti-Semitic Roots." *Science Nordic*, November 6, 2013. http://sciencenordic.com/butchery-law-anti-semitic-roots.

Maghen, Ze'ev. "Ablution." *Encyclopaedia of Islam*, 3rd ed., Brill Online. http://referenceworks.brillonline.com/.

Mahmud, Fahmi Mustafa. *Al-I'jaz al-Tashri'i fi Tahrim al-Khinzir*, part 1. Amman: Markaz Ibn al-Nafis li'l-Buhuth al-'Ilmiyya wa-Dirasat al-Mar'a, 2007.

Marcus, Kenneth L. "Jailhouse Islamophobia: Anti-Muslim Discrimination in American Prisons." *Race and Social Problems* 1, no. 1 (2009): 36–44.

Martinez, Patricia. "The Islamic State or the State of Islam in Malaysia." *Contemporary Southeast Asia* 23, no. 3 (2001): 474–503.

Masri, Basheer Ahmad. *Animal Welfare in Islam.* Markfield, UK: Islamic Foundation, 2007.

Mathew, Vloreen Nity, Ardiana Mazwa Raudah binti Amir Abdullah, and Siti Nurazizah binti Mohamad Ismail. "Acceptance of Halal Food among Non-Muslim Consumers." *Procedia—Social and Behavioral Sciences* 121 (2014): 262–271.

Matthee, Rudi. *The Pursuit of Pleasure: Drugs and Stimulants in Iranian History, 1500–1900.* Princeton, NJ: Princeton University Press, 2005.

Matthee, Rudi. "Alcohol in the Islamic Middle East: Ambivalence and Ambiguity." *Past and Present* 222, supp. 9 (2014): 100–125.

Matthee, Rudi. "Tutun." *Encyclopaedia of Islam.* 2nd ed. Brill Online. http://referenceworks.brillonline.com/.

Mattson, Ingrid. "Eating in the Name of God." *Islamic Horizons* 39, no. 2 (2010): 22–25.

Al-Mawsu'a al-Fiqhiyya. 2nd ed. 45 vols. Kuwait: Wizarat al-Awqaf wa'l Shu'un al-Islamiyya, 1983.

Mehta, Brinda J. "The Semiosis of Food in Diana Abu Jaber's *Crescent.*" In *Arab Voices in Diaspora: Critical Perspectives on Anglophone Arab Literature*, edited by Layla Maleh, 203–236. Amsterdam: Rodopi, 2009.

Melchert, Christopher. "al-Bukhari." *Encyclopaedia of Islam.* 3rd ed. Brill Online. http://referenceworks.brillonline.com/.

Meneley, Anne. "Resistance Is Fertile!" *Gastronomica: The Journal of Critical Food Studies* 14, no. 4 (2014): 69–78.

Michalak, Laurence, and Karen Trocki. "Alcohol and Islam: An Overview." *Contemporary Drug Problems* 33, no. 4 (2006): 623–562.

Michot, Yahya. *Against Smoking: An Ottoman Manifesto by Ahmad al-Aqhisari.* Oxford: Interface, 2010.

Milgrom, Jacob. "Food and Faith: The Ethical Foundations of the Biblical Diet Laws." *Bible Review* 8 (1992): 5–10.

Miller, H. D. "The Pleasures of Consumption: The Birth of Medieval Islamic Cuisine." In *Food: A History of Taste*, edited by Paul Freedman, 135–162. Berkeley: University of California Press, 2007.

Mintz, Sidney W., and Christine M. Du Bois. "The Anthropology of Food and Eating." *Annual Review of Anthropology* 31 (2002): 99–119.

Mohamed, Besheer. "A New Estimate of the U.S. Muslim Population." Pew Research Center, January 6, 2016. http://www.pewresearch.org/fact-tank/2016/01/06/a-new-estimate-of-the-u-s-muslim-population/?utm_source=Pew+Research+Center&utm_campaign=65c3bb5fd7-Religion_Weekly_Jan_7_2016&utm_medium=email&utm_term=0_3e953b9b70-65c3bb5fd7-400104481.

Mohamed, Maznah. "The Ascendance of Bureaucratic Islam and the Secularization of the Sharia in Malaysia." *Pacific Affairs* 83, no. 3 (2010): 505–524.

Mohamed, Maznah. "Legal-Bureaucratic Islam in Malaysia: Homogenizing and Ring-Fencing the Muslim Subject." In *Encountering Islam: The Politics of Religious Identities in South Asia*, edited by Hui Yew Foong, 103–132. Singapore: Institute of Southeast Asian Studies, 2012.

Möhring, Marin. "*Döner Kebab* and West German Consumer (Multi-)Cultures." In *Hybrid Cultures—Nervous States: Britain and Germany in a (Post) Colonial World*, edited by Ulrike Lindner, Marin Möhring, Mark Stein, and Silke Stroh, 151–166. Amsterdam: Rodopi, 2010.

Muhamad, Nazlida. "Fatwa Rulings in Islam: A Malaysian Perspective on Their Role in Muslim Consumer Behavior." In *Handbook of Islamic Marketing*, edited by Özlem Sandıkcı and Gillian Rice, 34–54. Cheltenham, UK: Edward Elgar, 2011.

Mukherjee, Romi. "Global Halal: Meat, Money, and Religion." *Religions* 5 (2014): 22–75.

Morewedge, Parviz ed., *Neoplatonism and Islamic Thought*. Albany: State University of New York Press, 1992.

Muzaffar, Chandra. "Malaysia: Islamic Resurgence and the Question of Development." *Sojourn: Journal of Social Issues in Southeast Asia* 1, no. 1 (1986): 57–75.

Myers, Trisha Marie. "*Kitabu Mesalihi'l Muslimin* and Counsel for Sultans: Text and Context in the Nasihatname Genre of the Ottoman Empire, 16th–17th c." MA thesis, Ohio State University, 2011.

al-Najaf, 'Abd al-Karim. *Al-Halal wa'l-Haram fi'l Shari'a al-Islamiyya*. Tehran: al-Majma' al-'Alami li'l-Taqrib bayna al-Madhahib al-Islamiyya, 2008.

Najiha, A. Anis, et al. "A Preliminary Study on *Halal* Limits for Ethanol Content in Food Products." *Middle East Journal of Scientific Research* 6, no. 1 (2010): 45–50.

Nakyinsige, K., et al. "Stunning and Animal Welfare from Islamic and Scientific Perspectives." *Meat Science* 95 (2013): 352–361.

Nasir, Kamaludeen Mohamed, and Alexius A. Pereira. "Defensive Dining: Notes on Public Dining Experiences in Singapore." *Contemporary Islam* 2, no. 1 (2008): 61–73.

Nasr, Seyyed Vali Reza. *Islamic Leviathan: Islam and the Making of State Power*. Oxford: Oxford University Press, 2001.

Nassar, Heba. "The Economics of Tobacco in Egypt: A New Analysis of Demand." World Bank HNP Discussion Paper, 2003. http://www-wds.worldbank.org/external/default/ WDSContentServer/WDSP/IB/2004/05/19/000265513_20040519171838/Rendered/PDF/ 288920Nassar010The0Economics010whole.pdf.

Nor, Nor Amna A'liah Mohammad, and Mohamad Hifzan Rosali. "The Development and Future Direction of Malaysia's Livestock Industry." *FFTC Agricultural Policy Platform Articles*, October 10, 2015. http://ap.fftc.agnet.org/ap_db.php?id=529&print=1.

Nor-Zafir, M. S. "Establishing Shariah-Compliance [*sic*] Hotel Characteristics from a Muslim Needs Perspective." In *Theory and Practice in Hospitality and Tourism Research*, edited by Salleh Mohd Radzi et al., 525–529. Croydon, UK: CRC Press, 2015.

Onaran, Burak. "Le débat sur le porc halâl en Turquie au début de la période républicaine (1923–1950)." In *Les sens du Halal: Une norme dans un marché mondial*, edited by Florence Bergeaud-Blackler, 31–45. Paris: CNRS Éditions, 2015.

Orlandi, Tito. "A Catechesis against Apocryphal Texts by Shenute and the Gnostic Texts of Nag Hammadi." *Harvard Theological Review* 75, no. 1 (1982): 85–95.

Özdestan, Özgül, and Ali Üren. "Biogenic Amine Content of Kefir: A Fermented Dairy Product." *European Food Research and Technology* 231, no. 1 (2010): 101–107.

Parker, Chad. "Transports of Progress: The Arabian American Oil Company and American Modernization in Saudi Arabia, 1945–1973." PhD diss., Indiana University, 2008.

Pellat, Ch., et al. "Ḥayawān." *Encyclopaedia of Islam*. 2nd ed. Brill Online. http://referenceworks. brillonline.com/.

Peterson, J. E. "Oman's Diverse Society: Northern Oman." *Middle East Journal* 58, no. 1 (2004): 31–51.

Petticrew, M., K. Lee, H. Ali, and R. Nakkash. "'Fighting a Hurricane': Tobacco Industry Efforts to Counter the Perceived Threat of Islam." *American Journal of Public Health* 105, no. 6 (2015): 1086–1093.

Phillips, Rod. *Alcohol: A History*. Chapel Hill: University of North Carolina Press, 2014.

Pilcher, Jeffrey M. "'Tastes like Horse Piss': Asian Encounters with European Beer." *Gastronomica: The Journal of Critical Food Studies* 16, no. 1 (2016): 28–40.

Poppe, J. "Gelatin." In *Thickening and Gelling Agents for Food*, edited by Alan P. Imeson, 144–168. London: Blackie, 1997.

Putzger: Historischer Weltaltlas. Berlin: Cornelsen Verlag, 1992.

al-Qaradawi, Yusuf. *The Lawful and the Prohibited in Islam*. Indianapolis: American Trust, 1999.

Qasmi, Mujahidul Islam. *The Islamic Concept of Animal Slaughter*. Beirut: Dar al-Kotob al-Ilmiyyah, 2009.

al-Rabi', Walid Khaled. *Ahkam al-At'ima fi'l-Fiqh al-Islami: Dirasa Muqarna*. Amman: Dar al-Nafa'is, 2008.

al-Ramlawi, Muhammad Sa'id Muhammad. *Al-Halal wa'l-Haram wa'l-Mughlib Minhuma fi'l-Fiqh al-Islami: Dirasa Tatbiqiyya Mu'asira*. Cairo: Dar al-Jami'a al-Jadida, 2008.

Rarick, Charles, Gideon Falk, Casimir Barczyk, and Lori Feldman. "Marketing to Muslims: The Growing Importance of Halal Products." *Journal of the International Academy for Case Studies* 18, no. 2 (2012): 101–106.

Rasul, Ghula, and Abdul Majid Khan. "Patterns of Trade among Muslim Countries." Pakistan Institute of Economic Development, 1977. http://opendocs.ids.ac.uk/opendocs/bitstream/handle/123456789/2437/RRS104.pdf?sequence=1.

Regenstein, J. M., et al. "The Kosher and Halal Food Laws." *Comprehensive Reviews in Food Science and Food Safety* 2 (2003): 110–127.

Reid, Megan H. *Law and Piety in Medieval Islam*. Cambridge: Cambridge University Press, 2013.

Renard, John. *Friends of God: Islamic Images of Piety, Commitment, and Servanthood*. Berkeley: University of California Press, 2008.

Reynolds, Gabriel Said. "The Sufi Approach to Food: A Case Study of Adab." *Muslim World* 90, no. 1/2 (2000): 198–217.

Rezai, Golnaz, et al. "Can Halal Be Sustainable? Study on Malaysian Consumers' Perspective." *Journal of Food Products Marketing* 21, no. 6 (2016): 654–666.

Riaz, Mian N., and Muhammad M. Chaudry. *Halal Food Production*. Boca Raton, FL: CRC Press, 2004.

Rippin, Andrew. "Abrogation." *Encyclopaedia of Islam*. 3rd ed. Brill Online. http://referenceworks.brillonline.com/.

Robinson, R. K. "Snack Food of Dairy Origin." In *Snack Food*, edited by R. Gordon Booth, 159–182. New York: Van Nostrand Reinhold, 1990.

Robinson, Sarah E. "Refreshing the Concept of Halal Meat: Resistance and Religiosity in Chicago's Taqwa Eco-Food Cooperative." In *Religion, Food, and Eating in North America*, edited by Benjamin E. Zeller, Marie W. Dallam, Reid L. Neilson, and Nora L. Rubel, 274–293. New York: Columbia University Press, 2014.

Rodinson, Maxime. "Ghidhā'." *Encyclopaedia of Islam*. 2nd ed. Brill Online. http://referenceworks.brillonline.com/.

Rodinson, Maxime, and A. J. Arberry, eds. *Medieval Arab Cookery*. Devon, UK: Prospect Books, 2001.

Roolvink, Roelof, et al. *Historical Atlas of the Muslim Peoples*. Amsterdam: Djambatan, 1957.

Rosenblum, Jordan. *The Jewish Dietary Laws in the Ancient World*. New York: Cambridge University Press, 2016.

Rosenthal, Franz. *The Herb: Hashish versus Medieval Muslim Society*. Leiden: Brill, 1971.

Roth, Laurence. "Toward a Kashrut Nation in American Jewish Cookbooks, 1990–2000." *Shofar: An Interdisciplinary Journal of Jewish Studies* 28, no. 2 (2010): 65–90.

Roy, Olivier. *Globalized Islam: The Search for a New Ummah.* New York: Columbia University Press, 2004.

Rozen, Minna. "A Pound of Flesh: The Meat Trade and Social Struggle in the Jewish Istanbul, 1700–1923." In *Crafts and Craftsmen of the Middle East: Fashioning the Individual in the Muslim Mediterranean,* edited by Suraiya Faroqhi and Randi Deguilhem, 195–234. London: I. B. Tauris, 2005.

al-Rumi, Jalal al-Din, and William C. Chittick. *The Sufi Path of Love: The Spiritual Teachings of Rumi.* Binghamton: SUNY Press, 1983.

Sabír, Nadirah Z. "Healthy + Halal + Humane." *Azizah* 6, no. 2 (2010): 69–72.

Safi, Omid. *Memories of Muhammad: Why the Prophet Matters.* New York: HarperOne, 2010.

Sai, Yukari, and Johan Fischer. "Muslim Food Consumption in China: Between Qingzhen and Halal." In *Halal Matters: Islam, Politics, and Markets,* edited by Florence Bergeaud-Blackler, Johan Fischer, and John Lever, 160–174. London: Routledge, 2015.

Salvio, Paula M. "Dishing It Out: Food Blogs and Post-Feminist Domesticity." *Gastronomica: The Journal of Food and Culture* 12, no. 3 (2012): 31–39.

Sariyannis, Marinos. "Law and Morality in Ottoman Society: The Case of Narcotic Substances." In *The Ottoman Empire, The Balkans, The Greek Lands: Towards a Social and Economic History,* edited by Elias Kolovos et al., 308–321. Istanbul: Isis Press, 2007.

Schacht, Joseph. "Ibāḥa." *Encyclopaedia of Islam.* 2nd ed. Brill Online. http://referenceworks. brillonline.com/.

Schyff, Gerhard van der. "Ritual Slaughter and Religious Freedom in a Multilevel Europe: The Wider Importance of the Dutch Case." *Oxford Journal of Law and Religion* 3, no. 1 (2014): 76–102.

Shechter, Relli. *Smoking, Culture and Economy in the Middle East: The Egyptian Tobacco Market 1850–2000.* London: I. B. Tauris, 2006.

Shemesh, Yael. "Vegetarian Ideology in Talmudic Literature and Traditional Biblical Exegesis." *Review of Rabbinic Judaism* 9, no. 1 (2006): 141–166.

Shirazi, Faegheh. *Brand Islam: The Marketing and Commodification of Piety.* Austin: University of Texas Press, 2016.

Simoons, Frederick. *Eat Not This Flesh: Food Avoidances from Prehistory to the Present.* Madison: University of Wisconsin Press, 1994.

Skovgaard-Petersen, Jakob. *Defining Islam for the Egyptian State: Muftis and Fatwas of the* Dār Al-Iftā. Leiden: Brill, 1997.

Smith, Alison K. "National Cuisines." In *The Oxford Handbook of Food History,* edited by Jeffrey M. Pilcher, 444–460. Oxford: Oxford University Press, 2012.

Smith, Dennis E. "Food and Dining in Early Christianity." In *A Companion to Food in the Ancient World,* edited by John Wilkins and Robin Nadequ, 357–364. West Sussex, UK: John Wiley, 2015.

Socha, Kim. *Animal Liberation and Atheism: Dismantling the Procrustean Bed.* Minneapolis-St. Paul: Freethought House, 2014.

State of the Global Islamic Economy 2014–2015 Report. Developed and produced by Thomson Reuters. http://www.flandersinvestmentandtrade.com/export/sites/trade/files/news/ 342150121095027/342150121095027_1.pdf.

State of Global Islamic Economy Report 2016/2017. Developed and produced by Thomson Reuters. http://www.iedcdubai.ae/assets/uploads/files/SGIE%20Report_f1_DIGITAL_1477897639. pdf.

Stilt, Kristen. *Animal Welfare in Islamic Law.* Clinton, WA: Animal People, 2008. http:// animalpeopleforum.org/wp-content/uploads/2016/09/Animal-Welfare-in-Islamic-Law-EN.pdf.

Stilt, Kristen. *Islamic Law in Action: Authority, Discretion, and Everyday Experiences in Mamluk Egypt*. Oxford: Oxford University Press, 2012.

"Al-Sukr." *Al-Mawsu'a al-Fiqhiyya* 25:90–104.

Swenson, Rebecca. "Domestic Divo?" In *Food and Culture: A Reader*, 3rd ed., edited by Carole Counihan and Penny Van Esterik, 137–153. New York: Routledge, 2013.

Şimşek, Murat. "Helal Belgelendirme ve SMIIC Standardı." *İslam Hukuku Araştırmaları Dergisi* 22 (2013): 19–44.

"Tabgh." *Al-Mawsu'a al-Fiqhiyya* 10:101–113.

Tadros, Mariz. "Scapepigging: H1N1 Influence in Egypt." In *Epidemics: Science, Governments, and Social Justice*, edited by Melissa Leach and Sarah Dry, 213–238. London: Routledge, 2010.

"Takhdir." *Al-Mawsu'a al-Fiqhiyya* 11:33–38.

Talin, Habibah Abdul, and Khairul Anuar Mohd Ali. "An Overview of Malaysian Food Industry: The Opportunity and Quality Aspects." *Pakistan Journal of Nutrition* 8 (2009): 507–517.

Tamime, Adnan Y., ed. *Fermented Milks*. Oxford: Blackwell Science, 2006.

Teramoto, Y., et al. "Characteristics of Egyptian Boza and a Fermentable Yeast Strain Isolated from the Wheat Bread." *World Journal of Microbiology and Biotechnology* 17, no. 3 (2001): 241–243.

Tieman, Marco. "Convergence of Food Systems: Kosher, Christian, and Halal." *British Food Journal* 117, no. 9 (2015): 2313–2327.

Tieman, Marco. "Halal Diets." *Islamic and Civilisational Renewal* 7, no. 1 (2016): 128–132.

Timothy, Dallen J., and Amos S. Ron. "Religious Heritage, Spiritual Ailment and Food for the Soul." In *Heritage Cuisines: Traditions, Identities and Tourism*, edited by Dallen J. Timothy, 104–118. London: Routledge, 2016.

Tlili, Sarra. *Animals in the Qur'an*. Cambridge: Cambridge University Press, 2012.

Tlili, Sarra. "All Animals Are Equal, or Are They? The Ikhwān al-Ṣafā''s Animal Epistle and Its Unhappy End." *Journal of Qur'anic Studies* 16, no. 2 (2014): 42–88.

Tomson, Peter J. "Jewish Food Laws in Early Christian Community Discourse." *Semeia* 86 (1999): 193–211.

Trépanier, Nicolas. *Foodways and Daily Life in Medieval Anatolia: A New Social History*. Austin: University of Texas Press, 2014.

Tripp, Charles. *Islam and the Moral Economy: The Challenge of Capitalism*. Cambridge: Cambridge University Press, 2006.

United Nations Office Drugs and Crime. *2014 World Drug Report*. http://www.unodc.org/wdr2014/en/interactive-map.html.

Usmani, Shaykh Taqi. *Legal Rulings on Slaughtered Animals*. Translated Mufti Abdullah Nana. Karachi: Maktaba-e-Darul-'Uloom, 2005. https://ia800804.us.archive.org/15/items/LegalRulingsOnSlaughteredAnimalsByShaykhMuftiMuhammadTaqiUsmani/LegalRulingsOnSlaughteredAnimalsByShaykhMuftiMuhammadTaqiUsmani-.pdf.

Varisco, Daniel M. "On the Meaning of Chewing: The Significance of Qat (*Catha edulis*) in the Yemen Arab Republic." *International Journal of Middle East Studies* 18, no. 1 (1986): 1–13.

Varisco, Daniel M. "The Elixir of Life or the Devil's Cud? The Debate over Qat (*Catha edulis*) in Yemeni Culture." In *Drug Use and Cultural Contexts "Beyond the West": Tradition, Change and Post-Colonialism*, edited by Ross Coomber and Nigel South, 101–118. London: Free Association Books, 2004.

Waarden, Frans van. "Taste, Traditions, Transactions, and Trust: The Public and Private Regulation of Food." In *Where's the Beef? The Contested Governance of European Food Safety*, edited by David Vogel, 35–59. Cambridge, MA: MIT Press, 2006.

Waarden, Frans van, and Robin van Dalen. "Halal and the Moral Construction of Quality: How Religious Norms Turn a Mass Product in a Singularity." In *Constructing Quality: The Classification of Goods in Markets*, edited by Jens Beckert and Christine Musselin, 197–222. Oxford: Oxford University Press, 2013.

Waines, David. "Abu Zayd al-Balkhi on the Nature of Forbidden Drink: A Medieval Islamic Controversy." In *La alimentación en las culturas islámicas: Una colección de estudios*, edited by Manuela Marin and David Waines, 111–126. Madrid: Espanola de Cooperacion Internacional, 1994.

Waines, David. "Dietetics in Medieval Islamic Culture." *Medical History* 43, no. 2 (1999): 228–240.

Waines, David, ed. *Food Culture and Health in Pre-Modern Muslim Societies.* Leiden: Brill, 2010.

Waines, David. "Food in Antiquity: Islamic Dimension." In *A Companion to Food in the Ancient World*, edited by John Wilkins and Robin Nadeau, 383–392. West Sussex: Wiley Blackwell, 2015.

Waines, David. "Food and Drink." *Encyclopaedia of the Qur'ān.* Brill Online. http://referenceworks. brillonline.com/.

Wallenbrock, Nicole Beth. "'Almost but Not Quite Eating Pork: Culinary Nationalism and Islamic Difference in Millennial French Comedies." *Performing Islam* 4, no. 2 (2015): 107–127.

Walters, Kerry S., and Lisa Portmess. *Religious Vegetarianism: From Hesiod to the Dalai Lama.* Albany: State University of New York Press, 2001.

Ward, Walter D. *Mirage of the Saracen: Christians and Nomads in the Sinai Peninsula in Late Antiquity.* Berkeley: University of California Press, 2014.

Waskow, Arthur. "And the Earth Is Filled with a Breath of Life." *Cross Currents* 47, no. 3 (1997): 348–363.

Welty, Jeff. "Humane Slaughter Laws." *Law and Contemporary Problems* 70 (2007): 175–206.

Wensinck, A. J. "Nadjis." *Encyclopaedia of Islam.* 2nd ed. Brill Online. http://referenceworks.brillonline.com/.

Wensinck, A. J., and J. Sadan. "Khamr." *Encyclopaedia of Islam.* 2nd ed. Brill Online. http://referenceworks.brillonline.com/.

WHO (World Health Organization). "Global and Regional Food Consumption Patterns and Trends." N.d. http://www.who.int/nutrition/topics/3_foodconsumption/en/index2.html.

Winchester, Daniel. "Embodying the Faith: Religious Practice and the Making of a Muslim Moral Habitus." *Social Forces* 86, no. 4 (2008): 1753–1780.

Wright, Clifford A. *A Mediterranean Feast: The Story of the Birth of the Celebrated Cuisines of the Mediterranean from the Merchants of Venice to the Barbary Corsairs, with More Than 500 Recipes.* New York: Morrow, 1999.

Wright, Clifford A. "The History of Macaroni." CliffordAWright.com. N.d. http://www.cliffordawright.com/caw/food/entries/display.php/id/50/.

Wszolek, M., et al. "Production of Kefir, Koumiss and Other Related Products." In *Fermented Milks*, edited by Adnan Y. Tamime, 174–205. Oxford: Blackwell Science, 2006.

Yalof, Ina. *Food and the City.* New York: Putnam, 2016.

Yeğin, Sırma, and Marcelo Fernández-Lahore. "Boza: A Traditional Cereal-Based, Fermented Turkish Beverage." In *Handbook of Plant-Based Fermented Food and Beverage Technology*, 2nd ed., edited by Y. H. Hui et al., 533–542. Boca Raton, FL: CRC Press, 2012.

Zakaria, Zalina, and Siti Zubaidah Ismail. "The Trade Description Act 2011: Regulating 'Halal' in Malaysia." Paper presented at International Conference on Law, Management and Humanities. Bangkok, Thailand, June 21–24, 2014. http://icehm.org/upload/8779ED0614020.pdf.

Zaouali, Lilia. *Medieval Cuisines of the Islamic World: A Concise History with 174 Recipes.* Translated by M. B. DeBevoise. Berkeley: University of California Press, 2009.

BIBLIOGRAPHY

Zellelew, Tilahun Bejitual. "The Semiotics of the 'Christian/Muslim Knife': Meat and Knife as Markers of Religious Identity in Ethiopia." *Signs and Society* 3, no. 1 (2015): 44–70.

Zilfi, Madeline. *The Politics of Piety: The Ottoman Ulema in the Post Classical Age (1600–1800)*. Minneapolis: Bibliotheca Islamica, 1988.

Zook, Darren. "Making Space for Islam: Religion, Science, and Politics in Contemporary Malaysia." *Journal of Asian Studies* 69, no. 4 (2010): 1143–1166.

INDEX